MW01148372

WARDSHIP AND THE WELFARE STATE

**New Visions in Native American
and Indigenous Studies**

Margaret D. Jacobs
Robert J. Miller

Wardship and the Welfare State

Native Americans and the Formation
of First-Class Citizenship in
Mid-Twentieth-Century America

Mary Klann

CO-PUBLISHED BY THE UNIVERSITY OF NEBRASKA PRESS

AND THE AMERICAN PHILOSOPHICAL SOCIETY

The University of Nebraska Press is part of a land-
grant institution with campuses and programs
on the past, present, and future homelands of
the Pawnee, Ponca, Otoe-Missouria, Omaha,
Dakota, Lakota, Kaw, Cheyenne, and Arapaho
Peoples, as well as those of the relocated Ho-
Chunk, Sac and Fox, and Iowa Peoples.

Library of Congress Cataloging-in-Publication Data
Names: Klann, Mary, author.
Title: Wardship and the welfare state : Native
Americans and the formation of first-class citizenship
in mid-twentieth-century America / Mary Klann.
Other titles: Native Americans and the
formation of first-class citizenship in mid-
twentieth-century America | New visions in
Native American and indigenous studies.
Description: Lincoln : Co-published by the
University of Nebraska Press and the American
Philosophical Society, [2024]. | Series: New visions
in Native American and indigenous studies |
Includes bibliographical references and index.
Identifiers: LCCN 2023054308
ISBN 9781496218179 (hardback)
ISBN 9781496239693 (epub)
ISBN 9781496239709 (pdf)
Subjects: LCSH: Indians of North America—
Government relations—1934– | Citizenship—United
States—History—20th century. | Indians of North
America—Public welfare—History—20th century. |
Indians of North America—Legal status, laws,
etc.—History—20th century. | Racism in public
welfare—United States—History—20th century. |
BISAC: SOCIAL SCIENCE / Ethnic Studies / American /
Native American Studies | POLITICAL SCIENCE /
Public Policy / Social Services & Welfare
Classification: LCC E93 .K58 2024 | DDC
361.6/508997—dc23/eng/20231213
LC record available at https://
lccn.loc.gov/2023054308

For my family

And for all my
fellow adjuncts

As Indians had for generation after generation, they were attempting to understand a white man reading endlessly from a sheaf of papers.

—Louise Erdrich (Turtle Mountain Ojibwe), *The Night Watchman*

You don't have to collapse just because there's federal law in your way. Change it!

—Ada Deer (Menominee)

CONTENTS

ACKNOWLEDGMENTS

I talk often with the students in my classes about joy. Finding joy in teaching, for me, is a conscious choice, a manifestation of the iterative relationality required for sharing and cultivating learning. Though much more solitary in practical terms, I think of research (and writing) in the same way. All aspects of my historian-self are impossible without conversation, commiseration, support, excitement, *joy*. Though I wrote this book myself (and take responsibility for all mistakes therein), I did not do anything alone. I thank all those who engaged in conversation and communion with me over the course of the nine years it has taken to bring this project to fruition.

First, thank you to the five people who read the entire manuscript when it wasn't anywhere close to being a book, for their essential comments, feedback, and guidance—my dissertation committee at University of California, San Diego: Rebecca Jo Plant, Ross Frank, Nancy Kwak, Natalia Molina, and Nicole Tonkovich. Foremost thanks go to my dissertation adviser, Rebecca Jo Plant. Rebecca has challenged me intellectually, supported me emotionally, and made my writing much, much better. She has been my tireless advocate since 2011, when I started my doctoral research, through the hellscape of the academic job market, and now as a colleague. Ross Frank introduced me to Native history and Native American studies. His kindness and generosity are one of my models of how to be a teacher. At my dissertation defense in 2017, he brought me a copy of Ella Deloria's *Waterlily*, likely from one of his own over-stuffed shelves. It ultimately became a foundational text for my own Native American history course, inspiring conversations with students and compelling me to rethink the way I could, as a non-Native person, engage with Native voices in my classes. This is just one small example of the way Ross has shaped my academic work. In addition to guiding my research and writing process, Nancy Kwak encouraged me to write my first published book review, helped me find work as a graduate assistant, and—something I will always be grateful for—donated baby supplies to my family as we were preparing for our first daughter.

I am especially grateful for the archivists and librarians who helped me locate and access the source material for this project. Special thanks to Matthew Law at the National Archives and Records Administration in Riverside, California; Adam Berenbak at the NARA Legislative Archives in Washington DC; Nathan Sowry at the National Museum of the American Indian Archive Center; and Michael Maher at the Nevada Historical Society. Thank you to the fantastic staff at the Harry S. Truman Library, the Arizona Historical Society, the Labriola National American Indian Center and the Law Library at Arizona State University, the Special Collections at University of Nevada, Reno, the Center of Southwest Research at University of New Mexico, and the National Archives branches in Atlanta, Georgia, and San Bruno, California.

This book would not be possible without the generous funding I received as a graduate student from the Charles Redd Center for Western Studies at Brigham Young University, the Harry S. Truman Library, the Coordinating Council for Women in History, the UCSD Center for the Humanities, and the UCSD Department of History, which funded several research travel grants and a dissertation writing fellowship. The American Association of University Women's American Dissertation Fellowship funded my final year of research and writing in graduate school. The American Philosophical Society's Phillips Fund for Native American Research Grant allowed me to make my first archival research trip after finishing my PhD, leading me to the treasure trove of resources at the NARA branch in Atlanta. A 2021–22 American Council of Learned

Societies Fellowship allowed me to finish writing this book. It is not an overstatement to say that I would never have finished this without that fellowship.

While a graduate student at UCSD, I benefited from the support and mentorship of other faculty in research, writing, and teaching, including Nayan Shah, Rachel Klein, Michael Parrish, David Gutiérrez, Heidi Keller-Lapp, and Stanley Chodorow. My skills in historical research and writing have been indelibly shaped by the guidance of the faculty in the Women's History MA program at Sarah Lawrence College, including especially Priscilla Murolo, Komozi Woodard, and Mary Dillard. Tara James invited me to give a talk at Sarah Lawrence in 2021, and Seth Cotlar and Leslie Dunlap invited me to Willamette University in 2017; I am grateful for those opportunities and ensuing conversations.

Ever since I met her at the 2016 Ethnohistory conference, Katherine Osburn has believed in this project and enthusiastically supported me. I am forever grateful for her energy and care, and I am fortunate that she has read and commented on this book. Kyle Ciani's thoughtful review of this book was immeasurably helpful, and I thank her for her close reading and suggestions. Thanks to Matthew Bokovoy, my editor at University of Nebraska Press, for his enduring support, feedback, and patience. Thank you to Heather Stauffer and the production team at University of Nebraska Press and to Jane Curran for thoughtful and thorough copyediting.

Rebecca Plant, Kate Flach, and Samantha de Vera closely read and commented on several chapters of this manuscript, and I appreciate their thoughtful feedback and questions. Kate, Ulices Piña, and Manuel Morales Fontanilla provided critical feedback on chapter 4. Patrick Lozar read and provided valuable feedback on the epilogue. (I am so thankful we met at the 2017 Ethnohistory conference.) In addition to all of her other contributions to my pedagogical and intellectual development, Laura González at Miramar College read and commented on a draft of chapter 6. So many thanks to Farina King, who is the epitome of intellectual generosity and an expert at facilitating collaboration. I think her coordination of the Native History Nerds group, an informal monthly gathering of historians and scholars in Native American studies for Zoom discussions during the pandemic, was a salve for every single participant. I know it was—is—for me. Working with Judy Wu, Rebecca Plant, Kacey Calahane, and the *Women and Social Movements in the United States* editorial team on a document project on Native women's challenges to termination policies helped me clarify and articulate key pieces of this book project.

Invaluable comments on various iterations of this project at conferences have come from Cassidy Acheson, Monika Bilka, Marisa Chappell, Maurice Crandall, Heather Ponchetti Daly, Farina King, Brooke Linsenbardt, Patrick Lozar, Haleigh Marcello, Jennifer Mittelstadt, Roger Nichols, Katherine Osburn, Jenny Pulsipher, Marc Arsell Robinson, Nicolas Rosenthal, Patricia Schechter, Rose Stremlau, Sasha Maria Suarez, Jennifer Talerico-Brown, Becca Wellington, Jessie Wilkerson, and Victoria Wyatt. I so appreciate the academic communities I have found through the American Society for Ethnohistory, the Berkshire Conference of Women Historians, the Western Association of Women Historians, the Western History Association, and the Pacific Coast Branch of the American Historical Association. I am also grateful for the feedback given in the UCSD Center for the Humanities Interdisciplinary Dissertation Workshop in 2015–16, and I thank Natalie Aviles, Amanda Cachia, Ivana Guarrasi, Lisa Ho, Mark Kelley, Audrey Lackner-Price, and Salvador Zarate for their comments. For their kindness, intelligence, and advice on the work that would eventually become this book, I extend heartfelt thanks to my fellow UCSD historians, Mayra Avitia, Stephanie Fairchild, Kate Flach, Laura Gutiérrez, Jorge Leal, William McGovern, Alina Méndez, Manuel Morales Fontanilla, Mychal Odom, Ulices Piña, Ryan Reft, Luis Sánchez-López, Kelly Silva, Elizabeth Sine, Maki Smith, and Camielyn West.

As an adjunct faculty member at UC San Diego, San Diego Miramar College, Cuyamaca College, and San Diego Mesa College, I have benefited from the connections and friendship of many fellow scholar-teachers, including Nathanael Aschenbrenner, Mira Balberg, Foster Chamberlain, Laura González, Javier Gonzalez-Meeks, Moriah Gonzalez-Meeks, Mark Hendrickson, Dan Igou, Gloria Kim, Denise Maduli-Williams, Patti Manley, and Camielyn West. I have nothing but appreciation and love for the curious and bright students in my women's history, digital history, U.S. history, and Native history courses at these institutions, whose insightful questions and comments have made me a better historian.

I'm not sure how to possibly begin to thank Kate Flach. Kate is one of my closest confidantes and intellectual sounding boards. I am immeasurably grateful for her friendship. Not only has she earnestly read and discussed my academic work for more than a decade, but she has provided emotional sustenance and support as I navigated the academic job market, motherhood, and adjuncting. In addition to her feedback on many pieces of this book, she has read cover letters and teaching statements, helped with interview prep, hashed out lesson plans, and listened to all my rage and sadness, breakthroughs and joy.

Unlimited thanks go to Leslie Dunlap. Leslie's women's history class at Willamette University changed my life. I was a senior, preparing to apply for graduate programs in psychology (my undergraduate major), and as a result of her class, I scrapped my plans and applied to one MA program in women's history instead. Leslie's skills as a teacher inspired me to take that risk. Her continued friendship and support allow me to be who I am. I owe her so much, not least for the comments she's provided on multiple drafts of critical pieces of this book. All the best parts of this book are because of conversations with her.

My family is my support system. Not only have they provided comfort and care, but many family members have directly assisted and enabled my research, sitting side by side with me in the archives, helping me photograph documents and talking through ideas. My mother, Sarah Klann, accompanied me to Reno, Nevada, to sort through records; my sister, Sally Klann, drove me all the way from San Diego to Phoenix when I was seven months pregnant to scroll through microfilm and turn pages upon pages of documents; Ham, Ana, Elizabeth, and Maria Keddie hosted me in Phoenix; and Kimi Sato was my tour guide in Washington DC. Sarah and Brad Klann, my parents, and Sally Klann, Jane Gajsiewicz, and Woody Klann, my siblings, have given me the confidence to do this and have always nurtured my love of history. I'm thankful for their love, humor, generosity, and support. My daughters, Nellie and Sarah Lam-Klann, are simply the best. Their creativity and chaos inspire me daily.

Being their mother is exhausting, exhilarating, and joyful. Eric Lam, my partner in parenting, friendship, and more, first deserves credit for noticing the way welfare showed up in the archival record of the Bureau of Indian Affairs. He's the one who called my attention to the conversations about Social Security while I was hunting for something else that didn't even make it into the dissertation, let alone the book. Moreover, Eric accompanied me all over the country to do research, photographing hundreds of documents as my research assistant. I am awed by the love he has for our daughters and the care he shows for his family and mine. I can't thank him enough for his love, patience, and belief in me.

And finally, to all my fellow adjuncts: I didn't think I'd finish this. There were months where I never opened my documents to write. There were *many* days where I felt the weight of all the unexamined sources, the unrevised notes, the detailed schedules and plans to which I had failed to adhere. I wrote this book without any financial support to do so from the institutions where I teach as an adjunct. I wrote this book in spite of what those departments expected of me. This is not to say I did not receive personal support and encouragement from colleagues and friends, especially those I've noted above. But this book wasn't in my job description. As an adjunct, I teach. Writing this book made me a better teacher because it made me a better historian. But writing this book did not and will not increase my paycheck. It did not get me health benefits. It will not guarantee that I have classes to teach each term. It will not get me tenure. It won't even get me a "full-time" job.

The ACLS fellowship (and my decision to leave the academic job market) gave me, for the first time since graduate school, time—time to think, to read, to write, to rewrite. Time to *talk*, with trusted colleagues and friends, to test out ideas, to delete. I was freed from a writing schedule that was constantly interrupted, truncated by teaching, parenting, and the relentlessness of the job market. I was freed from the guilt I felt whenever I found time to write what I essentially began to consider a "vanity project." I was freed from undermining my own self-worth and confidence, because I was freed, for that year, from the most humiliating and dehumanizing parts of adjuncting. The fellowship was $65,000, more than I've ever made for a year's worth of work.

To all my fellow adjuncts, and to all the graduate students reading this who may become adjuncts: You are essential. Your ideas matter as much as your labor. (Research and writing are labor, just as teaching is intellectual.) Our research and our teaching work together. That we think of them as separate at all is ludicrous. That we pay people to perform just one and assume they'll give up the other—or maybe that they don't deserve the opportunity to do the other at all unless they miraculously "write their way out" into a better-paying job—is outrageous.

To all my fellow adjuncts, you are not failures. The myth of an academic meritocracy—and those who adhere to and perpetuate this myth—failed us. We should get paid more. We need more respect. We need opportunities for scholarly thought, writing, process. All of these things make us better teachers.

And, we should get paid more.

We should get paid more.

We should get paid more.

So, to all my fellow adjuncts, you are essential. Not auxiliary. Not disposable. Not ghost-able. Not supplementary. Not temporary, contingent, part-time, *visiting*. You are essential.

NOTE ON TERMINOLOGY, USAGE, AND POETRY

My practice for terminology is as follows: whenever possible I utilize the specific names of the tribal nations to which the historical subjects in this text belong. In epigraphs and extracts I indicate the speaker's tribal citizenship in parentheses. When discussing Native people as a whole, or federal policy's impacts on Native people across tribal nations, I utilize "Native" or "Indigenous," to, as Devon Abbott Mihesuah writes, "make a statement: Natives were created on this hemisphere and did not migrate from another continent."[1] When discussing law, policies, and wardship created by the federal government, I utilize the terms "Indian law," "Indian policy," and "Indian wardship." This is in part due to practicality and contemporary convention—Indian policy and law are referred to as such in current debates and conversations. Describing federal policies such as termination and allotment as "Native policies" would also imply that these policies were created by and for Native people, which is inaccurate. Indian wardship, laws, and policies, while bureaucratic processes that impact and are shaped by Native people, are also, on the whole, created by legislators, government agents, and the courts in racialized and colonial contexts and frameworks. At the heart of this book is the slipperiness of these historically contingent terms and how listeners and speakers differentiated between what was said, what was heard, and what was meant.

Before 1947 the Bureau of Indian Affairs was known as the Office of Indian Affairs, the Indian Service, or the Indian Bureau. For clarity and consistency throughout this text, I use the term "Bureau of Indian Affairs" or BIA.

Throughout the text and in chapter epigraphs, I have engaged with contemporary Native poets and fiction writers, to whom I am indebted for their own deft engagement with slippery language. As a non-Native historian, poetry and fiction have helped me understand the intricacies, layers, and impacts of Indian policies more than any other forms. Policy is made by humans and thus requires an analysis that is expansive, theoretical, and engaging. Many policies and their resulting bureaucratic processes envision a linear path, with a concrete beginning and end. In practice, things are rarely so simple. Poetry and fiction allow for complication, pauses, blank spaces, reflection. In short, policy requires the discomfiting clarity that poetry and fiction can provide.

ABBREVIATIONS

AAIA   Association on American Indian Affairs
AB   Aid to the Blind
ADC   Aid to Dependent Children
AIDA   American Indian Defense Association
BIA   Bureau of Indian Affairs
ICA   Indian Citizenship Act
IRA   Indian Reorganization Act
NCAI   National Congress of American Indians
NOLEO   Notice to Law Enforcement Officials
OAA   Old Age Assistance
OAI   Old Age Insurance
ODB   Office of Dependency Benefits
SSB   Social Security Board
VA   Veterans Administration
WRA   War Relocation Authority

WARDSHIP AND THE WELFARE STATE

Introduction

Whereas there are no "classes" of citizenship in America, and Indians already are citizens and have political equality, *now therefore be it resolved* that we ask that Congress not abandon its legal responsibilities under the guise of "freeing" Indians from so-called "restrictions and disabilities."

    —Resolution of the Council of Laguna Pueblo, 1953

Who supports the Indians?

    —Bureau of Indian Affairs, *Answers to Your Questions on American Indians*, 1948

In 1948, in conjunction with the Haskell Institute, the Bureau of Indian Affairs (BIA) published a pamphlet purportedly containing "answers to your questions on American Indians." The response to question 22, "What is meant by 'Set the Indian free?'" contained a revealing clerical error: "This statement implies that the Indian is in some ways restricted in his person, or is not a citizen. Neither of these things is true. All Indians born within the United States became full citizens in 1942 by an Act of Congress (43 Stat. 253)."[1] The Indian Citizenship Act, passed in 1924, not 1942, universally declared all Native people to be American citizens. The error is a singular occurrence—elsewhere in the pamphlet the BIA used

1

the correct date. But its presence isn't surprising and perhaps wouldn't even be questioned by the pamphlet's target readership, the general public of non-Native citizens. In the mid-twentieth century there were many Americans who did not know that Native people were citizens, or who believed that those who lived on reservations weren't eligible for all the benefits of citizenship. There were even more who understood Native people to be "second-class" citizens, restricted or disabled in some way by their relationship to the federal government. The tone of the supposedly "frequently asked questions" of the BIA paints a very clear picture of how non-Native people understood (or misunderstood) Natives' place in the midcentury American polity:

> Are Indians still kept on reservations?
> Is it true that Indians pay no taxes?
> Have the efforts of the Indian Service to rehabilitate Indians been productive?
> What is meant by "Set the Indian free"?
> What is meant by "Emancipate the Indian"?
> What is meant by "Terminate Wardship"?
> Do Indians receive public assistance under the Social Security Act?
> Do Indians receive general assistance from their local communities or from county welfare departments?
> Do Indians receive money from the Government just for being Indians?
> Why doesn't the Government take care of needy Indians?
> How are Indians financed?[2]

Native people were understood to be restricted in their movements and legal rights—but guaranteed money or financing from the government; to be unfree in wardship—but free from taxes; to be cared for by the government—except when not cared for by the government; and, maybe most clearly from this compilation of questions, to be poor. Were Native people citizens? Yes. But were they "first-class" citizens? Certainly not.

Despite the efforts to provide short, accessible answers to these questions (as the BIA advertised on the pamphlet's cover, "checked, for your convenience!"), these queries cannot be answered simply. In an era where conversations about the citizenship status of racially marginalized groups in the United States were viewed through a lens of integration and equal access to civil rights, the BIA attempted to confront the loaded meaning behind seemingly positive ideas such as "emancipation" and "setting Native people free." But these ideas were—and are—complicated, especially when they are applied to Native people in the United States, a population whom non-Native Americans have long romanticized and dehumanized. Another supposedly "frequently asked question" in the pamphlet: "Are Indians naturally lazy?" The BIA's unsatisfying response simultaneously acknowledged the legitimacy of the question and provided reassurance to an American readership perpetually concerned with work ethic: "Some are lazy and many are industrious."[3]

The pseudo-legalistic conceptions of "first-class" and "second-class" citizenship seem to mean something official. The expression "first-class" citizenship first entered the American lexicon in earnest around 1940, growing in popularity as a rallying cry for opportunity into the late 1960s as the civil rights movement intensified.[4] It has since been adapted as an indicator of the highest level of political and social status.[5] "Second-class" citizenship works similarly, from the opposite end of the spectrum, as an implication of how certain groups have been prevented from accessing all the rights and benefits of citizenship. These terms are shorthand for all the rights we consider inalienable when we think of the idealized version of the United States. And they have staying power. In June 2022 the Supreme Court handed down their decision in *Oklahoma v. Castro-Huerta*, circumscribing the 2020 win for tribal sovereignty in *McGirt v. Oklahoma* by granting states jurisdiction over crimes committed by non-Natives on Native land. In his opinion for the majority, Justice Brett Kavanaugh asserted, "Castro-Huerta's argument would require this Court to treat Indian victims as *second-class citizens*. We decline to do so."[6] But as the Council of Laguna Pueblo argued in a 1953 resolution, "there are no 'classes' of citizenship in America."[7] First-class and second-class citizenship aren't real legal categories; they are rhetorical devices. During the 1963 March on Washington, marchers carried signs demanding school integration, equal voting rights, equal pay, and first-class citizenship. It was effective. The terms have become so ingrained in our vocabulary that they have some hold on our sense of actual legal rights—even Supreme Court justices aren't immune.

Clearly first-class citizenship also has a history. At the same time civil rights activists marched for the idea, non-Native legislators appropriated the term in order to propel their own Indian policy agenda. The Council of Laguna Pueblo emphasized that there were no "classes" of citizenship in America because they understood clearly how and why "first-class" citizenship was being deployed *to undermine* Native people's legitimate legal relationships with the United States government. The council stated it plainly: the midcentury policies proposed and enacted upon Native people were an abandonment of Native nations framed as the bestowal of first-class citizenship, "under the guise of 'freeing' Indians from so-called 'restrictions and disabilities.'"[8] This book engages with how Native representatives of tribal nations and intertribal organizations articulated their own political philosophies in their refutation of the illogics of first-class citizenship. By employing the relationships they had formed with government agents and utilizing a political grammar that those agents would have—or should have—understood, Native people, tribes, and organizations claimed both tribal sovereignty and American citizenship.

FIRST-CLASS CITIZENSHIP VERSUS INDIAN WARDSHIP

In the context of the mid-twentieth-century expansion of the federal welfare state, state agents and legislators idealized first-class citizenship as a political and social status available only to those who met proper qualifications of independence from government oversight and aid. In their policy conversations and negotiations, legislators, state agents, and citizens situated first-class citizenship against its apparent "opposite": the much older and fraught idea of Indian wardship. As positive as first-class citizenship was, wardship was negative, epitomizing the dangers of overdependency upon welfare benefits. To anyone who needed proof of the inherent risks in expanding the state's reach into ordinary citizens' lives, they had to look no further than Native American wards. By definition, wards could not be first-class citizens. Indeed, many non-Natives weren't sure whether wards were citizens at all. Wardship precluded access to first-class citizenship and prevented

Native men and women from fulfilling expectations of work, family, and political membership. This language only thinly masked how government officials used long-standing racialized and gendered anti-Native stereotypes to portray Native wards as perpetually impoverished and incapable of self-sufficiency.

But to Native people, wardship was not welfare, and welfare was not wardship. Native nations and organizations saw through non-Natives' desires to bestow first-class citizenship and "emancipate" them from wardship, arguing that non-Natives wanted to free tribal land from trust restrictions. They insisted that wardship was a legal and historical relationship that the United States was obligated to honor. Moreover, as American citizens and as humans with basic needs, Native people were entitled to welfare benefits.

Reaching the legal and political benchmark of equal access to so-called first-class citizenship implied that Native people—and, by extension, all citizens who utilized welfare benefits—had to conform to regulated and controlled ideals of individualism, economic independence, and gendered self-sufficiency. Thus, rather than an "achievement" of social and legal equality, for Native people, first-class citizenship was a restrictive categorization that undermined and threatened the legal and relational boundaries of wardship and tribal sovereignty. Indeed, legislators and state agents intended to terminate wardship. As the idea of first-class citizenship became more commonplace, legislators and some BIA officials lobbied to dissolve the trust relationship between tribes and the federal government and incorporate Native people into the American polity solely as individual citizens of the United States. These evolving Indian "termination" policies coincided with heated debates about Native people's eligibility for and access to welfare benefits and their status as American citizens. Although Native people were citizens, state governments, especially in the American West, denied Native people access to welfare benefits because of their misperceptions that Native people's welfare was the sole responsibility of the federal government. Additionally, federal welfare agencies granted the BIA power and oversight over Native people's receipt of benefits. As a result BIA agents employed the concept of first-class citizenship in service of their enduring pursuit of

Native people's assimilation into the American polity. Thus, *Wardship and the Welfare State* engages with both wardship and welfare, not just as historical policies, but as sets of intersecting bureaucratic and familial relationships weighted with gendered and racialized ideas about American values and morality.

This book is a history of politics and policy but maintains that politics and policy cannot be divorced from human relations. Non-Native legislators often collapsed and ignored the relationships that Native people built with BIA personnel and members of Congress through wardship and welfare, characterizing and generalizing both as "gratuitous" and "oppressive." But policies are made by people informed by culture and ideology. People are impacted by policies. People also resist policies, embrace them, adapt to them, and carry them out with gusto, ambivalence, and opinions of their own.

Wardship and welfare were not stagnant policy directives. They were constituted by relationships: between Native people and BIA agents, between Native people and social workers and welfare caseworkers, between bureaucrats at different federal and state agencies, between Native people and the military, between Native people and tribal governments, and between Native people and their own family members.

BRINGING TOGETHER WELFARE POLICY AND INDIAN POLICY

Both welfare and Indian policies have long histories as bureaucratic arms of the American morality police.[9] Indelibly shaped by the assimilative impulses of their administrators, at their cores, welfare and Indian policies were about molding "un-American," "abnormal" or otherwise "undeserving" populations into more "appropriate" versions of themselves. Money and resources channeled toward the subjects of these policies came with settler colonial and racialized strings attached. In many cases these resources provided recipients with a safety net—albeit weak—in exchange for behavioral change, abdication of culture, removal of children, and a particular vision for the future: first-class citizens, white (or as close to white as they could get), unencumbered by government oversight (and not in need of government benefits), independent heads of household (male), owners of property (individual, not tribal), and able to financially provide for dependents (a small, nuclear group: wives and children) through agricultural or wage work. Wardship and welfare sit at an uncomfortable nexus: distinct policies swirled together in a whirlpool of misconceptions and historical ignorance, both propped up by agents of the state, moral arbiters who clung to an ideal of first-class citizenship that the subjects of these policies could only rarely attain. Very few stopped to ask whether the targets of these policies even desired that ideal in the first place. In this book I draw upon Margot Canaday's definition of "the state" as visible "through its practices," essentially "what officials do." Canaday defines officials as "not only top decision-makers but bureaucrats at all levels."[10] Similarly, as Natalia Molina has argued, "low- and high-level bureaucrats and other functionaries of the state often interpreted and implemented race-making mechanisms from the ground up."[11] In this book the term "agents of the state" refers to a diverse group of personnel at the Bureau of Indian Affairs, state and county welfare offices, the Veterans Administration, the Social Security Board, and members of Congress.[12]

"Who supports the Indians?" the BIA asked itself in *Answers to Your Questions on American Indians*. In the response the BIA first sought to reassure the reader, the same reader who may have asked if Native people received money from the government "just for being Indians": "The great majority of Indians support themselves."[13] "Support," in this case, was defined as financial support. The rest of the response broke down sources of income of Native families on reservations—livestock and livestock products, wage work, arts and crafts, "unearned" income from land leases and mineral royalties, and, finally, relief (which was only 4.3 percent of "total Indian income" in 1948). This question was framed with a presumed understanding that Native people were needy. In most of the non-Native and government sources with which I engage in this book, Native poverty is similarly taken as a given. But this question can be made more useful if we stretch our understanding of "support" to reflect Indigenous understandings of relationality. To support, *to give assistance to*, can also mean providing with a home and necessities; producing enough food and water to be capable of sustaining; giving approval, comfort, and encouragement; being actively interested in and concerned for the success of. Home, basic needs, sustenance, comfort, active interest, concern. These are all more generative understandings of "support" than a breakdown of how much money Native people made in a particular year, indicating that they did not need anyone's economic support other than their own. And as I argue in the chapters that follow, in many cases this much more nuanced understanding of support was often more important than the specific dollar amounts the state disbursed.

Welfare policymakers and caseworkers, Veterans Administration personnel, and BIA agents subscribed to a framework of gendered economic ("first-class") citizenship wherein male breadwinners should earn enough outside of the home to support their dependents. In return for certain types of wage work, the federal government disseminated entitlement benefits: "tangible, publicly provided rewards."[14] Thus, as Alice Kessler-Harris notes, "employment emerged as a boundary line demarcating different kinds of citizenship."[15] Welfare policymakers clung to the idea of the "family wage," even as it failed to sustain many poor working families, including single mothers and their children, who turned to Aid to Dependent Children.[16] In the mid-1940s, welfare reformers and social workers incorporated work as part of their policies to "rehabilitate" welfare recipients. Welfare reformers understood the psychological benefits of work to be the "value of not being dependent."[17] Essentially, welfare reformers viewed welfare recipients' poverty, not as a symptom of larger structural inequalities, but as the result of individual failings.[18] Because they were more likely to be eligible for "needs-based" aid, women and racialized men who applied for welfare benefits were stigmatized as lazy and unable to participate in the idealized economic structure of the American family.

Similarly non-Native agents and reformers contrasted Native "savagery" with racialized ideals of "American" civilization that hinged upon each member of the nuclear family unit playing their part to achieve economic self-sufficiency. Campaigns to "civilize" Native people were made up of, in Robert Porter's words, "a four-pronged attack that served as a kind of Four Horsemen of the Indian Apocalypse," which included conversion to Christianity, coerced Western education for Native children, allotment of tribal lands, and the extension of citizenship to Native people.[19] Driven by the desire to assimilate Natives into Americanized ideals of property ownership, gendered labor, language, and religion, reformers and state officials forcibly attempted to educate Native people to become "proper" citizens.[20] For example, under the 1887 Dawes Allotment Act, state agents and reformers divided Native communities into patriarchal nuclear family units to allot tribal land, disrupting existing systems of community and family governance.[21] Citizenship was involuntarily "granted" to Native people who conformed to assimilationist ideals—that is, it did not require Native consent.[22]

However, as Frederick Hoxie argues, assimilationist policymakers and reformers did not envision citizenship to elevate Native people to the status of white Americans. Rather, by 1920 "a new, more pessimistic spirit governed federal action."[23] Native people were to be incorporated into the nation, but "their new status bore a greater resemblance to the position of the United States' other nonwhite peoples" than it did to idealized notions of "full," or later "first-class" citizenship.[24] Scholars have shown that throughout the early twentieth century whiteness remained the prerequisite for citizenship.[25]

CITIZEN CAREGIVERS

Historian Jessica Wilkerson poses a radical question in her study of Appalachian women's movements for social justice in the mid-twentieth century: "what would it mean to imagine the average American not as a citizen worker, as has been the case in modern U.S. political history, but as a citizen caregiver?"[26] Ever since I read this question, I've had trouble getting it out of my head. Indeed, I return to it several times in the chapters that follow, mulling it over as I consider the perspectives of Native women and governmental agents. If caregiving was at the center of our understanding of citizenship, that would change everything. Our discomforting definition of the "first-class" citizen—white, male, head of household, property owner, independent—would no longer matter. If we defined citizenship not as work (of breadwinners supporting dependents), but rather as *care*, we'd suddenly have an expansive opening, a valuing of women's unpaid labor in the home, the role women have played in sustaining their communities and neighborhoods, the work they've put into cultivating land and keeping families safe. We'd think of those who perform the work that is persistently devalued in American history and society—service workers, domestic laborers, teachers, support staff, those who provide the comfort, the humanity, the emotional labor—as the providers, the fulfillers of duty, the ones who make things run, the ones who deserve respect. We'd *support* them, both in the largest sense of the word (homes, basic needs, sustenance, comfort, encouragement) and in the smallest (financial assistance).

Wilkerson's question is also impactful because it brings together two things that seemingly don't mix: politics and care. Wilkerson focuses on the intersection between political organizing and labor, between home care and community care. Historians have shown how women welfare recipients actively challenged the widespread belief that they were "unworthy of support," by recasting themselves as mothers, consumers, citizens, and feminists.[27] In their efforts to defy racialized stereotypes of their laziness and immorality, these women, many of them Black, called attention to racism within the welfare system and demanded a "share in the economic abundance that had come to define American society."[28] Thus, they challenged popular notions of gendered economic citizenship and citizens' relationship with the state, by asserting that their chance at economic opportunity in the United States should also be safeguarded by governmental protection. These kinds of claims on the state echoed those of workers and consumers in the 1930s and 1940s, who saw government protection as "something they deserved."[29] In *Wardship and the Welfare State,* I also bring together politics and care, as the policies that this book interrogates—Indian policies and welfare policies—are ostensibly all about care. However, that care has historically never been neutral. Those who administer welfare and Indian policies enacted the "right" kind of care, the "right" amount of care, to the "right" people who needed it for the "right" purposes. Thus, there are two sides to caregiving, both of which are interrogated in this book. Care is relational: care sustains communities, it can be provided and accepted. But care can also be coercive, withdrawn, imposed, and withheld. Care can be both needed and resisted. Care is never neutral. Care is political. In many cases in this book, care is *demanded* (and still refused). In this book I historicize care as both an ingrained policy practice and a response to policy failures, as an expression of governmental bureaucracy and an assertion of tribal sovereignty and self-determination.

Thus, *Wardship and the Welfare State* has two goals: to understand the rhetoric and assumptions that undergirded terms such as "first-class" citizenship, "wardship," and "welfare dependency"; and to tease out the granular aspects of the relationships (mis)represented by those terms. Both of those goals meet at the illusion of a shared definition of these political concepts. But there was no such definition. Native people and non-Native state agents did not share the same perspectives or goals, even as they utilized the same language. Thus, Native people engaged in political maneuvering, utilizing these ideologies in a public sphere—testifying before Congress, issuing resolutions, lobbying politicians—in order to gain recognition and invite the state into care work; and in a private sphere—communicating with BIA agents and caseworkers, adjudicating family disputes—to gain access to the benefits they needed and to which they were entitled. In essence *Wardship and the Welfare State* interrogates the limitations of the state's definitions of "first-class" citizenship, "wardship," and "welfare dependency" and provides a counter-conceptualization of those ideas, rooted in historical Native understandings of self-determination and relationality.

The records of the BIA are the primary cache from which I drew to trace the colonial and interpersonal relationships that Native people formed with state agents. I also found these relationships in the papers of congresspeople and senators, the records of Senate and House subcommittees, the testimonies of Native people to Congress, tribal council records, and the records of the National Congress of American Indians. I visited four locations of the National Archives and Records Administration (Riverside, San Bruno, Atlanta, and Washington DC); one presidential library, the Harry S. Truman Library; two state historical societies (Arizona and Nevada); four university library special collections (Princeton University, Arizona State University, University of Nevada, Reno, and University of New Mexico); and the Smithsonian's National Museum of the American Indian Archive Center. As this list makes clear, *Wardship and the Welfare State* analyzes many examples from states in the American West, but like so much of the history of federal Indian policy, it is a national story, necessarily attuned to the intersections of federal, state, tribal, and local community politics.

The book begins with a contextual introduction of two policy (and historiographical) areas that do not often intersect in historical scholarship: Indian policy and welfare policy. Chapter 1, "Red Tape: An Introduction to Native Dual Citizenship in the Mid-Twentieth Century," provides background information useful for understanding how Indian policy and welfare policy interact and how Native people experienced both. Chapter 1 provides a succinct overview of Indian wardship as a legal and political category from its appearance in Chief Justice John Marshall's 1831 opinion in *Cherokee Nation v. Georgia* to the twenty-first century. The chapter also provides short introductions to the three key pieces of welfare legislation this book explores: the Social Security Act (1935), Servicemen's Dependents Allowance Act (1942), and the Servicemen's Readjustment Act, or GI Bill (1944).

Chapter 2, "Indian Poverty Knowledge: Defining First-Class Citizenship through Competency Legislation," explores non-Native politicians' definitions of "first-class" citizenship in the 1940s and 1950s. This chapter examines a set of termination bills proposed between 1944 and 1954 that would have implemented a process by which individual Natives could have applied for a "decree of competency" to achieve "first-class" citizenship and "emancipation" from their tribes. Through the conversations and correspondence generated over proposed competency legislation, non-Native politicians and state agents developed a definition of first-class citizenship that betrayed their concurrent fears of Native poverty and tribal sovereignty. The definition of first-class citizenship that terminationists developed was based on a body of knowledge I am calling "Indian poverty knowledge," after Alice O'Connor's definition of "poverty knowledge," the body of research generated on poverty in the twentieth century by think tanks, public agencies, and research institutes.[30] Indian poverty knowledge—research and data collected by the BIA, Congress, reform organizations, and scholars—was a specific set of ideas about Native poverty employed by the some agents of the BIA, members of Congress, and the media that was used to prop up a restrictive racialized and gendered understanding of first-class citizenship. Native activists challenged competency legislation, which ultimately failed to pass into law, by critiquing the ways in which the proposed bills would undermine tribal sovereignty and the legal relationships between Native nations and the United States.

Those legal relationships are the subject of chapter 3, "Every Day with the BIA: Welfare Applications and Wardship's Definitions," which turns to definitions of wardship. Wardship, a slippery concept that historically has no clear definition, is also a lived experience, constituted by the everyday bureaucracy Native people navigated to access resources and protect their legal rights as citizens of tribal nations. Native people formed actual relationships with members of the state, relationships that were shaped by Indian poverty knowledge *and* by the difficulties many Native people had accessing need-based welfare benefits such as Aid to Dependent Children (ADC), Old Age Assistance (OAA), and Aid to the Blind (AB) under the Social Security Act and benefits for military servicemembers and their families during and after World War II. Through chapter 3 I interrogate where two mutually exclusive sets of red tape met: how Native people accessed (or were restricted from accessing) welfare benefits *through* the relationships that constituted wardship. In other words, what did the BIA have to do with Native people's welfare benefits? And how did Native people's access to welfare shape wardship?

Chapter 4, "Gender and Wardship: Surveillance, Dependency, and Welfare's Limitations," continues the exploration of where wardship and welfare intersected. I interrogate what Nancy Fraser and Linda Gordon have called the *doxa* of dependency as a "keyword" in United States welfare policy—beliefs we understand to be common sense.[31] The *doxa* of dependency both contributed to and exacerbated the messy way historical actors understood wardship. Chapter 4 specifically engages with the understanding of dependency as a gendered term and investigates how Native women and men navigated both the *doxa* of welfare dependency and the *doxa* of Indian poverty knowledge to obtain welfare benefits. Welfare itself is gendered, and so were the ways in which the BIA interacted with Native people within wardship. Chapter 4 demonstrates how Native women and men negotiated with bureaucratic assumptions about their dependency with varying degrees of success. While Native women were subject to BIA oversight and surveillance of their receipt and use of benefits received under the 1942 Servicemen's Dependents Allowance Act, they did utilize the BIA to put pressure on family members serving overseas to facilitate their receipt of those benefits. Native men worked with the BIA to circumscribe wartime benefits due to their dependents and adjudicate family disputes. In the postwar period Native women faced enormous difficulties accessing ADC—in many cases despite the intervention of BIA agents on their behalf—while Native men received BIA assistance in obtaining GI Bill benefits and fulfilling the goals of that expansive welfare program.

Similarly, chapter 5, "Improving Farms and Homes: Assimilation and the GI Bill's Educational Provisions," also explores the relationship between advocacy and oversight, the coercive aspects of care rooted in the BIA's long history of assimilative programming. Chapter 5 focuses specifically on the educational provisions of the GI Bill and Native veterans' access to and participation in such programs. Agents within both the BIA and the Veterans Administration (VA) adhered to definitions of first-class citizenship that shaped Native veterans' experiences with the GI Bill, a welfare program that was simultaneously a measure employed to reduce the risk of a postwar nationwide economic depression and an assimilation program that promoted a gendered vision of gainfully employed, independent, male, first-class citizens. Many Native veterans used their GI Bill benefits at Indian boarding schools, where the BIA used resources received from the VA to energize existing programs in agricultural and vocational training, in a striking application of welfare benefits as a solution for Indian poverty knowledge. However, Native veterans critically engaged with this dynamic of opportunity and restriction—they may have been taking courses in the same institutions from many of the same instructors as Native students had before the war, but their GI Bill benefits went directly to them and their families.

Chapter 6, "Nebulous Shame, Innocent Taxpayers, and the Native Plight: Native Land and the Welfare State," zooms out from the details of wardship's relationships and examines broader assumptions about Native people's place in the midcentury American polity, especially in the context of politically charged conversations about the expansion of the federal welfare state. Chapter 6 examines how Native people, and reservations especially, became foils for anti-welfare rhetoric and activism, which manifested in refrains of Native people and other welfare recipients "taking" more than they deserved from an "innocent taxpaying public." Non-Natives who opposed welfare employed Indian poverty knowledge to undermine Native people's citizenship, arguing that because reservation land was tax-exempt, Native people did not deserve welfare benefits from the states. Instead, they reasoned, the federal government—a growing behemoth of unchecked power—was responsible for Native people's "plight." Anti-welfare conservatives acknowledged that Native poverty existed, and even acknowledged that many Americans felt guilty about it. But in their application of a definition of wardship rooted in Indian poverty knowledge, they simultaneously undermined Native land rights, supported termination policy (so Native people could be first-class citizens and pay their fair share), and opposed expanding the welfare state for all Americans. Chapter 6 demonstrates how Indian poverty knowledge reinforced an expectation of Native poverty (the so-called plight of Native people on reservations) that ultimately dehumanized them and deprived them of legitimate legal relationships and rights (both welfare and wardship).

Chapter 7, "Care Taken to Inform: Relational Wardship, Welfare, and Sovereignty," examines how Native people forcefully engaged with those sorts of assumptions and tried to change racist and sexist definitions of wardship through their personal interactions with state agents. The chapter explores how Native activists, namely Helen Peterson (Oglala Lakota), Ruth Muskrat Bronson (Cherokee), and others working within the National Congress of American Indians (NCAI) engaged a political grammar of first-class American citizenship to put forth their own definitions of wardship, welfare, and citizenship rooted in relationality. In their lobbying work and congressional testimonies, Peterson and Bronson took care to inform state agents of Native history, inviting the state into their relational worldview that incorporated the political and legal rights to wardship and welfare as elements of relational kinship. By defining wardship in terms that the state should have understood, they invited the United States to be a good relation to Native people. Whether the United States listened was another story.

> Listen, I have been educated.
> I have learned about Western
> Civilization. Do you know
> what the message of Western
> Civilization is? I am alone.
>
> —Eileen Myles, "An American Poem"

In "An American Poem," Eileen Myles masterfully distills the myths of "Western Civilization" clung to by the champions of first-class citizenship as the ideal path for Native people in the mid-twentieth century: "I am alone."[32] But first-class citizenship is a fiction. Or, rather, the idealized understanding of first-class citizenship shared by state agents, legislators, members of the media, and many non-Native citizens—an individual (white male) independent head of household, unencumbered by state interventions, economically self-sufficient, not in need of state benefits—is a fiction. Even the most individual of all individual rights of citizenship, the right to vote, and the most individual of all individual duties of citizenship, military service, are not unmediated or unencumbered. Women's historians have long argued that communities have shaped each individual's relationship(s) to the state. Membership within communities, families, and networks of kin are also political relationships.[33] In other words, no citizen exists in a vacuum of individualism. No person's relationship to the state is unmediated, completely divorced from some sort of collective—the family, the neighborhood, the tribe, the county, the community, the region, shared resources, language, land, values, religious beliefs. In a sense, what this book is trying to do—to tease out the complexities between wardship and citizenship, to interrogate wardship as a nuanced term that meant both something very specific and everything very general, to situate Native people in a larger national conversation about dependency and rights—all of these things come down to one idea: *we are not alone.*

> This treaty was later replaced by another (more convenient) treaty, and then another.
> I've had difficulty unraveling the terms of these treaties, given the legal speak and congressional language.
> As treaties were abrogated (broken) and new treaties were drafted, one after another, the new treaties often referenced old defunct treaties, and it is a muddy, switchback trail to follow.
> Although I often feel lost on this trail, I know I am not alone.
> —Layli Long Soldier (Oglala Lakota), "38"

Tribal sovereignty is at once a messy topic and one that is incredibly clear. Sovereignty connotes political respect and recognition. Sovereign nations are recognized as such by other sovereigns. Sovereignty is power—power over land, culture, language, membership, religion. In my U.S. and Native history courses I often ask students which of the following is more important for a nation to maintain its sovereignty: people or land. They are always divided. "There are small countries!" some students offer. Small land bases don't mean lack of sovereignty, as long as the people are there! "But the land!" the other side responds. Without the land, do you have a nation? Ultimately though, this question is impossible to answer (something my students quickly realize). Even with both land and people, if other nations do not recognize one nation's sovereignty, is that nation sovereign?

Tribal sovereignty is, like everything else in this world, relational. For sovereignty to mean anything, it must be understood and recognized by others. In the poem "38," quoted above, Oglala Lakota poet Layli Long Soldier describes the treaties between the United States and the Dakota Nation as "turbid treaties." "Synonyms for turbid include muddy, unclear, cloudy, confused, and smoky," she writes.[34] The United States has used *turbidity* to undermine Native sovereignty for centuries. In the mid-twentieth century, termination policies were ostensibly created to clear up the cloudiness. So many treaties, treaties on top of treaties, treaties broken, treaties drafted but unratified, treaties ratified but ignored, treaties abrogated again and again. Long Soldier's description—"it is a muddy, switchback trail to follow"—is perfect. In the mid-twentieth century, many non-Native actors—those who worked for the BIA, the VA, state and county welfare boards, members of Congress, and ordinary citizens—attempted to bypass all the switchbacks. They wanted to go straight up the mountain, carving a new, more "efficient," more "equal" trail. Even the language they used to describe this process was short and seemingly simple: "'Emancipate' Native people!" "Let them go!" "Set them free!" The winding switchback path of wardship, a historical relationship rooted in treaties and agreements, was unnecessary, oppressive, "gratuitous."

But what seemed to them like the simplest path to the top undermined health and safety. With no attempt to understand the mountain, to observe why the path has been carved in the way it has, to quietly respect the way humans maneuver through the land on this imperfect and muddy (turbid) trail, people can die. Land can be destroyed. History can be trampled and forgotten. The switchback trail is confusing and laborious. It requires *support*: meeting basic needs, comfort, active interest in the well-being of others, concern, a sense of home. But, as Long Soldier reminds us, "Although I often feel lost on this trail, I know I am not alone."

We are not alone.

CHAPTER 1

Red Tape

An Introduction to Native Dual Citizenship in the Mid-Twentieth Century

I am a citizen of the United States and an enrolled member of the
Oglala Sioux Tribe, meaning I am a citizen of the Oglala Lakota
Nation—and in this dual citizenship, I must work, I must eat, I must
art, I must mother, I must friend, I must listen, I must observe, constantly I must live.

—Layli Long Soldier (Oglala Lakota), *Whereas*

The red man has been so fettered with red tape that he is suffering
with age-long rope burns.

—Zitkala-Ša (Yankton Dakota), "Red Men Who Taught
Pilgrims How to Exist" (1934)

This first chapter is a brief reference resource on the history of Native
people's relationships to wardship and welfare. Because the following chapters integrate two historiographies that are not often analyzed
alongside one another, this chapter provides a short overview of the
history of Indian wardship and the three pieces of welfare legislation
discussed in this book: the Social Security Act (1935), the Servicemen's
Dependents Allowance Act (1942), and the Servicemen's Readjustment
Act (1944), also known as the GI Bill.

As a general term "wardship" implies incompetency by virtue of age (immaturity) or mental incapacity. Wards are under the protection, tutelage, or surveillance of guardians. It is impossible to disentangle wardship as a concept from the racialized and gendered connotations to which it is attached. Simply put, women, children, and people of color (those assumed to be dependent) needed to be wards; white men (those assumed to be independent) were eligible to be their guardians. Throughout the eighteenth and nineteenth centuries, these assumptions were reiterated and propped up by scientific racism, legal precedent, and political philosophies of liberalism. To challenge wardship was to challenge coverture, racial segregation, and scientific theories of evolution.[1] To challenge wardship was also to challenge a history of racial paternalism and enslavement of Native children, only thinly veiled as "apprenticeship" or "servitude."[2] Throughout the nineteenth and early twentieth centuries, wardship was deployed against Native people as a racialized and gendered concept to further their assimilation into the bottom rungs of non-Native society and further non-Natives' theft of land.[3] The ward-guardian relationship was tenuous, characterized by a tension between protection and control.

But the citizen-state relationship was also tenuous. What is the relationship between wardship and citizenship? Both political affiliations, both markers of identity and belonging, the two are not mutually exclusive. Indeed, Long Soldier's description of her "dual citizenship"—living, working, eating, mothering, observing, and more in both the United States and the Oglala Lakota Nation—reveals the extent to which her dual political memberships are all encompassing and entwined.[4] Zitkala-Ša's critique of how "fettered" Native people have been by this duality—or rather, by the administrative manifestation of this duality, the "red tape"—reminds us that dual (and sometimes *dueling*) political relationships are fraught.[5] The sections below provide a historical overview of that thorny red tape and the inescapable duality of both political relationships for Native people.

WARDSHIP AND CITIZENSHIP

Before 1924

In his 1831 *Cherokee Nation v. Georgia* decision, Chief Justice John Marshall ruled that the Cherokee Nation was not a "foreign state" under the terms of the Constitution. Rather, Marshall reasoned, the Cherokees, and by implication all Native people, should be considered "domestic dependent nations" and "in a state of pupilage. Their relation to the United States resembles that of a ward to his guardian."[6] *Cherokee Nation* marks the first application of the term "ward" to describe Native people within the United States. The chief justice's words were quite vague. He defined neither "ward" nor "guardian" and did not describe the relationship between Native people and the United States in concrete language—it only "resembled" that of a ward to his guardian. As "domestic dependent nations," tribes were situated in an area of "colonial ambivalence," where sovereignty was both codified and restricted.[7] However, state agents, historians, and the courts have used Marshall's terminology to interpret the relationship between tribes and the U.S. government ever since. As legal scholar Frank Pommersheim notes, the notion of tribes' statuses as "domestic dependent nations," sovereign entities also reliant on the federal government, continues to exist in the present day, although "its particulars, its contours, and its borders remain elusive."[8] The ambiguous definitions of this relationship between "ward" and "guardian" drastically affected all subsequent exchanges between Native people and the government (both federal and state).

Throughout the nineteenth century, wardship was linked with a racialized understanding of Native people as uncivilized and savage, needing "protection" by the government not only from unscrupulous whites but also from each other.[9] This racial and colonial ideology is clearly exemplified in the 1886 Supreme Court case *United States v. Kagama*. In *Kagama*, the court ruled that the Major Crimes Act of 1885 was constitutional. This act made it a federal offense for Native people to commit any of seven specific crimes against another Native person on a reservation.[10] The court removed jurisdiction for these offenses from tribes and placed it squarely under the purview of the federal government. *Kagama* challenged the Major Crimes Act because it undermined tribal sovereignty, since the federal government was exerting the power to regulate law and order and adjudicate disputes between Natives on sovereign Native land. Overruling the sovereignty argument, the court determined that since Native people were "remnants of a race once powerful, now weak and diminished in numbers," the federal government had the responsibility to exert its power over Natives living on reservations. Chief Justice Samuel Miller wrote that this was "necessary for their *protection*, as well as to the safety of those among whom they dwell."[11] The *Kagama* decision cemented wardship deep into the structure of the relationship between Natives and the federal government with legitimate legal and practical consequences. After *Kagama* the state had the right to intervene to punish individual Native people as they saw fit—to safeguard Natives from themselves.

Cases such as *Kagama* and the 1903 case *Lone Wolf v. Hitchcock* utilized wardship to formally solidify congressional power over tribes in matters of law and order and treaty enforcement.[12] In the late nineteenth century individual Native people living in the United States also sought to define the parameters of their identity and status as "wards." For example, in 1884 John Elk (Ho-Chunk) brought a suit in the Circuit Court of the United States for the District of Nebraska against an Omaha registrar who had refused to register Elk as a voter in a city election. In the case, *Elk v. Wilkins*, Elk challenged that under the Fourteenth Amendment, he was legally a citizen of the United States and therefore entitled to vote in the election. Elk had severed his relationship with his tribe and was living off-reservation when he attempted to register to vote. He argued that the only reason he was denied registration was because he was Native.[13] The court disagreed with Elk's claim to the Fourteenth Amendment and argued that although technically Native people were born within United States territory, they were no more subject to U.S. jurisdiction than children of ambassadors or other officials of foreign nations born on U.S. soil.[14] The court ruled that an individual Native person, even one like John Elk who had severed his or her relationship with his or her tribe, could not claim U.S. citizenship. Rather, Native people's status could only be altered "by the nation whose wards they are and whose citizens they seek to become." Thus, *Elk v. Wilkins* more clearly defined wardship as the opposite of citizenship. Following the court's logic in *Elk v. Wilkins*, individual Native people could not renounce their own wardship, and wardship was viewed as "an impediment to citizenship."[15]

In 1916 the court reversed their decision in *Elk v. Wilkins* and conferred a more ambiguous, dual status upon Native people. In the case *United States v. Nice*, the court determined that "citizenship is not incompatible with tribal existence or continued guardianship, and so may be conferred without completely emancipating the Indians."[16] The results of the *Nice* case contradicted much of the rhetoric surrounding allotment as a path to Native citizenship. Even if Native people were living on allotted land and had received citizenship as laid out in the 1887 Dawes Act, they remained legally "wards" because the federal government retained power over many aspects of their lives.[17] Chapter 2 investigates the relationship between allotment policy and first-class citizenship in more detail.

The Indian Citizenship Act (1924)

In 1924 Congress extended the dual "citizen-ward" status to all Native people who had not been declared citizens through allotment, marriage, or military service.[18] The Indian Citizenship Act (ICA) universally declared all Native people in the United States to be citizens, stating "that all noncitizen Indians born within the territorial limits of the United States be, and they are hereby, declared to be citizens of the United States: *Provided*, that the granting of such citizenship shall not in any manner impair or otherwise affect the right of any Indian to tribal or other property."[19] Although the act was sweeping and declarative, it was also mediated by the assurance that American citizenship would not infringe on Native people's rights to tribal property. Thus, the ICA "neither denied [Natives'] citizenship in tribes nor fully incorporated them into the American polity."[20] The act has been commonly referred to in historical literature as repayment for Native people's efforts in World War I, but it also reflected Progressive legislators' political efforts to minimize bureaucracy in the federal government and calculations on the part of Republican politicians hoping to court the Native vote.[21] The timing of this piece of legislation was also significant. In 1924 Congress also passed the most restrictive immigration law in the nation's history, the Johnson-Reed Act. Thus, while Native people were universally declared American citizens, with the assumption of their eventual assimilation, Congress decided to drastically restrict the immigration of people from

Eastern and Southern Europe and Asia, privileging the immigration of those who were associated with common perceptions of whiteness in the early twentieth century.[22]

Why, when so many were restricted from entry into the United States and a path to naturalized citizenship, were Native people declared citizens? Citizenship, in this case, was a method of coercive assimilation, undermining tribal sovereignty and classifying Native people as individuals rather than members of distinct tribal nations.[23] At the same time, the ICA further codified Native people's "citizen-ward" status into the law, enshrining nineteenth-century ideology of guardianship into twentieth-century politics. The ICA thus created a status of "dual citizenship" for Natives (both as Americans and as members of Native nations) and further served the U.S. government's goal to "eliminate Indian Country from the maps altogether."[24] The ICA has a messy legacy that did not clear up questions over where Native people belonged in the American polity. Yes, they were citizens. But they were citizens with rights to tribal property. And crucially, their citizenship did not connote whiteness, or equality with those considered to be white. Thus, the persistence of wardship precluded full assimilation of Native people into American society.

After the passage of the ICA, most of the public and even many in Congress did not realize that Native people were American citizens. For many in the early to mid-twentieth century, "ward" status trumped Native people's "citizen" status, and conversations abounded over how to extend citizenship to Native people and whether they were eligible for the benefits of citizenship. For example, the extension of social welfare provisions in the mid-1930s posed problems for state welfare workers who questioned whether Native people were citizens and residents of their states, eligible for such benefits as Old Age Assistance, Aid to the Blind, or Aid to Dependent Children under the 1935 Social Security Act. Lawyers working with the Department of the Interior and individual states reached similar conclusions—the ICA assured that Native people were citizens and eligible for welfare benefits. However, that eligibility did nothing to dissolve or clarify wardship status. State agents issued statements such as, "All Indians, ward or non-ward, who were born within the United States meet the citizenship requirements of our social welfare laws, for all are made citizens of the United States by the Act of Congress of June 2, 1924."[25] Or, "But an Indian ward, whether a ward because of his trust property or the maintenance of tribal relations, as a person and a citizen of the State where he resides, has the benefit of and is subject to State laws in manifold phases of his life. The necessity of proving abandonment of tribal relations in order to show an Indian a citizen and entitled to a citizen's rights is unnecessary in view of the citizenship act of June 2, 1924."[26] Thus, the ICA and subsequent interpretations of the act solidified Native people's simultaneous status as "wards" and "citizens." Supposedly, as interpreters of the law at both the federal and the state levels found, wardship status did not disqualify Native people from some benefits of citizenship.[27] However, as this book demonstrates, the ambiguous status of "citizen-ward" also allowed certain states to claim it was legal to restrict Native people from welfare benefits.

Thus, the ICA both propelled assimilation efforts and permanently attached wardship to Native people's citizenship status. Its ambiguity left a lasting impression on the twentieth century, spurring conflicts over both Native people's rights to the benefits of citizenship and their responsibilities to fulfill the duties of citizenship. Citizenship (and, in turn, revocation of wardship) continued to function as the proverbial "carrot" for Native assimilation and abdication of land—even when it was not necessary—well into the mid-twentieth century.

Indian Reorganization Act (1934)

U.S. Indian policy underwent a major change in 1934, with the passage of the Indian Reorganization Act (IRA). This key piece of legislation, also known as the "Indian New Deal," was created by John Collier, commissioner of Indian Affairs from 1933 to 1945. The IRA was undergirded by the argument that Native tribes should be recognized by the federal government as culturally distinct entities.[28] The IRA abandoned assimilation as an official policy, ended the practice of allotment, and encouraged tribes to adopt constitutions and exercise self-government.[29] Though the IRA represents a significant shift in federal Indian policy, the legislation has been critiqued by scholars who argue that it perpetuated the reach of the BIA over Native tribes through the use of suggested constitutions prepared by BIA personnel.[30] Thus, the IRA further extended Native people's ambiguous status in the American polity. Although Collier and his supporters halted the process of allotment and instituted protections for Native cultural, religious, and artistic expression, the IRA did not grant tribes full sovereignty or alter Congress's plenary power over them.[31] Furthermore, BIA officials presumed that federal supervision was necessary for those tribes that wished to achieve federal recognition as incorporated tribes under the IRA, "as Indians gained more experience" in self-government, before government officials could "fade away."[32]

Collier framed the IRA as a bill to reinforce and expand Native people's experiences of American citizenship. The first line of Collier's bill stated, "That it is hereby declared to be the policy of Congress to grant those Indians *living under Federal tutelage and control* the freedom to organize for the purposes of local self-government and economic enterprise, to the end that civil liberty, political responsibility, and economic independence shall be achieved among the Indian peoples of the United States."[33] Collier constructed the IRA as an end to the practice of "Federal tutelage and control." At the same time, he saw the act as an effort to support Native integration or assimilation into the democratic ideologies of the United States. Thus, although the bill was interpreted by critics as a "socialist" or "communist" endeavor, Collier proposed ending federal guardianship over Native people after they had adopted what he saw as the benefits of American "civil liberty, political responsibility, and economic independence."[34] Collier's goal was to alleviate Native poverty and the damage done by allotment, but he also wanted to remind state agents and the public that Native people were American citizens. A 1933 press release on the IRA from the Department of the Interior hailed the goals of the act: "conservation and development of Indian lands and resources, the establishment of a credit system for the Indians, the arrangement of scholarships in institutions of higher education for Indian youths and the formation of Indian business organizations."[35] However, the provisions set out in the IRA were not proposed as "aid" to a dependent and uncivilized population. Instead, the press release reads: "These are certainly elemental privileges to be sought for American citizens. However, curious, as it may seem, many Americans do not realize that

Indians are citizens."[36] By framing federal spending for Native people's economic and educational opportunities simply as "elemental privileges" for American citizens, Collier emphasized Native membership in the American polity as citizens and wards. Through the IRA, the federal government fulfilled its responsibility to its wards by providing what was due to them as citizens.

The IRA did not resolve any issues about wardship status. Indeed, in the same press release where Native citizenship was highlighted, the Department of the Interior claimed that "Thousands of copies were called for by Indians who termed this their 'Proclamation of Emancipation.'"[37] If the IRA was Native people's "Emancipation Proclamation," the government was liberating Native Americans who had been "enslaved" by the government itself. Furthermore, the press release claimed that Native people had equated the IRA with the document that would lead to the Thirteenth, Fourteenth, and Fifteenth Amendments to the Constitution, which had, at least on paper, institutionalized the full, legal citizenship of formerly enslaved African Americans. The IRA was depicted as an act that signaled a clear, linear path for Native people, from "wards" to "citizens."

Was the IRA as "emancipatory" as the Department of the Interior had claimed? Debates between John Collier and Congressmen Theodore Werner of South Dakota and Theodore Christianson of Minnesota during the 1934 House hearings on Collier's bill reveal persistent ambiguities surrounding the nature of Indian wardship and whether the IRA officially ended "guardianship." Collier argued, "The guardianship of the Indian is definitely ended by this plan." Congressman Werner seemed to agree, stating, "A man cannot maintain the right of citizenship and still be subject to guardianship." However, Werner qualified his strict delineation between citizenship and guardianship: "He remains a *ward* nonetheless." Collier attempted to clarify, arguing that Native people would still be under guardianship, but not the type of guardianship that would infringe upon first-class citizenship, "tak[ing] away from him his initiative, his self-respect, his power, his liberty and self-support."[38] Congressman Christianson attempted to establish a distinction between "two classes of guardianship which the law recognizes, guardianship of the person and guardianship of the estate." He asked Collier, "Is not the guardianship the Government is exercising here more in the nature of the estate of the Indian than the person?" Collier confirmed, stating, "It becomes that under this bill."[39] Therefore, Collier asserted that the IRA would retain the federal government's powers of guardianship over Native *land* but would cease to serve as a guardian over Native *people*. Although this distinction seemed simple, it was not easy to separate estate from person, especially considering decades of policy doctrine that had specified that Native people must be deemed "competent" by the state to take full ownership of their land without restrictions.[40] Indeed, Congressman Christianson's next comment to Collier revealed this complexity: "Ordinarily when a guardianship is established over his estate, that guardianship terminates whenever the incompetent becomes competent to manage his own affairs, and is resumed if he becomes incompetent again, but I presume that the policy of the Government in this instance is to assist the Indian until he develops full competency and then terminate the guardianship."[41] Christianson's assumption that the government would continue to assist Native people until they developed competency demonstrated that despite Collier's emphasis that the IRA would help Natives establish their citizenship, these politicians continued to understand Native people predominantly as wards. Ultimately, Congressman Werner was correct: Native people remained wards nonetheless.

Termination Policies (1940s–1960s)

John Collier left the BIA in 1945, and his departure, coupled with the context of post–World War II political discourse about race, ushered in a new era in Indian policy, known as the Termination and Relocation Era. As Donald Fixico has noted, midcentury politicians and state agents ascribed to "an undaunted devotion to conforming all segments of society into one unified nation" and the "dream of creating an America of one people."[42] They saw the trust relationship between Natives and the federal government as a negative impact on this vision of a unified nation. With these philosophies in mind, they proposed to "terminate" the relationship between tribes and the BIA. "Successful" termination policies included the passage of Public Law 280 in 1953, which authorized the states of Alaska, California, Minnesota, Nebraska, Oregon, and Wisconsin to assume civil and criminal jurisdiction over reservations without tribal consent, and the "relocation" programs of the mid-1950s, which provided job training and other incentives for Native people to move off of reservations and relocate in urban areas.[43] Terminationists were motivated by their desire to fully assimilate Native people into American society. However, though their rhetoric was reminiscent of nineteenth-century assimilation, twentieth-century politicians and policymakers couched termination squarely within language of midcentury celebrations of American liberty, equality, and prosperity. In this way termination was not necessarily an abrupt "backtrack" to the policies of the nineteenth and early twentieth centuries, interrupted by the IRA, but rather one additional stop on a long line of policies centered on ambiguous conceptions of Native citizenship. Wardship was an essential part of the practice and rhetoric of termination. Terminationists argued that before Natives could fully integrate into the "unified nation," wardship must be eradicated.

To advocates of termination, ending the relationship between Native people and the federal government meant ending the "dependency" implicit in the "ward-guardian" relationship. If Native people were no longer "dependent" upon the federal government, they would be able to achieve the same levels of prosperity and economic success as other American citizens. However, questions lingered over the role of the special relationship between Native tribes and the federal government and racialized tropes associated with wardship. In 1948 the Committee on Indian Affairs organized by the Commission on the Organization of the Executive Branch issued a report that engaged with Native racialization and citizenship. The committee asserted, "Assimilation must be the dominant goal of public policy." They supported this strident statement by pointing to the separation between (dependent) Natives and "reasonably prosperous non-Indians." Although the committee assured that Native people would "preserve some of their own values and attitudes," it was clear to them that Native people "d[id] not want to be 19th century story-book Indians."[44] In this case the committee did not represent assimilation as a coercive policy backed by the threat of extinction. Rather, they asserted that assimilation "must" be the policy goal because *Natives* wanted to "master and benefit from the culture of our times."[45] The committee utilized the familiar racial trope of "19th century story-book Indians" to highlight the danger of failing to enact assimilation as policy. In their eyes, if the government did not do something to bring Native people up to speed, there was a danger that this group of American *citizens*, despite their own desires, would be unable to access the benefits of living in the postwar United States.

Formulated in the language of postwar equality, the committee's report drew upon wardship to support Native people's citizenship status. For example, the committee asserted, "Regardless of treaties and agreements with Indian tribes in which a good many specific commitments have been made as to both educational and economic assistance toward assimilation, the Indian deserves at least a fair break because he is a human being and a citizen of the United States."[46] The committee acknowledged treaties made with tribes only to bring up the duties of the federal government as "guardian" to its "wards," educational and economic assistance toward assimilation. However, the committee pitched assimilation as something that the United States owed Native people, as a "fair break," not because of those treaties, but because of their humanity and citizenship. Ultimately, the committee reasoned, regardless of their status as wards, because Natives were citizens, Congress should promote assimilation policies.

The committee argued that wardship hampered Native progress. Crucially the committee situated Native people's failure to break free of the control of the federal government within a naturalized narrative of Manifest Destiny. It stated: "The thing that has been most lacking and most needed is Indian motivation. For 150 years policies have been imposed by the government. The policies have been Indian policies, not Indians' policies. If Indian tribes resisted, they could win battles, but they always lost the wars. If they retreated and withdrew to the west, they were always overtaken by the tide of westward migration."[47] Although the committee represented "westward migration" as a "tide" taking place independent of human action, Natives were both human casualties of it and humans who did not resist *enough* to stop it. The committee argued that the biggest problem (what was "most lacking" and "most needed") was Native *motivation*. In the context of federal wardship (and receipt of federal benefits in general), "motivation" was a decidedly racialized term. (Think of the BIA's "frequently asked question" published in 1948, the same year, cited in the introduction: "Are Indians naturally lazy?") Postwar assimilation—ironically, a government policy—would supposedly allow Native people to gain the strength they had needed for the past 150 years to resist the imposition of government policies.

In the 1940s and 1950s, legislators, reformers, and policymakers asserted that Native people needed to be emancipated because as wards whose resources were provided by the BIA, they were more likely to "shirk" their duties of citizenship. To be "free" of the BIA would mean that a Native person was "free" of wardship. In 1953 the passage of House Concurrent Resolution 108 institutionalized these impressions of wardship. This resolution mandated that Natives living in the states of California, Florida, New York, and Texas, as well as the Flathead Tribe of Montana, the Klamath Tribe of Oregon, the Menominee Tribe of Wisconsin, the Potawatomie Tribe of Kansas and Nebraska, and the Chippewa Tribe living on the Turtle Mountain Reservation in North Dakota, would be released from the supervision and control of the BIA.[48] This legislation drastically affected the relationship between members of these Native nations and the states in which they resided.[49] This resolution proposed "to end [Natives'] status as wards of the United States, and to grant them all of the rights and prerogatives pertaining to American citizenship."[50] Notably, in addition, the bill also declared that Native people "should assume their full responsibilities as American citizens."[51] Thus, Congress proposed that if Native people broke free from the chains of wardship, they could access the rights due to them as citizens. At the same time, politicians implied that thus far, wardship had precluded Native people from fulfilling their obligations as American citizens.

Wardship Continues

During a 2014 community meeting in Flagstaff, Arizona, Republican congressman Paul Gosar caused an outcry. While addressing concerns about construction of a copper mine on the land of the San Carlos Apache

Tribe, Gosar dismissed White Mountain Apache tribal member Paul Stago's apprehensions about the mine's impact on tribal sovereignty, claiming that Native people were "still wards of the federal government."[52] Stago asserted that Gosar's use of the "antiquated" term "ward" revealed "the true deep feeling of the federal government: 'Tribes, you can call yourselves sovereign nations, but when it comes down to the final test, you're not really sovereign because we still have plenary authority over you.'"[53] Former U.S. Attorney Troy Eid spoke out against Gosar's use of the term, deeming it inappropriate and outdated, and accused Gosar of "race baiting."[54] Indeed, Eid asserted that the 1924 Indian Citizenship Act had made Indians citizens, not wards, and the 1934 Indian Reorganization Act had "pushed the concept of tribal sovereignty and self-determination."[55] Paul Gosar insisted that his comments revealed the hidden truth about the relationship between tribes and the U.S. state. He clarified his comments further to *Indian Country Today*, arguing, "The federal government's dirty little secret is that Native American tribes are not fully sovereign nations in today's society as many people are led to believe."[56]

The legal and social construction of wardship has a convoluted and controversial relationship with the concepts of both citizenship and sovereignty. Ultimately, whatever Gosar's rationale, the media response to his comments simplified and generalized the historicity of wardship. "Ward" is not an antiquated term that has been banished to the corners of early American history. The media coverage of this incident downplayed the living history of wardship's continued impact on tribal sovereignty, racial identity, and Natives' place within the American citizenry. Although it is commonly associated with the nineteenth century, "ward" is not a term that politicians, state agents, members of the American public, or Native people can leave in the past. Indeed, in the "Frequently Asked Questions" section of the BIA's current website, some of the same questions in the 1948 *Answers to Your Questions on American Indians* appear. Notably, non-Natives are still frequently asking, "Are American Indians and Alaska Natives wards of the Federal Government?" and "Are American Indians and Alaska Native citizens of the United States?"[57]

The New Deal and World War II led to an expansion of the federal state in the 1930s to 1950s. Expanded welfare programs caused Americans to reassess how citizenship functioned as a "reciprocal relationship" between the federal government and individual citizens.[58] Citizens who fulfilled their increased obligations to the state began to understand themselves as entitled to state social welfare benefits as "rights."[59] This understanding of a "right" to welfare was not one-sided. New Deal policymakers and administrators also "spread rights language throughout the nation," changing the way Americans thought about relief and aid to the poor.[60]

As Cybelle Fox has written, the historiography of social welfare in the twentieth century has focused on "an American welfare state in black and white," leaving out (or lumping in) the experience of non-white and non-Black people.[61] Likewise, historians have mainly focused on Native people's relationships to state policy as their relationship to *Indian* policy. These scholarly assumptions mirror the policy assumptions that historical actors made about wardship in the mid-twentieth-century. "Welfare," or need-based aid administered by state and county welfare boards wasn't *for* Native people. Since they were "wards," the federal government took "care" of them. But, despite these misconceptions, welfare was certainly for Native people, and, moreover, wardship wasn't so simple.

Social Security Act

The 1935 Social Security Act ushered in a major change in American government and politics. Most notably the Social Security Act signified formation of a more centralized and expansive administrative state, which was increasingly interlaced with the lives of ordinary American citizens.[62] The act established provisions for maternal and child welfare, public health, and welfare benefits in five key categories: Unemployment Insurance; Old Age Insurance (OAI), a contributory program for wage earners in covered occupations financed by a payroll tax; and public assistance programs administered by the states and funded through federal grants-in-aid to states including Old Age Assistance (OAA), a program to assist needy citizens over sixty-five years of age, Aid to Dependent

Children (ADC), a program to assist needy parents of minor children, and Aid to the Blind (AB). Historians of welfare have analyzed how the Social Security Act and other aspects of the New Deal solidified a "two-track" system of welfare within the United States. Within this system, mostly white male wage earners were viewed as "entitled" to benefits guaranteed by the national government (in the form of OAI), and mostly non-white or female needy populations were viewed as "dependent" upon benefits administered by the individual states.[63] Race and gender have fundamentally impacted citizens' abilities to access benefits from federal and state governments.[64] For citizens applying for need-based programs such as OAA, ADC, and AB, local prejudices and discrimination at the hands of state officials impacted who was deemed eligible for aid and the amount of assistance granted.[65] Although many view the Social Security Act as one of the major achievements of Franklin D. Roosevelt's New Deal, historians have challenged that for those who were not able to access the social safety net the act enshrined for American citizens, the act revealed that "not all citizens are equal, nor are they entitled to equal rights and protections."[66]

Except for legal historian Karen Tani, scholars have not analyzed the impact of the Social Security Act on Native Americans.[67] Instead historians have mainly focused on the IRA. The IRA did not function like other New Deal programs for public welfare. The act stipulated appropriations for education (primarily vocational and trade school education) and established a revolving credit fund to lend money to the tribes that had elected to adopt constitutions and voted to accept the IRA. Funds could be lent to Native individuals through their respective tribes. The IRA also concentrated on increasing the land base of Native people. Although John Collier intended the act to improve tribes' economic situation, it did not function as Social Security, where individuals applied to bureaucratic agencies for needed funds.[68] Moreover, although the IRA was undoubtedly important, it was not the *only* piece of New Deal legislation that affected Native people.[69] Native people experienced the reach of the mid-twentieth-century expansion of the state through the familiar agency of the BIA and through state and county welfare offices responsible for administering and processing claims for Social Security benefits.

Servicemen's Dependents Allowance Act

Under the Servicemen's Dependents Allowance Act of 1942, wives, children, and other dependent relatives of men in the lower grades of the military were eligible for a monthly allowance consisting of a contribution from the soldier's paycheck and a contribution from the federal government.[70] These allowances were also referred to as "dependency allotments." A similar program to provide support for soldiers' dependents had been adopted in World War I. However, during World War I wives directly applied for benefits, whereas during World War II the soldiers applied for dependency allowances or allotments through their commanding officers. This severed the "unmediated relationship between women and the national state," which, as historian K. Walter Hickel has shown, provided women with considerable leverage during World War I.[71] Because the World War II soldier himself was tasked with applying for benefits, conflict naturally arose between families, servicemen, and bureaucratic state agents. The resulting red tape was not necessarily something unique to Native families. However, Native wives and parents did face challenges in claiming benefits due to their ambiguous status as both citizens and wards, which often meant that their claims were funneled through additional layers of bureaucracy and surveillance.

Servicemen's Readjustment Act (GI Bill)

The 1944 Servicemen's Readjustment Act, or GI Bill, was a massive veterans' benefit package that provided unemployment benefits, low-interest guaranteed loans for the purchase of homes, businesses, or farms, and tuition and stipends for up to four years of education or vocational training to those World War II veterans who had served at least ninety days, with a discharge other than dishonorable.[72] As a result of these programs, 4.3 million veterans purchased homes, 200,000 purchased farms or businesses, and 7.8 million (51 percent of all World War II veterans) utilized educational and training benefits.[73] Historians credit the GI Bill for a boom in the construction industry, as nearly "one-third of new housing starts nationwide" were backed by the Veterans Administration (VA) by 1955, and substantial changes to American colleges, as veterans made up half of the undergraduate population by 1948.[74] Historians Glenn Altschuler and Stuart Blumin have described the bill as "without question, one of the largest and most comprehensive government initiatives ever enacted in the United States."[75]

The bill provided the sixteen million people who had served the United States in World War II with opportunity for "upward mobility."[76] However, as many historians have noted, this was an exclusive opportunity—unavailable to nonveterans and easier to access and more advantageous for some veterans than others. For example, women veterans, who made up 2 percent of the total military personnel in World War II, received less information about their entitlements, were less likely to take advantage of educational training, and were unable to access the same kinds of benefits as men. Unlike male veterans, women did not receive living allowances for dependent spouses while in school.[77] Additionally, although the bill's language appeared to apply equally to veterans across racial and ethnic groups, the GI Bill did little to combat institutionalized and structural racism within the United States. Many more white veterans than Black veterans attended institutions of higher learning, in part because the law granted authority in admissions criteria to universities, which adhered to existing quotas and segregation policies.[78] Suzanne Mettler has further contextualized this discrepancy, noting that many African American veterans had less education than whites prior to entering military service and were thus more likely to take advantage of vocational training or subcollege programs.[79] Mettler asserts that the bill "opened the doors to higher education for many from the lower and lower middle classes," and "higher proportions of nonwhites than whites used the education and training benefits."[80] However, as Ira Katznelson has noted, because the law "left responsibility for implementation mainly to the states and localities, including, of course, those that practiced official racism without compromise," Black veterans often faced discrimination in their dealings with local VA officers in charge of unemployment benefits, job placement, and home loans.[81] Thus, though the GI Bill is unmistakably one of the largest and most influential government programs in U.S. history, it did not challenge American institutions of racism and sexism.

Historians of both the GI Bill and Native people's participation in World War II have largely neglected to examine both Native men's access to GI Bill educational programs and loans and the impact of wardship on Native veterans' lives.[82] Rather, scholars have focused on Native men's motivations for joining the war effort and, more broadly, the relationship between Native military service and assimilation. Mid-twentieth-century terminationist policymakers argued that military service signaled Native people's "readiness" to integrate into the "white world." Historian Al Carroll has criticized some non-Native scholars for recapitulating this kind of "assimilationist propaganda" in their own work, at the expense of examining "Natives' own words."[83] Scholars such as Alison Bernstein, Kenneth Townsend, and Jere' Bishop Franco have argued that military service led Native veterans to see the limitations the BIA placed on their lives and encouraged them to understand themselves as a minority group seeking opportunity and rights *within* the United States polity, ignoring the legal and political interactions between Native servicemen's wardship status and their agitation for rights as citizens.[84] In so doing, these authors have underemphasized Native people's identities as members of tribal nations, focusing solely on their military service to the United States as an expression of American patriotism and point of entry into mainstream American society.

Other historians *have* explored more of the multifaceted motivations and implications of Native military service. For example, Carroll asserts that World War II provided an arena for veterans and their communities to create "permanent and far more widespread tradition[s]" that "allowed veterans to make military service meaningful to them according to traditional dictates."[85] Thus, rather than a pure expression of service to the United States, World War II military service expanded existing military traditions among tribal nations. Paul Rosier argues that Native servicemen did express American patriotism, but at the same time they fought for recognition of the rights of their own Native nations. Rosier defined this dual expression of national loyalty as an "ideology of hybrid patriotism—both Indian and American."[86] Noah Riseman has also complicated Native people's relationship with the U.S. military by assessing how military service perpetuated American colonialism. He argues that the use of "indigenous soldiers as weapons in the Second World War was a process rife with colonial exploitation, where the colonizers' interests reigned supreme at the expense of indigenous agency and civil rights."[87] All three of these studies have created a valuable and nuanced picture of Native service, especially within the confines of war itself. However, scholars have not devoted the same attention to veterans' experiences after the war's end, especially in terms of how Native veterans worked within and outside of state programs to readjust to civilian life, as Kasey Keeler writes, navigating both "BIA and VA bureaucratic structures."[88]

Four years before the passage of the Indian Citizenship Act, Zitkala-Ša wrote a pamphlet called "Americanize the First Americans," calling for the replacement of the oppressive bureaucracy of "prolonged wardship" with democracy for Native people: access to education, citizenship, enfranchisement, and leadership from progressive Natives. Native people were not the ones who needed the oversight of an "autocratic discretionary power." Instead, she asserted, "I would suggest that Congress enact more stringent laws to restrain the unscrupulous white men." Zitkala-Ša proposed the replacement of the existing "bureaucracy wheel" with a "democracy wheel," its spokes "alive with growing community interests and thrift activities of the Indians themselves."[89] The universal bestowal of citizenship on Native people through the ICA did not do away with the discretionary power of BIA agents nor its congressionally enshrined bureaucracy. If anything, the bureaucracy wheel grew larger and more complex, as state agents, politicians, non-Native media and the public, and Native people themselves navigated the intersections between wardship and citizenship in the disbursement or restriction of welfare benefits. But although Zitkala-Ša's conceptualization of a "democracy wheel" powered by a hub of organized progressive Native citizens did not come to pass, the community interests and thrift activities of Native people surely did. Coupling the history of the expansion of the federal welfare state with the development of mid-twentieth-century Indian policies allows us to understand how Native people *moved* the bureaucracy wheel, insisting "upon [their] recognition by America as really normal and quite worth-while human beings."[90]

CHAPTER 2

Indian Poverty Knowledge

Defining First-Class Citizenship through
Competency Legislation

Design policy with intentional marketing titles.
Assimilation; Relocation; Termination.
Enough to talk about a vanishing race
in front of you as theory and practice.
> —Trevino L. Brings Plenty (Minneconjou Lakota),
> "Red-ish Brown-ish"

How do we know the Secretary of the Interior is competent
to declare us competent?
> —Diego Abeita (Isleta Pueblo), 1954

In 1944 the House Select Committee to Investigate Indian Affairs and
Conditions argued that Bureau of Indian Affairs (BIA) regulations and
procedures impeded "Indians who have the capacity to lead competent, independent lives." They recommended changing the process so
Native people could "at their own volition be certified as full-fledged
citizens."[1] Throughout the 1940s and 1950s, non-Native legislators and
state agents increasingly expressed similar concerns about Native people's access to "full-fledged" or "first-class" citizenship. Legislators and
state agents who favored terminating the trust relationship between
Native nations and the federal government argued that it was Native

people's relationship with the BIA that prevented them from accessing first-class citizenship. They spoke of "emancipating" competent Native people from wardship, ostensibly freeing Native people from the disabilities associated with government regulations and procedures to which they were subject.

But what *was* first-class citizenship? Legislators weren't concerned with all Native people—only those who were judged competent were understood to be held back from the social and legal categorization. By examining the debates over proposed legislation to decree Native people's competency, this chapter examines how legislators and state agents who supported termination defined first-class citizenship in the mid-twentieth century based upon their fears of both perpetual Native poverty and Native sovereignty.

In 1953 the House Committee on Interior and Insular Affairs reasoned that if a Native person was declared competent, he or she could "withdraw completely from the tribe, obtain his share of tribal property, and go his way—as a truly 'first-class citizen.'"[2] Between 1944 and 1954 legislators proposed eleven bills that would have implemented such an administrative process to adjudicate the competency of Native people who wanted "emancipation" from wardship. Because first-class citizenship was undergirded by securing individual property rights and legally separating from a Native nation, it was simultaneously a legal status, an indicator of financial self-sufficiency, and a marker of assimilation into midcentury American values of gender and race. Only certain Native people possessed the qualifications necessary to "go his way" as a "truly first-class citizen." As legislators debated and adjusted the threshold by which competency could be adjudicated, they developed a definition of first-class citizenship that reflected their assumptions and misperceptions about wardship and welfare dependency. Politicians who supported competency legislation discussed the dangers of wardship using the same language as they used when discussing how poor welfare recipients needed to learn to "value" work and to desire not to be "dependent."[3] A first-class citizen was someone who was free from wardship—defined as oppressive government oversight—and also was not in danger of becoming dependent on any other government benefits.

Competency is itself a term long associated with Indian policies. Since the 1887 Dawes Act politicians have touted plans to abolish the BIA and "emancipate" "competent" Native people from wardship.[4] Historians have described how nineteenth- and early twentieth-century competency boards of commissioners charged with allotting tribal land evaluated Native people based on their perceptions of their intellectual abilities, blood quantum, and potential to integrate into the American polity. If Native people were deemed competent, they would receive an allotment and embark on a path from "wardship" to "citizenship."[5] Mid-twentieth-century definitions of competency were reminiscent of allotment policies that defined "competent" Native people as moral, intelligent, and members of nuclear family units. However, in the 1940s and 1950s, competency signaled not only that one would be able to hold onto property in a responsible manner, but also would be unlikely to utilize welfare benefits. Scholars have only briefly considered competency bills as part of the widespread effort in Congress to terminate the BIA and extend citizenship rights to Indians in the postwar period.[6] The goal of termination policy, like allotment, was to integrate Native people into the American polity by severing the trust relationship between Native nations and the federal government and by distributing land and resources to individual Native people.[7] Through conversations and conflicts over competency legislation, politicians who supported termination deployed the ideology of first-class citizenship as a method to divide tribal property among individuals and deprive Native nations of their political relationship with the United States.

Thus, when associated with Indian policy, first-class citizenship was not a racially neutral achievement of political equality, although it was pitched as such by legislators and state agents in favor of termination. This was because legislators who drafted competency bills assumed that Native people were incompetent until proven otherwise. Likewise, they understood the BIA's oversight and control over Native people to be the reason why they could not access first-class citizenship. Therefore, they defined "Nativeness" itself in part as dependency upon the BIA. Joanne Barker has noted how during the administration of allotment policy, BIA officials would adjudge individual Native people's "competency" to determine if they were "ready" to manage the "demands of private property ownership." Individuals with less "Native blood" were more likely to be considered competent.[8] Thus, as Native people moved farther away from the perception of the "authentic Indian," whether that was through biology or behavior, they were in more danger of losing their rights as tribal members. In turn, tribes themselves were stripped of the power to determine who was eligible for membership. Mid-twentieth-century competency proposals demonstrate the endurance of these assumptions about authenticity and citizenship. Thus, these bills did not just have the power to affect Native people's "full" or "first-class" *American* citizenship; they also had the power to impact Native nations' sovereign authority over tribal membership and land.

Between 1944 and 1954 Republican congressmen Francis Case of South Dakota, Hugh Butler of Nebraska, and Wesley D'Ewart of Montana proposed eleven bills in the House and Senate that would have implemented a system whereby individual Native people could be declared "competent," emancipated from wardship, and enabled to sell their property if they so desired.[9] Although there were slight procedural variations within the bills, all eleven generally followed the same format. First, an individual Native person would apply for a "certificate of competency" from an authority (depending on the bill, either the secretary of the interior or a naturalization court judge). The adjudicator would examine the applicant's "moral and intellectual qualifications" and ability to manage their business affairs to determine whether the decree of competency could be granted. If judged to be "competent," the applicant would be freed of the "disabilities" caused by wardship and would no longer be eligible to receive any of the "gratuitous" services extended to Natives by the BIA, including, most importantly, the trust restrictions on property. Many of these proposed bills stipulated that when applicants received their decree, their spouse and minor children would also be declared competent. "Competent" Native people were judged on their likelihood to become a "drain" on state welfare resources. Many bills required that representatives from local welfare departments be present at competency hearings to weigh in on whether an individual applicant should be granted his or her certificate.

Lawmakers understood competency as a signal of individual Native people's deserving achievement of first-class citizenship due to their demonstrable "responsibility," "self-sufficiency," and ability to manage their own affairs. Although these bills were unsuccessful, persistent proposals of this type of legislation, hearings on the topic, and copious amounts of correspondence about the bills reveal the importance of the imagined category of competency in defining first-class citizenship in opposition to postwar fears of wardship and welfare dependency.[10]

The stipulated "moral and intellectual qualifications" needed to access competency between 1944 and 1954 were reminiscent of long-standing practices of regulating and controlling all needy citizens' receipt of state benefits. Crucially though, because those who supported competency legislation believed wardship to be "gratuitous," the tightly guarded "state benefit" was the "decree of competency." However, though supporters of competency legislation were unable—or unwilling—to do so, it is essential to separate the trust relationship between Native nations and the federal government from welfare benefits to which Native people were entitled as American citizens. As Native nations and organizations asserted in this period, wardship was not a "government benefit." Wardship was not welfare.

Legislators' fears of a specifically racialized form of entrenched and permanent "Indian poverty" fed into their conflation of wardship with welfare dependency. They worried that the trust relationship between Native nations and the federal government ultimately created and sustained Native dependence. Competency legislation provided administrative safeguards to ensure that when emancipated from wardship, competent Native people would not burden the welfare rolls. First-class citizens, as they were understood in the 1940s and 1950s, would not receive any government assistance, because they were supposedly "competent" enough to control their own property and were "free" from governmental control. Inherent in this definition were assumptions about citizenship and gender: "competent" Native people who would avoid welfare dependency were assumed to be men.

Non-Natives did not fear just the poverty associated with Native "dependence" upon the federal government, but also the idea of Native' sovereignty. Because legislators and state agents conceptualized first-class citizenship as the opposite of wardship, they resisted calls to maintain wardship as a way of protecting Native land and safeguarding treaty rights. Although an ideal first-class citizen was independent and self-sufficient, the same traits reflected in a Native *nation* were deeply troubling to non-Native legislators and state agents, because they called attention to the debt the United States owed to Native people.

This chapter demonstrates that first-class citizenship was not an objective category that all marginalized people in the United States attempted to obtain. As legislators and state agents attempted to define Native people's American citizenship and terminate Native nations' relationships with the federal government in the 1940s and 1950s, they simultaneously constructed the larger idealized category of first-class citizenship. Eligibility for the seemingly positive signification was limited and regulated by "competence": access to property ownership, freedom from government oversight, and lack of financial need. As a result first-class citizenship was undergirded by fears of both racialized "Indian poverty" and Native nations' sovereignty.

"MORAL AND INTELLECTUAL QUALIFICATIONS"

In the four bills he proposed in the House between 1944 and 1947, Representative Francis Case (R-SD) established the specific qualifications Native applicants had to meet before being "emancipated" from wardship. Two of Case's bills, H.R. 3681 (1945) and H.R. 2165 (1947), would have emancipated only Native veterans of World War I and World War II. The other two bills, H.R. 5115 (1944) and H.R. 2958 (1947), also proposed emancipating those with high school diplomas, certificates of competency from the superintendent of their reservations, or documentation that they had lived off-reservation for a period of five years. Senator Hugh Butler's (R-NE) 1948 bill, H.R. 1113, shifted criteria for competency. In this and five subsequent bills, judges and officials were instructed to "consider significant factors bearing upon the applicant's moral and intellectual qualifications and his ability to manage his own affairs."[11] These supposedly judicable capabilities were rooted both in welfare policies that required recipients to meet standards of morality and self-sufficiency and established Indian policies geared toward Native people's "successful" property management.

In 1954 Representative Arthur Miller of Nebraska argued that the phrase "moral and intellectual qualifications" "may give the Secretary or the courts too great a latitude in ruling against competency."[12] Miller proposed that judges instead evaluate whether the applicant could "manage his or her business affairs, including the administration, use, investment, and disposition of any property turned over to such person and the income or proceeds therefrom, with such a reasonable degree of prudence and wisdom as will be apt to prevent him or her from losing such property or the benefits thereof."[13] Miller's suggestions implied that if Native people lost their land after receiving a certificate of competency, it would be due to their lack of "prudence and wisdom," rather than non-Native land-grabbing. Thus, competency decrees also represented an understanding that "competent" Native people would show moral responsibility and shrewdness in managing their assets, specifically land. Proponents of competency legislation drew upon established welfare policy standards of "morality" and "intelligence" to judge whether Native people were competent enough to be "emancipated" from wardship. However, they also drew upon specifically racialized assumptions about Native people's mental abilities and potential to assimilate.

Alice O'Connor defines the body of research on poverty created by public agencies, think tanks, and research institutes in the twentieth century as "poverty knowledge." Poverty knowledge rested on several premises, including a belief in the power of empirical investigation to improve social conditions, the understanding that the state has a role to play in protecting citizens from "extreme concentrations of poverty and wealth," and a commitment to maintaining a capitalist economy. Importantly, poverty knowledge was also based on the idea that poverty was an individual condition.[14] This focus on the individual was also reflected in the importance Americans placed on individual rights to citizenship in the context of the United States' fight against fascism during World War II.[15] If something was holding back an individual from accessing their rights of citizenship, it was the state's job to fix the problem by finding what was wrong with the individual impoverished person. However, behind the state's seemingly positive role was the assumption that poverty itself did not match up with core American values, including "capitalist markets, political democracy, self-reliance, and/or a two-parent, white middle-class family ideal."[16] State agents and welfare officials were responsible for finding ways for impoverished people to achieve those core American values. Thus, the welfare state has also served as a "mechanism of social control" in its ability to regulate seemingly "un-American" behavior.[17]

In the mid-twentieth century, Indian termination policies were based upon the same assumptions that undergirded poverty research. Namely, in their arguments for terminating the BIA, proponents of these policies placed great emphasis on allowing individual Native people to fully access their rights of citizenship. This sentiment was the driving force behind competency legislation: supposedly the bureaucratic process where individual Native people would demonstrate their "moral and intellectual qualifications" would allow officials to discover which individual Native people matched closely with core American values and then release them from tribal membership and wardship, thus allowing them to access property ownership.

Proponents of competency legislation stipulated that until Native people sufficiently proved their abilities to manage their financial affairs and support their families without government assistance, they would be perpetually dependent on government resources. Thus, non-Natives assumed that if "competent" Native people were to take their place as full citizens, they would participate in American citizens' "value obligation to work" instead of becoming a drain on public resources.[18] Willingness to work "served as the defining characteristic of male citizenship . . . and divided the deserving from the undeserving poor."[19] The rationale behind competency legislation mirrored similar efforts in the late 1940s and 1950s to "rehabilitate" poor women welfare recipients' families through work, teaching the "value of not being 'dependent.'"[20] Additionally the language shares similarities with reformers' assumptions that welfare "dependence" was rooted in recipients' individual moral failings.[21] Crucially though, Native people's "competency" did not rest solely on employability in wage work. For Native people to be declared competent, they had to demonstrate that they deserved independence from government oversight through their moral and intellectual ability to manage their own property.

However, Native people were not only affected by poverty knowledge. Additionally they faced assumptions supported by decades of research and data collection by the BIA, Congress, reform organizations, and scholars of federal Indian law that sought to explain the reasons behind *Native* poverty—essentially *Indian poverty knowledge*. These two bodies of poverty knowledge intersected at many points. However, key to Indian poverty knowledge was state agents' and legislators' association of wardship with Native people's mental deficiencies. As Douglas Baynton asserts, all people are "defined in some way by disability, by its presence or ostensible absence."[22] Native people were no exception— much of nineteenth- and twentieth-century Indian policies were based on perceptions of inherent Native dependency, savagery, and mental inability to function in "civilized" American society.

Since the early nineteenth century, wardship was employed by white American legislators, state agents, and the public as shorthand for Native people's mental disabilities. As lawyer and activist Felix Cohen argued in 1953, wardship was deployed as a "magic word," used to justify "any order or command or sale or lease for which no justification could be found in any treaty or act of Congress." "Wardship," Cohen asserted, "always made up for any lack of statutory authority."[23] Throughout the nineteenth century this use of wardship was linked with a racialized understanding of Native people as uncivilized and savage, needing "protection" by the government not only from unscrupulous whites but also from each other.[24]

However, beginning in earnest in the late 1880s, state agents argued that by separating from their tribe, individual Native "wards" should and could attain citizenship. Thus, policymakers and reformers believed that in contrast to common legal and social practices that separated African Americans from whites, individual Native people had the potential to be incorporated into the white American polity.[25] The most significant piece of legislation designed to accomplish this goal was the General Allotment Act of 1887, commonly known as the Dawes Act. The Dawes Act set into place a policy of allotting reservation land into individual plots, to be held in trust by the federal government for a period of twenty-five years, after which the trust restriction would be lifted and individual Native allottees would assume ownership of the plot. Any "surplus" reservation land could be sold to white settlers after allotment was complete. By the policy's official end in 1934, two-thirds of all Native lands held in 1887 were lost to white settlers.[26] The ideology behind allotment was built upon the Jeffersonian model of private land ownership. At the turn of the twentieth century, ownership of land by individual nuclear families conformed to American social and economic ideals.[27] Policymakers and reformers reasoned that if Native people were forced to give up communal land ownership and assume individual property rights, they would become "civilized" and easily assimilated into the American citizenry.

Wardship's association with poverty and dependency upon government aid was woven into the fabric of the Dawes Act. In his agitation for the passage of the bill, Senator Henry Dawes of Massachusetts insisted that if allotment policy was not applied, the United States would continue to be responsible for Native "paupers." Dawes viewed allotment as the method through which Native people would cease to burden the government by assuming individual ownership of land. However, Dawes also pitched allotment policy as a method by which the United States government could "pay back" Indigenous people. In 1885 he told the Mohonk Conference, "Every dollar of money, and every hour of effort that can be applied to each individual Indian, day and night . . . is not only due him in atonement for what we have inflicted upon him in the past, but is our own obligation towards him in order that we may not have him a vagabond and a pauper, without home or occupation among us in this land."[28] Thus, Dawes and other politicians and reformers envisioned allotment as a program that would simultaneously benefit the country and individual Native people by creating self-sufficient citizens who did not require assistance or regulation from the state. Reformers and state agents who endeavored to make Native people into "productive" citizens believed that allotment would wipe the U.S. slate clean, as the policy would "make restitution to the Indian for all that the white man had done to him in the past."[29] However, the Dawes Act's goals of protecting

Native people from undue hardship (or "pauperism") and guiding them toward "civilization" resulted in the opposite of "restitution"—the massive decrease of Native-owned land.[30]

Assimilation policies, whether allotment of reservation land, education of Native children, prohibition of Native cultures and religious traditions, or eradication of Native languages, were geared toward remaking Native tribal members into *individual* members of the American polity—similar to the importance placed on an impoverished individual's adherence to core American values that undergirded twentieth-century poverty knowledge. In 1889 Commissioner of Indian Affairs Thomas J. Morgan emphasized: "The relations of the Indians to the Government must rest solely upon the full recognition of their individuality. Each Indian must be treated as a *man*, be allowed a *man's* rights and privileges, and be held to the performance of a *man's* obligations."[31] Not only did Morgan's choice of the word "man" represent a gendered understanding of who the "ideal" American citizen was (male, not female), but it also signified that to assume the obligations and privileges of citizenship, one needed to advance to a certain level of responsibility or maturity. A "ward" was not a "man." A "ward" was incapable of fulfilling obligations to the state, and in turn, a "ward" could not expect rights and privileges from the state. However, a "ward," like a child, would eventually *become* a man. As a man, Morgan argued, each Native person would be "entitled to his proper share of the inherited wealth of the tribe, and to the protection of the courts in his 'life, liberty, and pursuit of happiness.'"[32] As American citizens, Native people would still be able to access and use the resources they were entitled to as tribal members. However, Morgan purposefully used the term "proper share," indicating his vision of the culmination of Native people's progression to citizenship was individual Native men owning individual plots of land.

Morgan also stressed that as a man, a Native ward was "not entitled to be supported in idleness."[33] Supposedly, as wards of the government, Native people had no incentive to become self-sufficient. Idleness was also viewed as the opposite of "manliness." To transform Native people from an "uncivilized" people to members of the American citizenry, they had to adopt the characteristics of the "American race," which, as public figures such as Theodore Roosevelt argued, was built upon both "racial superiority and virile manhood."[34] As Gail Bederman has shown, Roosevelt's ideology of the ideal American was based upon a strong sense of a racialized, strenuous work ethic. To uphold American civilization, American men could not fall victim to "unmanly racial sloth" or "over-civilized decadence."[35] Native men were far removed from Roosevelt's conception of ideal American manhood because their economic and social status was firmly entwined with the federal government. Wardship was incompatible with manhood and, therefore, was something to be "outgrown," if Native men were to achieve citizenship status. If a Native man could overcome his "idleness" through the U.S. government's practices and policies, he would be one step closer to being considered as an individual racialized American citizen.

Indian poverty knowledge was built upon the perception that wardship epitomized idleness, poverty, and lack of manly ability to manage land and finances. Competency legislation drew upon this well-established set of perceptions, resurrecting some of the language and assumptions of allotment policy, including a fear of Native "pauperism." Supporters of competency legislation continued to associate wardship with dependency on government aid.

SOLVING NATIVE POVERTY THROUGH COMPETENCY

Legislators and state agents who advocated for competency legislation drew upon the large body of Indian poverty knowledge created in the nineteenth and early twentieth centuries. Additionally the mid-twentieth century also marked the expansion of the federal welfare state, which, scholars have shown, did not equally apply to all Americans.[36] As Cybelle Fox has noted, the way racial groups were incorporated into the welfare state reveals how those same groups "fit into America's racial hierarchy."[37] In her examination of Mexican Americans' access to welfare benefits, Fox illustrated how nativism and racism fed into rumors about "illegal" aliens' abuse of welfare programs and the "illegitimate burden" they placed on the welfare system.[38] Thus, as more and more Americans gained access to welfare benefits, debates emerged about who was "undeserving" of government aid. The stated goal of competency legislation was to grant Native people access to first-class citizenship, removing their "dependence" on the federal government. Intertwined in this goal was the assumption that some "competent" Native people were benefiting unfairly from their wardship—these Native people were "Indian" in name only and, since they were capable of thriving without the oversight of the BIA, should be emancipated. However, in their plans for judging and dispensing decrees of competency, legislators laid bare their racialized fears of inherent Native dependence and perpetual poverty.

Supporters of competency legislation understood wardship to be welfare dependency. This misperception clouded their understanding of Native people's entitlement to welfare benefits as American citizens, completely separate from the services, government provisions, or tax exemptions on trust property safeguarded by formal agreements and treaties. Beginning with the 1947 bills, if individual Native applicants were granted a decree of competency, they would "no longer be entitled to share in any of the benefits or gratuitous service extended to Indians as such by the United States."[39] This language reveals how non-Native legislators recast Native people's legal relationship with the United States as a relationship between a group of minority citizens who were unfairly privileged because they received supposedly unearned "gratuitous" benefits.[40] According to this logic, wardship impeded Native people's ability to fully engage in the reciprocal relationship between the state and its citizens, because Native people were not fulfilling the duties that merited such benefits. For example, because tribal property was tax-exempt, non-Natives accused Native people of profiting from state welfare resources without paying their fair share of taxes.[41] Native people's "privileged" position as "protected" wards worked to deprive them of their right to public assistance as citizens.

It was difficult for proponents of competency legislation to disentangle a vision of "competent" "first-class" Native citizens from Indian poverty knowledge, most specifically the assumption that Native people were somehow inherently dependent. This was revealed especially significantly in legislators' conversations about how competency would be ascertained and what would happen after an applicant received his or her decree. For example, proponents of competency legislation reasoned that even if they were no longer wards, Native people could still potentially drain public resources. After 1947, bills specified that the court was responsible for notifying governmental heads of towns and counties, superintendents from applicants' reservations, heads of tribal councils, and representatives from "the local welfare department of the State, county, and city government" to testify in favor or against the applicant.[42] Wesley D'Ewart, chairman of the House Committee on Public Lands, asserted in 1947 hearings over H.R. 1113, "We felt the county commissioner should have an opportunity to be heard because in the event the Indian is not competent he might become a county charge, and therefore a lien on the welfare funds of that county."[43] Later D'Ewart argued that judges who rashly bestowed competency certificates upon Indians who did not deserve them would face dire consequences: "If he loads the tax rolls of the welfare funds of that county with undue charges, those circumstances will be known, and if it is because of releasing Indians who should not have been released, he will not long remain Judge of that county."[44] The main goal of D'Ewart and others was to guard the welfare system from truly incompetent, perpetual Native wards.

Opponents of competency legislation also worried about potential problems if Native people were released from wardship and later fell on hard economic times. Would they be able to access welfare benefits as citizens or be followed by the racial stigma of their former wardship? In his 1953 testimony before the House Committee on Interior and Insular Affairs, Felix Cohen contended, "Indians all over the country are worried at the prospect of a sudden cut-off of Federal services before arrangements have been made with the states for a taking over of the school, health, and other public services that are now rendered by the Federal Government."[45] In their 1953 resolution against H.R. 4985, the All Pueblo Council claimed that competency legislation "does not offer any practical remedy for discrimination attitudes to which Indians may be subjected by their neighbors."[46] Rather, as the Oglala Lakota [Sioux] Tribal Council asserted, competency legislation could lead to Native landlessness, which meant that "far too many [Natives] become a burden on white communities and this breeds ill-will, contempt, prejudice, and discrimination. These feelings are not good either for Indians or the communities into which they go."[47] Proponents of competency legislation offered Native people no protection from racial discrimination and denial of welfare benefits once they were "freed" from wardship.

Competency supporters wanted to find a way to relieve so-called Native dependency on the federal government, arguing that the trust relationship in part caused Native poverty and held Native people back from first-class citizenship. In 1947 Hugh Butler argued before Congress that the BIA should be terminated because Indians "from every tribe, in every state and in every community where Indians reside, have beseeched their representatives in the Senate and the House to pass legislation granting them equal rights of citizenship with their white neighbors."[48] Further, Secretary of the Interior Douglas McKay asserted that competency legislation would remove barriers to responsible citizenship that had been imposed solely because of race. In a 1955 letter, McKay wrote, "We do not believe that a man who has demonstrated his competence and seeks control of his property should be denied that privilege merely because he happens to be Indian."[49] Terminationist politicians consistently returned to the idea that the BIA's oversight of competent Native people forced them to live, as Hugh Butler claimed, in conditions of "racial segregation," "inferior status," and subject to "control by race legislation."[50] They argued that the association of "Indianness" with incompetency held Native people back from living their lives unencumbered by federal oversight.

At the same time that proponents of competency bills argued that the United States needed to lift its racialized burden on Native people who themselves wanted to be emancipated from wardship, they also tapped into another familiar racialized refrain in order to justify severing the trust relationship between tribes and the federal government. Echoing common concerns about Black and Mexican American welfare recipients taking "more" welfare than they actually deserved, supporters of competency legislation rationalized that the BIA was unnecessary because it was "handling the affairs of many completely competent and oftentimes financially independent Indians."[51] Legislators asked whether competent Native people could even be identified as "Indian." In 1953 Commissioner of Indian Affairs Dillon Myer wrote a memo to the secretary of the interior expressing his fears about continued BIA responsibility for "competent" Native people. Myer argued that many of the individually allotted trust lands were owned by "highly competent Indians who insist on maintaining their lands in trust," because they had "certain advantages," including "being free from property taxes," "priorities in the purchase of other Indian lands, borrowing tribal and Indian Bureau loan funds, and using other tribal resources without adequate payment."[52] Myer accused "alleged tribal leaders with a modicum of Indian blood" of exploiting "other tribal members (who are less competent than they are) through shady real estate deals."[53] Those Native people who insisted on maintaining the trust relationship to reap the advantages of tax exemption and access to tribal loan funds were, in Myer's eyes, too competent to be wards and too competent to be *Native*. He asserted: "A great majority of the Indians are opposed to having the Bureau get out of business. This is particularly true of those Indians who are profiting through the exploitation of their less competent neighbors."[54] Myer reasoned that "competent" Natives were opposed to termination policies because they were benefiting from wardship at the expense of others.

Champions of competency legislation argued that it would provide a path to first-class citizenship for Native people capable and willing to embark down that path *and* that it would weed out any Native people who shirked their citizenship duties by maintaining a relationship with the federal government. In a 1954 letter to the executive director of the Association on American Indian Affairs (AAIA), a reform organization committed to Native issues, Oliver La Farge noted how the AAIA's own version of a competency bill would help to resolve the issue of competent Native people who avoided the duties of first-class citizenship through the use of the legal status of "Indian." He wrote: "I have real sympathy with the desires of [Barry] Goldwater and many others to cut off the free list those persons who are Indians only by legal definition and who have no true claim upon the federal government. Perhaps we should give some consideration to this problem in working up a competency bill."[55] La Farge's use of the term "free list" implied that he believed one could become "legally Indian" with no trace of Native ancestry, purely for the benefits of wardship.

Competency supporters were also reluctant to recognize forms of land ownership that fell outside idealized "American values." Native people, well acquainted with Indian poverty knowledge, questioned whether "competent" families would truly profit from receiving fee patents for their land. Or, as in previous policies, would more land pass into the hands of non-Natives? In response to a 1954 survey administered by the pan-Native organization the National Congress of American Indians (NCAI), the Omaha Tribe of Nebraska stated that they were opposed to H.R. 4985 because, thirty-five years prior, "some Omahas came to Washington and told the Indian Commissioner that they were competent and could handle their own business and it wasn't long that those thought, they were issued patent fee to their land holdings and even to those some didn't want it. Those sold their lands." The Omaha statement continued: "So we lost 3/4 of our good agricultural land to the white man. So we're afraid if this bill come to be a law, we'd lose the rest of our land. So therefore we are opposed to this bill."[56] During a 1954 meeting of the House Subcommittee on Indian Affairs, Cheyenne River Sioux chairman Frank Ducheneaux voiced his concerns that competency legislation would lead to increased poverty. "If I wanted to get a patent in fee for my land to get the restrictions removed," Ducheneaux stated, "I could go out there and have the court declare me competent whether I was competent or not, and I could spend my family poor and my children poor."[57] Native groups did not trust that competency legislation would free them from poverty. Rather they saw competency legislation as a path to poverty and landlessness.

Defining First-Class Citizenship through Competency Legislation

As they determined what qualifications Native people had to meet to receive decrees of competency, legislators and state agents defined first-class citizenship: first-class citizens were able to manage their own individual property, were male heads of household, and neither profited from nor suffered under governmental oversight. Conversations between the bills' authors and supporters between 1944 and 1954 demonstrate how legislators utilized Indian poverty knowledge to construct the parameters of first-class citizenship in opposition to wardship.

Although employability and a "value of work" were important markers of "productive" citizenship in the mid-twentieth century, in order to determine Native people's competency, legislators and state agents continued to focus on their abilities to maintain individual property ownership. With a certificate of competency, Native applicants would receive a patent in fee for their land, and trust restrictions would be removed on their land and other financial property. Ostensibly, proponents of competency legislation wanted to establish a process for determining competency that would ensure that Native people would be able to *retain* their individual property and utilize it to support their families, despite the removal of trust restrictions. Earlier bills did offer some protection for Native nations' use of tribal property. For example, H.R. 2958, Francis Case's 1947 bill, stipulated that before any Native "homeland" was diminished, the tribe had to grant approval.[58] However, in subsequent bills these safeguards disappeared. The bills proposed between 1947 and 1954 authorized the secretary of the interior to partition tribal land to release a "competent" person's physical property or the financial share of the property. For example, in H.R. 1113 (1947) the secretary of the interior was instructed to make every effort to divide land "held jointly or in common with other heirs." However, if it was "impracticable to divide the same according to their inherited interests he shall sell the interest or interests of the individual Indian applicant who has been adjudged competent and pay to him or her the net proceeds of such sale."[59] Hugh Butler's 1949 bill, S. 186, imbued the secretary of the interior with even more power, stating, "If the individual Indian who has been adjudged competent holds jointly or in common with other heirs an undivided interest in land the Secretary may in his discretion partition such land."[60] All subsequent bills contained the same language. Thus, the legislation invested the secretary of the interior with the power to divide land among individuals or even to sell tribal land altogether, in the interest of dissolving the trust relationship between Native nations and the federal government and reconceptualizing Native people solely as individual citizens.

Native critics of competency legislation contended that freeing land from trust restrictions wasn't about allowing Native people to access first-class citizenship, but rather served as a conduit for Native land to pass into non-Native ownership. For example, in 1953 the Council of the Pueblo of Laguna issued a resolution against H.R. 4985, asserting, "The main motive power behind this new drive to remove federal protection of Indian rights comes from selfish interest who want the lands that are still left us."[61] Similarly, in a 1954 letter protesting the same bill, Moses Twobulls, president of the Oglala Sioux Tribal Council, argued: "Enactment of this bill would give more Indians the idea they could get patent fees easily, and even more Indians than already do would feel forced to try to sell their land to meet current emergencies. Wholesale issuance of 'competency decrees' would surely follow and then wholesale selling off of Indian land."[62] At the NCAI emergency conference in 1954, Diego Abeita, spokesperson for the All Pueblo Council, explicitly connected competency and loss of Native land and resources, asserting: "In order to get our lands, they are going to declare us competent. How do we know the Secretary of the Interior is competent to declare us competent? We discovered a while ago that we had found oil, and that disturbed a lot of people. Now we have discovered we're sitting on a pile of uranium, and that is driving them crazy."[63] Native critics looked back on the history of Indian poverty knowledge and saw the result of releasing trust restrictions—massive loss of tribal land. Therefore, they understood that competency legislation would surely "jeopardize the safety of ownership."[64]

Apart from dividing tribal land into individually owned plots, proponents of competency legislation were also interested in making Native wards into "productive" and responsible citizens. Part of what competency legislation would purportedly fix was how, as wards, Native men and women unfairly avoided taxation. Some critics argued that competency legislation was a blatant attempt to tax Native property. For example, in 1951 lawyer James Curry sent a memo to Ruth Bronson of the NCAI, asserting: "We have a day to day fight with respect to the taxation of Indian lands. Most of the so-called emancipation bills are for the purpose of bringing Indian lands under taxation."[65] In his 1953 statement opposing competency, NCAI president Joseph Garry warned that taxes posed additional threats of land loss, foreshadowing the disastrous impact House Concurrent Resolution 108, passed the same year, would have on nations such as the Menominee. He predicted, "This bill, if enacted, would immediately take away the greater per cent of individual allotted Indian lands by forced sales of inherited lands through partition or for non-payment of taxes, thus paralyzing any plan of economic development which would insure the Indian's future security."[66] Land ownership was explicitly tied to first-class citizenship because it implied fulfillment of the responsibilities of citizenship through taxes independent of government oversight.

The definition of "competency" was also shaped by gendered assumptions about male responsibility and female dependency. In the four bills he proposed from 1944 to 1947, Francis Case suggested criteria based on gendered fulfillment of citizenship duties, which, if met, would automatically bestow competency upon Native applicants. For example, politicians and the public believed that if Native veterans had been honorably discharged from the armed services, they should be eligible for "full citizenship rights."[67] Case's 1944 bill (H.R. 5115) and 1947 bill (H.R. 2958) also specified that those applicants who possessed a high school education, had received a recommendation from an agency superintendent or tribal council leadership, or had lived away from a reservation for a period of five years should also receive competency decrees automatically. Although these three criteria applied equally to men and women, all four of Case's bills focused on veterans. To Case, military service was such a clear fulfillment of the duties of citizenship that it merited direct conferral of competency onto a Native applicant. There was no such equivalent for Native women to demonstrate fulfillment of their duties of American citizenship. Most likely, proponents of competency legislation assumed that the applicants for decrees of competency to be judged would be Native men.

This assumption was made clear at the 1947 House Subcommittee of Indian Affairs of the Committee of Public Lands hearings on Indian emancipation.[68] In those hearings legislators raised questions about the relationships between "competent" Native men and their wives.[69] Frank Barrett, Republican Representative from Wyoming, asked if wives should automatically receive decrees of competency when their husbands were deemed competent. Barrett argued that just as the United States owed "an obligation to the man and the wife as wards of the government and also an obligation to the children," "the man owes an obligation to his wife and to the children to provide for their support. He is the natural guardian of his own children."[70] Barrett continued, "It seems to me that if a man is competent that the whole family should be released."[71] Barrett understood that male heads of nuclear family households were the "guardians" of their wives and children. Other congressmen agreed with Barrett. Francis Case argued that before granting competency, the court needed to determine "whether this man is competent not only to manage his own affairs, but competent to take the place of government in looking after his family and children."[72] Thus, if they received a declaration of competency, Native men would be recognized as responsible patriarchs of their nuclear family units, adhering to one of the core "American values"—a patriarchal, two-parent household—necessary to obtain governmental support, or, in this case, would be "released" from government support.

Automatically conferring competency onto spouses of applicants would also safeguard competent Native men's individual property ownership. In July 1953, the House Subcommittee on Interior and Insular Affairs issued a report that highlighted the practical problems that would arise if one member of the family was declared competent, but the rest of the family's land continued to be held in trust. Some saw this division of family competency as counter to the terminationist goal of abolishing the BIA. Assistant Secretary of the Interior Orme Lewis argued, "It would not be practicable to terminate the rights of the head of a family to special Federal benefits while leaving the spouse and minor children eligible for such benefits."[73] Thus, the subcommittee proposed that "applications by married persons for certificates of competency should be considered only on a family basis." They argued that applications of married people would be considered "only if the spouse also files an application." This signaled legislators' desires to prevent possible familial disputes about tribal property. However, the subcommittee specified that "if one of them is determined to be a competent person, patents in fee should be issued to all the trust land of the applicants, their minor children, and any other minor children in the custody of the applicants."[74] Therefore, although husbands and wives would apply for competency together, both spouses did not need to be judged competent for all members of the family to receive decrees. This stipulation further reflected the subcommittee's belief in patriarchal family structures. It was unlikely that a court or the secretary of the interior would find a Native wife competent and her husband incompetent and bestow her with the power of guardianship over the rest of the family.

Members of the AAIA also presumed that most Native people who received competency decrees and gained access to first-class citizenship would be men. For example, in 1954, AAIA members drafted their own version of competency legislation that proposed three distinct criteria to judge individual Native competency. The first two criteria were that an applicant must show that "he has been graduated from an accredited high school," or that "he has, in each of the three years immediately preceding the date of application, earned more than $3600.00 from wages, salaries, fees for services, or net profits on a business operated by him without supervision by the Bureau of Indian Affairs."[75] These stipulations demonstrate that the AAIA also assumed "competency" to be the gendered responsibility of male applicants to generate enough income to provide for their family's future. The AAIA assumed that if Native applicants had earned enough to live independently from the BIA, they would also have earned enough to prevent them from relying on needs-based welfare programs.

The AAIA's version of the competency bill also tapped into gendered and racialized assumptions about marriage as a path to citizenship. In order to extend competency eligibility to "housewives who do not have the opportunity to earn the required amount of money," the third criteria proposed, "in the case of a married woman, that her husband, to whom she shall have been married for five years immediately preceding the date of application and with whom she has shared a household during such period, is, on the date of application, a person other than an Indian having special status under the law."[76] In this proposal Native women— specifically, those who had demonstrated that they were in a long-term marriage and were currently sharing a house with their husbands—were able to achieve competency only if their husbands had already done so. The language of "a person other than an Indian having special status" in this stipulation was vague enough to include both non-Native men and those Native men who had already applied and been granted decrees of competency. In either case, if their husbands had demonstrated through their racial identity or their financial earnings that they would not be dependent upon the federal government, the AAIA assumed that their wives would also not be dependent. Though this proposed language did not end up in the final versions of H.R. 4985, it demonstrates how deeply patriarchal assumptions about responsibility and independence were woven into definitions of Native competency and first-class citizenship.

COMPETENCY AND SOVEREIGNTY

In *Black Is a Country*, Nikhil Pal Singh describes how Black liberation activists reconceptualized racially stigmatized spaces to provide a defiant counterpoint to the "reassuring teleological narrative of black uplift through citizenship."[77] Native people also defied this teleological narrative, which undergirded all eleven proposed competency bills. Competency legislators proposed to "uplift" Native people, but only if they could prove their worthiness of first-class citizenship. In their definition of citizenship, legislators institutionalized the "ideal" self-sufficient nuclear family headed by a man who provided for his spouse and children, managed his land and finances responsibly, and never relied on public assistance. This version of first-class citizenship denied Native people recognition of their legal agreements with the United States as tribal nations and reconceptualized their relationship with the federal government as one of "gratuitous" benefits.

Proponents of competency legislation wanted to eventually terminate the BIA. They believed that terminating the BIA would lead Native people off the path of perpetual "welfare dependency," reclassify Native people solely as individual citizens, and dissolve the legal recognition of Native nations. If, as Native critics argued, wardship was not dependency, it was something far more threatening to supporters of competency legislation: an acknowledgment of the United States' historical relationship with Native nations and a recognition of Native sovereignty. Competency legislation, thus, was designed not only to combat a vision of Native dependency reinforced by decades of Indian poverty knowledge, but also to undermine Native sovereignty and release the United States from its legal responsibilities to Native nations.

Native nations and representatives were wary of language that claimed competency legislation would bestow a legal and social status upon Native people that they did not already possess. At the NCAI's 1954 emergency conference, Joseph Garry asserted, "Indians consider themselves first-class citizens; they do not want or need 'emancipation.'"[78] In his 1953 statement opposing H.R. 4985, Garry argued, "The only 'freeing' feature in this 'Competency' bill is to free the Indian of the trust status of his land which has been his sole protection against further exploitation of his land and property by selfish interests." Critiquing the assumption that wardship induced dependence, Garry asserted: "His tax freedom, which he will in time lose completely through the enactment of this 'Competency' bill, should not ever be and should never have been looked upon as a good-will handout to the Indian. This privilege of tax freedom for property is part of the price the U.S. Government has given the Indian for the valuable land that was taken from him."[79] Garry and other Native leaders emphasized that under the guise of "emancipation," competency legislation would only deprive Native people of land and protections that they earned as a result of their historical relationships with the United States.

Critics of competency legislation maintained that first-class citizenship did not necessitate emancipation from wardship. In a petition to the president and Congress against H.R. 1113, the AAIA asserted that "although many of the Congressmen who voted for H.R. 1113 thought they were voting citizenship to Indians," in fact, Native people were not "legally slaves or serfs; they are citizens and have been citizens for many years."[80] In his 1953 statement on competency, Garry argued that legislators' seemingly lofty desires to enhance Native people's lives with first-class citizenship was a facade. "Why this sudden over-enthusiasm for freeing an alleged subjugated minority group, numbering only 400,000 in population, unless other motives are involved?" Garry questioned. "Who is to gain? The Indians feel it will be the exploiters and land hungry citizens who will gain by this bill at the Indians' expense."[81] Garry exposed the underlying motives behind competency legislation—to further deny Native people's distinct claim to land and a legal arrangement with the U.S. government.

Nearly all competency bills contained a phrase that protected the "competent" Native person from losing any of the rights "to which he would otherwise be entitled as a member of any Indian tribe."[82] Beginning with H.R. 1113 in 1947, the language became more specific, allowing the applicant to "continue on the tribal rolls, as a member of the tribe," and safeguarding that the applicant would "in no manner be deprived of his or her tribal rights or treaty benefits."[83] Thus, Native people who had been decreed competent would not have been financially divorced from their tribe but would be allowed to maintain a stake in tribal assets and resources. For some tribes, the protection of "tribal rights or treaty benefits" would have safeguarded continued provisions for health care and education by the federal government. Indeed, in a 1949 letter to Senator Joseph O'Mahoney opposing H.R. 2724, Oliver La Farge of the AAIA pointed out, "To the extent that educational services, for example, are called for in treaties, these provisions are clearly mutually contradictory and would lead to utter confusion."[84]

Moreover, critics of competency legislation also pointed to how the bills threatened the relationship between tribal nations and the United States constituted through treaties. In 1954 Martin Vigil, chairman of the All-Pueblo Council, wrote to President Eisenhower to argue that competency legislation would enlarge the power of the BIA, increase confusion, and perpetuate a series of hearings and investigations that "would never end." "Pending Indian legislation is the most ruinous in the black record of one hundred and fifty years of broken promises by the Federal Government," Vigil wrote. "You swore to protect our rights."[85] Vigil reminded Eisenhower that according to the Declaration of Independence, "government is derived from the *consent* of the governed," and that not only had Native people not consented to competency legislation, "we have not even been consulted."[86] By emphasizing the "promises" the federal government made, Vigil pointed to the legal relationship between tribes and the United States. However, he also reminded Eisenhower of the American political promise of citizens' rights to be "governed by consent."

Competency legislation crystallized legislators' and state agents' assumptions about Native people's lack of first-class citizenship. However, in their efforts to "emancipate" Native people from wardship, politicians and state agents who supported competency legislation attempted to force Native people to assimilate into the American polity. This process of assimilation was cast as the removal of "disabilities" and the bestowal of individual rights of property and financial management. In reality, competency, based on Indian poverty knowledge, undermined tribal sovereignty, community, and family structures.

Historiographically, competency bills provide an unexamined way to explore the rationale behind termination policies. Designed as individualized, case-by-case evaluations, the process of granting competency decrees would have subjected Native applicants to judgment of their abilities to be "responsible" and "self-sufficient" citizens. Competency criteria, including Native people's service to the country, ability to demonstrate they would not become "drains" on public resources, and willingness to obtain fee patents for their land (even if that meant partitioning jointly held property), help historians fully unpack what legislators and state agents meant when they touted the benefits of first-class citizenship as if Native people were not already full American citizens. By analyzing competency protocols, we can also understand how closely wardship was linked to ideologies of welfare dependency. Legislators believed that individual Native applicants—mainly assumed to be men—who could prove to a judge or to a high-ranking federal official that they possessed the "moral and intellectual qualifications" to manage their affairs, take ownership of their financial resources and possible future financial failures, and provide for their families were no longer "Native" enough to continue to be wards. These procedures drew upon decades of Indian poverty knowledge that assumed "Nativeness" was in part defined by dependence and undermined the sovereignty of Native nations.

Legislators asserted that the application process for "competency" would have "weeded out" those Native people who were benefiting from wardship in ways they did not deserve or need—very similar to conservative politicians' arguments about poor, non-white single mothers receiving Aid to Dependent Children in this same period.[87] By focusing on competency as an individualized process, politicians tapped into the poverty knowledge of the mid-1940s to mid-1960s: poverty or dependence was the result, not of widespread economic or societal issues, but of "an individual's inadequacy."[88] If Native people—who as a group, were defined by Indian poverty knowledge as dependent upon an overprotective and bumbling federal government—could be evaluated one by one, those individuals (and, by extension, their dependent family members) could be "rehabilitated" from dependence and succeed as American citizens. Only those truly Native people, incompetent by definition and in need of perpetual governmental oversight and protection, would remain wards. As Native and non-Native critics of competency legislation asserted, this definition of competency threatened existing treaties and agreements. Moreover, it reinforced a non-Native conceptualization of wardship that equated Native identity with racialized dependence and special treatment, rather than recognizing and safeguarding Native sovereignty and humanity.

CHAPTER 3

Every Day with the BIA

Welfare Applications and Wardship's Definitions

The BIA is a great resource, if you know how to use 'em.
And we know how to use 'em.

—Larry Calica (Confederated Tribes of Warm Springs),
quoted by Valerie Lambert

Two decades after the passage of the 1924 Indian Citizenship Act, how
did Native people simultaneously live as "wards" of the government
and as citizens? Native people experienced wardship in the everyday
bureaucracy they navigated to access necessary services and resources
and protect their legal rights as citizens of tribal nations. Specifically,
with the expansion of the federal welfare state, Native people experienced
citizenship with their application for welfare benefits. Like other people
of color, Natives faced difficulty accessing benefits under need-based
programs such as Aid to Dependent Children (ADC), Old Age Assistance
(OAA), and Aid to the Blind (AB) under the Social Security Act, and
benefits for military servicemembers and their families, including GI Bill
loans and dependency allowances. However, the problems Native people
had were not solely based upon the institutional racism woven into the
welfare state.[1] Native people also faced the powerful assumptions—held
by agents both within the Bureau of Indian Affairs and other federal and
state agencies—that wardship was comparable to welfare dependency.

This belief was undergirded by agents' sense that Native people needed the state's protection and oversight, even when pursuing benefits to which they were entitled as American citizens. However, Native women and men living on reservations in the mid-twentieth century frequently engaged and negotiated with the BIA and representatives from welfare agencies both to gain access to those benefits and to articulate their own definitions of wardship, which directly conflicted with the definitions of terminationist legislators, BIA agents, and welfare administrators.

State agents defined wardship as a status of gendered dependency. Built into assimilative Indian policies were efforts to replace Native kinship and family systems with "a heteronormative and patriarchal Eurocentric kinship model of the nuclear family."[2] Thus, when agents attempted to help Native women and men access welfare benefits, they did so from within this gendered settler colonial framework. Social workers and officials who administered and determined eligibility for welfare benefits also understood the nuclear family as the ideal American standard.[3] Welfare recipients were often surveilled to determine if they had deviated from state officials' expectations. Indeed, welfare historian Annelise Orleck has noted that policymakers understood mothers enrolled in the welfare system to be "closely supervised *wards* of the state."[4]

However, as Premilla Nadasen has shown, welfare recipients formulated their own visions of citizenship and challenged the racism and sexism within the welfare system. Welfare rights activists fought for recognition of their contributions to their families and society and "attempted to assert some economic control over their lives."[5] Likewise, Native people did not maintain static relationships with the state agents in their lives; they pushed back against and subverted power dynamics because they held a fundamentally different definition of wardship. To Native people, wardship was not dependency. Instead, wardship was a legal relationship between sovereign entities.

Like the interactions and conflicts between those who received and those who administered welfare benefits, wardship's negotiations were often fraught. Many BIA agents assumed that as wards, Native people needed guidance and supervision in order to conform to Americanized family structures. Terminationist legislators contended that wardship itself was defined by "gratuitous" BIA supervision and should be abolished. Local welfare officials and many state legislators believed in a strict binary: Natives were either "wards" or "citizens," in an attempt, as Kevin Bruyneel argues, to impose order and boundaries on Indigenous peoples within the United States.[6] However, Native people maintained that under the legal terms of wardship as a reciprocal relationship between tribes and the state, BIA agents were required to safeguard tribal land and political rights.

As a legal status, wardship necessitated that Native people and BIA agents form relationships. However, those relationships were subject to competing interpretations. As explained in chapter 2, terminationists equated wardship with welfare dependency, arguing that the BIA held "competent" Native people back from "first-class" citizenship. To welfare caseworkers and many BIA agents, the BIA provided necessary guidance to Native people and served as a valuable intermediary between Native people and personnel from other governmental agencies. To Native people, the BIA was responsible for safeguarding the legal relationship of wardship—protecting tribal property and resources guaranteed by sovereign agreements. However, as this chapter shows, Natives utilized the connections they had with BIA agents—and indeed, made the most of the BIA's impulse to provide guidance and oversight—in order to obtain needed welfare benefits as citizens. Though far from perfect, those relationships were familiar, and the BIA acted as a powerful link to other areas of the federal government and a vehicle for Native people to amplify their concerns.

Non-Native welfare caseworkers' conflation of wardship with welfare was based on two primary misconceptions: BIA agents were essentially Native people's welfare caseworkers and thus all Native welfare issues needed to be funneled through the BIA; and Native people should not be able to access "more" welfare than they deserved, in the form of other need-based programs designed for all citizens. However, although non-Native caseworkers—and terminationists—conflated the two, and BIA agents did play a role in the administration of both, Native people actively affirmed that wardship and welfare were distinct entities. Thus, through their efforts to access welfare, Native people, organizations, and tribes ultimately contributed to a vision of tribal self-determination in the 1940s and 1950s.

This chapter examines how Native people navigated daily bureaucracy to define wardship by examining the red tape surrounding Native people's access to benefits under the 1935 Social Security Act, the 1942 Servicemen's Dependents Allowance Act, and the 1944 Servicemen's Readjustment Act (GI Bill). First, the chapter explores just how involved the BIA was with welfare issues. When Native people accessed welfare benefits, they had to contend with the assumptions and stereotypes of welfare caseworkers, who maintained that they required the BIA to interpret or translate for Native applicants. Regardless of the difficulties they faced as a result of caseworkers' misperceptions of wardship, Native people persisted in their efforts to access welfare. Second, the chapter examines how Native people used the BIA to serve as a "bridge" between themselves and other governmental agencies. In this vein Native people worked within the gendered settler colonial framework of the welfare state in order to maintain their right to welfare benefits. Although in many cases it was useful to engage with the BIA as a "bridge," they maintained that the BIA should not have oversight or authority over their benefits. Third, the chapter examines how Native people worked with entities outside of the BIA in order to define and preserve wardship as a legitimate legal relationship in the context of conflict over welfare. Tribal councils communicated concerns to welfare officials and negotiated for tribal sovereignty. Native people also mounted legal challenges in order to access welfare and pointed to their military service in an effort to safeguard both wardship and their access to welfare. Ultimately, by advocating for their right to welfare benefits in the termination era, Native people also advocated for continuation of wardship as they defined it.

EVERY DAY WITH THE BIA

In the mid-twentieth century, the BIA remained a large presence in Native families' lives. Correspondence related to Native women's challenges in obtaining monthly dependency allotments from relatives serving in the military demonstrates just how heavily BIA employees were involved in Native families' affairs. The extent of the bureaucracy involved in dispensing benefits to Native families was tinged with state officials' gendered assumptions about the BIA's responsibility to protect and supervise Native people.

For example, the paper trail generated by the efforts of Sarah Moore, a Paiute woman living on the Pyramid Lake Reservation in the mid-1940s, to obtain monthly dependency allowances from her husband, Howard, stationed at Fort Bragg in North Carolina, illustrates the extent to which the BIA was involved in Native women's lives. Sarah Moore's benefits were the official business not only of herself and her immediate family, but also of members of the tribal council, military officials, and the superintendent and social worker associated with the Carson Indian Agency in Nevada. Part of the reason for all of the correspondence was because bureaucrats in the Office of Dependency Benefits (ODB) needed to verify the "validity" of Sarah's marriage to Howard, as she had previously been married to Martin Lopez from 1929 to 1933. Her marriage to Lopez had been common-law, leaving no record "according to tribal custom."[7] Before Moore and her four children (two of whom were also Lopez's children) could obtain their monthly assistance, ODB representatives communicated with officials from the Pyramid Lake Tribal Council to ascertain "whether or not she was divorced from Martin Lopez before her marriage to Private Howard Moore."[8] Letters back and forth from the chairman of the tribal council and the ODB verifying her marriage to Howard Moore were dated in late August 1945. By mid-October of the same year, Moore had still not received any payments. A letter from Ralph Gelvin, the superintendent of the Carson Agency, to Steve Ryan, a BIA representative in Nixon, Nevada, relayed a message from Moore's mother: Howard had "informed [Sarah] of his attempts to secure an allotment; that deductions have been made from his wages therefore but she has to date received none."[9] Gelvin wrote to ask the representative to "visit Mrs. Moore and ascertain the full story."[10] Since this letter is the last piece of surviving correspondence related to this matter, it is unclear as to how long it took for Moore to finally receive her benefits.

This story, with its varying cast of official and informal characters, is not unique to Sarah and Howard Moore. Sarah Moore—speaking through her mother's message to Superintendent Gelvin—communicated that her husband Howard had taken the proper steps to secure her dependency allotment. Soldiers were expected to apply for family allowances through their commanding officers. From there, the application was sent to the Allowance and Allotment Branch in Washington DC, where each case would be investigated. If approved, dependents could expect to receive benefits in the next month, which would continue "up until 6 months after the present war ends."[11] Assuming that all application forms had been properly filled out and submitted—and because deductions were already being taken from his monthly paycheck, we can assume that they were—Private Howard Moore would have expected to have $92 sent to Sarah and the four children in his household each month, made up from both a contribution from his own paycheck and the rest from the government.[12] Sarah Moore's previous common-law marriage introduced a hiccup in the bureaucratic process, stalling the payments that the Moores needed. However, even after the tribal council verified Sarah's marriage to Howard, Sarah was still waiting for payments and had to reach out to both a family member and BIA employees to assist her in receiving her benefits. Sarah's benefits were significantly delayed, and BIA personnel were intimately involved in the Moore family's affairs as they attempted "to help her out of this uneasy situation."[13]

Although Gelvin's letter instructing Steve Ryan, the BIA representative in Nixon, Nevada, to visit Moore and "ascertain the full story," possibly revealed good intentions, those intentions were backed by a sense of distrust of Moore and her claims. Furthermore, while Moore's mother had written to Gelvin on August 29, he had waited until October 17 to respond to their concerns and had not communicated directly with Sarah Moore or her mother, but asked Ryan to visit Mrs. Moore. Sarah Moore's mother noted that Howard had been in the service for four months at the time of her letter. Thus, Sarah and her children were waiting on hundreds of dollars in dependency benefits. Those funds likely would have significantly impacted their livelihood.

Native women's receipt of welfare benefits was filtered through both the BIA framework of gendered settler colonialism and the distrustful notion held by state officials that welfare recipients could be taking more than they deserved.[14] For example, in 1944 C. H. Gensler, superintendent of the Colorado River Indian Agency in Arizona, wrote to the ODB to report that the daughter of Henry Dock, a soldier from the Colorado River Reservation, had died in 1943, and her mother, Ione Dock, had been "receiving dependency payments for her child for almost a year now to which she is not entitled."[15] We cannot know why Dock did not report her daughter's death to the ODB. However, whether it was an administrative task Dock had overlooked because of her grief or had done so purposefully to support herself with her husband stationed way from home, the fact remained that Dock's benefits were subject to Gensler's oversight. Gensler instructed the office to "advise the amount of refund that [Dock] should make" and to address future correspondence to Dock herself, but to include copies for Gensler's own files.[16] Gensler was heavily involved with Dock's benefits, going so far as to retain copies of ODB's correspondence with Dock in his possession. Cases like Sarah Moore's and Ione Dock's illustrate the often uneasy relationship between the BIA and Native people. While Moore enlisted Gelvin's help in order to obtain the benefits due her, both Gelvin and Gensler also operated as arbiters of the dependency allowances, acting as the spokesmen for the Native women under their jurisdiction in communication with other governmental agencies.

It was not unusual for BIA staff to facilitate communication between Native people and other governmental agents. In fact, this practice was the subject of much conversation and debate surrounding benefits under the Social Security Act in Arizona and New Mexico in the mid-twentieth century. As a result of an agreement reached in February 1948 between representatives from the BIA, the Social Security Administration, and the state welfare departments of Arizona and New Mexico, Native applications for need-based benefits such as OAA, ADC, and AB were forwarded to the BIA before being processed by state and county welfare caseworkers. The main reason for this was a stipulation within the agreement that the BIA was responsible for providing the funds for welfare benefits for eligible needy Native applicants.[17] However, welfare officials also delegated the screening of Native applications for errors and omissions to the BIA because they argued that they needed BIA "translation" to fully understand Native resources. A circular released by the commissioner of Arizona's State Department of Social Security and Welfare explained why:

> An Indian applying for OAA might tell the social worker that he has a small plot of corn and a few sheep and horses. Since the social worker might not know the value of these resources to the applicant, he would merely note the facts in the summary and allow the standard items in the assistance plan. The Indian Service might, however, recognize that the corn and stock furnish one-half of the applicant's food needs. In this hypothetical instance, the Indian Service would make a notation to this effect on the PA-101 and the social worker would reduce the food allowance by the appropriate amount.[18]

Welfare caseworkers needed the BIA agents to translate just how many resources were available to Native applicants, to prevent over-disbursing aid. Native livestock *could* negatively impact the amount of relief granted by state welfare offices. For example, a representative from the New Mexico nonprofit organization Navajo Assistance, Inc., asserted that the New Mexico State Welfare Office had established in October 1947 that one Navajo family's need—with an elderly husband, blind wife, and two small dependent children—should have granted them $144.09 per month. However, in May 1948, because BIA social workers on the reservation had informed the State Welfare Office that the family "owned 21 sheep and 10 goats," their monthly benefit was drastically reduced: "the old man would be given $7.50 and the blind wife $20.00 per month."[19] Because welfare caseworkers defined wardship as dependency on the federal government, they deferred to BIA administrators to translate Native applicants' needs. In cases like the Navajo family described above, this practice could negatively impact the benefits needy Native citizens were able to receive.

In certain states, especially Arizona and New Mexico, state and local welfare workers adopted a contentious attitude toward Native applicants and actively worked to separate themselves from Native people. In response Native people sought aid from the BIA to combat stalling tactics. For example, state welfare workers claimed that they lacked the staff needed to handle intake and processing of Native applications.

Alfred Jackson of the Pima-Maricopa Indian Community in Arizona noted that social workers in Pinal County had advised the community that "we should not send any more Indians into the county office to apply, because there will probably be no one there to take applications." Pinal County decided to send one worker to take applications on the reservation, "to review 10 applications only and no more."[20] The director of the welfare office of San Juan County in New Mexico limited staff to processing one application per week. According to Sam Ahkeah, Navajo Tribal Council chairman, "at this rate it would take approximately seven years to put the case load which is around 378 on Social Security here in the Shiprock vicinity."[21] In order to even get their applications into the hands of state and county welfare workers, Native applicants turned to employees of the BIA. On Native people's behalf, BIA employees expressed frustration and confusion over the lack of progress and cooperation with county welfare boards. Mary Woodruff, BIA social worker for the Pima Indian Agency, complained, "We have had to wait for months for the Welfare county offices to complete the processing of the Indian Applications."[22] Stalling tactics by the state welfare boards had potentially devastating effects for needy Native people whose applications languished in "suspense files" or who were turned away by caseworkers who stated that it was "humanly impossible" to process Native cases as well as white cases.[23]

Despite the resistance they faced, Native people persisted in their attempts to access benefits they were entitled to as American citizens. Through the quotidian administrative tasks required to apply for benefits, including visiting welfare offices, sending paperwork to government agencies, or seeking assistance from entities such as the BIA or the Red Cross, Native people defined their reciprocal relationships with the American state.[24] By applying for welfare benefits, Native people clearly separated wardship and citizenship. Although caseworkers saw them as dependent and undeserving of welfare benefits and relied on the BIA to "translate" Native need, Native people continued to assert their rights to welfare as American citizens and the protection of land and provision of services guaranteed them under the terms of wardship.

Although caseworkers actively resisted processing Native applications, Native people continued to maintain their eligibility for welfare benefits.

For example, in 1948, Sam Ahkeah wrote to the Navajo Nation's lawyer, Norman Littell, about a group of Navajos who had been turned away by welfare workers after traveling a long distance from the reservation to apply for OAA and ADC benefits in person. When they returned the following day, "they were informed that it would be necessary to furnish birth certificates for each member of the family, but, at the same time, were advised by the welfare worker that it wouldn't be worthwhile to go to all that trouble," because the payments "wouldn't amount to anything." Ahkeah contended this conversation had "discouraged them to such an extent that they went home the second time and dropped the matter."[25] He argued, "It is very discouraging when we see, for instance in a daily newspaper on November 11th, 'WELFARE PAYMENTS TO BE INCREASED FOR NEW MEXICANS', and then the same paper the next day shows: WELFARE PAYMENT TO BE REDUCED FOR NAVAJO TRIBE."[26] Ahkeah's letter clearly illustrates that despite the fact that Navajo applicants had been denied benefits, they understood that welfare workers' resistance to them to be unjustified. The maintained their right to benefits, keeping citizenship separate from wardship.

Native people did not passively accept denial or delay of benefits. Rather, they utilized BIA employees to assist them in obtaining the benefits they were owed. Lizzie Youngbird (Eastern Band of Cherokee) visited Cherokee Indian Agency clerk William Ensor "several times regarding the non-receipt of her check for dependency allowance from her son, Private Edmond Youngbird." Due to Youngbird's persistence, Ensor wrote to the U.S. Marine Corps to inquire about her check's whereabouts.[27] She received a response from the Marine Corps the next month.[28] Nina Winnemucca, a Paiute living on the Pyramid Lake Reservation, ran into challenges obtaining the benefits owed her from the life insurance policy of her son, Stanley Winnemucca, after he was killed in action while serving with the Marine Corps in 1943. Because Stanley's father, Pete Winnemucca, was originally listed as the beneficiary, Nina was left with "no means of support" when Pete passed away in 1942. She enlisted several BIA employees to help her write to the Social Security Board and the Veterans Administration in order to obtain any benefits that Stanley had accrued through his military service.[29] After Pete's death and prior to Stanley's, Nina had attempted to obtain a monthly family allowance from Stanley, but she was told that the soldier must be the one to file an application for an allowance through his commanding officer.[30] Before she was able to obtain any monthly payments, Stanley was killed in action.[31] A large collection of correspondence reveals that Nina was required to submit notarized affidavits attesting to the fact that she was dependent on Stanley in order to receive "death gratuity pay."[32] Obtaining the money from Stanley's life insurance policy proved to be more challenging. Nina was required to submit affidavits swearing to her own birth, because she did not have a birth certificate. In addition, since she was unable to read and write, she was required to place her mark on official papers and identification materials in the presence of others.[33] The legal complications of Nina's case caused her local BIA representative to turn it over to the Veteran's Commission in Reno, who then enlisted the help of the American Legion.[34] In the end, although it took an additional five months, Nina Winnemucca eventually heard that she would receive $45 per month from Stanley's death pension and a $55.10 monthly payment from Stanley's life insurance policy, which were to continue over the course of her lifetime.[35]

Nina Winnemucca faced extensive logistical challenges in order to obtain the financial assistance due to her. It must have taken extreme strength to persist in her struggle to gain access to her monthly checks, especially after the deaths of both her husband and son. Winnemucca's case demonstrates her individual perseverance and her expectation that she was entitled to benefits. Like Lizzie Youngbird, in order to access benefits, Winnemucca effectively engaged the BIA to serve as a bridge between herself and other governmental agencies.

THE BIA AS A BRIDGE

Native people enlisted BIA employees to advocate for them when they faced difficulties obtaining benefits or payments. However, administrative personnel still consistently viewed Native people as dependent wards, and the BIA's interference in Native people's financial lives could be intrusive. By utilizing the BIA as a "bridge" between themselves and other governmental agencies, Native people worked within state agents' assumptions that wards needed assistance and guidance to circumvent the roadblocks they frequently encountered when accessing welfare.

BIA personnel did consider themselves to be bridges between Native people and other governmental agencies. BIA agents wanted to spread information about programs and ensure Native access to benefits to which they were eligible, but they did so through a gendered settler colonial framework. For example, in October 1943, Don Foster, superintendent of Nevada's Carson Indian Agency, issued a memo to all BIA field employees and tribal councils that described a *San Francisco Examiner* newspaper article published the previous month. The article explained that to obtain a monthly dependency allowance for families of servicemen, Private Kee S. Kaibetony, twenty-two, and his wife, Nora Griggs, twenty-one, had been married in a Presbyterian church. Though the couple had first appealed to the Red Cross, ultimately the "Government had refused to recognize their union by traditional tribal rites on a reservation in Arizona." Foster urged other Native men eligible for the draft to "take this information seriously and take the necessary steps to protect the welfare of their families."[36] By relaying Kaibetony and Griggs's story, Foster acted as a bridge between Native communities and other offices of the federal government and the military, ostensibly to ensure that Native servicemen received the same benefits as other citizens. However, Foster's message was that Native servicemen should conform to Americanized marriage customs, something that Kaibetony and Griggs had challenged by first appealing to the Red Cross. The administrative correspondence between BIA agents and Native people often reflected the tension of wardship—while the BIA could, and did, provide assistance to Native people who were entitled to welfare benefits, it also promoted or enforced assimilation.

However circumscribed Native people were by their relationship with the BIA, utilizing the BIA as a bridge between themselves and other federal agencies was often the only choice they had. For example, when Sarah Moore (Paiute) did not receive her monthly dependency allowance, she employed the BIA's network of social workers and superintendents to follow up with the ODB. As is addressed in further detail in chapter 4, the ODB assumed that as a Native woman, she might be unable to responsibly make use of her benefits and would be better off entrusting them to a BIA agent. But, in turn, Moore might have assumed that she was more likely to see the money if official communication came directly from the BIA. As Linda Gordon has shown, that governmental and welfare agencies are not only institutions of "social control" but are influenced by clients and beneficiaries of aid.[37] Because Native people understood wardship as a legal relationship between tribes and the federal government, asking a government representative to file paperwork, inquire after benefits, or write official correspondence should not be viewed as Native women's capitulation to a state of *dependence* upon the federal government. Sarah Moore and her mother wrote directly to Superintendent Gelvin, and he took steps to solve the problem. Although the Moores' relationship with Gelvin cannot solely be classified as positive—after all, his actions were late and his letters paternalistic—communicating with the ODB through him was likely the Moores' best option.

Similarly, in 1943 Josie French (Paiute) utilized the Carson Agency's social worker, Tephia Slater, in order to fix a mistake with her monthly dependency allowances. Cornelius, French's husband, was serving with the U.S. Navy and had failed to list all his eligible children on his application. French directly requested that her family allowance be increased by communicating with Slater, who passed the message to another BIA employee to alert Cornelius's commanding officer.[38] Additionally, French had requested her husband's release from the navy due to the financial hardship she was facing at home. Through her correspondence with the BIA, she discovered that her husband would be able to receive a higher monthly salary by staying in the service than by returning to his previous job, since Slater had communicated with his former employers. Slater's language can be read as paternalistic. She did not expend her efforts on French's behalf purely because French was entitled to her benefits as a citizen and a wife of a serviceman. Rather, as an employee of the BIA Slater had the power to communicate with Cornelius's employers and make judgments about how Josie could "keep her accounts straight" with the increase she was due in her allowances.[39] Overall though, Josie French's attempts to increase her monthly allowances and care for her family by any means possible overshadows Slater's opinions on what was best for the French family. Familiar with the daily bureaucracy of wardship, French asked for Slater's assistance to obtain the benefits to which she and her children were entitled—and she received them.

Josie French's case also illustrates how through matters of financial welfare and government support, the BIA could also connect family members far apart in the context of war. For example, bureaucracy related to welfare benefits provided assurance to parents that their children serving overseas were still alive. In March 1944 Paiutes Joe and Bessie Greene enlisted the assistance of the BIA and the Red Cross in obtaining information about the whereabouts of their son Pike. They had recently received notice of the death of their other son, Scott, and after Joe had received a notification from the War Department alerting him that his family allowance checks from Pike had been discontinued, they were "greatly worried" about Pike.[40] Two months later, the Red Cross received a telegram from Pike Greene, expressing that he had canceled the allowance, "as he felt his family would get along without the allowance."[41] Although Pike claimed in the telegram that he had written his father to explain the discontinuance of the allowance, it appears as though Joe Greene never received such a letter. Therefore, though the bureaucratic chain of correspondence delivered unfortunate news, it at least proved useful for Joe and Bessie to ascertain Pike's well-being.

Perhaps Pike wished to stop the monthly deduction from his paycheck and figured that an allowance from his brother Scott would be sufficient for his parents to get by in their absence. It is unclear if Pike had knowledge of his brother's death. In any case the Greene parents were left without a steady stream of financial support and embarked on an effort to obtain the benefits entitled to them due to Scott's death overseas. Correspondence between the BIA and the Veteran's Administration, Quartermaster General, and General Accounting Office reveals that Joe Greene sought to cash out his son's savings bonds and life insurance to support himself and his wife. Unfortunately, the Veterans Administration disallowed the Greenes' application for death pension payments as dependent parents since "the veteran's death was not incurred in line of duty but was due to injuries received under circumstances that are not pensionable."[42] The Greenes pursued alternate avenues for accessing some sort of financial support from Scott's service. By September of 1944, nine months after Scott's death, E. B. Hudson, the BIA staff member assisting the Greenes with correspondence, received word that Joe Greene would start to receive a monthly check from the National Life Insurance Policy for the balance of his life.[43] The assurance of this payment was not obtained easily, as it took several letters back and forth between the Veterans Administration's Insurance Division and the BIA to explain why Joe lacked a birth certificate and why he was not sure of his exact birth date. Because they were born in the 1870s, Joe and Bessie Greene lacked easily accessible birth certificates. Unfortunately, Joe passed away before receiving any payments, and Hudson embarked on naming Bessie the beneficiary of Scott's life insurance policy.[44]

It is easy to get lost in the administrative and perfunctory language of all of the governmental correspondence surrounding the Greenes' family situation. If one steps back and examines their circumstances, what lies under the surface of the daily bureaucracy of wardship are two significant family tragedies within nine months of each other, with the deaths of Scott and Joe, and the reality of financial hardship facing aging parents whose children were thousands of miles away, separated by both oceans and governmental agencies. Bessie and Joe were left to deal with the pieces of their lives left from one son's death, while the other had discontinued their monthly allowances. Was Pike able to learn of his brother's death and reinstate his family allowances so that his parents could get by in their time of grief? Was Joe's health failing throughout the process of applying for the life insurance benefits? How did Bessie handle the death of her husband so close to that of her son?

Historians have shown that servicemen and women who had spent time in Indian boarding schools found it easier to adapt to military life.[45] Perhaps Native people on the home front who had dealt with colonial paternalism and bureaucracy for years were equally equipped with useful knowledge and expectations when they attempted to access welfare benefits. They were familiar with paternalistic superintendents and social workers intruding into their lives and homes and the red tape associated with correspondence between their local agency and higher authorities of the BIA. The Greenes accessed the benefits they were entitled to by employing state agents to advocate for them. This tactic could have drawbacks as well as benefits, but it was often the only available choice.

Thus, for Native people, welfare benefits were intimately connected to the daily bureaucracy of wardship. However, although they employed BIA agents to assist them in navigating through administrative hurdles to access welfare, Native people actively critiqued proposals that officially funneled the maintenance and funding of their welfare benefits through the BIA. Under the legal terms of wardship, the BIA did not have the responsibility to disburse need-based benefits. In fact, Native people opposed conflating resources and services under wardship and citizenship in this way. This critical distinction was made plain through debates over S. 691, a 1949 bill proposed by senators in Arizona and New Mexico, which would have amended the Social Security Act to stipulate that the federal government would be the source of funds for Native people for programs usually administered by the states, including OAA, ADC, and AB. The secretary of the Treasury would have disbursed funds to both Arizona and New Mexico to cover 80 percent of welfare benefits for any "needy individuals residing on lands which are exempt from real property taxes by virtue of Federal laws and treaties in the States of New Mexico and Arizona."[46] When they introduced it, the senators from Arizona and New Mexico framed their bill as a solution for suffering on reservations. By "embracing our Indian wards of the Government into the Social Security plan," proclaimed Dennis Chavez of New Mexico, "this bill would provide the means for an immediate response from the Government in taking care of the elderly, dependent children and the blind."[47] With this proposed bill, the senators separated needy Native citizens from other Arizonans and New Mexicans, explicitly linking their funds to the federal government, and the BIA.

Native critics of the bill argued that it constituted "special treatment" or a "special handout" for Native people and fell outside the bounds of wardship as a legal relationship. For example, David Jackson, representative for the Pima-Maricopa Indian Community on the Gila River Reservation, wrote to Ruth Bronson, secretary of the National Congress of American Indians (NCAI), in 1949 expressing his dissatisfaction with the bill. "We do not want to be handled separately or even set apart in separate class the social security as it should be dealt with on equality and not on the basis of special treatment," Jackson wrote. "If the amendment passes, it will be another bill passed by Congress without the consent of the governed. JUSTICE?"[48] Significantly, Jackson emphasized that as citizens, Native people were entitled to Social Security benefits on an equal basis with other citizens. To support his argument, he cited both a 1936 opinion by the solicitor of the interior of the applicability of the Social Security Act to Natives and the 1924 Indian Citizenship Act. Jackson's concerns echoed a 1946 statement issued by a group of Crow veterans objecting to the creation of a "separate office for Indian veterans" by the BIA, "on the grounds that this will merely continue the arbitrary power of the bureau 'over our property and our lives and continue to deny us the right to be citizens of the country we gladly fought for.'"[49]

In a letter to the Federal Security Agency soon after S. 691 was introduced, Ruth Bronson claimed that the bill meant Native people in New Mexico and Arizona would have to "beg special favors from Uncle Sam," and that they did not "want to be a party to this raid on the federal Treasury. We are against racial discrimination of all kinds, either that contained in Senate Bill 691 or that which is inherent in the present anti-Indian policies of New Mexico and Arizona."[50] Crucially, both Jackson and Bronson did not assert that the federal government was obligated to fulfill Social Security benefits under wardship. Rather, Native people were entitled to Social Security as citizens. Indeed, in his analysis of the bill for the NCAI, lawyer James Curry urged Native people to protest it. Curry believed the bill could engender further racial antagonism toward Natives due to the "special handout" they would receive, which could potentially exacerbate stereotypes about Native wards benefiting from their relationship with the government in ways other citizens did not.[51] Thus, the bill had the potential to undermine both Native people's citizenship status and also the legal arrangement of wardship. S. 691 did not progress further than the Senate Committee on Finance, due to a compromise reached in April 1949 between representatives from the Federal Security Agency, the BIA, the attorney generals of the states of Arizona and New Mexico, and the state welfare departments of Arizona and New Mexico.

Into the 1950s Native people in Arizona and New Mexico continued to maintain their right to welfare benefits as citizens rather than wards. In 1950 Congress adopted a new category for public assistance under the Social Security Act: Aid to the Permanently and Totally Disabled.[52] As they had done for other needs-based programs such as OAA and ADC, Arizona and New Mexico refused to issue these benefits to Native applicants, despite the language of the Social Security Act, which prohibited discrimination based on race in the administration of benefits to citizens, and exterior agreements such as the one reached in April 1949. Clarence Wesley, chairman of the San Carlos Apache Tribal Council, critiqued the decision, arguing that, rather than accepting a program that "the State finances with Federal help," Arizona refused "hundreds of thousands of dollars of Federal aid." Wesley asserted, "There are some politicians in the State who would rather throw away hundreds of thousands of dollars than give help to one crippled Indian kid."[53] Through these conflicts over access to welfare benefits due to citizens, Native people maintained the distinction between the boundaries of wardship and their right to need-based welfare benefits as citizens.

DEFINING WARDSHIP AND WELFARE OUTSIDE THE BIA

Native people also articulated their understandings of wardship and welfare with the relationships they formed with other entities, including tribal governments, the courts, and the military. Tribal government played an essential role in the administrative relationships of wardship and welfare. When they were able, tribes stepped in to provide relief when Native applicants were shut out of state and local programs. Additionally, they acted as official mouthpieces for Native welfare issues, articulating Native people's definitions of wardship while advocating for tribal citizens' eligibility for welfare benefits.

By providing resources out of their own budgets to the elderly, blind, and dependent children within their tribes, tribal governments recognized Native need when state governments did not. In 1938 the Colorado River Tribal Council issued a resolution to budget $3,000 "in order to provide for the old age among the members of the Colorado River Indian tribes who are not on the old age pension list under the Social Security

Act."[54] Within the next ten years, the Pima-Maricopa-Gila, Fort McDowell, and Salt River tribal councils also instituted their own relief programs.[55] Native citizens looked to tribal governments in response to the difficulties they faced in accessing welfare benefits as citizens. For example, a 1946 article published in the *Great Falls Tribune* reported that Native veterans gathered at a conference in Montana "went on record as urging legislation which would authorize tribal councils to make loans to Indian veterans," because, they asserted, "provisions in the GI bill of rights for making loans are too cumbersome to be practicable."[56] Native veterans agitated for increasing the power and purview of tribal government because they saw tribes as more attuned to the needs of their citizens than the United States government. During a 1945 meeting of the Navajo Tribal Council, Kizzie Yazzie relayed the concerns of a Navajo veteran: "I have been in battle and places of danger and I have returned and need to live on. I need assistance. I want you and the Councilmen to be for us veterans, with the Superintendent and others, that something be done with acquiring land or something from which we can make a living."[57]

However, the funds tribes were able to provide often did not meet all of the needs. Tribal councils recognized this and utilized the administrative relationships they had with BIA agents to voice these concerns to welfare officials. For example, in a 1948 letter to the director of welfare for the Office of Indian Affairs, A. E. Robinson, superintendent of the Pima Agency, argued that the tribal governments did not have enough available cash to support the relief cases. Robinson asserted: "They feel that no other community or group of people are required to carry a like burden and neither should they be called upon to do so. I find it difficult to disagree with them on this point."[58] Some tribes had no extra resources to grant to needy members, instead relying on the family members of those in need to help. Taos Pueblo governor Antonio Mirabal noted in a 1948 letter that need in his community was "severe to the extent that the aged and needy children receive only what can be supplied by near relatives. The food and clothing they receive from the relatives are of the barest necessities."[59]

Thus, even though some tribal councils could step in and provide a modicum of relief payments to needy tribal citizens, they argued that because Native people were entitled to need-based welfare benefits under the Social Security Act, it was not the tribe's responsibility to provide this type of aid. Moreover, some tribes argued that the funds they expended to aid needy tribal citizens would be better spent in other ways. In 1948 Jicarilla Apache Tribal Council chairman John Mills Baltazar wrote that although the "tribe as a whole has not neglected its needy" and had in fact spent "approximately $10,000 per year" for relief, any assistance they could obtain in "securing relief aid and benefits from State social security boards will save our tribal funds for use in improvement of our reservation, instead of using it for relief."[60] In this way Native people asserted that their rights as citizens should not be undercut by the rights they maintained under wardship—namely, the stewardship and ownership of tribal land. As citizens of tribal nations, Natives could apply to tribal councils for loans or relief payments. As citizens of the United States, they could apply to state and county welfare boards for OAA, ADC, and AB. Membership in the tribe did not cancel out membership in the American polity, and vice versa.

By advocating for their tribal citizens in official communications and providing support and guidance to those pursuing welfare benefits, tribal governments embodied Native sovereignty. Tribal councils worked with BIA employees in their efforts to obtain welfare benefits for tribal citizens. Native people also appealed to tribal councils to provide support outside of BIA oversight. In 1949 the governor of the Gila River Pima-Maricopa Community, David Johnson, contended that his people were "entitled under the law" to benefits. As his community's elected representative, Johnson stated that he went with every applicant to apply for benefits, in order to "take action at once to end this shameful betrayal of my people."[61] Similarly, in 1948 Sam Ahkeah, chairman of the Navajo Tribal Council, described the dire situation some Navajos faced without Social Security benefits. Emphasizing how common it was for him to be asked about Social Security, Ahkeah asserted, "I do not go out in the out lying parts of the reservation that I am not accosted and begged for help by the aged, the blind, the crippled, the sick mothers with dependent children, and the helpless." He argued that "to delay Social Security one day longer" was "to deny life, to these, my people."[62] To humanize those in need and call attention to the legal relationship the United States had with their tribes, both Johnson and Ahkeah worked to obtain access to welfare benefits for needy members of their communities.

In addition to applying for benefits in person, enlisting BIA agents to inquire after their benefits, and voicing their concerns to tribal councils, Native people also pursued legal avenues to access welfare benefits. In 1948 eight Native people from Arizona and New Mexico (Pueblo, Tohono O'odham, Hualapai, Jicarilla Apache, San Carlos Apache, and Gila River Pima-Maricopa Indian Community) filed a class action lawsuit against Administrator of Federal Security Oscar Ewing, Secretary of the Interior Julius Krug, Secretary of the Treasury John Snyder, and Comptroller General Lindsay Warren in the U.S. District Court for the District of Columbia (*Mapatis v. Ewing*). The plaintiffs claimed that denying them Social Security benefits deprived Native people of their civil rights, and that as citizens of the United States and residents of the states of New Mexico and Arizona, Native Americans were entitled to OAA, ADC, and AB. Because the Social Security Act stated clearly that all applications for Social Security were to be "promptly considered without discrimination because of race or color," the Social Security Board (SSB) determined that New Mexico and Arizona had violated the conditions of the act and threatened the states with a "withholding of Federal aid grants amounting to more than 10 million dollars per annum."[63]

Felix Cohen, Royal Marks, and James Curry, lawyers for the plaintiffs, argued that unless Native Americans in Arizona and New Mexico were "accorded equality of consideration with their white fellow citizens," they would be "facing acute hunger in the coming winter."[64] The plaintiffs asserted that a conspiracy between federal officials had contributed to a failure of the SSB to force Arizona and New Mexico to make payments to Native people, and that federal funds had been misappropriated from the SSB to the Department of the Interior, making it seem as though Natives were amply provided for by the federal government. Furthermore, Krug and Ewing had agreed to postpone hearings between the welfare boards of Arizona and New Mexico and the SSB until after the elections on November 2, 1948.[65] The lawyers claimed that denying public assistance to Native people was politically motivated, and that politicians had promised non-Native voters that the states would pay out federal Social Security grants "exclusively to the non-Indian portion of the population of these two states, thus increasing the allotment to each non-Indian beneficiary proportionately."[66] The lawsuit presented Arizona and New Mexico's efforts to deny needy Natives public assistance as racially motivated by contributing to both the personal gain of politicians and non-Native applicants for Social Security in both states.

Senators and representatives from New Mexico and Arizona were forthright about their refusal to grant aid to Native Americans in their states. In a 1948 letter to the commissioner of the Social Security Administration, eight senators and representatives from both states wrote, "There is very substantial weight to be given to the contention of both States that the primary responsibility for Indian welfare, both legal and moral, rests upon the Federal Government and not upon the States."[67] While couched in legalistic, race-neutral language, their arguments drew from and evoked deeply entrenched racialized discourses not only about Native people, but about welfare recipients in general. In the eyes of the politicians, government assistance—whether it was wardship or welfare—was not just a legal or political issue, but a moral one. The "problem which now confronts the Indians who reside on reservations as wards of the Government," they argued, would not be fully solved by the "payment of social security benefits." Rather, "any kind of temporary assistance through State agencies will not in any way solve the permanent problem and might conceivably complicate it."[68] The vaguely described "problem" on reservations was Native poverty, exactly what OAA, AB, and ADC were designed to combat. The politicians asserted that paying Social Security benefits to needy Indians would only "increase the number of paupers on the dole," rather than helping "reservation Indians so that they may become qualified to take their part in the economy of the nation."[69] As welfare historians have shown, those responsible for dispersing benefits feared that applicants for need-based aid (mainly women and people of color) would defraud the government and take more than they "deserved."[70]

Arizonan and New Mexican politicians argued that Native people's dependence was due to the federal government's failure in its "legal and moral" responsibility for Native wards. They contended that their states should not have to make up for the federal government's failure. The All-Pueblo Council, Mescalero Apache Tribe, Jicarilla Apache Tribe, and the NCAI responded to this argument in their amicus brief in support of the *Mapatis* plaintiffs: "No white man is excluded from social security assistance in New Mexico because of the amount of his uncollectible accounts. He might have a cellar full of Confederate money and still receive social security assistance. All the Indian asks is equal treatment."[71] In this case Native Americans did not disagree that the federal government had a responsibility to protect them under the confines of wardship. Indeed, describing the relationship between the federal government and Native tribes as an "uncollectible account" reiterated a Native conceptualization of wardship as an arrangement with the federal government that had yet to be fulfilled. Furthermore, by comparing a Native person to a white man with a "cellar full of Confederate money," the authors of the amicus brief asserted tribal sovereignty and autonomy and claimed citizenship rights at the same time. The authors did not see wardship as superseding Native people's entitlement to Social Security benefits as citizens of their respective states. Rather, they understood that Native people legitimately held *both* wardship and citizenship status. Ultimately, as a result of the compromise reached in 1949 between the states of Arizona and New Mexico and representatives of the federal government, the plaintiffs in the *Mapatis* case dropped their complaint.

When they encountered difficulties accessing GI Bill benefits, Native veterans advocated for their right to welfare as citizens and maintained the legitimacy and sovereignty of Native nations, working within and around settler colonial assumptions of wardship. For example, when a group of Navajo ex-servicemen found that the nearest Veterans Administration (VA) offices were in Phoenix and Albuquerque, far away from more isolated Navajo veterans, they formed American Legion Post 52 at Fort Defiance and Window Rock on the Navajo reservation. "We did not want to become a burden on the government, on the Veterans Administration, the Red Cross, or on the Navajo Tribe," asserted Mr. Bennet, representative for the "all-Indian Legion post" at a 1946 meeting of the Navajo Tribal Council.[72] "We decided the best method was to form an organization to get the help of groups interested in the Navajo veterans."[73] Peter Yazza, an ex-Marine and chaplain of the American Legion Post 52, argued that "Indian people have a very different problem than the white people because the white people have everything solved and it is down in black and white for them, and the Indian people have no knowledge of this work among them."[74] Yazza conceptualized the role of Post 52 as a resource for Navajo veterans who faced uncertainty accessing the benefits to which they were entitled in return for their military service. Post 52 represented Navajo veterans in Washington DC and around the country at American Legion conventions.

Native veterans' activism for equal rights of citizenship, especially voting rights, has led historians to pit Native veterans against more "traditional" members of their tribal nations and to position citizenship as antithetical to wardship. For example, Jere' Bishop Franco empha- sized how participation in the war effort led Native veterans to demand equal treatment on par with their non-Native fellow servicemen.[75] Alison Bernstein argued that after fighting alongside white soldiers in the war, Native veterans began to agitate for the end of wardship itself, because they had "begun to see the ways in which white society controlled their lives either through discriminatory legislation or the paternalism of the Indian Bureau."[76] Media coverage from the postwar period reinforced this narrative of veterans' efforts to obtain equality with other citizens and freedom from government oversight. In 1946 Salish veteran Stephen De Mers was quoted in a radio feature on Washington DC's WTOP expressing frustration with the reach of the BIA in Indian lives. "We have freed the Philipinos [sic], and we have been generous to subjects outside the U.S. But a didactic Indian Bureau, with an arbitrary attitude and jammed with red tape, has sought to lead us like children. We want rights as citizens, not charges."[77] Pitting their military service against the bureaucratic administration of the BIA, these veterans spoke through mainstream media outlets to highlight the hypocrisy they saw in the differentiation of Native veterans' rights compared to other veterans' rights.

However, not all Native veterans drew such distinct lines between wardship and citizenship. By calling attention to their military ser- vice, Native veterans challenged settler colonial assumptions of their dependency. They balanced between advocating for their rights as American citizens by challenging racial restrictions placed upon them, and demanding that the United States fulfill its obligations to Native nations.

Native advocates used military service to draw attention to the state's failure to uphold the terms of wardship. For example, in a 1947 letter to Senator Pat McCarran, N. B. Johnson, president of the NCAI, criticized a severe cut in the appropriations for the BIA, by arguing "on behalf of more than 300,000 defenseless wards of the United States Government, to provide adequate funds to at least insure minimum health and educational facilities for them."[78] By using the term "defenseless wards," Johnson condemned McCarran and other members of the Senate who had cut Indian appropriations—a key component in the legal relationship between Native nations and the federal government—without obtaining tribal consent. To further emphasize his point, Johnson asserted: "The Indian people sent more than 30,000 of their boys and girls to the Colors in World War II to fight for our institutions and American way of life. Let us not deny them the health and educational facilities which have been freely accorded our other citizens."[79] Johnson drew upon Native military service as the ultimate expression of citizenship and used it to remind McCarran of the United States' obligations to its wards. Similarly, in 1951 a Sioux veteran named Lone Eagle wrote to President Truman appealing for aid to Navajos in Arizona and New Mexico: "I am a veteran of World War I. My son served 3 1/2 years in World War II. My son-in-law has recently returned from Korea maimed for life—All enlisted volunteers—all good loyal Americans."[80] Johnson and Lone Eagle both pointed to military service to the United States in order to claim specific appropriations for Native people. In other words, they emphasized their contributions as citizens at the same time as they advocated for their entitlement to protections and resources as wards.

Other Natives drew attention to the military service of their family members and themselves to oppose changes in legislation that would alter the legal agreements between the federal government and Native nations. For example, in 1952 Joseph Red Cloud, chief of the Oglala Lakota Nation on the Pine Ridge Reservation in South Dakota, sent a telegram to Harry Truman appealing to the federal government for aid, stating that his grandchildren had fought for the country, and three of them had "been killed and one a prisoner—yet the fathers at home are in want of food and Congressmen too busy to help out."[81] Red Cloud simultaneously highlighted Oglala service to the United States and reminded Truman that the federal government had not lived up to its obligations to the tribe. Additionally, at the 1954 Emergency Conference of American Indians on Legislation, hosted by the NCAI, Zuni veterans of World War II and the Korean War issued a statement opposing several bills that would alter or abolish wardship, including a bill that would bring Zunis under the jurisdiction of the state of New Mexico. The Zuni veterans pointed to their military service to support their demand that the federal government honor their obligations to the Pueblo of Zuni: "We fully understand that the passage of these bills will effect [sic] us individually, our property, our tribal ownership, our protection against our religion, our communities, and the things we fought for so dearly."[82] Reminding the federal government of their military service, the veterans asserted, "We have fought for democracy and we would like to have you show us this democratic way of life and not neglect us." Instead of utilizing military service to demand the abolishment of wardship, the Zuni veterans emphasized that military service necessitated that the government honor Zuni tribal property rights and protections. Thus, when Native veterans called upon their military service to demand recognition and support from the government, they did not do so solely to insist that their rights be granted in return for fulfilling the responsibilities of citizenship. Native veterans also used military service to call for the federal government to fulfill the obligations of wardship.

In the termination era, welfare caseworkers and legislators who supported competency legislation shared the same assumption: they believed that as wards, Native people were under the guidance and oversight of the BIA in all matters of government assistance. As a result, welfare caseworkers and employees of other state agencies engaged the BIA to translate and interpret messages about welfare benefits to Native applicants and recipients. Conversely, Native people claimed their rights to both welfare benefits and the protection of their land and resources guaranteed by wardship. To Native applicants for welfare, wardship did not preclude their access to either need-based benefits under the Social Security Act or benefits accrued as a result of military service under the Servicemen's Dependency Allowance Act or the GI Bill.

However, when Native people ran into roadblocks in accessing welfare benefits, they turned to the BIA for assistance. In many cases the BIA was the most useful tool Native people could utilize in order to yield necessary financial intervention. Although the BIA was not a perfect advocate, Native people worked *with* the authority that other governmental entities imbued in the BIA. However, by also engaging with tribal governments and the courts and drawing attention to their military service, Native people fleshed out a definition of wardship that did not obstruct their entitlement to welfare benefits. Moreover, as they emphasized their citizenship *and* wardship, Native people articulated a sense of tribal self-determination. By persisting in their attempts to access welfare and publicly maintaining their rights to benefits, they emphasized to government agents that their relationship with the BIA was predicated upon a legal arrangement between two sovereign entities, and that wardship was not welfare.

Considering how wardship was experienced by Native people in their attempts to access welfare provides allows us to further historicize the termination era. This chapter has shown that the fears held by opponents of competency legislation were very valid: wardship *would* impede Native people's ability to access welfare benefits that they needed and to which they were entitled. Wardship was conflated with welfare dependency, not just in an abstract way, but in ways that drastically impacted poor Native people's quality of life. For example, states such as Arizona and New Mexico actively resisted granting Native people access to benefits under the Social Security Act, despite their demonstrated need. However, in their interactions with the BIA and with caseworkers, Native people actively combatted the conflation of wardship with welfare dependency. Moreover, they began to articulate sovereignty using wardship as a nascent language of tribal self-determination.

CHAPTER 4

Gender and Wardship

Surveillance, Dependency, and Welfare's Limitations

Lastly, if you should ever doubt that a series of dry words in a government document can shatter spirits and demolish lives, let this book erase that doubt. Conversely, if you should be of the conviction that we are powerless to change those dry words, let this book give you heart.

—Louise Erdrich (Turtle Mountain Ojibwe), *The Night Watchman*

In October 1952 Mrs. Futch Cypress (Seminole) instructed her son, Henry Cypress, to write to Kenneth Marmon, the Bureau of Indian Affairs superintendent for the Seminole Agency, to see if he could "do something about" increasing her monthly Old Age Assistance grant from $31.00 per month. "Henry Bret's wife mother received $45.00 that reason my mother want same way too," Henry Cypress wrote, enclosing a copy of a flyer from the Florida Department of Public Welfare indicating that the state's maximum payments had been raised for Old Age Assistance, Aid to the Blind, and Aid to Dependent Children. Marmon's response may have been disappointing for Mrs. Cypress, who learned that there was nothing the Seminole Agency could do about the amount of her monthly benefits. "Her case will have to be reconsidered by the Welfare Department before she can get an increase," Marmon wrote. But, he offered hope, writing, "It may be that your mother will be getting an increase this month," and took concrete steps to increase the likelihood of Mrs. Cypress's benefits meeting those of Henry Bret's mother-in-law. He sent a carbon copy of his letter to the welfare visitor for the county.[1]

American state actors have long fashioned themselves as moral arbiters of Native people's behavior. In this way wardship's history coincides with that of the welfare state, where caseworkers have surveilled recipients' moral "failings," looking to expose behavior that might classify them as "undeserving" of government aid.[2] As chapter 3 explores, the relationship between the BIA and welfare caseworkers was based primarily on logistics. Welfare workers often relied on the BIA to serve as a bridge to Native people. There were also ideological overlaps between the bureaucratic institutions, even if they didn't always work seamlessly together. For example, both BIA personnel and welfare caseworkers used moral suasion to compel (or coerce) certain behaviors in decidedly gendered ways. This chapter explores how BIA agents and other government workers drew upon accepted gendered definitions of dependency as they walked the thin line between advocacy and oversight of Native people's receiving and spending of welfare benefits. However, as the above example of Mrs. Cypress and her son demonstrates, Native people also employed the BIA as a bridge to welfare offices. Thus, the BIA's advocacy and oversight over Native people were undergirded by the relationships that constituted wardship, relationships that were by no means consistently positive but, nonetheless, were cultivated and negotiated over time. "The next time you come to Dania [the Seminole Agency office location] I would like to see you," Marmon closed his letter to Henry Cypress.

In their article "A Genealogy of Dependency," Nancy Fraser and Linda Gordon explore the linguistic layers that make up the *doxa*—the common-sense beliefs we take for granted—of dependency in the United States. Fraser and Gordon tease out the historical and ideological context of the idea of "welfare dependency," a term that brings to mind pejorative moral and economic stereotypes of young, non-white mothers without a male breadwinner.[3] Wardship and welfare were undergirded by similar but distinctive *doxa*. When Native people's interactions with the welfare state were circumscribed, negotiated, and facilitated by the BIA, Indian poverty knowledge—the perception that wardship meant Native people were idle, impoverished, and unable to manage their land and finances—aligned with common gendered and racialized assumptions about welfare recipients as non-white single mothers whose bodies and choices were antithetical to "independence."[4] Native women and men persistently navigated these *doxa* in order to obtain needed welfare benefits.

Historians Brianna Theobald, Margaret Jacobs, and others have shown how Native women's reproductive choices and child-rearing were heavily scrutinized, judged, and surveilled by many state actors in the mid-twentieth century.[5] BIA personnel "ranging from agency farmers to lowly clerks to boarding school teachers" weighed in on policies that had real consequences not only for individual women's lives but for the future of Native nations' sovereignty.[6] This state coercion compares to the government's regulation of Black women's mothering and reproduction. Legal scholar Dorothy Roberts has exposed government agencies' pervasive assumptions about Black women's "pathological" need to reproduce, leaving the responsibility for their children to "innocent taxpayers."[7] Roberts asserts that due to "the picture of reckless Black fertility," government assistance "has become a tool of social control, a means of improving the behavior of poor families."[8] In chapter 3 the examples of Sarah Moore, Ione Dock, and Josie French reflect state agents' surveillance of Native women's financial and familial decisions. Though Native women were able to employ the BIA to correct mistakes in their dependency allowances, the BIA's actions were often marked by distrust and judgment.

Native women's—and men's—relationships with the BIA should thus be understood within the longer history of state surveillance and moral suasion to compel certain behaviors. When other state offices used the BIA as the vehicle to communicate with Native recipients of welfare, that oversight took on even more complex dimensions. However, although they struggled with multimodal surveillance of their actions and finances, Native women and men continued to strategically employ the BIA as a tool to advocate for themselves and the welfare benefits they deserved. In *Reproduction on the Reservation*, Theobald asserts that "policy and politics obtain meaning and import as they intersect with women's lives," rather than Native women's lives obtaining "meaning and import through their . . . engagement with colonial policies and practices."[9] Although the BIA's and welfare caseworkers' moral suasion, surveillance, and distrust is evident in these policies, what gave them meaning was Native people's negotiations and challenges within and among their own family members, BIA personnel, and other state agents. Moreover, to understand the full importance of welfare policies for Native people, it is essential to recognize that the BIA was *not* the state welfare board. Native women and men knew the BIA in a way they did not know other state agencies, and as a result, we can see how they employed the BIA to adjudicate disputes with welfare caseworkers *and* within their own families. There were intersecting gendered power dynamics at play in these interactions, shaped by the state's power over Native people, but also within and among Native families and bureaucratic institutions.

Historians of welfare have emphasized how the structure of the American welfare system has been split into two categories: "rights-based" and "needs-based." Rights-based welfare provisions are more respected, less intrusive, and masculine, whereas needs-based provisions are more intrusive, less stable, and feminine.[10] Therefore, men have been more likely viewed as "entitled" to benefits such as Old Age Insurance (what we commonly call "Social Security" today), Unemployment Insurance, and GI Bill loans, and women and racialized people have been viewed as "dependent" on government programs such as ADC or OAA. Rights-based welfare programs have been more safely enshrined within material structures and popular ideologies, while needs-based welfare programs have been subject to frequent criticism and cited as dangerous to the financial well-being of the nation. As Suzanne Mettler demonstrates, the structure of welfare itself perpetuated these divisions. Mettler notes that "white men were incorporated into the uniform domain of the national government and women and nonwhite men were left under the auspices of the states," leaving women and racialized men more vulnerable to local prejudices and attempts to preserve a gendered and racialized social order.[11] Karen Tani has further argued that although welfare administrators proliferated the language of "welfare rights," and the state "recognized all citizens, even the poorest, as rights-bearing members of the national polity," the rights of the poor were subject to the "ebb and flow of politics" and "continued to turn on exercises of local discretion."[12]

This chapter follows the gendered dynamics of wardship's intersections with welfare during and immediately after World War II and explores the ways in which complex relationships between parents and children, spouses, and extended family members intermingled with Native people's relationships to the state. Despite terminationist rhetoric that equated wardship with oppressive welfare dependency, both Native men and women maneuvered within their relationships with the BIA to access the resources they needed from both needs-based and rights-based welfare programs. Some of their efforts were more successful than others. Namely, Native people's experiences with welfare—mediated, facilitated, and at times disrupted by their relationship with BIA—were impacted by gender dynamics. Native women were scrutinized and supported differently (usually more harshly) than Native men. However, Native men did not have easy access to the benefits of rights-based welfare programs by any means. The chapter explores how Native people experienced both "tracks" of the "two-track" welfare system, from programs that were completely "needs-based" (ADC) to those that were completely "rights-based" (GI Bill loans). But first the chapter explores benefits that were somewhere in-between—dependency allowances administered by the Office of Dependency Benefits (ODB). Throughout and immediately following World War II, Native men and women drew upon their understanding and experiences of wardship in order to press other state agencies and family members for both access to and restriction from welfare benefits.

SURVEILLING "SQUANDERING"

In 1943 the BIA distributed a circular letter to all superintendents stating that the ODB had advised that "superintendents may be designated to receive the allotments for children payable under the provisions of the Servicemen's Dependents Allowance Act of 1942 where we are satisfied that the mother or other person receiving such funds is squandering or using such funds to the disadvantage or detriment of the children."[13] Viewed in the context of welfare history, this kind of racialized and gendered state power and oversight doesn't seem so unusual. The assumption that Native women may not be able to utilize funds responsibly—and that the BIA would be able to curb potentially detrimental behavior—coincides with a longer history of state surveillance and power over Native and other non-white recipients of government aid.

Native women's lived experiences of wardship, or the relationships they had with BIA agents, were defined by a tension between advocacy and oversight. Although Native women did employ the BIA to adjudicate and resolve problems with other governmental entities, BIA personnel still operated under gendered settler colonialism and distrust of Native women's choices. This tension comes through in a letter E. B. Hudson, a BIA representative in Nixon, Nevada, wrote to Doris Shaw (Paiute), while Shaw was visiting her mother-in-law in California. The Red Cross had asked Hudson to check on Shaw's dependency allotment checks.[14] He found that Shaw's mother had been holding the checks for her. Finding this less than desirable, Hudson asked Shaw's mother to take the checks to the post office to be forwarded to Shaw in California. Shaw's mother was reluctant to do this because Shaw "had a bill at the store." Hudson went to the store to investigate the situation and discovered that Shaw had asked the store to hold the checks until she returned from her trip, and *the store* had in turn given them to her mother, "thinking that it would be better to have her keep them." Hudson ended his letter by assuring Doris Shaw that he would send a colleague to make sure that Shaw's mother returned the checks to the post office, and he admonished Shaw for not paying her bill. "In all fairness to Mr. Crosby, who extended credit to you when you needed it," he wrote, "I think that you should pay him as soon as you cash your checks . . . In this way you will feel better because then you will owe no one."[15]

It is possible that Doris Shaw and her mother were not on the best terms, and Shaw herself had originally contacted the Red Cross about the whereabouts of her allotment checks. However, even if Shaw had sought to solve a family disagreement by appealing to outside authorities, the extent to which Hudson intervened deserves critical attention. Not only did Hudson involve himself intimately in Shaw's family business by investigating her and her mother's accounts of what had transpired; he also instructed her as to the "best" way to resolve her debt and spend the money she received from her monthly allotment checks. Hudson apparently had no qualms about involving himself in this way, even though Doris Shaw had left the reservation for personal business and had taken precautions to make sure her checks were held for her in a safe place—the very store she was indebted to—until she returned. In her discussion of the welfare reform policies of the mid-1990s, Dorothy Roberts writes: "In the new era of welfare, government assistance has become a tool of social control, a means of improving the behavior of poor families."[16] As Shaw's experience demonstrates, Native women were no strangers to governmental efforts to "improve" their behavior. According to Hudson, if Shaw changed her behavior to align with BIA expectations of financial and personal responsibility, she would "feel better."[17]

State agents' adherence to Indian poverty knowledge shaped their actions. Hudson assumed that Native people such as Shaw were not likely to have the abilities to manage their resources properly. The fact that Shaw was a woman further compounded Hudson's distrust. First-class citizens—those who weren't dependent upon government oversight and management—weren't women. However, Native wives who received dependency allowances occupied an ambiguous semantic and political space between "good" dependency (as dependent wives of servicemen carrying out a duty to the nation) and "bad" dependency (as Native people or welfare recipients in need of oversight).[18] But even in the context of war, state agents could not see past their belief in Indian poverty knowledge and their racialized definitions of Native women as dependent wards. As a result Native women's interactions with the BIA over their dependency allowances mirror the relationships many other non-Native women of color had with welfare caseworkers in charge of overseeing their eligibility for welfare benefits.

For example, in July 1942 Mrs. George Pete (Paiute) went to the Washoe County, Nevada, chapter of the Red Cross "asking for assistance in supporting herself and her children until November when the government contribution will go into effect along with an allowance made by her husband." Red Cross executive secretary Celestia Coulson asked the BIA to verify Pete's story and inquire further into her family's situation.[19] Pete went to the Red Cross to obtain help in paying debts of $60 at her local grocery store. Coulson wrote to E. B. Hudson, asking, "Will you please check with Mrs. Pete and see what the whole thing is about since we cannot see how a man with a wife and three children dependent on him could have joined the Army without saying he was single?"[20] From her language in this letter, is clear that Coulson doubted Mrs. Pete's understanding of her own financial and family situation. Coulson asked several follow-up questions of Hudson, including whether he thought assistance was necessary, and "what is the *least* this family can live on a month?"[21] Thus, while Pete had endeavored to help herself and her family get out of debt by making use of an organization explicitly designed to help soldiers and their families, the representative from that organization had no qualms about checking on the validity of her financial situation by utilizing the BIA as an "interpreter." Indeed, BIA personnel conducted investigations at the request of the Red Cross on a regular basis. For example, in several monthly reports between 1944 and 1946 to the superintendent of the Sells Agency, the agency "community worker" described conducting weekly investigations for the Red Cross as well as completing "Family Allowance papers," delivering checks, and "keep[ing] up with the ever-changing addresses of over 270 Servicemen."[22] Coulson used the BIA not only to verify Pete's story but also to judge whether Pete was entitled to benefits, revealing how all-encompassing the "combination of moral suasion and the coercive power of the state" could be for Native women seeking aid from state actors.[23] The efforts of Red Cross staff and BIA community workers to verify claims and administer benefits to Native women look similar to the ways in which state welfare boards enlisted the BIA in their administration (and restriction) of ADC benefits, which is discussed later in this chapter. However, dependency allowances and ADC were not the same kind of government benefit. The differences between the two types of government aid can be seen through the ways the BIA interacted with Native women and other state agencies and through Native familial relationships.

The gendered definition of "first-class" citizens as competent, responsible, and self-sufficient heads of household meant that in the eyes of the state, Native men were granted a degree of financial and political power over Native women. Native men exercised elements of this power through their interactions with the BIA. However, the *doxa* behind both Indian poverty knowledge and first-class citizenship intersected as BIA personnel pressured Native men to support their dependents in a way the state deemed acceptable and responsible. Native women capitalized on that pressure in *their* interactions with the BIA. BIA agents were not family. But they were a constant presence and could play significant roles in adjudicating—and exacerbating—family disputes.

In October 1945 Eastern Cherokee veteran Jonah Welch wrote to Joe Jennings, the superintendent for the Cherokee Agency in North Carolina and Eastern Band of Cherokee principal chief Jarrett Blythe to request that his wife's dependency allowance payments be transferred to Jennings. The letter, only a paragraph in length, was cryptic. Olive McCoy Welch, according to her husband, was "not using this money for the benefit of these children": Julie Inez, Francis Terry, Bernice, Calvin Eugene, and Kenneth Lane Welch. Jennings wasted no time in responding to the issue, forwarding Jonah Welch's letter to the ODB that same day. Welch's allotment, $106.25 per month, was to be redirected from Olive McCoy Welch to an Individual Indian Money account, an individual bank account controlled by the BIA, and paid out "as needed for food, clothing and other necessary expenses for these children." Jonah Welch wrote about developing custody arrangements six days later. The children would be living with his mother and half sister, and he requested that the money from the account maintained by the superintendent be paid out to them.[24]

As discussed above, Jennings, as BIA superintendent, had the authority from the ODB to take over the administration of Olive McCoy Welch's dependency allowance, if she was found to be "squandering" her benefits. However, Jonah Welch's role in this transfer was quite surprising. Welch reached out specifically to Jennings to take responsibility for the funds and pay them out as needed to the new custodians of his children. Olive's gendered dependency intersected with the confines of wardship to allow Jennings to act as the fiduciary for the Welch's family's dependency allowance. Jonah Welch's word was all that was needed for Jennings to determine that Olive had "squandered" her benefits.

Welch was not the only Native soldier to replace his wife with Jennings as the guardian of dependency allowance benefits. In November 1945 Ute Junior Jumper wrote to the U.S. Navy to stop the allotment for his wife and two children: "Reason that she is now living with another man which I found out when I came home on furlough. She is not taking care of my children."[25] Jumper redirected the allotments for his two children, Leroy and Dempsey, to the Cherokee Indian Agency, care of Jennings. In a letter to the navy he wrote just ten days later, Jennings confirmed he would be "willing to receive as Superintendent of this Agency the allotment made to these two children if you decide to discontinue sending allotments for these children to the wife of Ute Junior Jumper."[26] Similarly, in January 1945, Private Lloyd Johnson also requested that his allotment payments to his wife Betty Ann Johnson be stopped due to infidelity, requesting instead that "his child be cared for by the Indian Agency," which Jarrett Blythe, the principal chief, agreed to implement.[27]

The paper trail left by the dissolutions of the marriages of Welch, Jumper, and Johnson reveals the gendered nuances of wardship, constituted by multiple intersecting relationships. Through their role as "guardians," the BIA could wield economic power over Native women such as Olive McCoy Welch, Betty Ann Johnson, and Jumper's wife, Dianah Teesateskie. This power, sanctioned by the ODB, was the product of decades of colonial assimilation policies and mirrors similar dynamics of BIA oversight of women's reproductive choices and child-rearing and the gendered inequities in the history of welfare administration.

Additionally, since servicemen applied for dependency allowances through their commanding officers, Native men's power over their dependents intersected with their own relationships to the military. In a significant difference from the previous world war, during World War II it was up to the soldier to apply for a dependency allowance, and ultimately it was his choice to stop those payments, as Pike Greene had done when he stopped his allotments for his parents, discussed in chapter 3.[28] Johnson made the decision to stop his wife's payments when he heard from two friends that she had been unfaithful. Jumper had discovered his wife's infidelity when he came home on furlough. Welch gave almost no indication of what exactly Olive McCoy Welch had done with the money instead of using it to care for their children. In all of these cases, the Cherokee Agency had assumed guardianship of the payments (and reassigned custody of the children), seemingly on the petitions of the men alone.[29] The wives' voices on the matter of their dependency allowances are completely missing from the historical record. Thus, we can see that the power to define what it means to be "squandering" one's benefits belonged both to the BIA and to Native men.

However, the relationship between Native men and the military was also shaped by how the BIA acted both as "interpreter" and "guardian" for Native soldiers. Jennings wrote to the ODB and directly to the military branches where Welch, Jumper, and Johnson were serving in order to confirm his willingness to receive the dependency allowance payments. Thus, he became an additional intermediary between the soldier and the service, which in turn shaped the relationship between BIA staff and Native men. Although both the BIA and Native men had power over Native women, they were not equal. Jennings followed through on the requests of Welch, Jumper, and Johnson, but ultimately the Cherokee Agency held the responsibility for the money that would be paid out to the men's children. The convoluted trail of documents generated by these requests demonstrates the extent to which Native men depended on the BIA's willingness to cooperate.

Additionally, despite the growing separation between individuals and their families in this era, Native servicemen were subject to a level of bureaucratic oversight that did not necessarily mesh with increased individual freedom and choice.[30] For example, in June 1944 E. B. Hudson wrote two letters to two different soldiers, brothers Levi and Arthur Dunn, regarding dependency allotments for their mother and another family member named Wanda. The letters reveal Hudson's desire for Levi and Arthur to include both their mother and Wanda as dependents.

However, this request seems not to have originated from Mrs. Dunn or Wanda, but rather from Mrs. Coulson, the Red Cross secretary from Reno who had visited the family and "felt they were entitled to it."[31] Although Hudson told Levi that Coulson had interviewed the Dunn family "relative to a letter from Arthur," in his letter he revealed that Coulson's "personal study" was conducted at the "request from your Commanding Officer."[32] Perhaps Arthur had asked his commanding officer to communicate with the Red Cross in order to get in touch with his family. However, the language in both letters reveals the extent to which outside state agents were involved in the Dunn family's affairs. Hudson asked both Dunn sons to list their mother and Wanda as dependents, even though he was unsure as to whether military regulations would permit it. In addition, he mentioned that he had instructed Richard Dunn, another member of the family who just recently passed his physical examinations for induction into the service, to also claim them as dependents. Although Hudson stressed to Arthur that "you may use your own judgment about this matter," and that it was "merely a suggestion on the part of the Red Cross Secretary," the extent of involvement of these outside agents is obvious.[33] Though soldiers were responsible for applying for dependency allowances, they were under pressure from bureaucrats such as Hudson and Coulson. While the addition of dependents was only "suggested," the suggestion came from those overseeing the financial well-being of the Dunn family, so we can assume it carried significant weight.

However, soldiers were also under pressure from their own family members, who employed the BIA to communicate with their loved ones serving far away from home. For example, in a letter to Smathers Calhoun, who was training at Camp Edwards in Massachusetts with the Engineer Amphibian Command, William Ensor, the clerk for the Cherokee Agency, wrote, "Your mother has been in the office several times about getting an allowance for you."[34] Ensor also extended a message to Nick Driver about how his mother, Nanny Driver, "was in today and stated that you were willing to make an allowance to her under the Servicemen's Dependents Allowance Act of 1942." Ensor suggested that Driver "go to your Company Commander or Personnel Officer to make an application."[35] With three members of the family serving in the military away from the reservation, Wanda and Mrs. Dunn may have also benefited from an increase in their monthly payments and may have even welcomed the Red Cross's visit to their home. In these cases there is a clear tension between the BIA and other bureaucratic agents' *scrutiny of* both dependents' eligibility and soldiers' responsibility and the BIA's *advocacy for* those who were dependent on their family members serving in the military.

In the administration, receipt, and application for dependency allowances, we can thus see conflicting and overlapping examples of BIA advocacy and oversight of Native people, as well as ambiguity in the ways in which Native families employed the BIA to intervene in distributing or applying for benefits. Both the BIA's motivations for judging and compelling Native people to apply for and receive dependency allowances and Native people's motivations for applying and receiving those resources were shaped by gendered expectations of martial citizenship in the context of war, familial expectations, and economic necessity.

POSTWAR WELFARE SURVEILLANCE

Native Women's Receipt of Aid to Dependent Children

In some ways Native women's experiences aligned with those of other non-white women who applied to receive ADC. ADC was a wildly imperfect system of support for mothers with dependent children, and as many historians have written, the interactions between caseworkers and applicants reflected how government agents had internalized misogynistic and racist ideologies about Black women's "pathological" need to have more children in order to obtain more money from the government.[36] For example, Annelise Orleck has described the ways in which state welfare workers invaded the privacy of welfare recipients, conducting predawn raids in the hopes of "find[ing] an actual male body in the woman's bed" and searching for "evidence of a man's presence—men's clothing, razors, or after-shave."[37] Native women's experiences of welfare surveillance were interwoven with their experiences of wardship, as welfare caseworkers relied on the BIA to "interpret" Native women's familial and financial relationships in order to determine eligibility for welfare benefits. Encoded in their use of the BIA as a bridge to Native families was caseworkers' understanding of Native women as *wards* rather than understanding them as needy citizens. But although BIA personnel and Native women's relationships were often strained, Native women enlisted the BIA to help them obtain welfare assistance. In the examples of two Seminole women, Mary Tiger and Lucy Pierce, discussed below, we can see how wardship's relationships shaped Native women's experiences with ADC benefits like those of Native men's experiences with dependency allowances. Native women's receipt of ADC wasn't just a matter of welfare caseworkers overseeing and judging Native women's eligibility. There were power dynamics at play between caseworkers and Native women; between Native women and the BIA; between the BIA and caseworkers; between Native women and Native men; and between Native men and the BIA. These relationships overlapped and clashed with one another, but, taken together, they constituted the confluence of wardship and welfare.

In the mid-twentieth century, Mary Tiger (Seminole) supported herself and her two children by selling handcrafted dolls and skirts and performing seasonal agricultural work. The income was irregular, and she first sought ADC benefits in 1948 to help care for her children, Texas (born in 1944) and Dorothy (born in 1935). Beginning in 1951 her subsequent applications were rejected by the Florida Department of Public Welfare. Correspondence regarding her applications reveals a well-established line of communication between welfare caseworker Mattie Snell; Snell's supervisor, Eva Wilson; and BIA personnel at the Seminole Agency, superintendent Kenneth Marmon and teacher William Boehmer. Most of the correspondence reveals confusion over Tiger's and her children's relationships to the children's fathers (Johnnie Jimmie, Texas's father, and Bill Osceola, Dorothy's father).

When Tiger first applied for ADC, she indicated that Johnnie Jimmie had drowned in 1946. However, when Tiger reapplied for ADC in 1951, caseworkers discovered that Jimmie was alive, had remarried, and was residing on the Big Cypress Reservation.[38] On August 17, 1951, Snell wrote to Marmon to ask his assistance in locating Jimmie, as "in line with our present agency policies, we may not determine whether he has deserted and abandoned Texas without an interview with him." If the interview found that Texas was "*truly* deserted and abandoned," Tiger was welcome to reapply.[39] Marmon wrote back to Snell two weeks later after locating Jimmie: "Apparently from what Johnnie Jimmie told me, he said that Mary Tiger did not want to accept anything from him for Texas."[40] This seems plausible, especially since Tiger had first claimed that Jimmie was dead. It is unlikely that Marmon's letter yielded a positive result for Tiger. The correspondence trail picked up again over one year later, after Tiger reapplied for ADC in October 1952. In the course of processing that application, Snell wrote back to Marmon and acknowledged that she knew that *Tiger* didn't want to accept anything from Jimmie, but "in order to determine her eligibility we must consider what *the father himself* says."[41] Snell also charged Marmon with connecting Dorothy's father, Bill Osceola, with the welfare office, to determine "his present marital status, his average monthly income, and expenses incidental to his present family." The letter was both impersonally bureaucratic and deeply invasive. Mary Tiger's voice is missing, although Snell clearly knew her and was frustrated with her unwillingness to provide a neat and uncomplicated timeline of her life. "Mary's statements have sometimes been contradictory in that sometimes she says she was married and sometimes she says she was not," Snell wrote. "She states that she has never been married."[42]

Was it really *Tiger's* messaging that was inconsistent? In her August 1951 letter, Snell wrote that it was Tiger's interpreter, Lonnie Buck, who "believed Mary and Johnnie Jimmie had been married according to the Indian custom."[43] The message that Mary Tiger herself gave to welfare caseworkers (as well as apparently Jimmie) was that she wanted nothing to do with Jimmie and that she needed support for her children. Did she ever receive it? It took over one month for Marmon to respond to Snell's request to reach out to Bill Osceola for information about his willingness to support Dorothy. He only responded when Snell's supervisor, Eva Wilson, wrote to remind him that "we have not yet approved Mary Tiger's application," and noting that it was "not possible" for Snell to visit Jimmie "as planned," but they had written him another letter as well.[44] On December 15, 1952, Marmon sent a hand-written note to Osceola, "Will you please read the letter from the Welfare Department and let me know as soon as you can, what I can write Mrs. Snell. She wants to know if you will help support Dorothy. Answer yes or no, and I will write the letter."[45] It took only two days for Osceola to respond to Marmon. He denied he was Dorothy's father and argued that "since he has a family of four to support he does not feel that he should contribute towards the support of Dorothy, even though Mary may have indicated that Bill is the father."[46] Marmon's willingness to take Osceola at his word could reflect frustration over the role Snell and Wilson expected him to play in verifying Native family relationships. In addition, it reflects the inclination of BIA superintendents to accept the accounts of Native men over those of Native women when it came to government resources. Marmon's willingness to accept Osceola's denial of paternity is reminiscent of Jennings's quickness to transfer dependency allowances from Olive McCoy Welch, Betty Ann Johnson, and Dianah Teesateskie into the hands of the BIA, on the basis of Native men's words alone. Both inter-bureaucratic frustration and the *doxa* behind gendered first-class citizenship could be true. Either way, Mary Tiger didn't receive her benefits.

The last remaining piece of correspondence related to Mary Tiger's case is a letter written by Boehmer to Snell at the end of December 1952. He wrote: "Mary Tiger states that she has heard nothing concerning her application for ADC assistance which she made in October and has asked me to write you about it. Mary has had very little work this fall and is in need of help."[47] This short letter contained more of Tiger's own voice than any of the previous correspondence. Tiger must have formed a relationship with Boehmer as her children's teacher, since Boehmer also noted that "her two children have been very regular in school attendance." He had previously written to Snell in October to clarify details about Tiger's income from the dolls and skirts she created, and one year previously he had assured Snell that he had relayed a message to Tiger that she was to come visit the welfare office.[48] Tiger had utilized the confines of wardship to advance her case for welfare eligibility. Unfortunately, we don't know whether it worked.

Mary Tiger's welfare application story simultaneously reveals her persistence and bureaucratic retrenchment. Tiger negotiated interactions with bureaucratic agents and understood the systems of oversight to which she was subjected. She communicated her wishes through an interpreter, repeatedly reapplied for benefits, and enjoined Boehmer to write letters on her behalf. She was consistent in her message about what she needed—ADC benefits. The Florida Department of Public Welfare was also consistent in what they required—evidence that there were men who could provide financial support in place of the state. The lack of resolution in this case is especially frustrating, since both men refused to support the children and clearly Tiger wanted to keep her distance from them. If policies and politics obtain meaning and import as they intersect with women's lives, this policy meant that the state welfare board placed an unfair burden on Mary Tiger to constantly reapply for benefits, only to receive the same response—having the BIA follow up with her exes to confirm Tiger's need. The state did not trust Mary Tiger. Both the BIA and the state welfare board adhered to a model of female dependency and male financial support, even if that model didn't match up with Native women's lived realties.

Snell and Wilson's insistence on making contact with Jimmie and Osceola was likely due to the passage of Notice to Law Enforcement Officials (NOLEO), a 1950 amendment to the Social Security Act that compelled public assistance employees to "get information on deserting fathers from mothers who applied for ADC," so that law enforcement could force fathers to pay child support. The amendment was passed in the midst of other political attacks on ADC in the mid-1940s, as it became clear that the population most likely to utilize these benefits were non-widowed single mothers of color.[49] In the decades immediately following NOLEO's passage, the legislation was deemed a failure. Instead of effectively connecting welfare caseworkers to law enforcement and tracking down deserting fathers, it was just "mere words on paper." Moreover, the pressure it placed on mothers to cooperate with welfare caseworkers and law enforcement could lead instead to mothers withdrawing their applications for ADC and children not receiving the support to which they were entitled.[50] After all, it was in the financial interest of state welfare boards to locate absent fathers. In a legal report from 1950, Maxine Boord Virtue wrote of the complex entanglements between welfare agencies and the legal system in Detroit. If fathers were deemed liable for child support by the courts, "the welfare agencies are relieved of the necessity of supplying further relief to the family, and in some cases are reimbursed through the courts for relief already supplied."[51] However, Virtue wrote, the very existence of ADC benefits "removes the economic pressure which causes the mother to be willing to cooperate with the court in enforcing the father's legal liability to pay family support."[52] The U.S. political obsession with the inherent "morality" of nuclear family units headed by male breadwinners forced women to choose: assist with the "legal harassment" of the fathers of their children—who already had made clear their inability or unwillingness to provide financial support—or withdraw their applications for ADC.[53] In light of this almost impossible decision, Mary Tiger's choice to maintain her distance from Jimmie and Osceola and to enlist Boehmer to reapply for benefits and follow up on her applications is all the more striking. NOLEO's addition to the ADC system was designed to discourage women exactly like Tiger from reapplying, regardless of their need.

The BIA's role in this political and cultural situation also became very complicated as welfare caseworkers pressed them for information about Native families in their jurisdictions. For example, in June 1951 district welfare visitor Coleen Jones wrote to Marmon for information on three more deserting fathers of Seminole children. "Because of limited funds available for our program for Aid to Dependent Children," Jones wrote, "it is necessary for us to re-establish lack of parental support in those cases receiving this aid."[54] Marmon's response contains more than a hint of frustration. Native women's familial and cultural relationships did not always fit neatly into the welfare board's objective of locating fathers and discerning their "ability to render financial assistance."[55] Marmon wrote that one of the men in question, Joyce Osceola's husband, had died, but the other relationships were much more complicated. Regarding the father of Lucy John's children, Ellen and Harry Clay, he wrote: "Lucy Clay John was married to Henry Clay but they have been separated for some time. Henry Clay is the father of Harry Clay. We understand that Ellen is the daughter of a white man, who is unknown to us." On the father of Alice Billy's children, Robert, Raymond, and Mark Thomas Cypress, he wrote: "The children of Alice Billy (Cypress) are the children of John

Cypress, to whom Alice Billy was formerly married. John Cypress is the father of Robert, Raymond, and Mark Thomas. John Cypress had plural wives at one time, and as far as I know Alice Billy often lives in John Cypress' camp with his other wife, Mary."[56] At the end of his letter, Marmon declared that the welfare office would have "no chance of securing financial support" from the fathers in the case of Joyce Osceola and Lucy John. "As for the support of Alice Billy's children," he wrote, "that would be something for your welfare department to work out with John Cypress." I very much wish there was a record of Jones's reaction to the information that Alice Billy was one of John Cypress's plural wives.

How did welfare caseworkers in Florida think NOLEO applied to BIA personnel? Did they consider BIA personnel to be law enforcement for Native people's behavior? Did caseworkers assume the BIA would provide further oversight and pressure on Native applicants? In order to determine eligibility for benefits and determine the amount of monthly assistance, caseworkers wrote to BIA personnel such as Marmon and Boehmer with very specific questions about Seminole family dynamics and relationships. In just one letter to Boehmer in February 1951, Snell asked the distance from the reservation to grocery stores; whether the Seminole Agency could provide transportation for Seminole community members who needed to shop; what was a "reasonable share of gasoline and oil;" the Social Security number for another tribal member; and the identity of the father of another child eligible for ADC. She ended the letter asking, "Can the Indian Agency keep these white men out? I think something should be done about them."[57] These were questions of logistics, finances, identity, and morality. Boehmer referred Snell's letter to Marmon, who responded with a similar mix of financial consideration and moral judgment.

As wardship intersected with Native women's receipt of welfare benefits, BIA personnel cooperated with welfare caseworkers—though uncomfortably at times. We can see this tension in Boehmer's role in Tiger's case. Boehmer worked on behalf of both Tiger (following up on her benefits and expressing urgency) and the welfare state (using language that would increase the likelihood that Tiger would be deemed eligible for benefits). However, in certain cases in their role as "interpreters,"

BIA personnel disagreed outright with the decisions that welfare offices made, even as they maintained a level of oversight over Native people. In October 1950 Boehmer wrote to Snell regarding the cancellation of Lucy Pierce's (Seminole) ADC benefits. Pierce was receiving ADC to support her care of her six grandchildren, whom she had taken in after their mother, Annie Bowers, died in 1948. After receiving her notice of cancellation, Pierce reached out to Boehmer for help, just as Tiger had. To Snell, he wrote, "I do not believe that this is correct and wonder upon what information the decision is based."[58] In January 1951 Boehmer reported to Marmon that he had discussed the case with the Florida Department of Public Welfare District Office, who had insisted that they would not reconsider Pierce's case. The children's father, Andrew Bowers, had remarried, and the office insisted that he and his new wife take full responsibility for the children.

In May 1951 Marmon wrote to the director of the Florida State Welfare Board, Sherwood Smith, appealing the district's decision. In this correspondence Marmon advocated for Pierce and her grandchildren and simultaneously assured the welfare board that the BIA properly oversaw and validated the family's need. He wrote, "One of *our* Seminole Indians, Lucy Pearce [sic], at Brighton, Florida," had her grant canceled in September 1950. After the death of Annie Bowers, "according to Indian law and custom, the grandmother and an aunt took these children to their home. The father had no further custody of the children. It was then that our field workers were successful in obtaining an ADC grant for Lucy Pearce." Marmon urged Smith to "make an exception to your regulations in this case; taking into consideration the Seminole Indian law and custom." The family was "worthy and needy."[59] The state welfare board's response must have been disappointing but not surprising, given the passage of NOLEO and the emphasis they placed on locating the fathers of Mary Tiger's two children. Smith wrote back with a different version of events:

> When the investigation was made, we talked with Andrew Bowers, father of the children, who told us that he had no intention of giving his children away, but that he had left them with their grandmother so that he might continue with his work. He told us at that time he would contribute to

their support. Later it was found that Andrew Bowers and Annie Osceola had married in October of 1948. This date was prior to the time of the approval of the case and had we had that information at the time the case was approved, the children would not have been eligible for an assistance grant. When we learned that Mr. Bowers had remarried and that there was a mother in the family who could provide supervision for the children it became necessary for us to cancel the grant.[60]

There is a distinct parallel between Lucy Pierce's ADC cancellation and Mary Tiger's efforts to receive ADC benefits—in both cases the state welfare board relied on (their interpretations of) the father's responsibility to provide for the children. In the case of the Bowers children, there was no middle ground where both their maternal grandmother and father could play a role in the children's financial support and care. Either Pierce could take custody and receive nothing from the state, or Bowers (and the nuclear family unit he had formed with his new wife, the "mother who could provide supervision for the children") could take custody—and also receive nothing from the state. In the eyes of the welfare board, Pierce was not the parent, even if the Seminole community and the BIA saw her as the children's caregiver.

Even with the BIA acting as a bureaucratic (and cultural) interpreter, the state welfare board emphasized Andrew Bowers's gendered responsibility: "We could not be in a position of telling this family in whose home the children should be placed and it was their plan that the children be left with their grandmother. However, such a plan does not relieve the father of the legal or moral responsibility to support those children."[61] But by canceling the grant, the welfare board *was* in effect "telling this family in whose home the children should be placed," and ignoring "*their* plan." Furthermore, in his letter to the state welfare board Marmon indicated that the Bowers children's stepmother "would not consent to taking in the six children."[62] The welfare board justified their cancellation of Pierce's ADC benefits with the assertion that in order to "administer our program on an equitable basis," they could not take into account tribal customs. The welfare board made a judgment based on gendered political ideologies of fatherly responsibility that impacted other members of the children's familial network. The case of Lucy Pierce and her six grandchildren illuminates Jessica Wilkerson's question about gender and citizenship mentioned in the introduction: "What would it mean to imagine the average American not as a citizen worker, as has been the case in modern U.S. political history, but as a citizen *caregiver*?"[63] The arrangement that both Andrew Bowers and Lucy Pierce came to after the death of Annie Bowers was one that fit into Seminole cultural expectations. It was also one that safeguarded the children. Lucy Pierce (and her daughter, the children's aunt) provided something critical for her grandchildren *and* Andrew Bowers. The BIA saw her as the appropriate guardian for these six children and helped her obtain the financial resources necessary to provide such care. Although caregiving was something the BIA often regulated and surveilled, their understanding of what made sense for Native families did not necessarily match up with that of welfare caseworkers, who adhered to a gendered ideal of first-class citizenship.

In her discussion of Crow women activists' pursuit of access to health care, Brianna Theobald writes, "The BIA, for all its deficiencies, was a *known entity* for tribal members."[64] Wardship was an entanglement of relationships, many of those marked by tension and paternalism, but those relationships had been cultivated and complicated by years of interpersonal contact. The choice of Lucy Pierce and Mary Tiger to reach out to William Boehmer for help in communicating their needs to a different (and most likely much less familiar) governmental agency makes sense. This is not to say that the BIA saw inherent value in the caregiving practices of Native women—as mentioned earlier, they intervened when Native women's caregiving was questioned or challenged by Native men or other bureaucratic agents—but that they understood those practices differently than members of the state welfare board.

"HELPING THEM HELP THEMSELVES"

Native Veterans and Gendered Welfare

The final section of this chapter turns to the BIA's relationship with another governmental entity, the Veterans Administration. BIA agents were more likely to push back against the requests and decisions of the caseworkers administering ADC benefits than they were to disagree with VA personnel. Gender surely has something to do with this distinction. As is addressed in more detail in chapter 5, the BIA made an effort to "sell" the benefits of the GI Bill to Native veterans. While it is clear that they also assisted families with dependent children to access ADC, their rationale was different in their encouragement of Native men to apply for benefits under the GI Bill. ADC (needs-based) and the GI Bill (rights-based), both state welfare programs, were not understood in the same way, as many historians of the "two-track" welfare system in the United States have shown.

In 1947 a Laguna Pueblo veteran voiced the concerns of many returned Native servicemen in a meeting with Senator Dennis Chavez of New Mexico and representatives of the National Congress of American Indians. He argued, "Indians are not informed as to what they are entitled to" because "the Veterans' Bureau refuses to treat Indians as it does other GI's, thinking the Indian Service takes care of them."[65] In response to the assumption that wardship superseded individual Native men's citizenship, the Department of the Interior insisted that BIA agents should actively "encourage veterans to take advantage of the GI credit opportunities open to them wherever possible," and reached out to members of the Veterans of Foreign Wars to help eligible Native people obtain loans.[66] Some BIA officials assumed that upon their return from World War II, Native veterans supposedly would possess a "new sense of power," "impatience with existing institutions," "increased self-assurance," and "potentially, at least, capab[ility] of assuming greater responsibility."[67] In 1944 John Evans, general superintendent of the United Pueblos Agency in New Mexico asserted: "It is important that the Indian should become aware of the benefits to which he, as a veteran, is entitled. And he should also take full advantage of the opportunities which are offered him."[68] To Evans and other BIA personnel who viewed their work with Native veterans through the overlapping *doxa* behind poverty knowledge and Indian poverty knowledge, it was not only the responsibility of the BIA to help individual veterans locate and obtain benefits, but it was also the veteran's own duty.

Although military service symbolized a great commitment of citizenship, and perhaps did bring increased self-assurance and power to individual Native men, their path to GI Bill benefits was unclear. Many Native veterans looked directly to the BIA to help combat misconceptions about Native ineligibility for the GI Bill. For example, in 1946 an all-Navajo American Legion post issued a resolution that urged "the federal government to create a lending agency within the Indian Service for the purpose of making loans for Indian veteran housing on the reservation."[69] When faced with lending agencies' presumption that the BIA was solely responsible for Native veterans and subsequent reluctance to grant loans, Native groups looked to their relationship with the federal government as a way of accessing resources that could improve their homes and economic conditions.

Just as Native women enjoined BIA personnel to help them obtain missing dependency allowances or welfare benefits, Native male veterans also recruited BIA staff to help them secure subsistence payments or clarify processes for obtaining loans under the GI Bill. Joe Jennings, superintendent at the Cherokee Indian Agency, protested the "very long delay" Cherokee veterans experienced in receiving their certificates of eligibility from the VA Vocational Rehabilitation and Education Division.[70] He also appealed when the VA failed to dispense tuition for eligible Cherokee veterans, which delayed their subsistence payments. He wrote, "It is noted that in practically every case the Veteran referred to in these exceptions are not receiving their subsistence payments and in some cases this is causing a hardship."[71] When veteran George Roberts didn't hear back from the VA on the status of his application for a certificate of eligibility, Jennings wrote to the VA about Roberts's anxiety about his situation because his "family is in desperate need of subsistence funds."[72] When Shufford Maney could not get a response from the Federal Housing Administration on his application for building priorities on a house, he visited Jennings, who wrote a follow-up letter on Maney's behalf.[73] The BIA, as the known bureaucratic entity, was an effective interpreter for Native veterans with concerns about their benefits. The message that veterans received from the VA could be confusing and their correspondence slow. In 1948 the VA sent the Cherokee Indian Agency a copy of a "suggested talk" that they should deliver to student veterans at an assembly covering details about an increase in subsistence payments. In the talk the VA instructed veterans: "don't write to the Veterans Administration about any matter unless it's absolutely necessary," since it could "slow up the processing of papers."[74] Filtering concerns about their benefits through the BIA was one way Native veterans navigated this system.[75]

Both politicians and the media discussed the importance of encouraging Native veterans to think about their experiences in the war as a positive assimilative process.[76] For example, in a 1947 publication about Navajo and Pueblo veterans, John Adair worried that if the BIA did not step in and help guide Native veterans into appropriate employment, the "whole acculturating process," which had been "greatly accelerated by the war," would have been for nothing. "In a certain sense it is a race against time, for a great many of these veterans, possibly the majority of them will slip back into their old ways after a period of years."[77] However, in general, the BIA's role in helping Native men secure their benefits was more complicated than Adair depicted. For example, in a memo about the difficulties that "war weary" veterans were bound to encounter as they faced both racial discrimination from non-Natives and social and cultural pressure from within their Pueblo families and communities, Evans, superintendent of the United Pueblos Agency, wrote that in the veterans' readjustment to civilian life, "no clearer example ever existed of a specific need to 'help the Indian help themselves.'"[78] What did it really mean to "help the Indian help themselves?" Was Joe Jennings "helping" veterans such as Shufford Maney and George Roberts "help themselves" when he facilitated their communication with the VA and Federal Housing Administration? Jennings pointed out the "hardship" and "desperation" Cherokee veterans faced in his letters to the VA. He helped them gain access to a gendered postwar welfare state, access that would enable them to support their families in a way that was socially expected. However, his "help" did not *remove* the state from individual veterans' lives. Indeed, veterans such as Maney and Roberts enlisted the BIA for assistance under the terms of wardship, not citizenship.

In 1945 Assistant Commissioner of Indian Affairs William Zimmerman sent a memo to all BIA superintendents that urged each agency to appoint an employee to keep track of all new veterans' legislation, to better inform returned Native servicemen of their rights.[79] Though Zimmerman urged BIA personnel to be "patient and helpful," he also cautioned against BIA employees taking on too much responsibility for which they were not equipped. He wrote, "We do not want to get in the position of overloading ourselves with work for which we have neither the funds nor personnel, and in the end have the Indian veterans accuse us of doing an inadequate job for them."[80] Zimmerman encouraged BIA agents to be of "service" to Native veterans and alluded to the trust and responsibility that Native veterans put into the BIA to facilitate their receipt of benefits. BIA personnel *did* take that responsibility very seriously. After receiving word that training periods had been reduced for Cherokee veterans, Jennings and other BIA personnel inquired in person at the VA office in Winston-Salem in order to clarify confusion. Two veterans had "just received letters which had reduced their training time to two years without an explanation," and Jennings stopped in at the office because "rumors were flying thick and fast and we wanted to get the facts in order to relieve our trainees of any anxiety about their training time."[81] Jennings was not solely concerned with Cherokee veterans. As is addressed in chapter 5, he put an enormous amount of work into establishing a veterans training program at the Cherokee Agency boarding school and had his program's future in mind. However, his correspondence does demonstrate the level of care about the mental and financial well-being of Cherokee veterans was different from the treatment that Native women often received at the hands of BIA agents. The BIA, like other governmental agencies and politicians, championed a specific vision of gendered first-class citizenship, which was undergirded by the idealized economically self-sufficient male head of household. The GI Bill fit into that vision in ways that ADC (and even dependency allowances) did not.

The BIA intervened on behalf of veterans in order to facilitate Native men's ownership of their responsibilities as first-class citizens. However, this came with a critical caveat—if, for some reason, the veteran did not live up to those prescribed expectations, the BIA could disrupt their receipt of benefits. Thus, there was an unspoken (and sometimes loudly spoken) tension between Native veterans and BIA officials. They weren't always adversaries, but neither were they allies. For example, in early March 1949 Jennings wrote to the VA to report that Edwin Walkingstick, a trainee in the electrical department at the Cherokee Indian School, had been absent without explanation for four days, and recommended that his subsistence payments be stopped.[82] He was dropped from the program. Walkingstick had been the subject of previous correspondence between the school and the VA, as his health had precluded him from regular attendance twice before, in 1947 and 1948.[83] The extent to which he and many other veterans were tracked by the BIA and VA suggests a degree of oversight that is connected to the BIA's long history of assimilationist policies. Interestingly though, Walkingstick still employed the BIA to obtain subsistence payments he was missing. At the end of March 1949 (the same month he had been dropped from the electrical training program), he asked Jennings to write to the VA to check to see if all his subsistence payments had been made, since he did "not believe that he has been paid all that was due him for the month of February, 1949."[84] Walkingstick continued to employ the BIA as an interpreter and bridge to the VA, even after he had been dropped from the training program.

The relationship between the BIA and Native veterans doesn't fit into a tidy narrative. Although the power of oversight the BIA had over Native women's receipt of welfare benefits seems much more overt, wardship's intersection with the GI Bill meant that the BIA oversaw (and surveilled) Native men's behavior too. In October 1945 Jonah Welch had called on the BIA to redirect his wife's dependency allowances to Superintendent Jennings. Just a few months later, in February 1946, Welch enrolled in the arts and crafts training program for veterans at Cherokee Indian School. However, he was dropped from the program after only two weeks, after he stopped attending "for reasons unknown."[85]

The tone of the correspondence between Welch and the BIA underwent a significant shift between October 1945 and October 1947, when Welch attempted to reenroll at Cherokee. Whereas Jennings had been more than willing to speedily step in and reroute Olive McCoy Welch's dependency allowances on Welch's behalf, he seemed to just as quickly dismiss Welch as a worthy candidate for veteran's training. Jennings was concerned with the appropriate use of government funds in both cases. It was enough for Jonah to claim that Olive McCoy Welch wasn't using her dependency allowance appropriately for Jennings to intervene and reassign fiduciary duties to himself. But Jennings was also concerned about Jonah Welch's subsistence payments from the VA, and whether Welch would follow through with his training. Jennings wrote to the VA in October 1947, after Welch had reapplied for training, to explain that between the time Welch had dropped out of the program and the time the BIA had reported it to the VA, he likely had received two subsistence checks and needed to return them. In Welch's letter to the VA, he noted that he did receive two checks, that he would be willing to repay the amount, but that he would be unable to pay one lump sum and "would like to know what arrangements could be made."[86] However, the VA wrote back that there was "no record in the veteran's file indicating that he was ever notified by the Finance Office of an overpayment in subsistence allowance during his previous course of training," but that if Welch was sure that he was overpaid, he could repay the amount monthly during his new course of training.[87] It is unclear if the unreturned checks (of which the VA had no record) were at the root of Jennings's hesitancy to reenroll Jonah Welch, or if it was something else that made Jennings and Cherokee High School's veterans training adviser, Prentice Willett, uncomfortable. In March 1946, after Welch dropped out of the arts and crafts training program, Willett sent a heavy-handed letter to Welch encouraging him to conform to prescribed gender and societal roles. "Do not let this opportunity of a life time pass," Willett wrote to Welch. "It most likely will not come again." Willett explained that Welch would lose out on monthly subsistence payments, tuition, school supplies, and tools; moreover, "you would have acquired assets in knowledge and skills which no one could take from you. With any effort at all you would have been able to do better for yourself or to have made someone else a better qualified employee had you completed any course of training in the vocations that you are interested in."[88] We don't know what happened with Welch that caused him to drop out of his training the first time he enrolled. In October 1947 Willett expressed hesitancy in reenrolling him, and Jennings wrote to the VA that "we aren't particularly anxious to re-enroll this man."[89] However, ultimately Welch did reenroll.

Welch's strained relationship with Jennings and Willett played out at the same time as politicians debated competency legislation in the halls of Congress. The BIA staff at the Cherokee Agency tapped into the same framework for "competency" and "first-class" citizenship that legislators employed. Depending on the type of training that veterans undertook, the discussion was centered more on their employability than their ability to own property unencumbered. Chapter 5 addresses the role of agricultural training at Cherokee and other Native veterans training programs that extended considerations of competency even further.

The line between advocacy and oversight of Native people's welfare benefits was delicately maintained by both BIA agents and Native people. The history of assimilationist policies and paternalistic surveillance of Native people's behavior and "morality" should not be separated from the ways in which the BIA understood wardship. However, when it came to welfare benefits, the BIA's role in the wardship relationship was more ambiguous than overtly overbearing. BIA agents had the ability to intercept dependency allowance payments if Native women were found to be "squandering" the money. However, they also acted as intermediaries for other government entities and Native dependents in order to obtain necessary funds and resources. And both Native men and women applied pressure on family members via BIA correspondence and authority.

The overlapping *doxa* behind Indian poverty knowledge and gendered welfare dependency did not make it easy for Native women to receive needs-based welfare benefits such as ADC. However, despite this difficulty, Native women continued to employ BIA personnel in order to inquire after the benefits they needed to take care of their families. Because the BIA was a known entity, and one that did not always have the same mission as state welfare boards, this was a strategic choice that in many cases represented the best chance that Native women had to access needed benefits. With benefits from the VA, the relationship between the BIA and Native people was still more complex. BIA agents were at times allies and support systems to Native veterans, helping them access the postwar welfare safety net that helped so many other male veterans "help themselves" and their families. However, they also played a role in overseeing and critiquing Native veterans' behavior, tapping into the (continuing) legacy of assimilation policy.

Wardship, a legal and social system constituted by these complicated relationships between BIA agents, Native individuals, and tribal communities, interfered with the administration of the welfare state in the years surrounding World War II. Gender structured wardship in complex ways: it shaped relationships between Native men and women, it defined state expectations of male and female familial and work responsibilities, and it impacted the ways in which BIA agents interacted with Native people. It is impossible to understand the dynamics of either wardship or welfare without assessing the impact of gender.

CHAPTER 5

Improving Farms and Homes

Assimilation and the GI Bill's Educational Provisions

Back home, being Cherokee meant I fell into a role. Unfortunately, it also meant I had only a few options: I could farm. I could work for a white man. I could leave. I learned that pretty quickly in school. They instructed us in the trades, but they were trades to stay, to exist, to fit into a slot already carved out for me. Sure, it was safe in a lot of ways. I didn't worry that I would starve; my family and church and neighbors saw to it that no one starved. But oh, the hunger! I always felt half empty, like I was missing out on some grand feast just over the mountains. I was tethered in all the good ways and in all the bad.

—Annette Saunooke Clapsaddle (Eastern Cherokee), *Even as We Breathe*

In August 1946, while visiting friends on Bailey Island, Maine, Eastern Cherokee veteran Richard Bradley wrote a letter to Prentice Willett, his adviser in the veterans training program at Cherokee Indian High School in Cherokee, North Carolina. Willett had written two weeks prior, informing Bradley that he had been dropped from his arts and crafts course where he had been working toward becoming a cabinet maker. "I am sorry that you see fit to discontinue your training up here as it appeared that you were doing very well with your work at the time you attended classes," Willett wrote. In his response Bradley expressed confusion and frustration. Addressing Willett by his first name, he wrote,

"Prentice, So I am dropped from the training. Well are they [sic] any chance getting back on with the G.I. Bill?" Bradley explained that he would be returning home in September and on the way was planning to "stop at the VA in Winston Salem for I want to talk to some of these big shots I want to find out some things." He signed his letter to Willett, "A Friend, Richard Bradley."[1]

This was not the only instance in which Bradley interrupted his training. In October 1947 the Veterans Administration wrote to Bradley to "suggest" that for the forty-one months of training that remained under the terms of his GI Bill educational provisions, "you pursue your course to its completion insofar as possible," because "you have already interrupted training at the Cherokee High School, Cherokee, NC, two times of your own volition."[2] The packet of correspondence between the VA, Bradley, and Willett illuminates the logistics of applying GI Bill benefits to educational institutions maintained by the Bureau of Indian Affairs. Bradley's interruptions in training reflect his unwillingness or inability to conform to the training timeline imposed by the VA and reinforced by the BIA. But while he pushed back against the "big shots" at the VA, he reminded Willett that he considered him a friend. Native veterans such as Bradley confronted and experienced the concurrent assimilative philosophies of the GI Bill and federal Indian policy, since their experiences of their GI Bill educational loans were mediated by the BIA.

The BIA had long had a stake in encouraging (and coercing) Native men to take on certain economic and familial roles in order to more effectively assimilate into the American citizenry. As described in chapter 2, the proposed competency bills of the 1940s and 1950s were designed to draw out self-sufficient, individual Native heads of household who could take control over their land and dependents without oversight from the federal government, essentially absolving the government of their trust responsibilities. Though competency legislation was often framed primarily as the path to individual Native men's property ownership, the proposed policies weren't only about land—they were ostensibly about ensuring that Native heads of household could make a *profit* on that land, that the land could become an occupation for Native people who were "emancipated" from their tribes. In her work on the Agricultural

Extension Service, historian Angela Firkus has explored the long history of the BIA's emphasis on farming as the best occupation for Native people on their path to assimilation. Indeed, Firkus notes that in 1910, "79 percent of Indian men and 30 percent of Indian women reported agriculture, forestry, or animal husbandry as their main occupation."[3] Native children also received gendered education in agricultural and menial occupations at boarding schools in the late nineteenth and early twentieth centuries. Through "outing" programs where Native children were placed with non-Native families and through vocational programs at schools, Native children received training in occupations "often characterized as making them 'useful,'" including domestic service, laundry, building maintenance and repair, raising livestock, and other agricultural tasks.[4]

At the end of World War II, employment was also a major concern for policymakers concerned with the impending influx of all returned veterans. At the heart of the GI Bill were concerns about both the U.S. economy as a whole and individual veterans' employability. The bill has been described as "an anti-depression measure" and "focused on stabilizing the labor force," because of the need to "secure the postwar economy."[5] But it was discussed in terms of individual veterans' needs as well. In her description of postwar "GI jitter-literature," Laura McEnaney writes, "war could turn an ordinary man into a fascist, a psycho, a loner, a drunk, or a brute."[6] Both individual men's citizenship and U.S. democracy could be protected by the safeguards the GI Bill put in place for a smooth transition.[7] By assuring that veterans would have specific opportunities for educational advancement, employment, and housing through the GI Bill, the state further defined the terms of first-class citizenship. A veteran's employability and the fact that he would not be adding to crowding relief rolls indicated his self-sufficiency. The GI Bill's emphasis on ensuring and expanding veterans' employability meant that it "reinforced the gendered dichotomy of work and dependence."[8] Thus, although the GI Bill was expansive in its scope as a federal welfare program, the ideology behind it was the same as other welfare policies that reinforced a specific understanding of gender, family, and work: an emphasis on the two-parent nuclear family household with a self-sufficient male breadwinner.

The BIA also juxtaposed "useful" employability against Native people's receipt of need-based welfare benefits, especially in the context of the postwar expansion of the federal welfare state. In the late 1940s—before the formal passage of the Indian Relocation Act of 1956—the BIA made informal, voluntary, and local efforts to relocate Native people from reservations to urban areas on the basis of "bringing about permanent resettlement of families in areas or communities where *all-year employment* may be available."[9] The BIA sent a circular letter to all superintendents in 1948, urging them to "assist Indians in obtaining work" and to accumulate information on how many Native people on each reservation had found their own employment, resettled, or "for whom jobs had been found." The language in the circular described Native people as "employables."[10] Counting the number of "employables" was framed as a welfare issue—"the matter of placing Indians in employment so that they might be removed from the relief rolls." The form sent with the circular letter included prefilled categories of employment for BIA superintendents to utilize. The categories would have been very familiar to both BIA officials and Native people: agriculture, manufacturing, railroad, mining, construction, road work, and domestic work.

Native veterans' identities as husbands and fathers impacted both state agents' perceptions of them as potentially "employable" first-class citizens and the amount of money they were due from the state. Thus, they sat at the juncture between two racialized and powerful policy legacies. The BIA and the VA had similar goals—an employed ("first-class") citizenry, with all the gendered and racialized prescriptions that label entailed. For example, Eastern Cherokee veteran Jonah Welch— the veteran who, as described in chapter 4, had reported to Cherokee Agency superintendent Joe Jennings that his wife was "squandering" her dependency allowance payments—was the subject of much correspondence between Jennings and the VA in the late 1940s. In December 1948 the VA wrote to confirm that five of the Welch children were attending boarding school at Cherokee and to inquire as to whether Welch or his estranged wife, Olive McCoy Welch, had been "contributing to the support and maintenance of the children," because "it may be that the children are entitled to a share of the veteran's subsistence allowance while he was in training."[11] Welch himself was attending the boarding school at Cherokee under the terms of the GI Bill in their veterans' training program. The Welch family's experiences with the BIA and VA all coalesced within the walls of the same Indian boarding school where multiple members of the family were training in order to access better employment opportunities (under BIA instruction and guidance), and where government officials kept watch on family dynamics (in the Welch family's case, to actually give them money) in the larger service of the nation. In other words, both the BIA and the VA maintained a stake in the familial responsibilities of individual Native veterans. Indeed, it is in part because of their surveillance that we have a record of Jonah's educational progress and also a partial record of the experiences of Olive and their children throughout their difficult postwar transition period.[12]

As mentioned in chapter 3, familiarity with wardship likely prepared Native people for the bureaucratic intransigence that came with sorting out problems with dependency allowances or other state welfare benefits. Native veterans also drew upon wardship—their existing relationships with the BIA—to navigate the bureaucracy of the GI Bill. Indeed, the provisions of the GI Bill that Native veterans were most likely to take advantage of—funding for education and training—were fulfilled by the same people, within the same facilities, as the assimilationist education programs of the early twentieth century: boarding schools and day schools on reservations, like the one multiple members of the Welch family attended. And unsurprisingly agricultural training was a significant element in the education programming available to Native veterans.

But in other ways the educational provisions of the GI Bill were extremely different from the vocational training programs of the early twentieth century. Native veterans who utilized their GI Bill educational loans took advantage of two significant opportunities the GI Bill provided, which compared favorably to past BIA educational and training efforts: they received subsistence pay and tuition for training, and they could remain close to their land and family networks. Officials within the BIA and the VA worked to allow Native veterans to apply their GI Bill benefits to existing training and educational programs and institutions on reservations, linking a longer legacy of assimilative educational programming to a mid-twentieth-century ideal of first-class citizenship that many Native veterans seemed especially eager to access.

This chapter explores two distinct examples of veterans training programs administered by the BIA under the confines of the GI Bill: Cherokee Indian School in Cherokee, North Carolina, and the Veterans' Vocational School on the site of the Poston War Relocation Center on the Colorado River Reservation in Arizona. These programs were significantly different in their outcomes—Cherokee was largely considered a success while the Veteran's Vocational School at Poston failed to materialize. However, this chapter focuses on the similarities between the two programs: both in the ways in which Native veterans engaged with the GI Bill and with BIA staff and in the perspectives of the BIA agents who worked to establish both programs. Native veterans' experiences of the GI Bill are best described as a tension between opportunity and restriction. In her novel *Even as We Breathe* (quoted in the epigraph to this chapter), Eastern Cherokee writer Annette Saunooke Clapsaddle eloquently describes this tension. Within the Eastern Cherokee community in the mid-twentieth century, there were few options available for young men: "I could farm. I could work for a white man. I could leave."[13] It was "safe" (that safety maintained by family and community members) but left some with a sense of "hunger," feeling "half empty." In order to understand how Native veterans and their families experienced the GI Bill, we need to look at both the senses of safety and hunger to fully understand how new economic opportunities were tied to the restrictive legacies of assimilation.

THE GI BILL AND NATIVE VETERANS' EDUCATION

The final version of the GI Bill, passed in 1945, declared that the VA would provide to veterans the actual cost of up to four years of education and training—up to $500 a year—on top of monthly subsistence allowances ($65 a month for unmarried veterans and from $75 to $90 a month for those with dependents).[14] Eight months after the bill's passage, subsistence allowances were raised to $75 a month for single veterans, $105 per month for veterans with one dependent and $120 per month for two or more dependents.[15] Cultural memory of the GI Bill associates its educational benefits with four-year colleges and universities. But GIs also used their benefits to pay for other kinds of education, including correspondence courses and agricultural and manual training programs. The GI Bill provided access to higher education—widely considered one of the most effective pathways to upward economic mobility—to 2.2 million American veterans. As Lizabeth Cohen writes, veterans who entered colleges and universities "grabbed the biggest headlines." But Cohen also notes that 3.5 million veterans "enrolled in *other* schooling, 1.4 million chose on-the-job training, and 700,000 sought farm training."[16] Thus, most veterans who took advantage of the educational provisions under the GI Bill did not use those benefits for what we often consider "traditional" higher education.

Indeed, for many non-white veterans, the educational benefits of the GI Bill were *only* accessible through vocational or agricultural training programs. Policies of segregation and institutionalized racism account for many of those experiences. Historians Glenn Altschuler, Stuart Blumin, and Ira Katznelson have pointed to limitations on African American veterans, noting that even those who had completed high school were often funneled into "agricultural and manual training programs instead of the liberal arts."[17] For Native veterans, the history of assimilationist education policy fundamentally shaped their experiences with the GI Bill. During a 1947 meeting with Senator Dennis Chavez and Congresswoman Georgia Lee Lusk of New Mexico, a Laguna Pueblo veteran voiced concerns about Native veterans' access to the educational opportunities in the GI Bill. The veteran argued that "it is hard for Indians to take advantage of training offered under the GI Bill because they do not have high school educations." In response Lusk mentioned that "boys who do not have high school educations can go to trade schools or be apprenticed to shops under the GI Bill and learn a trade, and at the same time study school subjects without having to meet entrance requirements."[18] Although the trade school option certainly may have appealed to many returned Native servicemen, the Laguna Pueblo veteran's concerns point to how the educational benefits of the bill could reinforce rather than challenge societal class and racial stratifications, including those cultivated by federally run schools' racialized curricula and Native people's historical lack of access to higher education.

In its original drafts, the GI Bill specified that federal officials and agencies were prohibited from "directing or dictating in any way the servicemen's education."[19] However, this provision would have made it impossible for Native veterans to utilize GI Bill benefits to attend schools and participate in training programs operated by the BIA, a federal agency. Indeed, in a 1944 conversation on the floor of the House of Representatives, Arizona Representative John Murdock wondered how this would affect "Indians and *their* schools." Would the section of the bill "debar Indian veterans from making use of an Indian school, for instance, at Phoenix, Ariz., where there is a good school operated entirely by the Federal Government?"[20] John Rankin, representative from Mississippi, argued, "If the State did recognize the Indian school the Veterans Administration would, because those Indians would rather go to that Indian school that to try to go to the University of Minnesota. We are trying to bring this down to a practical level."[21] Members of Congress later amended the law to state, "Indian schools operated or supervised by the United States, shall not be ineligible to supply education or training under this title by reason of such Federal operation or supervision."[22] In order for Indian schools to be eligible to receive tuition payments from the VA, they had to obtain approval from the state Department of Education.[23] Murdock and Rankin's assumptions about what Native veterans would prefer and what was practical for them deserve some interrogation. On one hand they both associated Native veterans with a certain kind of educational institution—federal Indian schools. The University of Minnesota or an equivalent institution of higher education was not *"their"* school. But the differentiation was a little more complicated. Yes, practical concerns kept Native people close to home. But, these same concerns, including especially family responsibilities, impacted the educational decisions of many veterans.[24] The choice to attend a veterans training program at an Indian boarding school was also shaped by Native people's histories with BIA educational programming, their relationships with BIA personnel, and their understandings of what obligations the federal government should fulfill under the terms of wardship.

Indeed, some Native groups specifically highlighted Native veterans' ineligibility for university education in their petitions to the U.S.

government for more educational resources. For example, in 1946 the Navajo Veterans of Foreign Wars issued a resolution to immediately remedy the "deplorable state of existing educational conditions among our Navajo people," because "almost all of the returned veterans are unable to avail themselves of the privileges granted in the GI Bill of rights because of an inadequate elementary schooling."[25] The Navajo Veterans of Foreign Wars used their military service to press the United States, "for whose continuance we fought," to fulfill its obligations to the tribe—indeed, education was one of the stipulations in the treaty the United States signed with the Navajo in 1868—by instituting structural change in the education system. In other words, as much as the ideologies of first-class citizenship—economic self-sufficiency and gendered familial responsibility—shaped the GI Bill and Native people's receipt of their benefits, wardship also shaped the decisions that Native veterans made about their GI Bill benefits.

Cherokee Indian School (Cherokee, North Carolina)

Cherokee Indian School, a boarding school in Cherokee, North Carolina, was operated by the BIA between 1890 and 1954.[26] The boarding school was located on the land held in trust for the Eastern Band of Cherokee, the Qualla Boundary. In late 1945 the VA approved the school as a training center for veterans, and the program began in February 1946.[27] The school was considered to be a great success by the VA and by BIA personnel at other agencies, who wrote to Cherokee Agency superintendent Jennings for advice on how to set up similar programs in their own locations.[28] Before approval for veterans' training, Cherokee Indian School already employed instructors in shop, auto mechanics, and arts and crafts, a soil conservationist, an agricultural teacher, an electrician, and an engineer.[29] With the advent of the veterans' training program and corresponding VA resources, the school added six more agricultural instructors (five with college degrees) whose job was solely training GIs. Jennings described these instructors as "all men who are without race prejudice, who feel they are doing important work, and who do not count the hours when there is a job to be done." The GI instructors received advice and supervision from the soil conservationist and the agricultural extension agent, and each oversaw "not more than 15 trainees."[30] Although the veterans training program surely bore certain similarities to the existing educational programming at Cherokee, the way Jennings described the GI instructors revealed a significant distinction between the veterans training program and the boarding school curriculum. While both boarding school instructors and GI instructors were putting specific motivation into their work—they saw it as important, even as a form of "uplift" for Native families—GI instructors oversaw only fifteen trainees each and were well supported by the resources of the VA under the GI Bill.

The majority of veteran students at Cherokee embarked on a course of agricultural training, for "those men who [had] land which they want to use to the best advantage." Those "with insufficient land or land unsuited for agricultural purposes" took courses in trades, including handicraft work, woodworking, wood carving, ironworking, metalworking, plumbing, electrical work, carpentry, painting, stone masonry, or auto mechanics.[31] Many Cherokee veterans had not completed their elementary education, and some worked toward their high school diploma at the school.[32] The training appealed to many veterans. Supervisors at the school noticed that the "economical returns" were greater for agricultural trainees compared to those in trades, because in addition to the subsistence pay they received from the VA, "they get what they make on their farm during training." They also were able to "remain at home during their training period," a significant factor, as most of the veterans were "married men with children."[33] Training veterans in trades undoubtedly helped the school as much as it helped the veterans themselves, as they applied their new skills to the improvement of the school's physical plant: "The School depends upon current production work for Trade Training; that is, the carpentry trainees do all types of new construction and maintenance work at the school and agency under the supervision of the school Carpenter, and painting trainees likewise do all the painting under the supervision of the Painter. This is also done in all other trades."[34] Veterans in both agricultural and trades training also were encouraged to market their products—farm produce and handicrafts—to tourists passing through the adjoining Smoky Mountain National Park.[35] This kind of cultural economy was a familiar method employed by BIA agents in order to foster Native people's economic development in the early twentieth century. Alongside skills training in manual, agricultural, and domestic labor, students at boarding schools received instruction in the creation of crafts, dolls, textiles, and Native arts, which they often sold to tourists or collectors.[36] In the case of the Cherokee Indian School, the proximity to a national park and potential customers for Cherokee goods was another reason why the school was so highly regarded and successful. Students of the veterans training program not only contributed valuable labor to the building and maintenance of the school, but also contributed to the recreational and leisure economy of the region and built up the Cherokee community through their farms.

Poston Veterans Vocational School (Parker, Arizona)

Just over two thousand miles away from Cherokee, North Carolina, BIA agents on the Colorado River Indian Reservation in southwestern Arizona (home to the Colorado River Indian Tribes, which include Mohave, Chemehuevi, Navajo, and Hopi people) attempted to establish their own veterans' training program. The Colorado River Indian Reservation was the site of the Poston War Relocation Center, one of the camps that held incarcerated Japanese Americans during World War II. Poston was jointly overseen by the BIA and the War Relocation Authority (WRA) until 1943, when the WRA took on sole oversight.[37] Once incarcerated Japanese Americans and WRA staff left Poston at the end of the war, the barracks and buildings that had housed them remained. These structures were used in multiple ways—some of the barracks were sold to veterans and their families on the reservation for home building materials, an adobe building that had been used as a school for incarcerated Japanese American children was repurposed as an elementary school for children of the Colorado River Indian Tribes, and, as this chapter discusses, other barracks and structures were earmarked for a new Veterans Vocational School for Native people in the area.

The veterans' school never materialized, though not for lack of trying on the part of BIA staff nor for lack of interest on the part of Native veterans. Throughout 1947 the BIA superintendent of the Colorado River Agency, C. H. Gensler, worked to confirm that the buildings could be repurposed for vocational training. This was no simple task—the buildings had been under the management of the WRA, then transferred to the War Assets Administration, and then transferred to the Department of the Interior, which oversaw the BIA.[38] Well into the planning process there was still considerable confusion about whether the BIA actually owned the buildings.[39] Higher-ups at the BIA also proposed using the buildings as a way to pay down some of the claim that the Colorado River Indian Tribes had filed against the WRA for utilizing their land for the concentration camp.[40] Moreover, after years of being subjected to the desert elements, the buildings needed roof repairs and weather protection. For example, the "paper put on the sides to keep the dust from blowing through the cracks [was] about all off."[41] The BIA didn't have enough funds for necessary repairs. Gensler had made arrangements with the Federal Public Housing Authority to repair the living quarters for veterans and their families and with Public Works to repair the instructional buildings and classrooms, but both funding agreements fell through.[42] Colorado River Agency BIA staff then posited that the tuition payments they would receive from the VA could be received in advance to pay for building construction and repair, but they learned that "the VA cannot under the law pay for capital assets," such as housing and classroom facilities.[43] They had planned to utilize the labor of veteran students to construct the school, another way of saving on labor costs once the planned aid from the Federal Public Housing Administration collapsed.[44]

Gensler proposed that veterans receive "instructional work" training in "carpentry, plumbing, electrical, sheet metal," and other trades as they worked to rehabilitate the physical structures from the WRA camp. "It is not altogether necessary that these men shall intend to follow these particular building trades," Gensler wrote in a 1947 proposal, noting that even "agricultural men" could gain "instructional work" experience. "It is our opinion that a farmer needs to know how to drive nails, square a board and saw it off, and put it where it belongs, and to do a certain amount of plumbing, and at least to know enough about electricity to handle low voltage without getting hurt or setting fire to something."[45] Gensler and other BIA staff were trying to launch a veteran's training program without any resources besides the rapidly decaying WRA barracks and Native veterans' labor. Earlier Gensler had written to the VA to inquire whether "a combination of part-time institutional training and part-time supervised training on the job *without payment of wages* for Indians living on reservations [was] permissible as institutional training under VA policies."[46] The VA responded that in order for the program to be considered full-time institutional training, the school had to provide "a minimum of 25 hours per week of direct instruction (other than training on the job instruction)."[47] Without classroom buildings to provide this direct instruction, the Poston school could not fulfill this requirement.

This is not to say that Native veterans would not have participated in such a program had it taken off. In the Southwest, "on-the-job" training was hard to come by for Native veterans. In 1948 industrial consultant Max Drefkoff compiled a report on the Navajo reservation, which revealed that many Navajo veterans "do not now find sufficient opportunity for 'on-the-job' training on the reservation, for the reason that no industries currently exist where such training can be had."[48] Navajo leadership had made efforts to get information to veterans about opportunities for training in trades. In 1945 a representative from the Veterans' Service office in Phoenix spoke to a tribal council meeting and emphasized, "The thing to remember is that these veterans under this bill get that living expense account in addition to any pension they may be drawing, and they don't have to necessarily be in a school such as the college at Flagstaff. They may be working for a trader, silversmith, or taking some trade, but that trade must be part of the apprentice training program."[49] Staff at Colorado River wanted to create that type of program, while in the process of building the school itself.

ASSIMILATIVE RELATIONSHIPS

At the end of the war and in the immediate postwar period, Native veterans and the BIA worked together to ensure access to GI Bill loans for education and training. BIA agents tried to identify the educational needs and desires of returned servicemen by sending out questionnaires and surveys to gauge veterans' interest. For example, in 1945 Superintendent John Evans of the United Pueblos Agency sent a letter to Pueblos serving in the armed services that asked, "Just what kind of training will you want after the war? Will you want to finish a high school course, to have advanced vocational training, or to go on to college?"[50] Similarly, in preparation for the training program at Poston, staff at the Colorado River Agency sent out a survey to returned veterans soliciting specific information about the type of training programs veterans wanted to utilize, "in order that we may help you get into the kind of training you want under the GI Educational Law." Veterans were to choose between "on the job training," "high school," "business college," "college," and a variety of skills and trades, including cattle production, farming, roads, irrigation, carpentry, and electric work.[51] In compliance with a BIA circular requesting data on returned servicemen and women, BIA staff overseeing the Gila Bend, Papago, and San Xavier Reservations in Arizona reported that of 172 Tohono O'odham veterans, "23 have expressed their interest in the educational opportunities under the GI Bill of Rights." Only one was enrolled at a four-year institution, the University of Arizona. BIA staff expected that "the majority of these 23 will enter various High Schools, Trade Schools, and Business Colleges," as well as "take advantage of the Correspondence Courses."[52] Native veterans' choice of vocational training was likely due to a mix of factors: the historical failure of the BIA to provide education that prepared Native students to attend colleges and universities; their desires to translate new skills they had learned in the service to future careers; and their need to remain close to family members and land.

As noted in chapters 3 and 4, BIA agents acted as intermediaries between the VA and Native veterans. Not only were BIA agents explicitly instructed by leadership to assist veterans, but VA staff might have assumed that the best way to communicate with returned Native servicemen was through the BIA. Native servicemen, like their wives and parents during the war, might have also assumed that requests were more likely to be answered if the correspondence came from BIA agents. Social workers and field agents on reservations put effort into obtaining records of "each veteran's location, employment or vocational training plans," and BIA agents were required to submit reports detailing how many Native people had requested assistance in obtaining employment, education, and other GI Bill loans.[53] Thus, veterans must have logically assumed that the BIA was equipped to help them access the educational and training benefits of the GI Bill. And as both the Cherokee and Poston veterans' schools demonstrate, the BIA was providing bureaucratic and logistical support and also providing veterans with the actual institutions where they could carry out their training.

As a result the BIA advocated for Native veterans and their families in their correspondence with the VA. As mentioned in chapter 4, Cherokee veteran Edwin Walkingstick had trouble with both the BIA and VA in 1949, when he was dropped from the electrical training program at the Cherokee school due to attendance problems. Even after his removal from the program, Walkingstick continued to use Superintendent Joe Jennings to track down missing subsistence payments. He reentered his training in April 1950.[54] Unfortunately the VA factored in his previous interruptions in training and only granted him subsistence pay and support until October of that year, significantly reducing the time he had expected to be enrolled. Urging the VA to reconsider terminating Walkingstick's subsistence pay, Jennings argued for extending the contract through the end of December 1950. Jennings acknowledged that Walkingstick "has had several interruptions in training" but asserted that those should not count against the work he had accomplished since his last reenrollment. Jennings also directly spelled out how impactful subsistence pay was to Walkingstick and his family. "The small amount of tuition which this school will lose is small in comparison with what the subsistence payments will mean to the veteran and his family," Jennings wrote to the VA. "We are informed that it was necessary for him to buy food on credit during the month of December, since he had no opportunity to work to earn money for living expenses during the time he was in training."[55] In Jennings's response to the VA's decision to terminate Walkingstick's subsistence pay, he emphasized Walkingstick's attendance and work as a student but more prominently called attention to how the absence of subsistence pay had damaged his role as familial provider.

Employment and family dynamics are two lasting pieces of assimilationist ideology that show up continually in both Indian policy and welfare policy. Economic self-sufficiency would mean that fewer Native "employables" were on "relief," but it would also mean that Native familial providers would be able to take care of their dependents without government support. For veterans such as Walkingstick, employability was also about his future role in the Cherokee community. During an earlier period of enrollment at Cherokee, Walkingstick voiced a desire to find long-term employment in his hometown. In a short written response to the prompt "What the school could do," in 1946 Walkingstick wrote "Build bigger shops. And train the ones who would like to work around here. There'll be jobs of some kind. And we should find out what those will be."[56] The BIA's emphasis on tracking and reporting potential Native "employables" takes on additional connotations if we consider how Native veterans understood their subsistence pay. GI Bill subsistence pay wasn't considered to be "relief" by Walkingstick or Jennings (or the VA, for that matter), but rather the beginnings of true employability, rooted in the gendered responsibilities of first-class citizenship.

Walkingstick's desire to complete his training under the umbrella of the GI Bill was a practical financial necessity, but more than that, it was the beginning of the future he saw for himself and his family in Cherokee, North Carolina. Walkingstick's own voice in the record was positive and upbeat. His school essay expressed optimism ("there'll be jobs of some kind") and faith in the joint effort of Native veterans and school officials ("*we* should find out what those will be"). In his letter to the VA in January 1950, asking to be reenrolled at Cherokee High School, he wrote that he "would like very much to continue training in the electrical field," as he felt that he could "do well with this sort of work."[57] Within the educational provisions of the GI Bill and, indeed, within the conceptualization of assimilation more broadly, there is an inherent tension between opportunity and restriction. Supposedly, assimilation would allow "dependent" Native wards to realize their full potential as first-class citizens. But in order to access this opportunity, assimilation policy demanded acquiescence to certain behaviors and practices. As historians of Native people's resistance to Indian boarding schools have shown, that acquiescence is not at all straightforward. Neither was the ideology of the BIA, the administrators of assimilation.

Those veterans at Cherokee High School who changed their course of study definitely encountered the tension between opportunity and restriction. Cherokee veterans' educational decisions weren't theirs alone, or even those of their immediate families. The records of their voices appear sandwiched between bureaucratic procedures and opinions of the BIA and the VA. A veteran had to explain and justify his choice to switch educational tracks to the VA. In addition, educational administrators within the BIA usually provided further explanation and context. For example, in 1947 Cherokee Arnold Roland wrote to the VA's agricultural training adviser desiring to switch his course of study from agricultural training to auto mechanics: "As I see the situation now as pertaining to myself there is not a very good future in Agriculture, because of insufficient farming land." However, Roland noted that he "had quite a bit of experience while in the Army with mechanized equipment," and he believed that his "best opportunity lies in that field."[58] Attached to Roland's letter to the VA was a follow-up from Roland's agricultural instructor at Cherokee, Fred Brown. Brown wrote that Roland "has proven very satisfactory in every way," but "due to the fact that Mr. Roland's acreage is too small for him to continue his Agricultural Training," Brown recommended the VA grant permission for him to change to auto mechanics instead.[59] Brown's letter added nothing substantial to the conversation between Roland and the VA, except to provide the BIA's approval of Roland's decision.

At times the BIA didn't approve of veterans' decisions to change course. Buford Blanton wrote to the VA in 1947 wanting to switch from carpentry to auto mechanics, stating, "I do not have the educational qualifications which would permit me to acquire a full status as a skilled Carpenter. I find that it takes quite a bit of mathematics." Blanton had only "better than a fifth grade education." Prentice Willett, veterans training adviser at Cherokee High School, relayed to Joe Jennings, the superintendent, that he did believe that Blanton could become a carpenter, and that his "progress has been very satisfactory." Willett conceded that "it does take a good working knowledge of mathematics to make a finished carpenter," but argued that if Blanton "so desires," he could do so, if he put in "some extra work at home" and spent "a great amount of time in our Math classes."[60] Jennings forwarded all the correspondence to the VA, presumably to let them have the final say in whether Blanton should switch courses. These types of letters likely bear resemblance to many teachers' evaluations of their students' "untapped potential." Willett clearly believed that Blanton could finish his course in carpentry, though it would take extra work in exactly the area that Blanton specified as his weakness. What was the relationship between seeing someone's potential and utilizing a position of power to shape their future opportunities and actions? Moreover, how did veterans weigh the mission of the BIA against their own desires when they made choices about their GI Bill educational benefits?

Many veterans did not disrupt BIA expectations. Rather, they utilized the language of assimilation and progress in order to maximize their GI Bill benefits. For example, after having completed his course in painting and decorating at Cherokee High School in three years, Charlie Anthony wrote to the VA to request a supplemental certificate of eligibility and "entitlement for further training" to complete the arts and crafts course at the school as well. "I plan to remain in this section of the country," Anthony wrote, "and feel that a course in finishing new furniture, handicraft, etc. and refinishing antique furniture, along with my training in painting and decorating that I would be able to make a good living," especially considering the "great demand for new hand-made furniture from our native woods."[61] Superintendent Jennings attached his own letter to Anthony's, backing up Anthony's claims that he would benefit from additional training in Arts and Crafts. Jennings wrote, "At the present time there is a great demand for hand-made and re-finished furniture in this locality."[62] In this way there is a key distinction between the training that Native veterans received at federal Indian schools under the GI Bill and previous "instructional work" training they may have received earlier in life. As adult veteran students, they weighed the skills they had acquired in their vocational training (as well as during their time in the service), their families' needs and desires (illustrated by Anthony's assertion that he "plan[ned] to remain in this section of the country"), and where their desires intersected with the mission of veterans' training programs overseen by the BIA.

Among the veterans who were hoping to become students at Poston, we can see similar levels of enthusiasm for veterans' training opportunities where they could utilize new skills and accommodate family needs. "There is considerable discussion amongst the veterans about the Poston School," wrote Robert Bennett, a VA employee in Phoenix, to Superintendent Gensler in March 1947. "Many are desirous of being considered for enrollment there when the school is established."[63] Bennett suggested that someone be assigned to take applications from prospective students and take their educational desires into account in the setup of the school. Gensler pushed back. Though he conceded that "there may be but little, if any, doubt but that the Veterans School will be established," he cautioned against "unduly build[ing] our Indians up to a feeling that a thing is sure, until we know it is sure."[64] As the year progressed and it became increasingly difficult to pin down specifics on the likelihood of the Poston school materializing, Gensler continued to correspond with the VA about local veterans who were "anxious to enter on-the-job training" that existing institutions on the Colorado River Reservation could provide, such as irrigation and agriculture.[65] Indeed, the Poston veteran's school seems to have had widespread community support among tribal members.[66] Looking at the success of the Cherokee school, it is not hard to see why. It was supposed to be an institution that would provide a variety of training programs, from agriculture to auto mechanics; *and* Native veterans would be paid to participate; *and* it allowed Native people to envision a future role within their communities. This a strikingly appealing alternative to the 1948 circular encouraging the "voluntary relocation" of "employables" for low-wage labor far away from their families and homes.

ASSIMILATION, BY ANY OTHER NAME

But, however appealing they were for individual veterans, BIA-administered veterans training programs still took place in the context of mid-twentieth-century Indian policy. These programs were ensconced in the concept of first-class citizenship and were designed to enable veterans to take their place as self-sufficient members of a local economy, able to provide for their dependent family members. On one hand, the financial resources that veterans received from the GI Bill reinvigorated and transformed existing BIA educational programming, especially in agriculture. On the other hand, it was difficult to *fully* transform the existing framework of BIA educational programming into something that was truly driven by students' needs, as the same old assimilationist rhetoric seeped into the ways in which BIA staff discussed their veterans training programs.

At Cherokee, sticky older assimilationist ideologies clashed with newer critiques of the training that Native students received at Indian boarding schools. In a progress report written just over two years after the veterans training program began, H. A. Mathiesen, a BIA supervisor, simultaneously praised the veterans in the program and denigrated their previous educational efforts: "A visit to the Cherokee shops and classrooms will convince anyone that they are taking their training seriously. In many instances, these young men have admitted that they wasted too much of their time while they were in grade and high school. It is worthwhile to note that all of the students' time is expended in learning a trade and not in institutional ditch digging."[67] Mathiesen wrestled with the impact of educational trauma on Cherokee veteran students, at once recognizing their efforts—"they are taking their training seriously"—but also signaling that this was a change from their previous behaviors as students—they have "admitted that they wasted too much of their time" in the past. But *who* was responsible for that wasted time if all students did when they were younger was "institutional ditch digging?" Clearly Mathiesen differentiated the veterans' program from previous boarding school curriculum in "instructional work." The veterans were working for something valuable, cultivating their own farms or learning a trade. This is a marked contrast from the "useful" training Native students received in BIA schools in the early twentieth century.

Still, Mathiesen's report continued to reflect BIA assimilationist ideologies. "What has it taken to make the Cherokee Indian veterans school a success?" he asked. "First of all, it has been the desire of the returned Indian to *rehabilitate himself*."[68] This kind of rhetoric fit seamlessly into the larger conversation around competency and self-sufficiency discussed in chapter 2, as well as refrains directed toward other returned GIs.[69] Who was a first-class citizen if not someone who took initiative, who made progress in their own educational and economic growth?

This quote also shows tacit agreement with some of the worst assumptions that boarding school personnel made about Native students in the late nineteenth and early twentieth centuries: that they did not come with desires of their own, only as blank slates to be etched with markers of civilization; and that those who made their way in the world as professionals owed their success to the teachers and institutions who "educated" them.[70] However, it wasn't just self-starting veterans who made Cherokee a success. According to Mathiesen, "members of the entire staff at Cherokee have worked together. . . . The reservation soil and moisture conservation engineer, the extension agent, and the forester are as interested in the program as are the school men, and why not, since the veterans training program has given the Indian Service worker a full welcome to every home and farm on the reservation."[71] In other words, the veterans training program was beneficial for existing BIA efforts at the Cherokee Agency. The BIA staff had a "*full welcome* to every home and farm," *because* of the GI Bill.

Elsewhere in the country the educational benefits of the GI Bill also obviously boosted existing BIA agricultural programs. For example, in 1947 Omer Davis, the agricultural extension agent working with the Pima Agency in southern Arizona, noted that the sixty members of the veterans' farm project were "doing a very good job of planting fall gardens. In many cases, the veteran must clear and level the land necessary to put in these gardens, as they are taking up land that has not been farmed for many years and is now covered with mesquite."[72] With the help of the added GI Bill benefits, veterans were doing more to farm the land than they had done in the past. In 1955 Robert Hackenberg, a research associate with the Bureau of Ethnic Research, compiled a report for the John Hay Whitney Foundation about economic and political change among Akimel O'odham (formerly referred to as Pima) people on the Gila River Reservation. Hackenberg's report revealed that veterans' farm training programs had improved upon the BIA's agricultural extension services' previous efforts. "The percentage of younger men who completed this program and actually attempted serious farming was encouraging," Hackenberg wrote. "The agency superintendent compared this program with the extension service, attributing the success of the G.I. training to be the presence of one instructor for every twenty students, where there was only one extension man for nearly 10,000 Indians in the Pima jurisdiction."[73] Hackenberg highlighted the key differences in previous BIA programs and the veterans' training program, noting that the "instruction was carried on by Indians," and that veterans were paid to participate. He asked, "What extension program could compete with this?"[74]

In his progress report Mathiesen also emphasized the role of committed personnel to staff the veterans' program and, of course, the fact that Cherokee veterans were paid to undergo training. He noted that "since the day it was organized there has been a waiting list of potential students," and there is "complete Indian enthusiasm for the training school and its program." Why? "Because he receives $75 per month if single, $105 a month if married and can receive a maximum of $120 if he has more than one dependent."[75] The GI Bill provided what the BIA had always been after—in Mathiesen's words, "numerous improved farms and homes" and "a happier and more aggressive Cherokee Indian"—in no small part because veterans received a real paycheck for their participation.

When Mathiesen wrote about "improved farms and homes," he wasn't just concerned with aesthetics. He also cared about veterans and their families embracing first-class citizenship, an ethos of self-sufficiency and competency, something he assumed had been absent. For BIA personnel, establishing veterans training programs on reservations wasn't only about ensuring Native people direct access to GI Bill resources. It also coincided with long-standing goals to "improve" both tribal land and Native people's behavior.

The proposed Poston school was built explicitly on assimilationist foundations. Japanese Americans were incarcerated at Colorado River because John Collier, the commissioner of Indian Affairs from 1933 to 1945, saw the camp as an opportunity to develop an irrigation system that would improve the land for future Native residents who were to "colonize" the reservation.[76] The Colorado River Indian Reservation was established in 1865 for Mohave and Chemehuevi people living in and around the Colorado River basin. Between its establishment and the mid-twentieth century, the history of the reservation, as Sarah Krakoff writes, "consisted of repeated efforts by the federal government to settle greater numbers of Indians there, irrespective of tribal affiliation, or in the alternative, to open up the reservation to non-Indians." Krakoff emphasizes one of the primary reasons for repeated efforts to induce other Native people to "colonize" the reservation was the firm belief that "desert lands had no greater use than to be irrigated and farmed."[77] In a 1939 address to the Colorado River Tribal Council, Collier highlighted the government's irrigation goals in an effort to convince the council to agree to open up reservation land to Natives who were not tribal members. He asserted: "100,000 acres are going to be irrigated, and you, in the nature of the case, cannot use all of it. Impossible! It will be used either by Indians or white people. If used by white people, it will soon be owned by white people. From your standpoint and that of Indians as a whole, it is better that Indians be located here."[78] When the "opportunity" to locate a WRA camp on the Colorado River Indian Reservation presented itself, Collier seized it.[79] Incarcerated Japanese American laborers would contribute toward the goal to "improve" the reservation by performing "useful work" in developing the irrigation system, building roads, and constructing permanent school buildings "to be turned over to the Indian Service after the war."[80] The BIA looked ahead to the postwar period, where they would be able to utilize the barracks to "fit the needs of the Indian colonization program."[81] Before the end of World War II, 13 families (Hopi and Navajo) had relocated to the reservation. Between 1945 and 1951, a total of 145 Hopi and Navajo families were counted as "colonists."[82]

Thus, the GI Bill revitalized one of the BIA's longtime goals on the Colorado River Reservation: to guide and improve Native agricultural work. With that work came all the behavioral expectations that coincided with the BIA's vision of Native economic self-sufficiency. A 1945 summary report of irrigation projects at Colorado River read, "In carrying out its obligations to establish these Indians on a firm economic base . . . the first step of the government should be to develop fully their present resources and educate them in the utilization and protection thereof." The authors of the report asserted that after the war's end, most Native people "will continue to rely upon reservation resources for a livelihood. It is, therefore, urgent that all feasible Indian Irrigation Projects be developed fully at an early date."[83] In their planning stages BIA staff viewed the Poston veterans' training school as one piece of the longer colonization plan.

Moreover, veterans' training was not just about the individual veteran's economic future, but about family dynamics. BIA staff estimated that 90–95 percent of the veterans who would attend the Poston school would be married with children.[84] Thus, in addition to further development of the irrigation system and "instructional work" resulting in the construction of permanent structures, BIA staff envisioned that the veterans vocational training school would also be "an opportune place to carry on training with these GI families in suitable home life on the American plan," which meant that "considerable activity" should "be set up for the wives and children."[85] While tuition from the VA would be used to finance the veterans school, the BIA would "be involved in the expenses of such training as is given the wives and children of these veterans," including the future educational needs of the veterans' children "as they become old enough to go to school."[86] And after the veterans completed their training in "agriculture, stock raising, and gardening . . . land [could] be provided to these G.I.'s if they so desire, in 40-acre tracts for them to make their homes on."[87] Additionally the BIA acknowledged that "there may also be moral problems" among the veteran student population, and "a suitable building will have to be provided, strong enough to detain some of these young men when they get too much liquor and get hard to handle."[88] Thus, vocational training wasn't just vocational training. Rather, at Poston, veterans' training was explicitly understood as one element of long-standing BIA efforts to "train" Native families to work, live, and act appropriately, on the "American plan."

The BIA placed significant weight on agricultural training for Native veterans nationwide. Commissioner of Indian Affairs William Brophy described the BIA-operated veterans on-the-farm training programs in a 1946 letter to Senator John Chandler Gurney of South Dakota. Under these programs "a returned Indian veteran will work on his own farm two days a week under supervised instruction in good farming practices, and the Veterans' Administration allows him subsistence for the time spent in this activity."[89] In his 1946 annual report to the secretary of the interior, Brophy continued to laud programs that had been implemented "in cooperation with the Veterans' Administration and the Indian schools or, where possible, with the public schools." These agricultural training programs allowed Indians to "receive classroom instruction, and supervision and on-the-farm instruction by agricultural experts," as well as VA subsistence allowances under the GI Bill.[90] Cherokee Indian School operated one such on-the-farm training program. Jennings described the weekly one-on-one sessions between agricultural instructors and their trainees as "an ideal implement of the Extension Division" and "valuable to the trainee and to the instructor," as they allowed both to "check on progress made, consider problems and possible solutions, and plan further work."[91] In addition to the weekly meetings at each veteran's farm, students also attended short courses at the school on "all sorts of topics pertaining to farm life." However, these seminars were not limited to techniques in raising livestock, planning, or marketing. They also included topics such as "sanitation on the farm," "family relationships," and "home planning."[92] On-the-farm training was not just for individual veterans, but applied to their families too. This makes sense, given the history of the Agricultural Extension Service, which also provided home economics training through Home Demonstration clubs, workshops, circulars, and house calls to rural American women all over the country.[93] In the early 1940s Home Demonstration agents working with Native populations in Nevada and California wrote about their goals to arouse "a definite interest in food production, use, and preservation" among Native families, including teaching Native people how to garden to "build up interest in foods."[94] One agent in Bishop, California, wrote that the local "Ladies Home Improvement Club" would "improve the interior of each Indian home by friendly helpful suggestions."[95]

Indeed, one of the most potentially impactful aspects of on-the-farm training programs—the on-on-one relationships that developed between instructors and trainees—also was one of the most likely to be tinged with the legacies of assimilationist philosophies and evaluations of Native farming and home keeping. For example, at Cherokee, agricultural instructors tabulated and recorded the amount of each kind of livestock, the number of acres granted to each crop farmed, the size of the veteran's home, whether the roof, porch, outside, or inside needed

repairs, and other elements of the farm. Instructors left short evalua-
tive comments about some of the items on their checklists. Robert Reed
"need[ed] a porch," his poultry house was "not satisfactory," and his six
apple trees bearing fruit were in "poor condition." George Walker's barn
"need[ed] repair" and his house was in "fair condition" (although the
instructor added the comment, "toilet—no," to his assessment). Noah
Ledford had no acres cleared for permanent pasture but "plan[ned] to
clear about 3 acres."[96] There was an inherent tension in these kinds of
evaluations. On the one hand, in order to receive their subsistence payments from the GI Bill, the veterans were essentially "graded" on their
farming practices. However, these weren't just practice farms—they were
the actual homes of the veterans and their families. Thus, the Walker
family's lack of an indoor toilet wasn't just a neutral observation, but
part of the trainer's evaluation of Walker's educational performance.
In other words, on-the-farm training wasn't just about learning how to
plant and tend crops, raise livestock, or market goods. It was also training in ideas of competency and self-sufficiency. Veterans received GI
Bill resources for their participation, but that money came with certain
strings attached. Trainees were "required to spend some of their income
on permanent improvements for farm and home." They bought "cows,
hogs, horses, mules, oxen, poultry, bees, farm tools and machinery,
household utensils and furniture" or built new homes, barns, or buildings
on their property.[97] Just as the BIA staff at Colorado River envisioned
the Poston school continuing to "improve" the reservation's land and
community, Cherokee veterans' participation in the veterans' school
contributed to both individual and broader community "improvement."

The interactions that Native veterans had with their on-the-farm train-
ers were thus marked by both opportunity and restriction. For example,
on one visit an instructor at Cherokee remarked that the trainee "was not
out at work" and "should have been out helping his dad clean the weeds
of the potato patch," a judgment of what the veteran *should* have been
doing. But, just nine days earlier the same instructor assisted a different
trainee in working out an application for a Farmers Home Administration
loan, an incredibly useful tool for Native veterans to have.[98] Although
Native veterans were able to secure GI Bill funding for education, they

were much less likely to secure farm or home loans under the GI Bill. Many Native veterans who lived on reservations were unable to secure loans for housing, farming, or businesses because lenders understood that their property was owned by the tribe or the government. For example, in 1946 a representative for the Veterans Employment Service of Arizona wrote to the superintendent of the Sells Indian Agency to offer support and services to Native veterans seeking educational and employment benefits. However, the representative asserted that though they could "also discuss the matter of loan provisions of the GI Bill . . . there is not much opportunity for veterans living on the reservation where property is Government owned to take advantage of the loan provisions."[99] In their compilation of statistics concerning returned Tohono O'odham servicemen and servicewomen, BIA staff at the Gila Bend, Papago, and San Xavier Reservations found that although "one Veteran attempted to secure a loan to carry on his cattle industry," the loan was not granted because the veteran was "living on Tribal land."[100] In his 1948 BIA report on Navajo economic development, Max Drefkoff found that "banks in the vicinity of the reservation are reluctant to make loans to Navajos for the purpose of engaging in business."[101]

Within this climate of lenders' widespread resistance to granting Native people loans for farms or businesses, the Cherokee school's success is an aberration. Not only did individual instructors provide guidance and assistance to veterans applying for loans, but the school also instituted an instruction plan on farm loans. The lesson plan's purpose was "to examine the different sources of credit in order that we may decide which will best meet our particular needs."[102] Veterans who took this particular course would determine the differences in farm improvement loans from the FHA, local banks, and other federal loans. The distinction between the success that Cherokee veterans found with their loan applications may have been due to geographical differences. As a whole, the states of Arizona and New Mexico cited in the examples above were quite hostile toward Native people. Their misperceptions of Native land use may have played a part in the likelihood of Native people in those states receiving loans for farms and businesses. Indeed, the BIA staff at Colorado River explicitly planned to utilize the "credit department of the Indian Bureau" to "make loans" to veterans "if they find they cannot secure financing through regular G.I. channels with banks" for livestock, furniture, and building material.[103] The Cherokee program was so well established and popular that Cherokee veterans who participated may have been more likely to receive loans from local banks.

Though they shared much in their service, Native veterans experienced the GI Bill differently than non-Native veterans. The complementary assimilative elements of the GI Bill and long-standing BIA practices shaped both the types of programs Native veterans were able to access using the educational provisions of the GI Bill and how they interacted with those programs. Staff at the BIA and the VA envisioned a particular impact of the GI Bill on Native veterans—veterans training would move them closer toward first-class citizenship. That took on additional connotations in the context of termination policies, especially the competency legislation proposed between the mid-1940s and mid-1950s.

Exploring the unique experiences of Native veterans' interactions with the BIA and the VA complicates the one-dimensional image of Native veterans that many non-Native terminationist legislators espoused after the war. To many legislators and state agents, military service symbolized both Native "readiness" to leave behind tribal life and incorporate themselves into the American polity. For example, in 1944 a group of seven congressmen formed the Select Committee to Investigate Indian Affairs and Conditions, a group tasked with investigating living conditions of Native people in Nebraska, South Dakota, North Dakota, Montana, Minnesota, Oklahoma, Arizona, New Mexico, Washington, Idaho, and Alaska. In their report to Congress, the committee asked, "Will the Indian who has recently doffed the uniform of Uncle Sam be willing to don the blanket of his forebears?" The committee "most vehemently denie[d] that he should."[104] They saw a return to tribal life as a step backward and demanded that "the Indian who has fought to save freedom for humanity throughout the world should not be expected to subsist in an atmosphere which denies him freedom here at home."[105] To non-Natives, military service was a marker of Native competency.[106] Some advocates of termination pushed this type of argument further to justify the complete dissolution of the BIA. For example, in a 1947 article for the *Washington Times-Herald*, Frank Waldrop argued, "The Indians in 1947 are capable of looking after themselves. More than 22,000 Indians served with our fighting forces in the recent war. About 45,000 more worked in war industries."[107] If Native people could serve their country, Waldrop reasoned, "there is no excuse for the Indian bureau. Let 'em go."[108] Waldrop's assessment of the role of the BIA in Native veterans' lives does not accurately reflect their reality. As this chapter shows, the relationship between the BIA and Native veterans was much more complicated. The BIA (and its history of assimilation) was intimately interwoven into Native veterans' education and training, as well as their daily experiences of the GI Bill, including the logistics of subsistence pay, keeping track of their family relationships, and considering their future career paths.

Native veterans' use of the GI Bill for education was shaped by opportunity and restriction. They worked with the BIA. They sought out veterans training such as the successful program at Cherokee and the planned program at Poston. They used subsistence pay to care for their families and to invest in their land and communities. Some found success. However, that success was shaped by BIA policies with long histories of their own. Agricultural training was the most common training track taken by Native veterans. Agriculture was viewed as both employment and identity by the BIA. It had long been connected with ideas of "Americanness," self-sufficiency, and first-class citizenship. The GI Bill reinvigorated existing BIA programs in agriculture, allowing existing personnel—soil conservationists, extension agents, irrigation experts, and others—increased access to Native farms, homes, and labor. However, equally as important, the GI Bill also poured financial resources directly into the pockets of Native people themselves.

Waldrop's crass command—"Let 'em go," implies that there was somewhere *else* that Native veterans could go. One of the appealing aspects of BIA-run veterans training, especially on-the-farm training, was veterans' ability to *stay* in their homelands. Instead of moving their families to different, more urban areas to look for insecure and low-wage work, they could stay home, as Annette Saunooke Clapsaddle's quote from this chapter's epigraph reads, "tethered in all the good ways and in all the bad."

CHAPTER 6

Nebulous Shame, Innocent
Taxpayers, and the Native Plight

Native Land and the Welfare State

One of the finest things about being an Indian is that people are always interested in you and your "plight." Other groups have difficulties, predicaments, quandaries, problems, or troubles. Traditionally we Indians have had a "plight."

    —Vine Deloria (Standing Rock Sioux), *Custer Died for Your Sins*

"After stealing everything," he would rage, "now they want to blame us for it too."

    —Diane Wilson (Dakota), *The Seed Keeper*

In 1947 the author of an article in the Phoenix newspaper, the *Arizona Times*, asserted that Arizona could not support the "added burden" of Native applicants for need-based welfare benefits under the Social Security Act. But it was not "a question of discrimination by Arizona against a racial minority." Rather, the author contended, "It is a question of which is responsible for the care of the Indians—the federal government or the state of Arizona." After all, "The fact that thousands of Indians reside in Arizona is not of Arizona's doing. In the westward march of empire, greedy white men uprooted the Indians wherever they happened to be and cuffed them across the nation, to dump them finally on reservations in the West. They might have been left in Indiana or Ohio." The federal government, the author contended, had "treated the Indians shamefully" and was behind "the greedy white men's" forced march of Native people to Arizona. It would be "equally shameful" to "shift responsibility to Arizona for care of their aged, blind and dependent." With the state's limited resources, "our own citizens are the ones to whom the benefits should go."[1] To the author of this article, Native people in Arizona weren't citizens of the state, or even citizens of the United States. Rather, the state of Arizona existed before Native people were "dumped" there, not the other way around. The origins of Native nations in what became the state of Arizona were completely unknown—or more likely, willfully ignored. To that author, the aggrieved party in the debate over Native access to welfare benefits was the state of Arizona and the non-Native citizens who might be shortchanged should the state be forced to care for poor Native people.

Blatant historical inaccuracies aside, the *Arizona Times* piece perfectly encapsulated two intersecting misperceptions of wardship and Native people's citizenship in the mid-twentieth century: Native people were simultaneously victimized by the shameful history of white men's unfettered greed *and* unfairly benefited from their relationship with the federal government, specifically through the (tax-exempt) land that was held in their name. Allowing needy Native people in Arizona to access Social Security benefits meant that non-Native citizens would go without. Native people might have been poor, but that wasn't Arizona's fault (or responsibility). Welfare officials in New Mexico made similar arguments. Harry Hill, commissioner of New Mexico's Department of Social Security and Welfare, argued in 1947, "For us to consider accepting reservation Indians on the various programs would mean drastic cuts in practically every category of relief."[2] Similarly, in 1951 Alva Simpson of the New Mexico Department of Public Welfare asserted that if the department had not been charged with granting aid to Native people, they "would not have had to reduce standards of assistance for care of the blind and the permanently and totally disabled."[3] By separating Native citizens of Arizona and New Mexico from all others, state officials reified both a racial and (imagined) legal boundary between Native and non-Native citizens. In the eyes of state officials and non-Native commenters, when they applied for relief, Native people attempted to take something *away from* other needy citizens. Native people's relationship to the federal government meant that they were poor, but privileged.

Non-Native opposition to Native rights—whether those rights were guaranteed by treaty or by American citizenship status—has been mostly studied in the context of the late twentieth century, especially after the highly publicized intertribal direct action protests that began in earnest after the fish-in demonstrations in the Pacific Northwest in 1964.[4] Jeffrey Dudas asserts that non-Native backlash was primarily in response to tribes' abilities to "leverage the federal government's trustee responsibility to promote their interests."[5] This opposition swelled in the 1960s and 1970s, in part, as Dudas states, in response to a general cultural shift that "opened the American polity to a variety of historically excluded populations."[6] In the 1980s and 1990s, organized anti-sovereignty groups specifically targeted tribal gaming and wealth.[7] But conservative caricatures of Native people as "takers acting as a drain on the U.S. economy," also have roots in frustrations over the expansion of the welfare state and taxation as a result of the New Deal and World War II.[8] In other words, it wasn't against just certain tribes' gains in wealth and political power that anti-Native commentators mobilized, but also the nature of Native *poverty*. Wardship itself—or at least the misperception of wardship held by non-Natives hostile to the federal government's expansion of welfare programs—was the target of anti-Native racist rhetoric. Those who pushed back against Native people's "power" (albeit power they ultimately conceded was circumscribed by poverty) weren't as organized as the anti-treaty rights groups initiated in the 1960s. But the anti-Native racism that swelled in the late-twentieth century was alive and well in the termination era and can be seen clearly in conflicts over Native people's access to welfare benefits and in the support garnered for termination policy itself.

This chapter demonstrates how Native people became the perfect foil for conservatives' fears over the expansion of the federal government in the mid-twentieth century. As Molly Michelmore has explored, the Revenue Act of 1942, passed in the context of World War II, transformed the federal income tax "from a class tax to a mass tax" and mobilized most Americans as "taxpayer-citizens."[9] In the years following the war, Republican politicians took advantage both of Americans' understandings of themselves as individual "taxpayers" and of a "narrowed definition of welfare that comprised only cash assistance programs for the very poor."[10] Pitting welfare recipients against a larger, indistinct "taxpaying public" who deservedly guarded their wealth from a needlessly expansive federal government (and the "undeserving" recipients of welfare aid) became a familiar and powerful rhetorical and ideological device. State governments that resisted the federal government's reach into their affairs effectively deployed this rhetoric. As Karen Tani has written, in the 1940s "a new era was dawning in federal-state relations, and the states had something to gain by visibly standing up to federal welfare administrators." States chafed under the constraints of a "feminized, tax-sucking federal welfare state."[11] However, although the efforts of state legislators, politicians, and commentators were depicted as a battle of innocent taxpayers against an ill-defined and overpowering federal government, in reality it was the individuals who needed welfare assistance whose lives were truly impacted.

Non-Natives employed Indian poverty knowledge, the widely held assumptions about the expected ubiquity of Native poverty and its associations with incompetency and dependency, to reinforce and amplify the distinction between recipients of need-based welfare benefits and the "rest" of the population, the "innocent taxpayers." Ironically, even though most non-Native people did acknowledge that poverty was widespread on reservations, they were not inspired to push for extending welfare benefits to Native people. They assumed that Native people who lived on reservations were not full citizens, mainly because they conflated the tax exemption on trust property with exemption from all taxes. Indeed, the states' supposed lack of tax revenue from Native people was one of the most concrete excuses state officials employed to defend their refusal of Native applicants for public welfare assistance. Harry Hill asserted to Senator Carl Hayden in 1947, "Since the state cannot tax or require the Indian to assume any of the obligations of citizenship, and since he is not required to carry any portion of the burden of taxation, it does not seem reasonable that this state should be called upon to support the reservation Indians."[12] In a 1951 letter to New Mexico senator Dennis Chavez, Alva

Simpson argued against adding Native people to New Mexico's welfare caseload, given that "very few of them pay taxes and the lands are tax free."[13] As Joanne Barker has noted, the taxation clause of the Constitution connotes that tribes are separate sovereigns within the United States, not represented in Congress and therefore exempt from taxation by Congress.[14] The idea that Native people were getting *more* from the government than the average citizen was not rooted in an accurate legal understanding of wardship, an accurate understanding of taxation, or an accurate understanding of citizenship. Furthermore, aside from tax exemptions on trust property, Native people *did* (and continue to) pay sales, gasoline, and other state taxes.[15]

First, this chapter interrogates how Indian poverty knowledge provided evidence for Native people's "plight." Non-Natives—especially those who resisted the expansion of the welfare state—equated Native people with poverty and placed the blame for that poverty on the shoulders of the federal government. This resulted in a vaguely articulated idea of national "guilt," which was marked as both a poor excuse for wardship's persistence and as a legitimate problem that the government needed to address. Yet, anti-welfare sentiment circumscribed the extent to which a national reckoning of guilt over the U.S. treatment of Native people could take place. When non-Natives spoke of "responsibility," they were much more likely discussing it as something Native wards needed to learn rather than as something non-Natives needed to take.

Second, the chapter examines non-Natives' (mis)conceptions of reservations. Reservations epitomized so much of Native people's "plight." They were understood as both "protected" spaces, safe from the tax revenue that could be collected by state governments, and "prisons," places that kept Native people impoverished and segregated. Reservation land and its anomalous characteristics were key to non-Natives' perceptions of Native people's lack of first-class citizenship in the mid-twentieth century.

Third, the chapter assesses the intersections between anti-welfare rhetoric and anti–land rights sentiments. Anti-welfare ideology undermined Native people's land rights, including the trust protections on land that they expected from the federal government. At the same time, those who did not understand—or try to understand—the dynamics of Native land prevented Native people from accessing welfare benefits. Reservations were misunderstood by non-Natives, and this could have specific implications for Native welfare recipients. Reservation land was at once "overvalued," which could prevent needy Native people from receiving welfare, and deemed inadequate to serve as collateral for home loans under the GI Bill.

Ultimately, non-Natives deployed two main misconceptions that worked together to reinforce support for termination policy and reify the portrayal of Native people as perpetually dependent tax avoiders. First, Native people were victims of the vaguely defined but cursorily acknowledged "white men's greed." Their resulting poverty was a national shame. However, despite commonly deployed rhetoric of guilt over this disgraceful situation, non-Natives did not speak of Native poverty in specific terms and stopped short of recognizing the legal and political history of tribal sovereignty. Second, and seemingly illogically, the relationship that Native nations had with the federal government was characterized as unfair special treatment. Native people were poor and dependent (kept "segregated" on reservations), but they were also privileged (they didn't pay any property taxes on reservation land, which the government "maintained" for them). Thus, twentieth-century anti-Native racism has its roots in frustration over blatantly false misconceptions of wardship. These racist ideologies reinforced both support for termination policy (to push Native people toward first-class citizenship) and opposition to the expansion of the federal welfare state.

THE NATIVE "PLIGHT" MEETS THE TAX-SUCKING WELFARE STATE

Anti-welfare rhetoric exacerbated the assumptions at the root of Indian poverty knowledge. In 1950 the *Los Angeles Herald-Express* printed an editorial that read, "There could be no more damning indictment of the so-called welfare state than the standard of living to be found among our government-cared for American Indians."[16] The author's point was ostensibly to undermine the claims of the "New Deal government" and to warn against the dangers of "complete government control and patronage." However, the true targets of the editorial were those who had supposedly been victimized by "paternal government bureaucracy":

But see for yourself. Motor down toward Albuquerque and visit any of the 30,000 Navajo families in their government-supplied homes on the government-maintained reservations. Go into any of the Navajo "hogans" and see what kind of food the welfare state furnishes them. But perhaps you don't like goat meat. See what kind of windows there are. Look at the nice soft beds—which aren't to be found—and see what kind of clothing the government gives its wards. Investigate the hospitals. See what kind of medical attention is available. Do not be surprised if the children have never been to school.[17]

Relying on well-worn racialized poverty tropes to strike the fear of welfare dependency into the hearts of fellow non-Native taxpayer-citizens, this author used Navajo people purely as a foil, a way to prove what could befall Americans if the government had complete control.

This particular editorial was essentially an early version of what historian Margaret Jacobs, echoing Vine Deloria, identifies as the "plight narrative," the "litany of grim statistics on the poor economic and social conditions that afflicted most Indian reservations and urban communities."[18] The plight narrative was evidenced by Indian poverty knowledge. Widespread media coverage of the "plight" prompted both policy and public action. For example, Jacobs asserts that media coverage of hardships such as infant mortality, unemployment, and low life expectancy set the stage for the removal of Native children from their families in the 1960s and 1970s.[19] Adopting Native children was one way that non-Natives felt they could "help" address the "national shame" of Native poverty.[20] At the root of the plight narrative was a vague sense of conscience or guilt, mostly directed toward the damaging choices made by a historical federal government or the "country" in general. Jacobs quotes from Mary Davis, a supervisor at the Children's Bureau of Delaware, who lauded the bureau's work in placing Native children in non-Native homes: "I believe all Americans feel a certain sense of guilt about our country's treatment of the Indian," so she and other social workers were "glad of the chance to do something concrete to offset our nebulous sense of shame."[21] The author of the Los Angeles Herald-Express editorial who claimed that reservations were the "perfect example of the welfare state" tapped into that same nebulous sense of shame to project an anti-welfare message. Although the author's description of Navajo hogans was cruel and dehumanizing, and Davis and her coworkers supposedly were motivated to "help" Native families, both examples of the plight narrative assumed two things: to be Native was to be poor, and Native poverty was—at least in part—the federal government's fault.

Recognizing that responsibility for Native poverty lay with the federal government did not mean that non-Natives acknowledged or respected Native nations' relationships with the government or the nuances of Native sovereignty. Guilt was a poor motivator for authentic assessment of necessary social change. It was an even poorer rationale for the specific acknowledgment of past wrongs. Mixing the rhetoric of guilt and shame with mid-twentieth-century welfare policies resulted in politicized conflict about the nature of citizenship and dependency. Those who opposed the expansion of the federal government saw the expenditure of federal funds on Native people as an example of the government being blinded by guilt. In his 1944 article for the Association on American Indian Affairs (AAIA) publication the *American Indian*, anthropologist H. Scudder Mekeel wrote: "Regardless of class or region, our collective guilt as a Nation because of our past treatment of the Indian has seriously prevented an objective attitude toward him. Such guilt reinforces a sentimental viewpoint and helps maintain a sizeable budget for the Office of Indian Affairs in Congress, but it does not lead to a solution of the fundamental problems involved."[22] Furthermore, to some conservative politicians, wardship did not solve the plight, instead perpetuating a state of dependence and discouraging Native "responsibility." In 1950 Senator Hugh Butler of Nebraska inserted into the *Congressional Record* the full text of a speech given by Dean Russell at a Montana "convention on individual liberty." After comparing the "bondage of a welfare state" with the bondage of slavery, Russell asserted that while individual responsibility had been granted to freed slaves, it had never been extended to Natives. He claimed, "Now compare the remarkable progress of those former slaves to the lack of progress of the American Indians who were made wards of the Government; who were given State-guaranteed 'security' instead of freedom with responsibility."[23] In

Russell's view, the government's extension of benefits had created a total state of dependence for Native wards. "It has been claimed that many thousands of Indians will actually die of starvation unless the Government feeds them," he claimed. "If this is true, why is it so?"[24] Ultimately, Russell's main point was about the dangers of governmental overreach, not actually providing food to starving Native people.

Similar logic extended past that Montana convention to state governments. In 1961 the United States Commission on Civil Rights reported that certain states refused to extend general assistance programs to Native people because they contended that, since Natives were "Federal 'wards,'" "the plight of the Indian is largely of the Federal Government's own making."[25] Conservative politicians and policymakers saw unchecked dependency on the federal government as dangerous, not only for Natives, but for the whole nation. Russell expressed this viewpoint in his 1950 speech, stating bluntly: "If we free Americans continue to turn to Government for our security, we, too, will surely become dependent wards instead of responsible citizens. . . . Instead of calico and blankets, we may be promised a hundred dollars every month. But since the principle is the same in both cases, the results will also eventually be the same."[26] Similarly, in a 1956 article Oklahoma teacher Essie Skillern wrote: "Some say the present unfortunate plight of the Indian American is indicative of what will happen in the United States of tomorrow if present trends toward an all-powerful welfare government continue, and each citizen becomes a 'ward of the government.' This reason alone, critics claim, is enough to warrant termination of federal supervision and control of the red man."[27] Wardship was equated with a large, unwieldy, expensive, and unproductive welfare state, directed by feelings of guilt rather than rooted in goals of economic self-sufficiency for Native men and women.

At the same time, as the above quote from social worker Mary Davis suggests, non-Natives did not discount the idea of national guilt. Even the *Arizona Times* editorial acknowledged that Natives had been treated badly by "greedy white men." However, the recognition of ill-treatment (by vague and depersonalized sources) did not mean that non-Natives questioned American ownership of Native land. Rather, guilt coexisted uneasily alongside a narrative of the United States' "inheritance" of that land. Skillern wrote: "Do we ever stop to think that the very land of America was *contributed* to the white man by the Indian? Even the trails and paths which white men have converted into roads and great highways were first made by Indians."[28] Skillern simultaneously downplayed the violence inherent in the United States' history with Native nations—Native people simply "contributed" their land to white settlers—and sanctioned a narrative of America's predestined occupation of Native land. However, in doing so, she tapped into a sense of collective national guilt. Because Natives had contributed their land to the United States, the American people owed them something in return. First-class citizenship for Native people could help assuage non-Native guilt.

But guilt could only go so far in the pursuit of Native people's "emancipation" from wardship and assumption of first-class citizenship. Anthropologist L. S. Cressman emphasized that the BIA had instituted a "standing offer" to "work constructively with any tribe which wishes to assume either full control or a greater degree of control over its own affairs."[29] Thus, Native poverty and dependency could not be blamed solely on the extensive role of the federal government in Native people's lives. Skillern wrote: "Many Americans have a kindly attitude toward Indians. They are prepared to help him on occasion by appropriations in Congress to avert starvation, by gifts to missions, and by approving bills to end federal wardship. As a matter of fact, the Indians are helped in almost every way except in a way designed to help them help themselves."[30] Skillern claimed that because both Native and non-Native people had become so accustomed to the federal government "helping" Native people, Native people themselves had failed to capitalize on opportunities presented by the government to encourage "responsibility" and "self-sufficiency." Indeed, Skillern quoted Commissioner of Indian Affairs Glenn Emmons, who, in a 1956 speech, stated that he "wanted to get the government out of the business of playing nursemaid to its present Indian wards."[31] Advocates of termination such as Emmons, Cressman, and Skillern grossly misinterpreted Native people's relationship with the federal government, casting benefits and protections guaranteed by treaties and government-to-government agreements as well-intentioned "help" that Native people weren't willing or equipped to accept, foreshadowing bitter fights over land and wealth in the late twentieth and twenty-first centuries. In his assessment of the conflict over Oneida sovereignty in twenty-first-century Wisconsin, Doug Kiel writes of anti-sovereignty activists who "characterize Indigenous sovereignty as a privilege, even a gift, that can and ought to be revoked by the settler state when the tribal self-governance comes too close to actually existing."[32]

Guilt is a difficult feeling to honestly interrogate, especially if the guilty party is not easily identified. Non-Natives, especially those "innocent taxpayers" who held tightly to their land and money, couldn't truly pinpoint the guilty party. Was it the federal government? Or was it Native people themselves? Very few people claimed that Native people *hadn't* experienced extreme violence, loss of land, disease, and trauma at the hands of the United States. But by framing Natives' perpetual dependence as the result of vaguely defined federal incompetency, authors such as Cressman and Skillern also managed to undermine the legal complexities and legitimacy of wardship. In other instances, policymakers alluded to the weight of Native poverty on the conscience of ordinary Americans but simultaneously downplayed their responsibility. For example, in his 1954 speech at the annual meeting of the AAIA, Glenn Emmons contended, "Most reservation families are grubbing along" below "acceptable American standards," and "far too many are merely subsisting in rural slums under conditions which periodically shock the conscience of the Nation."[33] Emmons pointed to the recurring "shock" of Native poverty to support his goals for Native assimilation. Similarly, in a 1958 policy paper on termination, S. Lyman Tyler revealingly asserted, "Always the desire of the United States has been that the Indian would become more like us, that is like the predominant culture, or, failing this, that he would at least become enough like us so that he could live among us without giving us a guilty conscience."[34] Thus, Native assimilation into "acceptable American standards" of living would both "solve" the Native plight and assuage pesky, persistent non-Native guilt.

Equating wardship with "welfare" introduced an additional host of racialized assumptions about welfare dependency and fears of an expansive welfare state into conversations about the historical relationship between the United States and Native tribes. While serving as treasurer and consultant to the executive director of the National Congress of American Indians, Ruth Muskrat Bronson (Cherokee) illustrated the effects of mixing guilt and assumptions about race and dependency quite clearly in an essay entitled "Outreach." It is worth quoting at length:

> The average American is noted for his sympathy for the underdog. He is also apt to have romantic sentiment for the American Indian. These two admirable qualities, combined with a vague sense of guilt for having ousted the original inhabitant of a naturally rich land because of his own need for a new world, a *heritage of guilt*, too, for the long and shameful history of broken treaties with those he dispossessed, conspire to foster impulsive action, based on a desire to make amends but founded on superficial or inaccurate knowledge rather than on thoughtful study or familiarity with fact and reality. This is serious, indeed, for the Indian since it jeopardizes his very existence and unquestionably would lead to his eventual—literal—extinction.[35]

Terminationist policymakers understood the legal treaties and agreements Native nations had with the federal government as federal "overprotection" of Native citizens, motivated by a sense of guilt. That guilt, however authentic it may have been, was mistakenly understood to be a poor rationale for continuing an expansive welfare policy through wardship. Thus, although the American "heritage of guilt" implied at least some lip service paid to Native people's experiences of historical violence, it equated neither to a formal acknowledgment of settler colonialism nor to fulfillment of individual treaty stipulations. In fact, to terminationists, American guilt and conscience impeded Native integration and stalled the release of federal trust restrictions on Indian land. As Bronson underscored, this could have dire effects on tribes.

RESERVATIONS AND WARDSHIP

The myth of how "tribes dwell in primitive splendor," as Vine Deloria wrote in 1969, has a long history.[36] "To hear some people talk," Deloria argued, "Indians are simultaneously rich from oil royalties and poor as church mice."[37] Like so much in the history of Indian policy, contradictory misperceptions of Natives' simultaneous wealth and poverty come from non-Native desire for Native land. Native land was (and continues to be) highly valuable and, according to non-Natives who did not try or want to understand the relationships that Native people maintained with their environment, perpetually underutilized. Deloria asserted that non-Natives only recognized Native humanity so that their land could be "stolen legally and not blatantly," since Native people should "have the right to sell their lands."[38] This ideology undergirded federal policies that forced land cessions and allotted reservations and remained very prevalent into the mid-twentieth century. For example, in 1946 an assistant vice president at Valley National Bank in Phoenix wrote to Senator Carl Hayden to express his dismay at how "Indians are literally wasting our two greatest natural resources—water and land." He proposed leasing the land to non-Natives, who could implement the needed "improvements."[39] The implication was clear: Native people didn't know what they were doing, and maybe they didn't even *care* about the valuable land they occupied.

Of course, it wasn't just that Native people seemingly benefited from the land only "with the very minimum of effort."[40] It was also that the land was exempt from property taxes. In 1941 Colorado River Agency superintendent C. H. Gensler remarked that in the view of the "taxpaying public," Native people do not pay taxes and do not have to buy land and "pay for it from individual effort."[41] Deloria also described this misperception, stating, "Because taxation is such a nebulous and misunderstood concept, the general public usually believes that Indians *get away with* millions of dollars of tax-free money."[42] In the mid-twentieth century, non-Natives' failure to understand Native history *and* their general confusion about how taxation worked coalesced into dangerous assumptions about both Native land and the relationships Native nations had with the federal government.

Land ownership was the source of nearly all historical problems between the United States and members of Native nations. Societal racialization of Native people was based on assumptions about Native property. Reservations were completely misunderstood by many non-Natives, but especially those hostile to allowing Native people to access welfare benefits, who used reservations to justify denying welfare benefits to needy Native people. In 1946 Commissioner of Indian Affairs

William Brophy responded to terminationists' calls to "emancipate Indians from wardship" by asserting that Native people did not need to be "set free." Brophy explained, "The trusteeship which the Government exercises over Indian property is an obligation which the Government accepted from the Indians in order to protect their lands from further alienation."[43] Brophy also asserted that wardship applied "to the property rather than to the person of an Indian" and thus reasoned that the federal government's "protection" of Native people applied only to land.[44] To Brophy and, indeed, many in the BIA, Natives' citizenship and "freedom" were not impeded by wardship. Thus, although popular rhetoric pitched wardship as a racialized status that prevented Natives' access to full American citizenship, Brophy interpreted midcentury wardship purely as the fulfillment of the government's obligations to protect Native land.

However, since the mid-nineteenth century, one of the most common physical, visual, and epistemological tropes of "Indianness" had been reservation residence. In the nineteenth and early twentieth centuries, reservations acted as bounded spaces within which state agents could track and identify each Native person for the purposes of "education," administration, and legal control.[45] After the 1887 Dawes Act, policymakers attempted to allot reservations for use by individual nuclear family units. In their simultaneous efforts to dissolve reservations and "protect" Native land from sale to unscrupulous whites, state agents increased their systems of control and management of individual Native people, instituting systems to judge when they were "ready" to take control of allotted land and assume the rights and responsibilities of American citizenship.[46] Thus, reservations acted simultaneously as tools for state agents to "oppress" and "protect" Indians, seemingly created as much to keep Natives *in* as they were to keep others *out*. As the twentieth century progressed, reservations continued to symbolize to non-Natives how different Natives were from other citizens, whether that difference demanded increased control over their "lack of civilization" or protection from the outside world. Ultimately, as Barbara Welke argues, reservations served to relegate Native people to the outside of the "borders of belonging" in the American polity.[47]

But it wasn't just that reservations were geographically distinct from non-Native space. Reservations also represented a demarcation of federal jurisdiction that state governments could not penetrate—for taxation or welfare disbursement. During the protracted legal battle between tribes in Arizona and the state's Board of Public Welfare over whether Native people were eligible for state welfare funds under the Social Security Act, Arizona newspapers equated wardship with the reservation system. In 1953 the *Phoenix Gazette* argued: "The Indian problem is essentially a federal one. It can't be solved at the state level until the reservation system is abandoned."[48] Similarly, the *Arizona Republic* published an article that same year that contended, "This state's belief is that the privileges of citizenship must await the responsibilities. As long as federal wardship stands in the way of state tax revenue and jurisdiction with respect to the reservation, state payments of benefits should at the most be only nominal."[49] Thus, to many non-Native Arizonans, reservation land was what stood in the way of Native people assuming the full benefits—and responsibilities—of first-class citizenship.

To state and local governments, the reservation system epitomized how Native people were able to avoid state law enforcement and tax collection. As the 1961 United States Commission on Civil Rights report established, "Some States resent the fact that while on a reservation, Indians are beyond the reach of State law; this resentment is occasionally expressed in attempts at 'retaliation.'"[50] Certain states reasoned that because Natives were removed from the responsibilities of state citizenship in ways other citizens were not, a state did not have the obligation to "provide the same measure of care to Indians that it does to its other citizens."[51] Arizona even made a concentrated effort to remove certain citizenship rights from Natives living on reservations. In response to a 1959 case where the Supreme Court ruled that the state had no jurisdiction over a transaction that had occurred on the Navajo reservation, "the State sought to remove all polling places from the reservation."[52] In New Mexico state agents argued that since the Navajo Nation was held to be a "separate tribal nation and not subject to criminal laws or other laws of our State," "votes cast by Indians within the reservation are invalid because cast outside the State."[53] Thus, to particular states,

Native people on reservations were not subject to state laws or property taxes and, as a result, were restricted from the rights of state citizenship.

To state officials, reservations also symbolized Native people's "uncivilized" nature and supposed unassimilability. Dating back to the mid-nineteenth century, many Native people periodically left and returned to reservations, taking advantage of familial, economic, political, and cultural "opportunities for Indian mobility."[54] As Philip Deloria argues, this led to a new non-Native fear of "outbreak." "Outbreak was more rebellion than war," Deloria writes, "and more intimately concerned with the extent to which Indians had or had not been assimilated or forcibly incorporated into American civil society."[55] But even if Native people left reservations, and joined non-Native society, they did not cease to be Native. Even into the twentieth century, Bethany Berger writes, "Despite the advocacy of assimilation, Indians leaving reservations to join the broader community often found themselves shut out of public and social institutions."[56] Thus, because reservations were places where large groups of racialized Native people lived, reservations became symbols of racialized wardship. For example, in 1961 the authors of the Commission on Civil Rights report separated the Native "racial minority" into three groups: reservation, non-reservation, and off-reservation.[57] Reservations acted as racialized spaces that divided Native people into "degrees" of wardship. The racialized implications of former reservation residence followed any Native people who left, marking them with the status of wardship, even if they were removed from tribal property.[58]

State agents understood reservations as symbols of either federal wardship and dependence or dangerous incubators of Native nationalism and tribal sovereignty. Both dependence on the federal government and assertions of Native nationalism contradicted idealized notions of multicultural, democratic postwar American citizenship. Native people's American citizenship was seemingly limited by their "dual citizenship" in the United States and their respective tribal nations. For example, Thomas S. Shiya, an Indian Affairs consultant in Arizona, delivered a speech to the Phoenix Area Land Operations Conference of the BIA in 1955, where he described the limitations of reservations. Shiya argued,

"In isolating the Indian on reservations and in protecting his land on a tribal basis, we denied him the opportunity to find his rightful place in our competitive society."[59] Shiya's main critique was of the "artificial barriers between Indian tribes and the world surrounding them," which contributed to a "great contradiction of dual citizenship."[60] Native people needed to choose: "either a mutual working toward full fledged citizenship with his fellow American or else full fledged tribal citizenship on his reservation 'island.'"[61] For Shiya, reservations represented both physical and ideological isolation from American citizenship.

However, despite Shiya's depiction of reservations as "islands," reservations were not independent, fully functioning, national entities with built-in infrastructures. The federal government was enmeshed in reservation life. Furthermore, although states were restricted from reservations in some areas, government officials understood that "Indians who remain wards of the Federal Government are not in a water-tight compartment into which State laws and functions do not penetrate."[62] Lawyers arguing on behalf of Arizona tribes that wanted access to Social Security benefits claimed that "no Indian reservation in Arizona is self-sufficient and no resident of any such reservation can avoid travelling beyond its borders, nor can he escape ordinary State cigarette, gasoline, sales or use taxes."[63] Thus, to demand Native people separate their tribal membership, federal wardship, and state citizenship was not only an insidious denial of the history that Native nations had with the United States government, but it was also just logistically impossible.

Common political and media portrayals of reservations as "prisons" that held Native people back from full integration into the American polity obscured complicated histories of individual tribal treaties and removal. In 1947 Senator Hugh Butler of Nebraska defended one of his competency bills, arguing that Native people "are restricted in property rights. They live under conditions of *racial segregation*. They are subject to limitation and exemption because they are Indians."[64] In a 1950 letter to Commissioner of Indian Affairs Dillon Myer, the American Missionary Association argued that the reservation system was an "anomaly of segregation and dependency."[65] Similarly, when the Commission on the Rights, Liberties, and Responsibilities of the American Indian performed research for their report in 1959, they found that "more than one American has asked whether an Indian can leave the reservation at will," and that many members of Congress also believed that "Indians suffered far more restraints than they do."[66] In the midcentury, when many residential areas, public services, and private businesses *were* segregated and restricted on the basis of race, it is not completely shocking that the public believed reservations to be systems of segregation. However, Native people's experiences of "segregation" were viewed differently than segregation in the Jim Crow South. In the minds of non-Natives, reservations meant that Native people were controlled by the federal government, not restricted by individual business owners or state and local government bodies.

Essentially, to the mid-twentieth-century American public, reservations symbolized Native people's "plight." Reservations were continually positioned as the opposite of the comfortable, civilized space of the "white man's world." Vine Deloria sharply criticized this tendency in 1969: "To hear others, Indians have none of the pleasures of the mainstream, like riots, air pollution, snipers, ulcers, and traffic. Consequently, they class Indians among the 'underprivileged' in our society."[67] In 1943 the Senate Committee on Indian Affairs published a partial report of a survey of "conditions among the Indians of the United States." The committee argued that keeping Native land in trust limited their freedom: "There is no more justice in tying an Indian to a piece of land than there would be in selecting a group of whites or other racial group for such forced tenantry and handicap in freedom of movement."[68] The understanding that Natives were "tied" to reservation land unjustly was also expressed by those outside of Congress. In 1946 the American Indian Defense Association (AIDA) submitted a report on "the plight of the Navajo Indians" (there's the plight again) that was included in the record of Senate Committee on Indian Affairs hearings on a bill establishing a commission to study tribal claims against the United States and the administration of Indian Affairs. AIDA stressed that "50,000 human beings born and reared on this continent from time immemorial" were "still segregated, still within the so-called reservations." AIDA claimed, "No classes of other citizens are thus as segregated as are the American

Indians," adding, "This is certainly not America." Not only did "reservation life destroy independence," but, as AIDA claimed, "reservation Indians are made dependents and kept so."[69] What was at the root of Native people's plight? They were "kept" as "tenants" on reservations, forcibly dependent upon the government and shut off from first-class citizenship, which could be realized through outright property ownership or gainful, year-round employment.

OPPOSITION TO BOTH WELFARE AND NATIVE LAND

Because Native people's ever-growing "plight" was primarily understood as the result of the federal government's expansive power, state and federal agencies actively denied Native people access to *more* federal resources through welfare. This denial was based on a racialized anti-welfare ideology and reinforced by individual lenders' and state agents' unwillingness to challenge commonly held misperceptions about the nature of trust land. Thus, despite widespread recognition of Native people's "plight," Natives' access to welfare benefits remained elusive, in no small part due to the resistance of caseworkers and other state agents to fully understand the dynamics of wardship. In particular, reservation land did not conform to non-Native conceptualizations of poverty and wealth. Ultimately anti-welfare sentiment undermined Native land rights, and, in turn, anti-land rights ideologies undermined Native people's access to welfare benefits.

In 1953 the Hualapai and San Carlos Apache nations filed a lawsuit against Arizona over the state's refusal to extend benefits to disabled Native citizens under the Social Security Act. Kent Blake, counsel for the State of Arizona, argued that Native people on reservations were not eligible for benefits because they were wards. Specifically, he claimed that "reservation Indians" in Arizona had enjoyed a "peculiar and privileged status . . . over the past many years." He contended: "Reservation Indians . . . are maintained on lands that are held in trust for them by the Federal Government. Their hospitals, their schools, and their police protection are all provided for them by the Federal Government."[70] Significantly, Blake's choices of "maintained" and "provided" depicted the ward/guardian relationship as special treatment, as opposed to framing federal "protection" as something granted in exchange for land. Blake continued, "as to such Indians as are living *off the reservation*, as to such Indians as are living in the communities, that are *paying taxes*, that have become *emancipated* and form part of the regular communities in the State of Arizona, if those Indians are permanently and totally disabled, we are not attempting to exclude those Indians."[71] However, the "treatment that has been given the reservation Indians in the past by the Federal Government" meant that disabled Native people living on reservation land would be excluded from welfare benefits in the state of Arizona.[72] There is a sense in Blake's argument that by virtue of their relationship with the federal government, Native people had benefited in ways that other non-Native citizens of Arizona had not—particularly through trust land being exempt from state property taxes. In this sense reservations were a representation of how Native people received "special treatment" from the federal government as a racial group.

When it came to welfare eligibility, reservation land was both over-valued and misunderstood. For example, in her attempt to determine whether Mae Harris (Gila River Indian Community) was eligible for public welfare, Esther Koontz of the Yavapai County Board of Public Welfare in Prescott, Arizona, wrote to Pima Agency superintendent A. E. Robinson: "You advised us that our client has ten acres of irrigable land valued at $1000 and held in trust by the Federal Government. We are interested in knowing if Mrs. Harris may sell this land if she wishes to do so."[73] Koontz was most likely attempting to determine Harris's total wealth and was unable to determine whether trust land should be included. Robinson responded, "The land of Mae M. Harris is not transferrable." Furthermore, he continued: "This land was evaluated arbitrarily. As there is no way to sell the land for the $100 per acre valu-ation was made by comparison to off-reservation land."[74] Reservation land represented a conundrum for welfare officials such as Koontz. Did Harris "own" those ten acres if she technically was unable to sell them? Were they worth as much as off-reservation land? And did it even mat-ter, considering that Harris could not transfer the land to a non-Native person? Furthermore, even though she had ten acres of trust land, Har-ris was clearly in need of financial assistance from the state. By casting

Harris's land as an asset that might be sold, Koontz recast her situation as less dire because of her racial identity and status as a ward. Harris was sitting on a potential $1,000, but, of course, that valuable land was only available to her because she was Native. Even though Harris was poor enough to apply for public assistance, to Koontz and others at the Yavapai County Board of Public Welfare, Harris's land must have represented a privilege that disrupted the narrative of racialized poverty and welfare dependency.

Mae Harris's stake in tribal property negatively impacted her eligibility for benefits, despite her need. Similar issues arose when Native veterans attempted to access home loans under the GI Bill. In the postwar period, tribal leaders and political organizations devoted to Native issues frequently highlighted the poor quality of housing on reservations. In a 1950 newsletter the AAIA characterized reservations as "neglected slum areas" and "a disgrace to the nation."[75] Part of the reason why such "slums" were so widespread, the AAIA argued, was because Native people had been denied benefits under the Federal Housing Act of 1949, and, thus, "neither the State nor the Federal Government has or has had authority or funds for Indian housing."[76] Similar to battles between states and the federal government over Social Security benefits, this "jurisdictional no-man's-land" reflected the impact of wardship on Native people's receipt of much needed benefits.[77] In his role as lawyer for the All-Pueblo Council, Felix Cohen protested the absence of any loans to Native people within the "some 80 million dollars or more for repairing and rebuilding rural housing" appropriated by Congress in 1949, but the Farmers Home Administration "turned down [his] protest and refused to alter its discriminatory policy."[78]

After World War II, homeownership became a realizable dream for a significant number of American families.[79] By 1956, thanks to the GI Bill, which furnished low-cost loans to veterans to aid in the purchase of homes, farms, and businesses, 42 percent of World War II veterans were homeowners.[80] However, as historians have shown, the bill's effects were not equally distributed to all racialized veterans. Banks and VA loan officers had the power to deny loans to Black applicants purely based on race, and higher-level administrators of the VA's loan program reinforced racialized institutions about where money from the national treasury could be spent. As Glenn Altschuler and Stuart Blumin note, in addition to localized instances of bigotry, VA loan officers and bankers defined applicants' worthiness based on redlining, which ultimately "denied mortgage loan guarantees to most African Americans and actively promoted the continuing segregation of all-white neighborhoods."[81] These practices were understood to protect the nation's "public purse" by refusing loans to "perceived high-risk borrowers."[82] Thus, although in theory VA-backed mortgages and loans for small businesses were nondiscriminatory, in practice these loan programs reinforced structural racism.

Native veterans who lived on reservations were largely unable to secure loans for housing, farming, or businesses because lenders understood that tribal property was not owned by individual Native people but either by the tribe or by the government. For example, in 1946 W. C. Sawyer, a representative for the Veterans Employment Service of Arizona, wrote to the superintendent of the Sells Indian Agency to offer support and services to Native veterans seeking educational and employment benefits. However, Sawyer asserted that though they could "also discuss the matter of loan provisions of the GI Bill . . . there is not much opportunity for veterans living on the reservation where property is Government owned to take advantage of the loan provisions."[83] Kasey Keeler has argued that relocation policy was a way that terminationists worked to "gradually sever" the federal government's "relationship to Indian people while moving them to urban areas where they were expected to assimilate and integrate."[84] Keeler classifies relocation as a specific *housing* policy, noting that in the 1950s, when white families were moving into the suburbs, helped by the GI Bill, Native families, including veterans' families, were moved into poor, temporary housing in cities.

As mentioned in chapter 5, BIA officials asked agency superintendents to catalog information about "employable" Native people, with the idea that if they were unable to secure employment on reservations, they should relocate to areas where "all year employment may be available."[85] As Keeler's work shows, the government's mission to relocate Native people was not purely in the interest of employment but also served to advance assimilationist goals and disrupt Native people's connections to land. Rhetoric of "first-class" citizenship helped to bolster relocation policies. In 1947 Kimmis Hendrick wrote in the *Christian Science Monitor*, "The only way a reservation Indian can gain independence is to leave the reservation."[86] In the eyes of lenders, reservation land was more than just a symbol of governmental control—it was a poor source of loan security.[87] A 1945 article published in the *Great Falls Tribune* described a NCAI meeting where members had discussed the "question of whether trust-status land offered by Indians could be accepted as collateral for loans under the GI bill of rights." Stephen De Mers, Salish veteran and chairman of the Flathead Tribal Council, was quoted as asserting, "money lenders questioned the land as security for loans because it cannot be sold."[88] Similarly, in 1956 meetings with Commissioner of Indian Affairs Glenn Emmons, many tribal representatives expressed their concerns about the difficulty tribal members faced in obtaining loans for housing and equipment. For example, Mrs. Art Hooper, representative for the Yomba Shoshone Tribe on Nevada's Reese River Reservation, spoke of the difficulties her son had in getting a loan "because he lives on the reservation." Charlie Malotte of the Te-Moak Tribe of Western Shoshone asserted: "We would sure like to get loans for the boys. . . . They want to get loans. My son is one. He has got three kids. He has got an assignment and no machinery. He asked for a loan and couldn't get it."[89] The experiences of Native people on reservations who applied for public benefits, whether those benefits were needs-based welfare or GI Bill loans, but could not access them sharply contrasts with the impression given by commentators hostile to Native people's access to welfare. Although anti-welfare conservatives depicted wardship as the equivalent of welfare itself, clearly Native people on reservations who applied for public benefits experienced things differently.

The "plight" of Native people was commonly accepted across the United States, established by decades of publicly consumed Indian poverty knowledge. However, Native land occupied an ambiguous space within the plight narrative. Because land was so sought after by non-Native interests, Native use and care of that land was undervalued and misunderstood. The "plight" of Native people was tied to a misperception of the land as "segregated," "isolated," or "imprisoning." First-class citizenship was pitched as a way out of the plight—a way off of both Native land and welfare rolls.

That reservations were "free" from taxation was an essential piece of the conversation surrounding wardship and first-class citizenship. Native people were depicted as unfairly reaping something that other citizens could not even sow. In retaliation, state governments restricted access to welfare based on a nebulous conception of "taxpayer citizenship" that capitalized on more generalized anti-welfare sentiments. At the same time, though, non-Natives ultimately agreed that Native people were legitimately poor and placed responsibility for Native welfare in the hands of the federal government. States such as Arizona and New Mexico made this case explicitly when they refused to provide needs-based benefits to Native people under the Social Security Act. Lenders and the VA made this case implicitly when they failed to fully understand the dynamics of the trust relationship between Native nations and the federal government and refused to grant Native veterans home loans under the GI Bill. Anti-welfare and anti-Native commenters accepted the "nebulous sense of shame" over the federal government's historic treatment of Native people, while simultaneously depicting Natives as dependent, perpetually impoverished, and duped by the government. The solution they proposed was to limit the power of the government, terminate tribal power, and let others have access to reservation land.

Ultimately the "plight" narrative undermined Native sovereignty and individual Native people's humanity and basic needs. In his research on twenty-first-century conflicts over Oneida sovereignty in Wisconsin, Doug Kiel writes, "The expectation of poverty not only essentializes (and even dehumanizes) Native people as striving for bare survival but also implies that Native communities are not suited for competition in the marketplace."[90] The "expectation of poverty" was and is a powerful narrative. It coexisted with a nebulous sense of guilt that, left undefined and unaddressed, only served to further misclassify Native people's complex relationships with the United States. Not only did the "expectation of poverty" undermine economic and political opportunity, but as the history of the mid-twentieth-century welfare state reveals, it encouraged the growth of anti-Native racism.

CHAPTER 7

Care Taken to Inform

Relational Wardship, Welfare, and Sovereignty

First, Senator Ervin, I would like to say that although for almost 20
years, I have been trying to work in the field of *human relations*, I
have to be frank in saying that I do not know what the differences are
among civil rights or civil liberties or constitutional rights or special
Indian rights, and when we were invited by you to appear here, for
the first time in the 8 years that I have served our organization, I was
so afraid that you would have a lot of technical and legal questions
that I at first asked our general counsel, Mr. Cragun, to make the
statement for us.

> —Helen Peterson (Oglala Lakota), Testimony before Senate Judiciary
> Committee, 1961

In the tradition of the Old Ones, all children are deemed as ours.
We are all related.

> —Joy Harjo (Muscogee), "Prepare"

In February 1957, while serving as executive director of the National Congress of American Indians, Oglala Lakota activist Helen Peterson wrote
a letter to Lucille Hastings, assistant chief of the Welfare Branch of the
Bureau of Indian Affairs. Hastings had called to clarify—or, more likely,
critique—Peterson's use of the phrase "Indians starving to death" at a

talk Peterson had recently delivered before the Oklahoma State Society, a booster organization for Oklahoma located in Washington DC. Peterson dismissed Hastings's concerns about phrasing and asserted that she could "not recall making quite that statement," claiming that "starvation can mean different things to different people." Instead, she rerouted their conversation to the "increasing cases of hardship" among poor Native people and offered details of four different examples of Native welfare applicants who could not receive the assistance they required from either the BIA or the states in which they resided.

Peterson was an expert at using the state's political grammar to communicate Indigenous ideologies and propose alternatives to the entrenched Indian poverty knowledge in the BIA and Congress. In her letter she conceded that she "meant to refer in strong terms to Indian economic poverty" and did not see a problem with the word "starvation," regardless of the embarrassment her messaging might have caused the BIA. But she did not speak in generalities. Instead, she named specific Native people who had difficulties accessing needs-based welfare benefits and offered detailed accounts of their situations. Mr. and Mrs. Benton Rowland, who had been working as seasonal laborers in Nebraska and Colorado, were "turned down" by Marian Margrave of the Pine Ridge Agency Welfare Branch, because of "an insufficient work record for 1956." The widow of Chief Red Bird was going "from one house to another since the death of her husband, living however she can." A Kiowa, Comanche, and Apache man was denied general welfare assistance because he had land, "although that land brings him only $25.00 per year."[1]

By shifting the discussion to how specific people experienced the failures of state agencies, Peterson employed a relational framework of both wardship and welfare rights. Each of the people Peterson referenced in the letter had either written or spoken to Peterson through her capacity as NCAI executive director. She stitched together their stories to urge the BIA to address a general theme of poverty among Native populations, reminding Hastings of the relationships between each person, the welfare agency from which they had been rejected, and the BIA.

In addition to her advocacy on behalf of Native people in her communications with the BIA, Peterson was a strong, long-standing presence at congressional hearings. In a 1955 hearing on the potential termination of the Eastern Band of Cherokee Indians in North Carolina, James Haley's (D-FL) offhand remark revealed her persistence. After he "notice[d] in the audience Mrs. Helen Peterson," Haley noted: "She seems to have some interest in Indian affairs; as a matter of fact, about every meeting I conduct in Washington, she is there."[2] Peterson's relentless care work exemplifies and illuminates how discussions of both tribal sovereignty and Native people's welfare cannot be separated from the concept of relationality. However, Haley's reduction of Peterson's advocacy to "some interest in Indian affairs" reveals something too. Despite the care Peterson and other Native advocates invested on behalf of poor Native people in the mid-twentieth century, relationality was difficult for non-Native state agents to fully grasp.

Native people's understanding of self-determination was (and is) not separate from a framework of relationality. In fact, by defining and asserting their relationships with the state, Native representatives expressed tribal sovereignty in language state representatives should have understood. However, as Daniel Cobb reminds us, "It is one thing to talk the language of the larger world; it is something completely different to have your audience make the correct translation." In the examples that follow in this chapter, the "disparity between what was said and what was heard" is in full view.[3] What we should take away from these exchanges is not only how Native people adeptly spoke of the "language of the larger world," but how, despite Native people's clarity, non-Native state agents persistently refused to listen.

"Political grammar" characterizes the "techniques through which dominant stories are secured, through which their status as 'common sense' is reproduced."[4] In this way political grammar is similar to the *doxa* of dependency and welfare discussed in detail in chapter 4. However, while *doxa* is defined as a shared set of assumptions, political grammar can be understood as the vehicle through which those assumptions are expressed. In 1792 American statesman Joel Barlow put forth that a constitution should serve "as a political grammar to all the citizens," forming "the habits of thinking for the whole community."[5] This is not to say that influential documents or ideologies were (are) accepted across a population without debate or qualification. Rather, the existence of a political grammar implies a shared language and procedures that should ensure equality and operate "as a check, and control on the actions of the majority," constituting "the only weapon by which a minority can defend themselves against the abuses of a majority."[6] Thus, political grammar acts as a language and set of tools through which power is negotiated.

This chapter analyzes the ways in which Native activists engaged a political grammar of first-class American citizenship to advocate for both their nations' sovereignty and the welfare of their people. By taking care to inform members of Congress, state welfare agents, and the BIA of their understandings of wardship, Native activists were also doing something else—something much more radical than it would first appear. They were not only advocating for civil rights, equal access to welfare, and justice under the law. They were also communicating a vision of a relational understanding of wardship, welfare, and citizenship. In the epigraph above, a quote from Peterson's 1961 testimony before the Constitutional Rights Subcommittee, part of the Senate Judiciary Committee, Peterson's characterization of her work as "human relations" encompasses the wide range of relationships that shaped wardship and welfare: relationships between Native family and community members, relationships between towns, counties, states, and the federal government, and relationships between representatives of the U.S. state and Native people.

When Peterson explained her role to the Senate as one of "human relations," she was signaling to the non-Native state representatives that she understood what was at stake in these policy deliberations. Moreover, by listing in quick succession all the legal terminology that had been applied to Native people without their consent or consultation— "civil rights or civil liberties or constitutional rights or special Indian rights"—and indicating that she had brought the NCAI's lawyer with her, she communicated plainly that she fully expected to be subjected to familiar pseudo-legalistic manipulation. Peterson's care work was thus not only care taken to inform the congresspeople of her expertise in human relations and her knowledge of the history of U.S.-Native relations, but care taken to protect herself and the Native people the NCAI represented from that manipulation.

The year Peterson testified in front of the Senate, 1961, was a significant year for Native activism. Kevin Bruyneel argues that the 1961 American Indian Chicago Conference (AICC) marked a symbolic shift in the way Native people asserted sovereignty. The AICC demanded a "very distinct form of equality," which was neither explicitly a civil rights framework nor a 1960s–1970s Third World decolonization framework.[7] Termination policy provoked pan-Native activism. The dissolution of the BIA and integration of Native people into the U.S. polity solely as "citizens," as midcentury terminationists wanted, would have meant the dissolution of tribal sovereignty. In other words, to articulate self-determination and control over their cultural, political, and economic affairs, Native people needed to retain the construction of "wardship" in some form. Thus, far from symbolizing continued "dependency," for Native people, wardship functioned as a tool to remind the United States of the political relationships between it and distinct tribal nations. While termination advocates viewed wardship as an inadequate stepping stone to first-class citizenship—a manifestation of dependency—to many Native people, wardship signaled something different: the legitimacy of the relationships between the state and Native people. Those relationships signified Native tribes' distinct claims to land, American acknowledgment of colonialism, and a promise that the U.S. government would continue to pay its debt to Native people.

Thus, Native engagement with wardship functioned as tribes' and Native organizations' political assertion of the validity of treaty rights and acknowledgment of government-to-government relationships. But relations should also be understood within a broader context of care—care that was sustained and communicated by Native women. Even the language of "treaty rights," seemingly specific rights and benefits guaranteed by legitimate political agreements between sovereign entities, should be viewed within the larger context of care. As Brianna Theobald notes in her study of Crow women's reproductive health activism in the mid-twentieth century, when Crow women "evoked 'the spirit of the treaties,'" they were calling up "a history of land sales and land loss and of federal promises, broken promises, and shifting obligations."[8] In other words, relationality is a political concept, but it is also a concept rooted in the necessity of the care of kin and of individual, family, and tribal welfare.

Native women worked within the political grammar of citizenship quite well.[9] They understood the language that would get through to non-Native members of Congress and the BIA. In turn, they took care to inform those non-Native actors (mainly, though not always, white men) about relationality, urging the United States not only to uphold the political bargain they had struck with Native nations but also *to be a good relation to Native people.* Non-Native state agents did not (or could not, or *would* not) absorb that information.

Native people's relational frameworks of wardship and welfare acted as critical precursors to midcentury discourses around both sovereignty and welfare rights. By examining Native anti-termination activism and agitation for access to welfare benefits in the midcentury, we can connect Native political ideologies (many of which were expressed and developed by Native women) to more well-known movements for political recognition and human rights. For example, Native people's adaptation of the language of citizenship foreshadows the alternative frameworks of other poor populations who agitated for access to welfare. Specifically, the welfare rights movement of the mid-1960s also employed a relational philosophy, though it was not rooted in a specifically Native ethos. By centering Native women's ideologies, intellectual precedents, and organizing traditions, this chapter invites future scholars to consider how Native women's ideas of relationality can help us frame and analyze later movements in new ways.

In this chapter I first examine the concept of relationality, coming to a definition rooted in Native scholarship and poetry. Then I turn to how Native activists used a political grammar of citizenship to tease out a definition of wardship that state agents should have understood and respected—namely, a definition of wardship that would have safeguarded Native sovereignty. However, state agents—in this chapter, the state agents with whom Native people primarily engaged were members of Congress—did not accept that definition, repeatedly returning to Indian poverty knowledge and well-worn poverty tropes that undermined wardship. Next, the chapter turns to Helen Peterson's 1961 testimony in front of the Constitutional Rights Subcommittee of the Senate Judiciary Committee. I utilize Peterson's rich testimony as a consistent reference point throughout the rest of the chapter, examining how Peterson's direct challenge to Public Law 280 employed a political grammar of citizenship but also proposed an alternative framework based on relationality. Peterson pushed the committee to be better kin to Native people.

Following the deep analysis of Peterson's testimony, the chapter examines the deceptive language of the state. Native activists pushed back against the state's use of terms such as "fair play" to ostensibly lift the "limitations" of wardship on Native people's citizenship. Instead, they emphasized that the state should fulfill its obligations under the terms of wardship. The last two sections flesh out relational definitions of wardship and welfare. First I examine how Native activists compared wardship with "entitlements" instead of needs-based welfare programs, engaging with the language the state had used to undermine wardship to force the United States to honor its obligations. Then I examine Native people's reiterations of how the state failed to employ relationality in the refusal of welfare benefits to needy Native people. Not only was the state's understanding of welfare completely transactional, but state agents' purposeful confusion of wardship and welfare left Native people in need without basic care.

The chapter concludes with a discussion of welfare rights activism in the 1960s and 1970s and how the framework of poor women of color who spearheaded the welfare rights movement can be analyzed through a relational lens. Welfare rights activism was different from the anti-termination activism of Native people, but I argue that understanding Native people's relational frameworks can allow for new points of connection in scholarship and analysis.

DEFINING RELATIONALITY

Native people, historians, and scholars of Native American and Indigenous studies have long emphasized the importance of relations in Native epistemologies and ontologies. For example, Donald Fixico defines a "Native ethos" that "acknowledges the presence of all things and sees them as related to one another on the basis of mutual respect."[10] To explore Navajo self-understanding, Farina King uses the metaphor of the "earth memory compass," a method for Navajos to "know themselves, their people, and their relationships with all things around them."[11] Native studies scholar Kim TallBear juxtaposes an "Indigenous logic of relationality" against non-Native settler frameworks of property and possession. TallBear asserts that by disrupting Indigenous "social relations of all kinds—with other-than-human relationships, with place, with one another," settlers make "ownership claims" "in their desire to belong to this land." Citing Cheryl Harris's theory of "whiteness as property," TallBear argues that "settler relations with both humans and other-than-humans are also enacted as property relations." "Within an Indigenous logic of relationality," she writes, "this makes settlers very bad kin."[12]

"Welfare" is a term that should have been associated with relationality, though within the larger *doxa* of midcentury poverty knowledge, it was rarely considered this way. In a 1965 congressional testimony, Vine Deloria (Standing Rock Sioux) spoke specifically of the distinctions between Native and non-Native societal systems of welfare. "Now I think since World War II this society has been coming around to a society that is socially concerned about itself and about its citizens," he asserted. This was not foreign to Native systems of kinship and "social patterns," Deloria noted. "This is the type of society Indians have."[13] Historian Julie Reed has explored a powerful example of one such "socially concerned" Native society in her study of nineteenth-century Cherokee social welfare systems. Reed writes of Cherokee people's adherence to "*Osdv iyunvnehi*, roughly translated today as welfare, but more adequately defined as the continual act of perpetuating positive well-being for the community."[14] The Cherokee community's commitment to the welfare of all members was rooted in both matrilineal kinship and *gadugi*, which Reed defines as "coordinated work for the social good."[15] If an individual was in need, it was the responsibility of all other members of society to respond, according to the rules of kinship and *gadugi*.[16]

Poverty knowledge in the midcentury United States operated in direct opposition to the Cherokee concepts of *osdv iyunvnehi* and *gadugi* and Indigenous kinship relations more generally. At its base, poverty knowledge reinforced a belief that poverty was the fault of individual poor people, not of families, not of local governments, and not of society as a whole. Rather than signaling a commitment to safeguarding a larger social good, *welfare* was transactional. Welfare was equated with benefits an individual poor person received from the government and whether or not they "deserved" those benefits.

The second quote in the epigraph to this chapter is an excerpt from Muscogee poet Joy Harjo's "Prepare," which appears at the beginning of her 2021 memoir, *Poet Warrior*. In this poem Harjo defines relationality as human relationships sustained over generations by the connections between ancestors and their descendants. Her definition is wide-ranging and all-encompassing. She urges the reader to "come closer so I can feel your breath," positioning herself in relation to the reader:

> You could be my daughter,
> my son. My grandchild or great-grandchild. You might be
> my sister, cousin, uncle, or aunt.

For Harjo it is not only significant to recover "the tradition of the Old Ones," where "all children are deemed as ours," but to understand that all humans *are* someone's children. She writes to those who feel lost or alone, those "looking for words to sustain you, to counter despair." She speaks directly to those who lack basic needs, those who "could be wrapped in rags on the street, detained in a cage at the border."[17] Thus, relationality is familial, kinship ties nurtured across time and space. But even more than familial, relationality is *care*. Care can mean meeting basic needs, but also the feeling of connection and relation all humans crave. *"Come closer so I can feel your breath"*: Harjo reminds the reader that both she and they are not only alive, but they are related, too.

Elsewhere in her memoir, Harjo cites Kiowa poet N. Scott Momaday's "The Delight Song of Tsoai-talee." Similar to Harjo's approach, Momaday's use of relationality calls attention to the links between being in "good relation" with others and feeling alive. He writes:

I stand in good relation to the earth

. . .

I stand in good relation to all that is beautiful
You see, I am alive, I am alive[18]

Momaday's refrain, "You see, I am alive, I am alive," reminds readers that aliveness is cultivated and sustained by the care shown to and received from one's relations. Moreover, both Harjo and Momaday speak to the relations sustained between the past and the present, between ancestors and descendants, widely defined. Thus, in order to understand relationality, it crucial that we understand history. In their testimonies to Congress, Native people—Peterson and Deloria are just two examples—often returned to historical explanations, both of the United States' legal obligations to tribes and the necessity of relational care.

Native understandings of wardship and welfare cannot be separated from relationality. But for those who adhered to a belief in Indian poverty knowledge, it was easy to chop up relationality. It did not matter if one stood "in relation to all that is beautiful." It only mattered where one stood in relation to the individual patriarchal family unit. Indeed, that was the *only* relationship that mattered. If that relationship was "properly" maintained, there would be no need for wardship or welfare or any other sort of larger sense of "social concern," *gadugi*, or feeling of another's breath.

As noted in chapters 3 and 4, Native people understood wardship as a confluence of relationships between themselves and their family members, BIA agents, and agents of state and local welfare boards. Thus, Native people's understanding of relationality wasn't just limited to their Native family members. Indeed, as discussed in chapter 4, Eastern Cherokee veterans invited BIA agents such as Cherokee superintendent Joe Jennings into their intimate, familial disputes over welfare benefits, and Seminole women reached out to BIA teachers and employees for assistance in obtaining welfare benefits. Peterson's constant presence at congressional hearings reiterates just how hard Native people worked to bring the state into these understandings. For Peterson and many others, relationality— the obligation to care for human relations—extended to the state.

However, state agents' conception of Indian poverty knowledge fundamentally shaped their relationships with Native people and in many ways undermined Native definitions of both wardship and welfare. Even when Native organizers and leaders strategically employed the political grammar of the state, speaking in terms of taxes, citizenship, and legal obligation, state agents did not fully understand the intersecting relational definitions of wardship and welfare. Nonetheless, Native people's engagement with political grammar was not distinct from their understanding of relationality. Rather, welfare and wardship served as a nexus for Native people to assert the need for both care and sovereignty, the state's social responsibility and political obligation.

INTERPRETING THE POLITICAL GRAMMAR OF CITIZENSHIP

Native activists delicately navigated political conversations about citizenship, attempting to explain how wardship and citizenship were not mutually exclusive relationships with the state. In his 1954 testimony on behalf of the NCAI in front of President Truman's Committee on Civil Rights, D'Arcy McNickle (Salish Kootenai) attempted to define how Native people experienced violations of their civil rights as citizens. Though McNickle argued that Native people, like African Americans, faced "color prejudice," providing a familiar way for the committee to understand discrimination against Natives, he also attempted to tease out how the impacts of wardship and the impacts of racial discrimination intersected. He stated, "I don't mean to indicate that Indians are not segregated, as I said a while ago, because of skin color. That occurs, but the greatest difficulty that Indians face is that they are segregated because their situation is misunderstood."[19] He reiterated, "Indians occupy a situation which is not understood, and because of that lack of understanding they suffer certain disabilities." In response, the committee tried to separate their discussions of wardship from civil rights violations, arguing that Native experiences reflected "a lack of understanding, *not* a matter of prejudice."[20] However, in so doing, they misinterpreted McNickle's explanation and reified a false distinction between prejudice and misunderstanding. As is discussed in detail below, Peterson's 1961 testimony reveals how racial prejudice against Native people was intertwined with local state officials' misunderstandings of wardship.

Although different, wardship and citizenship were both statuses that conveyed certain rights and protections onto Native people. In their mid-century political conversations and debates over Indian policy, Native people used "wardship" to demand sovereignty, reminding representatives of the U.S. state of the nation's relationship with Native people. For example, in the 1947 report of President Truman's Committee on Civil Rights, Milton Steward and Rachel Sady remarked, "Not long ago an Indian complained that the 'Indians all over the country today have to sue the government to make them realize that the Indians are still wards of the government.'"[21] And in a 1954 speech, Oliver La Farge, president of the Association on American Indian Affairs, quoted the Northwestern Band of Shoshones, who released a statement that emphasized the tribe's dual claims to wardship and citizenship: "We desire for the time being to remain as wards of the Government and covet our title as Indians for as such we are recognized by other Indians elsewhere, and have the full rights as to the treaties made on our behalf by our forebears with the proper authorities, statutes made for our behalf we covet; constitutional rights given to Indians we covet, and to remain and retain these rights we want."[22] By choosing to "remain as wards of the Government," the Northwestern Band of Shoshones retained both their cultural and racial identity as Native and their legal agreements with the United States. Thus, while members of the public and politicians racialized "wardship" in this era, to Native people it was a term that signified their "government-to-government" relationship between the United States government and tribal nations. Both the author of the statement quoted by Steward and Sady and the Northwest Band of Shoshones took care to inform representatives of the U.S. government of the *relations* between the U.S. state and Native nations.

In a 1949 letter to Ruth Muskrat Bronson (Cherokee), a founding member of the NCAI, then serving as the organization's secretary, James Curry, a lawyer for the NCAI, asserted: "Whenever Indian appropriations come before Congress the fires of racial antagonism are ignited by complaints that the Indians want special treatment. The charge is not true. Indian appropriations are not favoritism. They are in payment of an honest debt of our government."[23] Curry returned to the "considerable amount of existing confusion" over the term "ward," which had been "loosely used."[24] In "Outreach," an undated midcentury essay written for the NCAI, Bronson further clarified what a "payment of an honest debt" meant. Bronson argued that Native people did indeed have "special privileges," due to the nature of trusteeship: "In the not so distant past the Indians agreed to end wars and cede lands to white settlers in exchange for certain defined, inalienable, lands and specified services which the Indians could not provide for themselves."[25] Thus, wardship was an ongoing legal relationship sustained by the debt of the United States government to Native tribes. This debt wasn't "favoritism" or "special treatment," in the sense of unearned or "extra" benefits, but something with valid legal roots, the agreements and treaties entered into by two sovereign entities.

However, throughout the termination era, state agents did not (try to) understand the nuances of wardship's relationships. This misunderstanding was on full display at the 1954 hearings conducted by the Subcommittee of the Committees on Interior and Insular Affairs in Reno, Nevada, over the proposal to terminate Nevada tribes' trust relationships with the U.S. government. Eleanor Myers, the representative of the Lovelock Paiutes from Lovelock Indian Colony, faced a barrage of pointed questions from members of the committee who weaponized the political grammar of equal citizenship to downplay her request that the government fulfill its (political and relational) responsibilities under the terms of wardship.[26] Myers testified in front of the committee to ask for government investment into her community before her tribe was terminated. She framed her request as one "for better preparedness," because her community was "merely existing on a 20-acre piece of Government-owned land."[27] To Myers, for the Lovelock Paiutes to be "better prepared" for termination, they deserved fulfillment of their basic needs under the terms of wardship, including running water, functional toilets, street lighting, and sanitary systems. In addition, she explained that because most jobs for Native men were seasonal, women were bringing home most of the family income through regular jobs as housekeepers. For

Paiutes in Lovelock Colony to access the basic resources they needed, Myers stressed that they needed more opportunities for regular employment. She claimed, "Our people live on this tax-free land because we cannot earn in 8 months the same as our neighbors earn in 12 months."[28]

In response the congressmen on the committee returned to the language of "equality," simultaneously downplaying the legitimacy of the requests and creating a perception that what Myers was asking for was some sort of extra, special treatment. In the following exchange, George Abbott, special counsel to the House Interior Committee, disregarded Myers's requests by asking complicated questions about taxes and property ownership.

> MR. ABBOTT: You appreciate, Mrs. Myers, that as it was indicated by the concurrent resolution, it is the sense of Congress that the Indians "should be entitled to the same privileges and responsibilities as are the non-Indians," and some of the basic responsibilities of non-Indian property owners—and your people would become property owners—is that they occasionally find themselves included within what we call taxing districts—sewer districts or sanitary districts. There may be paving districts, sidewalk districts, whatever you have, and on the basis of the improvements or increased value of your property—if curb and guttering is placed, for example, and a storm sewer main or sanitary sewer main—there is a direct assessment against the property that benefits from that in relationship to the benefits received. Now, if a district were formed and if the increased value of your property resulting from those improvements could be established, would your Indian people have any objection to entering into the same kind of obligation or finding themselves in the same kind of obligations that non-Indians do?
>
> MRS. MYERS: Well—
>
> MR. ABBOTT: In other words, it is certainly a challenge, of course.[29]

By framing Myers's request in the language of property taxes, Abbott tapped into one of the most racialized aspects of the American political grammar of citizenship—if someone did not pay any taxes, they were not deserving of any welfare benefits or public services provided by state and local governments. Under the guise of equal access to first-class citizenship, and "entitling" Native people to the "same privileges and responsibilities as non-Indians," Abbott asserted that as wards, not property owners, Native people were unable to understand or were not ready to receive those privileges and responsibilities. Abbott's long-winded technical questions also reveal a sexist refusal to consider Myers's requests as an elected representative from her community that the government govern Nevada tribes by consent. Myers could barely respond to Abbott's questions before he continued his dismissive "explanation" of how the Lovelock Paiutes could not possibly be entitled to governmental efforts to fix up their colony. Abbott asserted his power as a government agent and a white man to rehash racialized Indian poverty knowledge and tropes about wardship. Despite this, Myers continued to demand that the colony be "fixed up" by the federal government before termination:

MR. ABBOTT: Is your group suggesting a sort of Federal city be created; then once it is created, turned over to the city of Lovelock?

MRS. MYERS: No, they just want to be—well, *they want the colony fixed up.*

MR. ABBOTT: Surely.

MRS. MYERS: So that they could—

MR. ABBOTT: You understand in our system by cooperative contributions directly relating to the benefit you receive, you manage over a period of years 10-, 20-, 30-, or 40-year periods, under a bond issue—to borrow money secured by lien against the individual property directly proportionate to the benefits received. Surely if your people understand that, and you know that the load at given periods is not going to be too burdensome, then you certainly wouldn't object to finding yourselves in a sanitary district or paving district or lighting district? You mentioned street lighting there. Would you, with perhaps a little Federal assistance at the outset?

MRS. MYERS: Maybe.[30]

Myers and Abbott clearly operated under two completely different ideologies of both wardship and welfare. To Myers and her community, the request to have the colony fixed up made sense not only under the terms and conditions of wardship as the relationship between two sovereign entities, but because *poor Native people needed care.* Abbott did not approach Myers's requests from a relational framework. Instead, he conceived of the Lovelock Paiutes' welfare purely in a transactional sense. Unless they participated in the economic and political infrastructure responsible for public services, "just like everyone else," the colony was not eligible for what Myers was asking. But Abbott's conflation of a nebulous idea of "taxpaying" with citizenship ignored both legal reality and Native people's humanity. As John Cragun, tribal attorney for the Confederated Salish and Kootenai Tribes of the Flathead Reservation, wrote to the delegation of Montana legislators in Congress in 1957, the Montana Welfare Department's refusal to grant welfare payments to Native people because "they pay no taxes," "is wrong as a matter of fact and of law. Relief recipients are not current real-estate-tax payers in any event."[31] As explained in chapter 6, this kind of refusal to care for poor Native people on the basis of jurisdiction or taxpaying was only a thinly veiled foil for anti-Native racism.

HELEN PETERSON AND THE SENATE CONSTITUTIONAL RIGHTS SUBCOMMITTEE

In their statements to and exchanges with members of Congress, Native activists (working for the NCAI or on behalf of tribal governments) explained relationality as both nuanced history and a conception of family/kin. During Peterson's tenure as a leader of the NCAI (1953–61), her testimonies legitimized and signified the relationships between Native families, BIA personnel, and agents at state and local welfare agencies. These communications were explicitly political—meant to interject in the formation of new Indian policies and challenge existing policies. Moreover, Peterson connected individual and community relationships—in her terms, "human relations"—to a larger conception of tribal sovereignty.

Jessica Wilkerson's proposal to center women's caregiving as "political activity," to reimagine the average American as a "citizen caregiver" rather than a "citizen worker," takes on new connotations in the context of Peterson's testimony and work on behalf of the NCAI.[32] Peterson's care work served multiple purposes. Her communication of specific Native people's cases to important figures (whether it was a congressional subcommittee or BIA personnel) revealed her care for the health and welfare of both individual Native people and of tribes as sovereign entities. She gave concrete examples to inspire powerful state administrators to take action. Importantly, the action she demanded was legislative change—policies that would impact entire tribes. In so doing she disrupted Indian poverty knowledge (and poverty knowledge in general), which was based on a belief that poverty's roots were in poor people's individual shortcomings. Her emphasis on relationality challenged the erasure of care ingrained in individualistic American conceptions of economic self-sufficiency and growth. Peterson challenged an assimilative understanding of first-class citizenship based on gendered and racialized standards of individual success and possession, such as wage labor, property ownership, and paying taxes.

The NCAI, founded in 1944 specifically to combat termination policy, was a national organization, in Peterson's words, "of the Indians, for the Indians, by the Indians."[33] Though men dominated membership in the NCAI in its first decade, by 1955 Native women comprised "at least half" of the organization's membership.[34] Native women such as Peterson, Ruth Bronson, Elizabeth Bender Cloud (Ojibwe), and others tirelessly sustained the organization, performing every kind of task, from clerical work to research—driving across the country conducting surveys and interviews of Native people on reservations—to lobbying Congress.[35] Both Peterson and Bronson held early leadership roles in the NCAI. In their written and oral communication on behalf of the organization, Peterson and Bronson expressed a view of Native relationality that underwrote Native definitions of wardship, sovereignty, and welfare.

In 1961 Peterson made a statement on behalf of the NCAI before the Constitutional Rights Subcommittee of the Senate Judiciary Committee.[36] In her statement she directly challenged what Aileen Moreton-Robinson has called "the white possessive," colonists' ideology of rightful control and appropriation of land and bodies they understand to lack free will.[37] Peterson began her testimony by acknowledging the goals of the subcommittee, "to see how Indian citizens were faring in those areas where the federal jurisdiction has been specifically transferred," under the terms of Public Law 280.[38] She then immediately pivoted to a critique of PL 280, framing the law as an example of white possession. For the majority of her statement, her focus was on inadequate law enforcement for Native people residing in PL 280 states (Nebraska, California, Minnesota, Wisconsin, and Oregon).

Through her engagement with the grammar of constitutional rights and citizenship, Peterson simultaneously pushed for an alternative framework of understanding Native people's relationship to the U.S. government and critiqued the American legal system for its consistent failures to maintain both reciprocal relationships that Native people had with the state—wardship and citizenship, both undone by PL 280.

Peterson placed the blame squarely on the shoulders of the states that made no effort to incorporate Native people under their jurisdictions, to the detriment of Native health and safety. Omaha and Winnebago people in Nebraska, for example, had expended energy "to get for themselves what other citizens take for granted," having been denied law enforcement from the state for eight years. This was "particularly shameful to contemplate, particularly in view of the fact that the lands of the Omaha and Winnebago have been taxed all along."[39] Peterson understood how taxation worked as part of the political grammar of midcentury American citizenship, as discussed in chapter 6. In this case it could not be used as an excuse for denying Omaha and Winnebago people their access to law enforcement. Moreover, Peterson pushed the committee further, arguing that in states where "there is no connection whatsoever with any Indian tribal council or tribal court," Native people received poor "quality of law enforcement" "under the white man's law enforcement and court systems."[40] By transferring jurisdiction to states that were "obviously unable or unwilling to accept [their] new responsibilit[ies]," PL 280 deprived Native people of their rights of equal citizenship in the United States, their sovereignty as members of nations with their own judicial systems, and the care they required as human beings. In short, PL 280 exemplified how the state (and the states) were "very bad kin."

Peterson's vision of an alternative justice system was centered on Native relationality. "This Committee will want to know" about tribal courts, Peterson argued, especially as "enlightened white men who search for better answers to the problems of what to do with offenders against society." The committee needed to pay attention to the work that tribal courts were doing, despite—or perhaps because of—their significant differences to state courts. She asserted:

> While their procedures or records may not be in the same form as those of the white man, nevertheless their deep concern for justice, for compassion, for determining the kind of punishment that will come closest to helping a man restore his dignity as a person, the appealing concern for the family of the defendant, the *care that is taken to inform* the defendant of the provisions of the tribal code in a way that the defendant truly understands (and where this involves explanations in an Indian language, with 150 different languages still spoken by the Indians today this is something the white man's court could hardly provide)—these are truly attempts at justice that this Committee will want to know about.[41]

The "care that is taken to inform" defendants of the nature of tribal legal systems was the same care that Peterson took to inform the committee of the distinctions between tribal courts and state courts and what was at stake in PL 280 states for Native defendants. In her critique of PL 280, she repeatedly returned to tribal sovereignty, something that Native nations possessed long "before the white man came." She strongly critiqued the assimilative currents undergirding termination policies while reasserting the sovereignty of tribal governments, arguing: "The question is whether our country is bold enough to permit the survival of governments which do not necessarily conform to the white man's concept of what is an ultimate good. Otherwise, the tribes could be stripped of the last vestige of their original total rights of self-determination—just to make them over in the image of the white man."[42] Peterson simultaneously identified Native people as part of the United States ("our country") and reinforced the separate relationship between tribes and "the white man." As Moreton-Robinson writes, in Native writing and expression, the use of "white man" is "operationalized extensively as a metaphor for the nation-state and American culture."[43] For Peterson, wardship and citizenship were not mutually exclusive, and the state had failed at maintaining the relationships that undergirded both.

In her statement to the committee, Peterson cited ten specific examples of individuals or tribes that had been denied their constitutional rights, experienced racial violence, or were the victims of police brutality. Peterson gave testimony grounded in specificities, revealing her efforts to move the committee from overreliance on generalized, faceless poverty tropes into the establishment of real kin relationships. When the committee heard about two young Native men who had been sentenced to fifteen years in prison for stealing sheep in Idaho, or the death of Lakota World War II veteran Vincent Broken Rope at the hands of a town marshal outside Pine Ridge Reservation, were they more likely to absorb Peterson's larger points about the validity of tribal courts and the inadequacy of state law enforcement? Though PL 280 and other termination policies were implemented by legislators and supporters as ways to push Native people toward first-class citizenship, Peterson's examples repeatedly proved that the removal of wardship resulted in jurisdictional abandonment. In their individualistic conception of first-class citizenship, the state (at the federal, state, *and* local levels) failed to consider their responsibilities to Native people and the existing legitimate relationships between Native families and the state.

Peterson took care to inform the committee of an alternative definition of justice. She took care to critique an assimilative and generalized concept of first-class citizenship. She took care to reassert the legitimate relationships that Native people had with various levels of state government. And, importantly, she took care to utilize the political grammar of citizenship—in six separate instances she referred to Native people as "citizens," and in four places she called attention to Native people's "constitutional rights." In her closing statement she called Native people "first Americans."[44] She fit Native people into the committee's conceptions of citizenship, while at the same time broadening what the committee should consider to be the main issues facing Native people and the U.S. government's main failures.

FAIR PLAY AND RIGHTS: WARDSHIP AND CITIZENSHIP'S ENTANGLEMENTS

Peterson was one of many Native activists who consistently denounced non-Native legislators' claims that termination policies would "restore rights" to Native people, making them equal to "all other citizens of the United States."[45] Testifying on behalf of the NCAI in 1954, Peterson forcefully opposed a bill proposing the amendment of the commerce clause of the Constitution to remove the words "and Indian tribes." Peterson asserted, "Indians have repeatedly expressed bitter resentment at the trickery and unfairness of employing such words and phrases as 'restoring the same rights to the Indian tribes which are enjoyed by all citizens of the United States' which purport to give Indians something that they do not already have." In this case Peterson took care to inform Congress that their political and legal rhetoric of equal citizenship did not fool Native people: "We want to make it unmistakably clear that we know Indians have been citizens since 1924 and already have the rights of citizens."[46] For Peterson, the first step toward incorporating a relational view of wardship and citizenship was ensuring recognition that both relationships were legitimate and were not mutually exclusive. The second step was naming the state's obvious deception.

In "Outreach," Bronson established why non-Native people understood wardship as a limitation on full citizenship: "The casually informed citizen, dedicated to fair play, feels there is something definitely insulting in labelling an adult a ward of the government, as though he were being branded as too incompetent to function without a guardian."[47] "Fair play," though a synonym for justice and equality, is also transactional—it implies that two parties have treated each other equally. Bronson's emphasis on American citizens' *dedication to fair play* illustrates not only Americans' adherence to democratic ideals but also "equal" relationships on both sides (neither side receiving more than they should). In her 1961 testimony, quoted in the epigraph to this chapter, Peterson expressed her confusion over how "civil rights or civil liberties or constitutional rights or special Indian rights" should be differentiated. In response, Senator Ervin said, "I am sure that we would probably be more benefitted by getting some idea as to whether the Indians have been accorded fair play—I think that is a meaningful term—rather than whether they have been accorded all of their technical constitutional rights."[48] Boiling down Native people's complex relationships with the U.S. state to a simplistic idea of "fair play" was one way non-Native Americans reproduced a *doxa* of Indian poverty knowledge and dependency. Both wardship and welfare sat uneasily alongside "fair play," as relationships that could be (and were) easily spun by critics as "gratuitous" benefits bestowed on "undeserving" populations.

At the 1954 Emergency Conference of American Indians on Legislation, the NCAI mounted a unified response to termination policy, in part by correcting stereotypes about the limitations of wardship, asserting: "Reservations do not imprison us. They are ancestral homelands, retained by us for our perpetual use and enjoyment. We feel that many of our fellow Americans do not know that we are citizens, free to move about the country like everyone else."[49] The NCAI declared that wardship was structured by legal agreements that had been designed between independent nations "on a basis of full equality." Furthermore, the NCAI stressed that the relationship between tribal nations and the federal government should be one of "governing only by consent."[50] Similarly, in a 1956 meeting with Commissioner of Indian Affairs Glenn Emmons, representatives from Nambe Pueblo and Tesuque Pueblo stated clearly that they understood the obligations of wardship to be historically contingent on the relationships Native people had with the United States government: "Federal services now provided were given because of all the Indian gave up to the White Man when he overran our country." As a result, they stated further, "we believe it is not only a moral but a legal right to obtain the Indians' consent as well as to consult" on changes in policy.[51] Native people considered "government by consent" to be their right as nations that held legal agreements with the U.S. government.

The language of first- and second-class citizenship—concepts that were rooted only in political grammar and not in any official or legal code—undermined and devalued an actual set of relationships, wardship. Without wardship, or rather, if the United States failed to recognize the legitimacy of wardship's relationships, Native people could not, as the NCAI reasoned, "take our rightful place in our communities, to discharge our full responsibilities as citizens."[52] In 1949 residents of the Reno-Sparks Indian Colony foreshadowed Eleanor Myers's requests on behalf of the Lovelock Paiutes to have their colony "fixed up," when they petitioned the federal government for "welfare assistance," including improved housing, modernization of water mains, sanitation and plumbing, electricity, and recreational facilities for children. The petition stated, "Our Government has been pouring millions of dollars into foreign countries for rehabilitation, while right here in our own country, the *real Americans* are being neglected."[53] By directing their petition to the federal government, the Reno-Sparks Indian Colony demanded fulfillment of the obligations of wardship, yet they also called themselves the "real Americans." Clearly they did not view wardship and citizenship as mutually exclusive categories. The Reno-Sparks colony reiterated their desires in a 1956 meeting with Commissioner Glenn Emmons. Reno-Sparks tribal representative Hastings Pancho declared, "It is the obligation of the U.S. and the Indian Affairs to raise its subjects to the level of economic well-being and enjoyment as others do in the country."[54] Pancho and the other members of the Reno-Sparks colony pointed to Native people's basic needs that were not being fulfilled, taking care to inform the United States and the BIA of the significance of both entangled relationships, wardship and citizenship. In other words, it was not wardship itself that limited Native people's citizenship but the state's failure to fulfill their obligations that undermined Native people's basic welfare.

TOWARD A RELATIONAL DEFINITION OF WARDSHIP

In addition to informing Congress and the public that Native people were already citizens, Native activists and organizations also called attention to the similarities between wardship and other groups' relationships with the state, attempting to fit Native people into midcentury definitions of citizenship tied to the expansion of the American welfare state. Especially after World War II and the institutionalization of the GI Bill, the public understood that veterans deserved benefits and protected status from the federal government.[55] Felix Cohen, noted lawyer for many tribes and organizations devoted to Indian affairs, argued in 1952, "The fact that the United States has certain obligations to its Indian citizens no more removes their land from the confines of the State than do the special obligations of the Federal Government towards Government bond holders, veterans, members of the armed forces."[56] And, as midcentury welfare programs became "entitlements" for American citizens, some advocates claimed that Native people's receipt of protections and benefits from the state were no different from the protections and benefits to which all citizens were entitled. In 1961 the Commission on the Rights, Liberties, and Responsibilities of the American Indian made this comparison explicit in its report, *A Program for Indian Citizens.* The commission compared New Deal welfare benefits to the "help" Indians received from the government: "The United States has supplied comparable relief through Social Security, and aid to the old, the blind, and dependent, crippled children, and the unemployed as well as by free distribution of surplus commodities. In other respects also, it has been extending *to the entire population* the kind of help formerly given only to Indians."[57]

In her "Outreach" essay Ruth Bronson also argued that receipt of resources from the federal government was not something that was exclusive to Native people: "It is hard to see how federal benefits make a 'second class' citizen out of an Indian if preferential treatment does not jeopardize the status of veterans, farmers, subsidized airlines and steamship companies, the manufacturers protected by tariffs or the business men with rapid tax write-offs."[58] In so doing, Bronson exposed what Molly Michelmore has called the "hidden welfare state," indirect incentives and subsidies to private individuals and enterprises that expanded in the World War II era. This indirect spending was "not often recognized as emanating from government at all."[59] Bronson's exposure of this type of government spending pointed toward both the false equivalence of wardship with welfare payments that were often demonized and a wider definition of welfare itself.

In her 1961 testimony Peterson emphasized the similarities between Native and non-Native people in an effort to stave off additional pieces of legislation designed to "help" Native people receive first-class citizenship. Speaking to subcommittee chairman Senator Sam Ervin, she began, "I do not think, Mr. Chairman, our notions are legally so far apart, except we call them by different names." She then compared Yakima citizens' efforts to "keep Yakima ownership of property" to "our family corporations that restrict sale of stock in the corporation to members of that family." Applying a familiar, very American, and male-gendered concept—the family business—to her explanation of tribal land ownership and stewardship was a strategic move that Peterson employed to both humanize and legitimize Native people's legal rights. She went on: "So, if we think not that the Indian people did not encourage or permit or protect individuals and families' uses of land, but that they were *taking the same kind of care* a family corporation takes to see, when and if that Indian family does not any longer need that particular piece of land, then it is available to other members of the family, I think it would not be so far from what our non-Indian neighbors in such large numbers feel is a sensible way to do things."[60] Peterson steered the committee toward a familial, relational conception of land rights, reassuring committee members that Native people were not unknowably foreign, but fellow humans "taking the same kind of care" of their families as non-Natives took of theirs.

TOWARD A RELATIONAL DEFINITION OF WELFARE

A relational definition of wardship humanized Native people, as opposed to the transactional and bureaucratic conceptions deployed by state agents. This was especially clear in correspondence over Native people's inability to access welfare benefits and child welfare services, including foster care, from county and state boards of welfare in Montana in the middle of the 1950s. In 1957 the Montana Department of Public Welfare employed a legalistic rationale for denying welfare to Native people on reservations: "The legal interpretation we have is that the Indian reservation and its inhabitants comprise a sovereign unit of government; as such they have the right to handle their own affairs."[61] This was not an example of a government agency recognizing tribal sovereignty. It was just one in a long line of excuses used to deny relief to needy Native people.

In 1956 William Newton, BIA social worker in Billings, Montana, remarked that the general assistance welfare grants received by Native people were "generally lower than those of non-Indians," but that "such differences result from differences in the needs of Indians and non-Indians. For example, Indians frequently do not pay rent or have charges for water and other utilities."[62] Similar to the Arizona examples discussed in chapter 3, welfare caseworkers in Montana relied on their assumptions that Native people were benefiting in some way from their land held in trust. In reality the situation was not at all simple. Water alone was fraught with conflict, as many Native people on Montana reservations faced challenges to their water from the BIA, the Bureau of Reclamation, and private individuals. Just three years earlier Paul Charlo (Confederated Tribes of Salish and Kootenai) had testified through an interpreter in front of the Congressional Subcommittee on Interior and Insular Affairs during their "investigation" of what could be done to "fulfill that desire which the Indian tribes and members of tribes have been expressing so vociferously for a great many years of ending federal wardship."[63] Charlo's testimony exposed the multitudinous failed relationships between himself (and the Confederated Tribes of Salish and Kootenai more broadly) and various state agencies. He asserted:

> They come along now and then they violate our treaty rights. They went to work and made some boundary lines here and there. They even closed my water. Then they turn around now and want money for my water. Then the Commissioners, they wanted to buy our reservoirs and he didn't want to let go of them. He refused them. That way, when they take all this water away, everything, use it, maybe to drink that water will make us sick. Now the Reclamation took the water away from the Indians. If you didn't irrigate, you have to pay for the water anyhow, and then there's a delinquency on their land.[64]

Charlo described a continuous fight for access to water and land guaranteed by treaty rights, which put him and his tribe at financial and potential health risk. Poor Native people may not have had to pay a water bill, but they had to pay for water in other ways.

Charlo's testimony also reiterates just how many bureaucratic agents were involved in Native people's land and affairs, with seemingly little communication between any of them. It is hard to keep track of just which governmental agency Charlo conflicted with and when, a difficulty that reveals the impact of such a variety of bureaucratic characters all demanding access to Native resources. In his testimony Charlo also repeatedly characterized government agents, whom he called "you people," as "all in a hurry, in a rush," even ending his statement with "That's all he's got to say now because you're in a rush."[65] Charlo's critique was about water and land rights, but also about state agents' failure to build relationships.

Welfare caseworkers in Montana did not want to build relationships. In 1957 the Lewis and Clark County Welfare Board sent a letter to Montana congressman Lee Metcalf that stated clearly: "We are strongly opposed to aid for ward Indians, feeling they are the exclusive responsibility of the federal government. One of our principal objections is that if the ward Indians know they can leave the reservations and obtain relief, too many of them will flock to Montana cities and simply intensify the problem of Indian slums."[66] Through their racist refusal of welfare to needy Native people, caseworkers in Lewis and Clark County reified their physical (reservations vs. cities) and jurisdictional (federal vs. state responsibility) distinctions from Native people. However, they also noted that despite their strong opposition to doing so, there were a "a few cases where *common humanity dictated such relief*" to "ward Indians."[67] How bad must those cases have been? How poor must those "few" have been to have pushed welfare caseworkers to think of them in terms of "common humanity" rather than in terms of "the problem of Indian slums?"

These kinds of examples of non-Native resentment and misunderstanding of and resistance to wardship were why Helen Peterson, Ruth Bronson, and other Native activists took care to inform members of Congress and the non-Native public of Native people's humanity. In her conversation with Senator Ervin in 1961, Peterson stated, "It always goes back to the lack of resources," echoing Eleanor Myers from 1954: "they want the colony fixed up."[68]

As they debated the threshold for Native men's "competency" in the 1940s and 1950s, terminationist legislators laid bare their commitment to and exaltation of heteropatriarchal household organization and property transmission. As stated in chapter 2, in 1947 Frank Barrett equated the U.S. government's "guardianship" over Native wards with Native men's guardianship over their dependent wives and children, asserting "if a man is competent that the whole family should be released." Francis Case agreed, reasoning that competency should be bestowed when it was clear to an adjudicator that a Native man could "take the place of the government in looking after his family and children."[69] Legislators saw wardship as oppressive oversight over potentially competent heads of household. Government oversight was acceptable only if there was no competent man to look after the family.

Twenty-five years later, welfare rights activist Johnnie Tillmon published her article "Welfare Is a Women's Issue" in *Ms. Magazine*, where she stated plainly what white male members of Congress clearly believed: "Welfare is like a super-sexist marriage. You trade in a man for *the* man."[70] Tillmon and others within the National Welfare Rights Organization agitated for welfare recipients' autonomy, namely, their right to control their bodies, their finances, and their families. Not only a movement for individual rights and respect, the welfare rights movement was also about expanding access to first-class citizenship by challenging social stereotypes around what poor women, mainly poor women of color, contributed to society as a whole. Using a political grammar of her own, Tillmon spoke to the middle-class, feminist readers of *Ms.*, urging them to see how patriarchal ideologies structured not just family and interpersonal dynamics, but the basic framework in which women interacted with the U.S. state.

Welfare rights activists challenged the racialized understanding of welfare as a transactional relationship between poor women of color and the rest of society. In this unequal transaction, poor women could never hold up their end of the bargain. They were always deemed untrustworthy, their very subjectivities demanding surveillance of their behavior. The government's role in the welfare system was to protect the rights of the "innocent taxpayers" from the greedy advances of poor non-white women. Welfare rights activists foregrounded the relationships between themselves and their children, pressing conservative politicians, welfare caseworkers, and members of the public to see their value in relational terms, as mothers, citizens, and fellow humans.

In order to do this, though, they utilized a political grammar the state could more easily understand—they spoke of motherhood as work. As Premilla Nadasen has written, at a time when low-income Black mothers "were increasingly attacked as lazy, immoral women," welfare rights activists pointed to the work of motherhood and argued that they deserved "compensation for raising children."[71] This in itself challenged common interpretations of the reciprocal relationship between citizens and the state by reorienting the significance of citizens' individual contributions to the nation away from economic growth to caregiving.[72] Just as Tillmon used a political grammar of equality that would appeal to feminist readers of *Ms.*, welfare rights activists were strategic in their demands for equality and citizenship. Felicia Kornbluh writes that "the women and men of the welfare rights movement wanted *first-class citizenship* in the post–World War II United States. This meant gaining full access to its ballot boxes, its courtrooms, and its consumer marketplaces."[73] In order to legitimize their concerns to legislators and caseworkers deeply committed to heteropatriarchal household hierarchies, they framed their contributions in terms that were virtuously, competently male—work and political equality.

The welfare rights activists of the 1960s and 1970s, like Native anti-termination activists of the 1940s–1960s, were masters of political grammar. Both groups pushed against conservative politicians' and "innocent taxpayers'" definition of welfare as transactional—benefits in exchange for taxes, in exchange for morality, in exchange for assimilation. Understanding welfare as a relational system, albeit not one separate from legal obligations, opens up the possibility for discussions of care, kin, sovereignty, and human rights *within* the state's relationships with individuals and families. It is not surprising that some politicians, state agents, and media outlets supported termination and opposed welfare. They understood wardship and welfare as inherently unequal transactions. Native activists, and later welfare rights activists, reoriented wardship and welfare in relational terms, disrupting this definition.

As midcentury Native activists took care to inform state representatives of their specific concerns, they challenged the pseudo-legal terminology that those representatives took for granted. Their choices foreshadowed the political grammar utilized by welfare rights activists in the late twentieth century. By challenging first-class citizenship as a category and reframing welfare and wardship in relational terms, they pushed back against legislators and social workers who bureaucratized and depersonalized Native poverty. Native women and men spoke in terms of "legal obligations," but these obligations were not separate from relationality. Indeed, Native activists challenged the state's dehumanized view of poor people. Native people and welfare recipients of color were not incompetent citizens, but humans with a multitude of relationships, with the state, with their families, and with their sovereign nations.

I end this chapter with an invitation to find points of connection: between anti-termination activism and welfare rights activism, between welfare policy and Indian policy, and between historians of Native people and historians of the United States more broadly. Native activists in the 1940s through the 1960s invited others (including, importantly, state agents) *into* their care work, first through their use of the political grammar of first-class citizenship and then with their relational definitions of wardship and welfare. We, students of their histories, should accept that invitation. Recognition of Native people's humanity—*human relations*—is quite different from the action taken in the midcentury motivated by guilt and rhetoric of "fair play." Ruth Bronson put it simply in the title of her 1944 book, *Indians Are People, Too*. In the introduction, she writes: "Yet what Indians want most is for us to remember that they, too, are persons like ourselves, subject to the same psychological laws governing all human beings; touched by the same kindnesses as others; shaped and molded by the things that have happened to them over the years, just as we are patterned by our experiences. Our failure to apply this principle in our dealings with Indians has always resulted in increased difficulties for them."[74] Writing seventy-seven years later, Joy Harjo recounted, "I decided right then, during those long nights, that if my creative work did anything in this world, I wanted Indians to be seen as *human beings*."[75] It's time we listened.

In her essay on transgender feminism, Susan Stryker invited readers to find similar points of connection—without usurping power or dismissing difference—between themselves and transgender communities. Stryker found in her bodily experiences an intersection and connection with others of different backgrounds, political statuses, and positionalities. "These issues are my issues, not because I feel guilty about being white, highly educated, or a citizen of the United States," Stryker wrote. "These issues are my issues because my bodily being lives in the space where these issues intersect."[76] Peterson and Bronson and so many other midcentury Native activists took care to inform their non-Native contemporaries of their issues. Under Peterson's umbrella of *human relations*, these are our issues too.

Conclusion

Throughout the mid-twentieth century, wardship was deployed as a "magic word," as Felix Cohen asserted in 1953.[1] As *Wardship and the Welfare State* shows, "first-class" citizenship was a similar "magic word," a way to paper over legitimate political relationships and social obligations in the service of the United States' ongoing colonial project, desire for Native land, and adherence to a transactional definition of welfare. Both wardship and welfare were constituted by lived realities and negotiated relationships—the ones that were built and the ones that crumbled.

Chapter 1 examines the history of wardship as a nebulous legal and political term applied to Native people beginning in 1831. For state agents and policymakers, wardship stood in for racialized dependency, solidified the plenary power of the federal government over tribal nations, and justified the restriction of Native people from their receipt of welfare benefits. The advent of citizenship in 1924—and subsequent adaptations of citizenship through passage of major pieces of federal welfare legislation—did not replace wardship as the primary reciprocal relationship between Native people and the United States, but it did add more complications.

Chapter 2 explores the definition of first-class citizenship that emerged in the context of the eleven failed competency bills proposed in the House and Senate between 1944 and 1954. Non-Native terminationist legislators applied the *doxa* of Indian poverty knowledge—the assumptions, stereo-types, and ideologies that undergirded decades of Indian policy research and reform efforts on Native poverty—and their gendered and racialized notions of "independent," "self-sufficient" citizenship to termination policy. Drawing on a long-standing and loaded idea of "competency," these policymakers equated wardship with welfare dependency. Native critics of competency legislation understood wardship as a set of legal and social relationships backed by treaties and agreements between Native nations and the U.S. government. They did not want or need "emancipation" to become first-class citizens, because wardship did not make them dependent. "Emancipating" Native people from ward-ship was essentially a code for the United States abandoning its legal responsibilities to Native nations.

Chapter 3 examines the complexities of wardship as practice, rela-tionships, and behavior. Native people maintained that wardship—as a legal relationship—necessitated that BIA agents facilitate Native people's access to both land rights and political sovereignty. Moreover, they also employed the BIA as a bridge to other governmental agencies, especially to access welfare benefits to which they were entitled. The BIA was an imperfect bridge, as the historical relationship between Native people and the BIA was based on assimilative coercion and control. However, Native people knew BIA agents. And they knew that they might be more likely to find success dealing with other federal bureaucrats if they com-municated their needs *through* the BIA. Although welfare caseworkers and terminationist legislators understood wardship itself to be welfare dependency, Native people maintained that welfare and wardship were distinct, but that the BIA could (and should) play a role in safeguard-ing Native people's access to both. In so doing, they articulated both their rights as American citizens and a vision of midcentury tribal self-determination. Additionally, when the BIA failed to facilitate the receipt of the benefits to which Native people were entitled or when Natives were purposefully shut out by other state agencies, Native people found ways to assert their right to welfare benefits, whether it was through tribal governments, through the courts, or by drawing attention to their records of military service. In so doing, they differentiated between wardship and welfare, claiming both wardship and citizenship as legitimate, mutually exclusive relationships with the U.S. government.

Chapter 4 focuses on how wardship's relationships were gendered by examining the *doxa* of dependency and how it was applied and negotiated by BIA agents, welfare caseworkers, and Native people during and after World War II. Native men and women interacted with the BIA differently—whether they used the BIA as a bridge to obtain welfare benefits or were surveilled by the BIA and other welfare agencies. The Office of Dependency Benefits imbued the BIA with the authority to scrutinize Native women's spending of their dependency allowances. Native servicemen also utilized the BIA to adjudicate family disputes, removing the dependency allowances (and custody of children) from wives who they believed were "squandering" the money, or at least committing adultery. Native women, in turn, utilized their relationships with the BIA to remind (or put pressure on) their family members serving in the military so that they could obtain needed dependency allowances. Native women also tapped BIA personnel to assist them when they faced difficulty accessing Aid to Dependent Children (ADC) benefits. State and county welfare workers also used the BIA to "translate" Native women's eligibility and need. The *doxa* of dependency was applied differently in ADC cases than dependency allowances, as federal legislation and caseworkers reaffirmed a commitment to patriarchal nuclear family units at the expense of Native women's real experiences. Native men also employed the BIA to solidify receipt of benefits of their own under the confines of the GI Bill. While BIA staff were fully invested in facilitating Native veterans' assumption of first-class citizenship, Native men were by no means exempt from assimilative surveillance. Indian poverty knowledge and welfare dependency, operating as twin *doxa*, forced Native people to walk a delicate line between the BIA's advocacy for their rights and oversight of their behavior.

Chapter 5 continues this exploration of the concurrent dynamics of BIA coercion and care through a detailed examination of the way Native veterans accessed the educational provisions of the 1944 GI Bill. The BIA incorporated the larger mission of the GI Bill—facilitating an economically smooth transition from wartime to peacetime by ensuring the employability of individual male breadwinners—into their existing educational programming at Indian boarding schools. Both examples explored in chapter 5, the Cherokee Indian School in Cherokee, North Carolina, which served mainly Eastern Cherokee veterans, and the proposed veterans' training program at the site of the Poston War Relocation Center on the Colorado River Indian Reservation in Parker, Arizona, were organized around principles of "instructional work," where veterans' training overlapped with building and maintenance of each school's physical plant. Both the Veterans Administration and the BIA were concerned with male employment and familial responsibility. The GI Bill, an expansive federal welfare program, coalesced with the assimilative legacy of BIA goals, as both welfare and Indian policies touted the benefits of first-class citizenship: independent, employed male heads of household, imbued with responsibility over their dependent wives and children. However, the relationships that constituted wardship are also not so easily simplified. Native veterans enlisted BIA personnel to access their GI Bill benefits, in part because the benefits were substantially better than vocational training programs administered by the BIA in the early twentieth century. Native veterans were paid for training, and their families received subsistence pay. They could also remain close to their land and families, especially if they accessed their GI Bill educational loans at Indian boarding schools. In the termination era, when non-Native commenters shouted to "let Native people go," Native veterans eagerly embraced the chance to learn, earn, and *stay* in their homelands.

That relationship between Native people and land is the subject of chapter 6. Tribal land, especially in western states hostile to extending state welfare resources to needy Native people, was simultaneously a marker of Native people's ever-present "plight" *and* the immense "privilege" they received as a result of their relationship to the federal government. Chapter 6 demonstrates that the roots of anti-sovereignty organizing and anti-Native racism in the late twentieth century lie in Indian poverty knowledge and anti-welfare conservatives' conflation of wardship with a caricature of perpetual welfare dependency. In this view wardship, like welfare, became a threat to the good citizens of the "taxpaying public." Two main (contradictory) misconceptions worked in tandem to shore up termination policy and reinforce Indian poverty knowledge: Native people were poor—at the hands of an expansive federal government that had oppressed them—though the nation did feel guilty about it; and the federal government's relationship with Native tribes allowed them to take advantage of benefits that other citizens could not get, namely tax exemptions on reservation land held in trust. Both of these misconceptions lacked specificity, nuance, and clarity but were effectively mobilized by those opposed to Native land rights, to Native citizens' access to welfare benefits, and to Native people themselves. Those who willingly misunderstood wardship saw one solution to Native people's "plight" and welfare dependency: first-class citizenship.

Wardship and the Welfare State closes with chapter 7, an examination of wardship and welfare from a relational lens. As an Indigenous framework of understanding the world, relationality, the essential relationships maintained between people and the world around them, including the relationships between Native people and state agents, provides a counterpoint to Indian poverty knowledge. Not only is relationality a political concept, as the "government-to-government" relationship between Native nations and the United States implies, but it is also a concept that cannot be separated from care—the care of kin and individual, family, and tribal welfare. When relationality is applied to the history of welfare policy, we can easily critique how desperately anti-welfare policymakers and members of the public clung to a valorization of first-class citizenship, an individualized and transactional understanding of community membership. Chapter 7 assesses how Native people, particularly prominent Native women organizers such as Helen Peterson and Ruth Bronson, employed the political grammar of the state to communicate a relational definition of both wardship and welfare rights. Critiquing phrases such as "fair play" and the seemingly positive definition of "first-class" citizenship, Native women emphasized the legal legitimacy and social obligations inherent in wardship and welfare. Despite their persistent "care taken to inform" and the relentless care work they performed on behalf of Native nations threatened by termination policy, non-Native legislators often refused to hear their coherent and valuable message.

That message is one we *still* need to hear: the United States should be a better relation to Native people.

In 1961 Helen Peterson wondered whether the United States was "bold enough to permit the survival of governments which do not necessarily conform to the white man's concept of what is an ultimate good." Her question is still relevant, isn't it?

Epilogue

We do and we do not write of treaties, battles, and drums. We do and we do not write about eagles, spirits, and canyons. Native poetry may be those things, but it is not only those things. It is also about grass and apologies, bones and joy, marching bands and genocide, skin and social work, and much more. But who would know?

> —Heid E. Erdrich (Turtle Mountain Ojibwe), introduction to
> *New Poets of Native Nations*, 2018

In *The History of My Brief Body*, Cree poet Billy-Ray Belcourt describes non-Natives' assumptions about perpetual Native poverty as "the abstract you the white woman conjures from a bank of public ideas that are injurious."[1] As a white woman educator, I am committed not only to acknowledging that this "bank of public ideas" exists, but also to interrogating how it may materialize (in injurious ways) in class discussions.

I've taught a diverse array of students across a variety of institutions, but most of them are not Native. When I teach Native American history, I do a lot of unlearning—both intentionally and by necessity. This practice is cultivated by questions my students raise, by confronting (and re-confronting) my own assumptions, and by centering scholarship by Native authors, facilitating discussions about their arguments in my classes. As an educator, I am constantly reinventing my syllabi, inviting students into a mutual (and at times awkward) willingness to unpack some very sticky and complicated ideologies. My students are eager, brilliant, and ready to confront their own assumptions. All of us in the United States are immersed in a cultural and economic worldview shaped by "Indian poverty knowledge," an unwieldy bank of public ideas based on countless surveys, congressional investigations, social work and nonprofit work, and an accumulation of policy decisions and political applications of federal Indian law. Anti-Native racism and colonialism are on our buildings and mountains, in our governing documents, under our feet in the land upon which we walk, live, and learn. We also invariably drink up a powerful message about an "American Dream" accessible to all who can work hard enough. We denigrate and shame poor people. We assign poverty moral significance. As *Wardship and the Welfare State* argues, anti-Native racism, buttressed by Indian poverty knowledge, and a deep American ambivalence about all poor people have a long history as mutually reinforcing iterations of what we understand to be "common sense." Native people are poor. Even in the twenty-first century this is not a controversial statement among the general populace. But it should be.

We know this "common sense" when we see it. And we *like* to take photos of it—artful depictions of destitution, beauty in the "squalor," resilience through "hardship." These photos awaken a desire, also rooted in the "American Dream," to smooth away the chips in equality's facade. We don't like seeing "second-class citizens." But we can't help but blame them a little too. Because if we don't, we might have to admit that some of us benefit from poverty and colonialism, even as others suffer. As Saidiya Hartman asks, "Are we witnesses who confirm the truth of what happened in the face of the world-destroying capacities of pain," or "are we voyeurs fascinated with and repelled by exhibitions of terror and sufferance?"[2] Witness or voyeur? Participant or observer? Maybe both?

In fall 2020 I taught a course called "Native Americans and American Politics." I designed a whole week of instruction around the "Politicization of Poverty." I assigned two texts—an article published in a 1948 issue of *Look* magazine by Will Rogers Jr. on Navajo poverty, "Starvation without Representation," and a set of photos of Oglala Lakota people on the Pine Ridge Reservation by Aaron Huey published in 2012 by *National*

Geographic. In my mind these two texts would work well together, and the Indian poverty knowledge they evoked would be clear. I wanted students to dig into Rogers's text and accompanying photos of crying Navajo children alongside Huey's photographs and examine how depictions of Native poverty have remained so static over six decades. I wanted us to get into a discussion about how often it is that non-Native observers and mainstream media outlets "discover" Native poverty, as if Native people were kept secluded and hidden in poverty pockets of their own making. I wanted us to get into the assumption, as historian Margaret Jacobs has written, that "for most Americans, the glass of modern Indian life is empty of all but pain, suffering, and misery." And, I wanted us to consider Jacobs's counterpoint: "But what if we saw it as half full?"[3]

It was harder for us to do this than I thought it would be. Students were quicker to critique the word choice, captions, and photos in the 1948 *Look* article than they were to critique Huey's twenty-first-century photographs. The 1948 article opens with a half-page photograph of a crying Navajo child, clad in two blankets, standing in the snow without shoes. The caption pulls no punches: "Barefooted and virtually naked on the snow-strewn mesa, this unhappy Navaho Indian baby stands as an indictment of our cruel neglect of his people."[4] The reactions of the class varied. Some were understandably distressed by the way Navajo families were presented in the article. Many were frustrated at the inaction of Congress, one of Rogers's main arguments in the piece. A discussion emerged in our collaborative annotations about whether the naked crying baby photo was staged. Even if the photo "was probably staged by the photographer," one student wrote, "it's still kind of cruel to make a child wear so little in such weather." Another replied, "how could the photographer just snap the picture and feel fine?" This image is a difficult one. Paired with the caption, it is blatantly exploitative—indeed, the child "stands as an indictment" of colonialism! But who was the target of our complicated feelings? The child, for whom we might feel sadness or empathy; the child's family, for whom we might feel grief or sorrow or anger; the government, who has caused this suffering; or the photographer and magazine, whose presence may have aggravated the child so much it became upset? Or maybe we feel helplessness, guilt, and discomfort, looking back on an incident captured over seventy years ago?

One other photograph caught the eye of analytical students: a woman and three young children, two standing in front of her, and one in her arms. The caption reads, "The ragged family who live in this hut of timber and sod typify the primitive life of some 60,000 other Navahos."[5] This sort of caption and photograph are a familiar recapitulation of what Margaret Jacobs calls the "plight narrative," which I discuss in detail in chapter 6.[6] Students caught this framework quickly: "Really generalizing to call 60,000 Navajo ragged and primitive, not to mention demeaning," one wrote. Another remarked, "This is not an accurate portrayal or at least one that is well-rounded of Native issues," while another replied, "From the picture they chose to the headlines and bylines, it all just seems to be about the plight narrative."

The plight narrative is alive and well. The August 2012 *National Geographic* issue featured Aaron Huey's photographs from his time spent on the Pine Ridge Reservation in South Dakota and an article by Alexandra Fuller, "In the Shadow of Wounded Knee." The collection of photographs was not without controversy. Huey first published about half of the photographs on the *New York Times* "*Lens*" blog in 2009, where they appeared alongside an interview Huey gave to James Estrin and the headline "Behind the Scenes: Still Wounded."[7] Poverty was Huey's unmistakable, unapologetic focus of the first set of photographs. Huey had embarked on a "self-assigned photographic road trip to document poverty in America" but didn't make it farther than Pine Ridge. "My photos are a witness, not a solution. They are the dark and the light and every struggle between," Huey stated. The "struggle" Huey documented prompted conflicting feelings of sadness, guilt, and anger. In response to Estrin's question, "How about the children?" Huey responded:

> I remember calling home to my wife crying because I had just held a beautiful 3-year-old girl on my knee. She hugged me and called me uncle, and I love her so much. But I know that it is only a matter of time until she is broken. Soon she will be drinking, and pregnant, and abused, and dying. Right now she is still perfect, but no one can last in an environment

like that. That's the part I hate. Knowing that there is nothing I can do to change it . . . I know for sure that change has to come from within the reservation. It cannot be imported. I cannot run away with these children. Someone in their own town has to lead them, preferably someone from within their own home.[8]

Huey's emotional experience cannot be divorced from his whiteness and the long history of white interlopers who stumble upon Native poverty and engage with a desire to "run away with these children." This kind of language demands interrogation, not in the least because throughout the twentieth century, running away with children was very much the *government policy*—Native children were removed from their relatives and placed into boarding schools, foster homes, and non-Native adoptive families.[9] They were removed because white social workers and religious organizations and AmeriCorps volunteers and adoptive parents saw the "future," just like Huey: "*it is only a matter of time until she is broken.*"

Huey's photographs and the *Lens* interview received criticism, especially from Oglala Lakota readers. In August 2012 James Estrin wrote a new piece for *Lens*, detailing the responses, focusing on how, while "no one suggested that the images failed to portray important problems that exist on the reservation . . . some thought it was an incomplete view."[10] Estrin touted Huey's willingness to "listen and learn" from the critiques he received. "Mr. Huey's reaction was different than most photographers facing the disapproval of their subjects. He returned to the Pine Ridge reservation. And listened. A lot."[11] Huey felt that the story was incomplete too, that "the stories that [the photographs] were trying to tell . . . had not been heard," and that to do so, he would "have to go into much more traditional communities and photograph people who were not, at this point, likely to be open to him."[12] Huey published an updated collection of photographs in *National Geographic* and launched the Pine Ridge Community Storytelling Project, supported by a prestigious John S. Knight Journalism Fellowship from Stanford University.[13] The project was administered through the website Cowbird and embedded on the *National Geographic* website. Ten years after it first appeared, it is no longer available on *National Geographic*. The Cowbird site remained active until Cowbird stopped maintaining their digital archive in 2022.[14] The site contained 258 stories, including photographs and short text segments, from 105 Oglala Lakota contributors. Huey also collaborated with artist Shepard Fairey to design and print thousands of posters and billboards in a public art installation project focused on the failure of the United States government to uphold the terms of the Fort Laramie Treaties of 1851 and 1868.[15] Huey's 2010 TED talk, "America's Native Prisoners of War," has been viewed over 1.9 million times.[16] He ended the TED talk with this statement: "The United States continues on a daily basis to violate the terms of the 1851 and 1868 Fort Laramie Treaties with the Lakota. The call to action I offer today—my TED wish—is this: Honor the Treaties. Give back the Black Hills. It's not your business what they do with them."[17]

It seems like quite the turnaround for Huey—from holding a three-year-old on his knee and envisioning her future as alcoholic, abused, pregnant, and broken, to standing on a national stage proclaiming we need to "Honor the Treaties." But still, *the plight narrative is alive and well.* Though the revised photo spread in *National Geographic* is a much more varied presentation of Pine Ridge, including photographs of sacred ceremonies, teenage couples spending time together, and families gathered in their neighborhood, many of the original photographs from 2009 remain.[18] Instead of complete dysfunction, gang violence, and desperation, the new photo spread depicts dysfunction, gang violence, desperation, *and* ceremonies, families, horses, and traditions. The tagline of Alexandra Fuller's article that accompanies the photographs describes Huey's work as "a rare, intimate portrait [that] shows their resilience in the face of hardship."[19] What do we get if the cup is half full of hardship *and* half full of resilience? One of the most striking photographs included in the 2012 spread was taken by Huey in 2008 and depicts C. J. Shot, then three years old, who is bathing in a kitchen sink. An adult woman is visible in the next room, looking at her phone at the table, a plate of food in view. The kitchen counter is crowded with dishes, empty aluminum soda cans, and plastic cups. The caption reads, "Three-year-old C. J. Shot bathes among dishes. The Oglala concept of *tiospaye*—the unity of the extended family—means that homes are often overcrowded, especially with the severe housing shortage on the reservation. In 2008, when this photograph was made, 22 people lived in the three-bedroom house. 'These houses aren't who we are,' says Oglala activist Alex White Plume."[20] This caption contains multitudes. Shot appears to be the familiar lone Native child; although we can see an adult, Shot is alone in the sink. The caption introduces the term *tiospaye*—the only time this term is used in the piece at all—but in the same breath, implies that this concept is at least part of the reason for inadequate housing and overcrowding.[21] What comes through, despite the words of Alex White Plume, is poverty, the ever-persistent plight.

My students saw the collection of photos at Huey's website, without the accompanying article. The majority were much less likely to critique the plight narrative as distilled by Huey's images compared to the critiques generated by the *Look* magazine article from 1948. Descriptions from the collective annotations indicated that students saw in Huey's images a "depiction of the poverty and pain inflicted upon Natives," and in the Native subjects' facial expressions, "particularly children," an indication "that they're not ok with this." One student called out the resilience through hardship narrative: "While there is a mix of poverty/ hardship and beauty/resilience, I feel that the album as a whole focuses more on the poverty and hardship of the Natives." Another astutely wrote, "I assume that the goal was to make the reader upset at some level, and perhaps the collection should have featured some smiles somewhere."[22]

To his credit, Huey changed his approach after receiving criticism. His 2012 *National Geographic* photographs, with their mixture of "poverty/ hardship and beauty/resilience," opened up an opportunity for discussion of how Native people's lives are represented or consumed by mainstream American viewers. He is not the first—nor will he be the last—white or non-Native photographer to publish images of stoic Native beauty amid overwhelming poverty. Yet it is worth considering the partially clothed crying Navajo baby who "stood as an indictment of our cruel neglect" in 1948 alongside the photograph of C. J. Shot, just one member of a larger Oglala Lakota *tiospaye*, bathing in the sink. It seems that non-Native viewers are much more likely to accept the photographs that "stand as indictments" of poverty, disease, alcoholism, and neglect than we are to accept the photographs that celebrate family, friendship, ceremony, and joy. But the "indictment photograph" (of which there are many in the *National Geographic* spread) has long outlasted its shelf life. In 2014 Swinomish and Tulalip photographer and teacher Matika Wilbur noted in an interview with the *Santa Fe Reporter*: "I think that we have enough images that talk about the poverty, the struggle, the suicide, and I don't know if that actually helps our kids. One time I showed my students at the high school Aaron Huey's TED Talk, and you should have seen how deflated they were afterwards. I saw it with my own eyes. I watched them deflate."[23]

> Yet I feel forced to decide if *poor* really means brittle hands dust and candy-stained mouths a neighbor girl's teeth convenience store shelves Hamburger Helper a dog's matted fur a van seat pulled to the living room floor those children playing in the carcass of a car mice on the floor-board my sweeping chill hantavirus the ripe smell a horse chewed ripped its backbone exposed the swarms of do-gooders their goodly photos . . .
>
> I agree to let meanings and arguments with my head thrust into the punctuation of poverty here, breathe.
>
> —Layli Long Soldier (Oglala Lakota), "Waȟpánič̣a," 2017

My student's comment—*perhaps the collection should have featured some smiles somewhere*—says a lot about the sentiment behind the *National Geographic* spread as well as the ways in which the concepts of Indian poverty knowledge, welfare dependency, and wardship are still ingrained in mainstream media coverage of Native people and of the way that non-Native American audiences perceive Native life. Vine Deloria's 1969 classic *Custer Died for Your Sins* has an entire chapter devoted to "Indian humor." "One of the best ways to understand a people is to know what makes them laugh," he wrote. "People have little sympathy with stolid groups."[24] Moreover, Deloria historicized humor, explained how it could be used to find solutions to difficult problems, and argued that "any kind of movement," especially one that was pan-tribal, "would be impossible" without humor as a unifying thread. Humor could be a way to "awaken" an audience and "bring them to a militant edge."[25] In the *National Geographic* article, Fuller mentioned laughter, but only as further evidence of resilience through hardship, or maybe less generously, to suggest a timeless Lakota helplessness in the face of that hardship. Of her interview with Alex White Plume, Fuller wrote, "Then he laughed in the way of a man who knows that he cannot be defeated by ordinary disappointments."[26] But this view of White Plume's laughter both flattens his experiences and the care he took to inform Fuller and *National Geographic* readers of Lakota history. The "ordinary disappointments" Fuller referenced were violations of Oglala Lakota sovereignty. Fuller goes on to describe White Plume's "oddly unexcited view of history's injustices," which he "punctuated with laughter but also with pauses long enough to roll a cigarette."[27] Despite the interviews she conducted and the history she recounts, Fuller's article is one-dimensional. Impoverishment, rooted in both historical injustice and contemporary tragedy, is ever-present, always lurking in the background. Fuller's text and Huey's photographs are part of, as Long Soldier writes in the poem quoted above, "the swarms of do-gooders their goodly photos."[28] Readers and viewers never get the chance to breathe into the "punctuation of poverty." Despite White Plume's long pauses, the article contains no *pause* for the outsiders looking in—just a straight highway of tragedy, uncomfortable "fascination and repulsion," to echo Saidiya Hartman, that we want to get through as quickly as possible. Quick! Someone get the solution! "Emancipate" Native people! "Let them go!" "Set them free!"

Elsewhere in "Waȟpánič̌a," Long Soldier writes: *I intend the comma to mean what we do possess.*[29] Far from a flattened acceptance of "history's injustices," White Plume's "unexcited view" may instead be evidence of a deeper self-reflexiveness, an understanding of what Fuller expected, what he and other Lakota interviewees may have wanted non-Native readers to find in the article, and the long-standing relationships that Pine Ridge citizens have with the U.S. government, with the non-Native media, and with their own relatives. As the chapters in this book show, non-Natives have been quick to appraise wardship and Native people's inability to access first-class citizenship without fully examining or understanding the relational aspects of wardship and the dynamics between the United States and tribal governments or between individual Native people and state agents. Undoubtedly "history" has dealt Native people many injustices. But what should be just as obvious is that Native people fully understand what those injustices were, who perpetrated them, and why they continue to matter.

> I often counseled people to run for the Bureau of Indian Affairs in case of an earthquake because nothing could shake the BIA.
>
> Columbus didn't know where he was going, didn't know where he had been, and did it all on someone else's money. And the white man has been following Columbus ever since.
>
> —Vine Deloria (Standing Rock Sioux), *Custer Died for Your Sins*, 1969

What if we saw modern Native life—historically rooted in creativity, humor, relationality, an astute use of political grammar to negotiate with those in power, a self-reflexive acknowledgment of how Natives are seen by non-Natives, and how Native people understand themselves—what if we saw *all* of that, and saw it as *half full*?

NOTES

NOTE ON TERMINOLOGY

1. Mihesuah, *So You Want to Write*, xi.

INTRODUCTION

1. Bureau of Indian Affairs, "Answers to Your Questions," 20.
2. Bureau of Indian Affairs, "Answers to Your Questions," 16–17, 20–21, 24–29, 31.
3. Bureau of Indian Affairs, "Answers to Your Questions," 13.
4. I used Google Books Ngram Viewer, accessed at https://books.google.com/ngrams, to graph the appearance of the phrases "first-class citizenship" and "first class citizenship" (without the hyphen), and I noticed a strikingly clear increase in the use of these terms after 1940, peaking just after 1960. Additionally, I conducted searches through ProQuest Congressional to get a sense of how often this terminology came up in the *Congressional Record* and testimonies. The results were similar to the Google Ngram results, in that the term doesn't appear as a signifier of political and social citizenship until the 1940s. I have found instances of "first-class" being used as an adjective earlier in the twentieth century, but mainly just as a way to signal "great" or "stand-up," as in "He's a first-class citizen!"
5. For example, in her analysis of women's citizenship before and after the Nineteenth Amendment and the fight for jury service, Gretchen Ritter notes that "first class" or "full" citizens are understood to possess the highest level of civic status, including voting rights, jury service, and civil rights. Ritter, "Jury Service and Women's Citizenship," 482–83.

6. Oklahoma v. Castro-Huerta, 597 U.S. 20 (2022), emphasis added. In his dissent Justice Neil Gorsuch points out the majority's obvious paternalism, targeting the "second-class citizenship" idea specifically.

7. Council of Laguna Pueblo Resolution on H.R. 4985, December 12, 1953, NCAI, Series 4, Tribal Files, Box 111, Folder: Tribal Files Laguna (Pueblo, New Mexico), 1948–1961, NMAI.

8. Council of Laguna Pueblo Resolution on H.R. 4985, December 12, 1953.

9. Scholars have shown that citizens who accessed needs-based welfare benefits under programs highly susceptible to changing public opinion and local norms were also more likely to be scrutinized and policed, in case they were "undeserving" of such benefits. See Katz, *Undeserving Poor*; Gordon, *Pitied but Not Entitled*; Odem, *Delinquent Daughters*; Mink, *Wages of Motherhood*; Shah, *Contagious Divides*; Orleck, *Storming Caesar's Palace*.

10. Canaday, *Straight State*, 5.

11. Molina, "Race All Their Own," 168.

12. For more on the men and women who worked for the BIA, see Cahill, *Federal Fathers and Mothers*; Lambert, *Native Agency*.

13. Bureau of Indian Affairs, "Answers to Your Questions," 30.

14. Kessler-Harris, *In Pursuit of Equity*, 4.

15. Kessler-Harris, *In Pursuit of Equity*, 4.

16. Chappell, *War on Welfare*, 16.

17. Mittelstadt, *From Welfare to Workfare*, 59.

18. Mittelstadt, *From Welfare to Workfare*, 7.

19. Porter, "Demise of the *Ongwehoweh*," 108–9.

20. See Simonsen, *Making Home Work*; Margaret D. Jacobs, *White Mother*; Mitchell, *Coyote Nation*; Hoxie, *Final Promise*; Chang, *Color of the Land*.

21. Stremlau, *Sustaining the Cherokee Family*, 128.

22. Pommersheim, *Broken Landscape*, 163.

23. Hoxie, *Final Promise*, x.

24. Hoxie, *Final Promise*, xi.

25. See Ngai, *Impossible Subjects*; Molina, *Fit to Be Citizens?*; Haney-López, *White by Law*; Lee, *At America's Gates*; Roediger, *Working toward Whiteness*.

26. Wilkerson, *To Live Here*, 6.

27. Nadasen, *Welfare Warriors*, 14–15, xvii. See also Orleck, *Storming Caesar's Palace*; Rhonda Williams, *Politics of Public Housing*.

28. Nadasen, *Welfare Warriors*, 104.

29. L. Cohen, *Making a New Deal*, 289. See also Meg Jacobs, *Pocketbook Politics*.

30. O'Connor, *Poverty Knowledge*.

31. Fraser and Gordon, "A Genealogy of Dependency," 310–11.

32. Myles, "An American Poem."

33. See, for example, Barkley Brown, "Negotiating and Transforming," 124.

34. Long Soldier, *Whereas*, 50–51.

1. RED TAPE

1. See Kerber, *No Constitutional Right*, 24; Field, *Struggle for Equal Adulthood*, 8–9; Field, "Frances E. W. Harper," 112.

2. Risling Baldy, *We Are Dancing for You*, 63–64.

3. Ellinghaus, *Blood Will Tell*, 53.

4. Long Soldier, *Whereas*, 57.

5. Zitkala-Ša, "Red Men Who Taught Pilgrims How to Exist," in *Help Indians Help Themselves*, 174.

6. Frickey, "Marshalling Past and Present," 392.

7. See Bruyneel, *Third Space of Sovereignty*, xvi.

8. Pommersheim, *Broken Landscape*, 105.

9. Berger, "Red," 603–17. See also Williams, *Like a Loaded Weapon*.

10. The crimes covered by the Major Crimes Act were murder, manslaughter, rape, assault with intent to kill, arson, burglary, and larceny.

11. Bruyneel, *Third Space of Sovereignty*, 81, emphasis added.

12. Lone Wolf, principal chief of the Kiowa, sued the government for implementing an agreement to allot the Kiowa and Comanche reservation. While Congress had approved the agreement, the Kiowas and Comanches had not, citing the provisions of the 1868 Treaty of Medicine Lodge Creek, which "stipulated that all land cessions must be approved by the tribe." The Supreme Court ruled that Congress had the right to abrogate existing treaties with Native tribes, and that allotment could be carried out without tribal approval. The court used wardship to support the decision. Justice Edward Douglas White asserted: "The Indian tribes are the wards of the nation. They are communities dependent on the United States." The court recognized the role of the federal government in creating this "dependent" population but reinforced wardship and reemphasized the responsibility of the government to protect Indian people. Chief Justice White wrote, "From their very weakness and helplessness, so largely due to the course of dealing of the Federal government with them and the treaties in which it has been promised, there arises the duty of protection, and, with it, the power." Essentially, wardship was a foil for divesting Natives of land. Because Congress had plenary power over Native wards, allotment could be carried out without tribal consent. See Hoxie, *Final Promise*, 154–55; Porter, "Demise of the *Ongwehoweh*," 132. The relationship between the history of allotment, wardship, and first-class citizenship is addressed in chapter 2.

13. See Pommersheim, *Broken Landscape*, 164–66.

14. Porter, "Demise of the *Ongwehoweh*," 133.
15. Pommersheim, *Broken Landscape*, 166.
16. Porter, "Demise of the *Ongwehoweh*," 134.
17. *United States v. Nice* was a conflict over the federal regulations regarding sale of liquor to Native people. For more, see Porter, "Demise of the *Ongwehoweh*," 134–35; Pommersheim, *Broken Landscape*, 169.
18. In 1919 Native men who had served the United States in World War I were granted a path to citizenship. However, as Gary Stein asserts, few Native veterans took advantage of this option. See Stein, "Indian Citizenship Act of 1924," 264.
19. Indian Citizenship Act of 1924, Pub. L. No. 68-175 Stat. 253 (1924).
20. Bruyneel, "Challenging American Boundaries," 33.
21. Stein, "Indian Citizenship Act," 266. Thomas Grillot traces the Republican Party's political calculations behind the Indian Citizenship Act and the its connections to recognition of Native World War I veterans in *First Americans*, 167–70.
22. Capozzola, "Legacies for Citizenship," 725; for more on the Johnson-Reed Act see Ngai, *Impossible Subjects*.
23. Many Native critics of the ICA thought so too. See Bruyneel, "Challenging American Boundaries" for more.
24. Bruyneel, "Challenging American Boundaries," 31; Capozzola, "Legacies for Citizenship," 725.
25. Webb Opinion on Indian Eligibility 1936, Social Security Legislation Correspondence, Box 168, CRCC Files, Records of the Bureau of Indian Affairs, RG 75, NARA–Pacific Region (R).
26. Office of the Solicitor of the Department of the Interior, "The Applicability of the Social Security Act to the Indians," 1936, Social Security Legislation Correspondence, Box 168, CRCC Files, RG 75, NARA–Pacific Region (R).
27. Indeed, wardship was used as a rationale to restrict Native voting rights, especially in western states. For more, see McCool, Olson, and Robinson, *Native Vote*; McDonald, *American Indians*; Rollings, "Citizenship and Suffrage."
28. Some scholars refer to the IRA as the "tribal alternative." Rusco, *Fateful Time*, 115–16. Rusco borrows the term from Taylor, *New Deal*.
29. The concept of "self-government" has been critiqued by scholars who argue that it is not a "Native idea" but rather provides a limited means for tribes to exercise local control and responsibility within the U.S. political sphere. However, because of this characterization, self-government has proved to be a useful concept for Native people to use when dealing with government officials, because it provides a "context within which negotiations can take place." See Deloria and Lytle, *Nations Within*, 15.
30. Nelson and Shelley, "Bureau of Indian Affairs Influence," 182; Rusco, *Fateful Time*, xi, n. 7.

31. See Deloria and Lytle, *Nations Within*, 73; Philp, *John Collier's Crusade for Indian Reform*; Rusco, *A Fateful Time*.
32. Deloria and Lytle, *Nations Within*, 71.
33. Deloria and Lytle, *Nations Within*, 67, emphasis added.
34. For more on the critiques of the IRA as communism see Philp, *John Collier's Crusade*, 172; Taylor, *New Deal*.
35. Press Release on Opposition to Wheeler Howard Bill, Series III—Commissioner's Subject File, Part II—1933-1945, John Collier Papers (University Microfilms International, Reel 30), Arizona State University Law Library.
36. Press Release on Opposition to Wheeler Howard Bill.
37. Press Release on Opposition to Wheeler Howard Bill. The IRA was not the first piece of Indian policy legislation to be hailed by government agents as the Native "Emancipation Proclamation." The Dawes Act was similarly delineated in this manner, and Native students at boarding schools observed "Emancipation Day" on its anniversary. See Simonsen, "Object Lessons."
38. Deloria and Lytle, *Nations Within*, 84.
39. Deloria and Lytle, *Nations Within*, 85.
40. See Ellinghaus, *Blood Will Tell*, 74.
41. Deloria and Lytle, *Nations Within*, 85.
42. Fixico, *Termination and Relocation*, 76–77.
43. Fixico, *Termination and Relocation*, 112, 147; Deloria and Lytle, *Nations Within*, 199. See also Rosenthal, *Reimagining Indian Country*; Ramirez, *Native Hubs*; Goeman, *Mark My Words*; Miller, *Indians on the Move*; Keeler, "Putting People Where They Belong;" Blansett, Cahill, and Needham, *Indian Cities*.
44. Report of the Committee on Indian Affairs 1948, 54, Indians—Report of the Committee on Indian Affairs to Commission on Organization of the Executive Branch of the Government, October 1948 (1 of 3), Box 43, PNWH, HSTL.
45. Report of the Committee on Indian Affairs, 54.
46. Report of the Committee on Indian Affairs, 56.
47. Report of the Committee on Indian Affairs, 59.
48. House Concurrent Resolution 108, 67 Stat. B122 (1953).
49. See Fixico, *Termination and Relocation*; Philp, *Termination Revisited*; Arnold, *Bartering with the Bones*; Puisto, *"This Is My Reservation"*; Beck, *Struggle for Self-Determination*; A. Deer, *Making a Difference*.
50. House Concurrent Resolution 108. See also Harmon, *Rich Indians*, 214.
51. Virgil K. Whitaker, chapter 1, "Pictures and Policy," 24–25, Report of the Commission on the Rights, Liberties, and Responsibilities of the American Indian, 1959, Memo #110—Memorandum to Accompany Chapter 1 of Commission Report 11-11-59, Box 72, William Brophy Commission on the Rights, Liberties, and Responsibilities of the Indian Papers, HSTL.

52. Gale Courey Toensing, "Are American Indian Nations 'Wards of the Federal Government?,'" *Indian Country Today*, December 19, 2014 (updated September 13, 2018), https://ictnews.org/archive/are-american-indian-nations-wards-of-the-federal-government.

53. Toensing, "Are American Indian Nations 'Wards'?"

54. Felicia Fonseca, "Rep. Gosar's Native American Remark Causes Outcry," *AZ Central*, December 11, 2014, https://www.azcentral.com/story/news/arizona/politics/2014/12/11/congressmans-native-american-remark-causes-outcry/20258071/.

55. Fonseca, "Rep. Gosar's Native American Remark."

56. Toensing, "Are American Indian Nations 'Wards'?"

57. United States Department of the Interior, Indian Affairs, "Our Nation's American Indian and Alaska Native Citizens," Frequently Asked Questions, modified August 19, 2017, https://www.bia.gov/frequently-asked-questions.

58. Rosier, *Serving Their Country*, 70.

59. L. Cohen, *Making a New Deal*, 285. See also Sparrow, *Warfare State*, 4, 14; Meg Jacobs, *Pocketbook Politics*, 220.

60. Tani, *States of Dependency*, 8.

61. Fox, *Three Worlds of Relief*, 3.

62. Mettler, *Dividing Citizens*, 3.

63. See Mettler, *Dividing Citizens*; Gordon, *Pitied but Not Entitled*; Skocpol, *Protecting Soldiers and Mothers*.

64. See Mettler, *Dividing Citizens*; Katznelson, *When Affirmative Action Was White*; Poole, *Segregated Origins of Social Security*.

65. Chappell, *War on Welfare*, 10.

66. Poole, *Segregated Origins of Social Security*, 11.

67. Tani, "States' Rights, Welfare Rights." See also Tani's chapter "Claiming Welfare Rights: Fair Hearings, State-Court Claims, and a Forgotten Federal Case," in *States of Dependency*, which discusses Native claims to welfare alongside other groups.

68. See Deloria and Lytle, *Nations Within*, 144–49.

69. Native people also participated in other well-known New Deal public programs. See, for example, Parman, "Indians and the Civilian Conservation Corps"; Rosenthal, "Painting Native America in Public."

70. Monthly Allowances for the Dependents of Soldiers Pamphlet, Veteran's Rehabilitation, Box 165, CRCC Files, RG 75, NARA–Pacific Region (R).

71. Hickel, "War, Region, and Social Welfare," 1364. For a discussion of subsistence allowances and the concept of "military families" in the late twentieth century's all-volunteer army, see Mittelstadt, *Rise of the Military Welfare State*.

72. Mettler, *Soldiers to Citizens*, 6; Altschuler and Blumin, *GI Bill*, 71. On the longer history of the United States government providing social benefits for veterans, see Skocpol, *Protecting Soldiers and Mothers*.

73. Mettler, *Soldiers to Citizens*, 6–7.
74. Mettler, *Soldiers to Citizens*, 6. Lizabeth Cohen notes that combined with the Korean GI Bill, the legislation is responsible for financing of one-fifth of all single-family residences by 1966. See Cohen, *Consumers' Republic*, 141. For composition of American colleges, see Cohen, *Consumers' Republic*, 140.
75. Altschuler and Blumin, *GI Bill*, 83.
76. L. Cohen, *Consumers' Republic*, 137.
77. Altschuler and Blumin, *GI Bill*, 121–23; L. Cohen, *Consumers' Republic*, 138–39; Mettler, *Soldiers to Citizens*, 144–50.
78. Altschuler and Blumin, *GI Bill*, 134.
79. Mettler, *Soldiers to Citizens*, 56.
80. Mettler, *Soldiers to Citizens*, 53, 55.
81. Katznelson, *When Affirmative Action Was White*, 123.
82. An important exception is Keeler, "Putting People Where They Belong."
83. Carroll, *Medicine Bags and Dog Tags*, 6. For example, in the first book-length work on Native participation in World War II, Alison Bernstein contended that Native veterans' "sudden and unprecedented exposure to the white world contributed to a new consciousness of what it meant to be an American Indian, and a sharpened awareness of the gap between the standard of living on most reservations and in the rest of American society." Bernstein, *American Indians*, 17. Kenneth Townsend claimed that many Native people "perceived their involvement in the nation's war effort as the final step toward full assimilation with white society." Townsend, *World War II*, 3.
84. See Townsend, *World War II*, 215–21, 228; Bernstein, *American Indians*, 171–73. See also Franco, *Crossing the Pond*, 198–200. Franco argues that service to the country in World War II laid the groundwork for "an increase in civil rights among Native Americans," including the occupation of Alcatraz and BIA buildings in the late 1960s and early 1970s.
85. Carroll, *Medicine Bags*, 134.
86. Rosier, *Serving Their Country*, 9.
87. Riseman, *Defending Whose Country?*, 27.
88. Keeler, "Putting People Where They Belong," 71.
89. Zitkala-Ša, "Americanize the First Americans" (1920), in *Help Indians Help Themselves*, 106–7.
90. Zitkala-Ša, "Americanize the First Americans," 107.

2. INDIAN POVERTY KNOWLEDGE

1. Select Committee to Investigate Indian Affairs and Conditions in the United States, An Investigation to Determine Whether the Changed Status of the Indian Requires a Revision of the Laws and Regulations Affecting the American Indian

(H.R. 166), H.R. Rep. No. 2091, at 2 (1944), Folder 19, Congressional Report Addressing Changed Status of American Indian 1944, Box 16, William Zimmerman Papers, CSR-UNM.

2. Committee on Interior and Insular Affairs, Report to Accompany H.R. 4985, Providing a Certificate or Decree of Competency for United States Indians in Certain Cases, H.R. Rep. No. 836, at 7 (1953), NCAI, Series 6, Committees and Special Issues Files, Box 256, Federal Indian Policy and Legislation Files, Competency Bill (H.R. 4985), NMAI.

3. Larry Burt has stated that "conservatives gave the term 'ward' a welfare connotation in describing native dependence on material aid and services from the federal government," and Daniel Cobb has noted that by the end of World War II a number of policymakers compared the trust relationship between tribes and the federal government to "a socialistic welfare system that not only fostered dependency but betrayed American values of liberty, democracy, and individualism." Burt, *Tribalism in Crisis*, 20–21; Cobb, *Native Activism*, 12.

4. Katherine Ellinghaus notes that the "legal status of competency" was created by the 1906 Burke Act, which modified the process of releasing allotments from trust restrictions to allow individual Natives to obtain fee patents after "an application process that supposedly measured their level of acculturation and business acumen." See Ellinghaus, *Blood Will Tell*, 46. Legislators continued to propose emancipation bills in the early twentieth century both before and after the passage of the Indian Citizenship Act in 1924. In 1916 and 1917 Senator Harry Lane (D-OR) proposed two bills that would have bestowed citizenship upon Native people who had already received or would receive allotments, and reorganized the BIA "with a view to its speedy abolition." Bill for the Abolishment of the Indian Bureau, the Closing Out of Indian Tribal Organizations, and for Other Purposes, S. 4452, 64th Cong. (1916); Bill for the Abolishment of the Indian Bureau, the Closing Out of Indian Tribal Organizations, and for Other Purposes, S. 415, 65th Cong. (1917). After the passage of the Indian Citizenship Act, Representative John McGroarty (D-CA) proposed two joint resolutions in the House of Representatives in 1936 and 1937 that would have created an "Indian Emancipation Commission," with an eye to abolishing the BIA, annulling existing treaties, and transferring property to individual Native people. Bill to Abolish the Bureau of Indian Affairs, to Abolish the Office of Commissioner of Indian Affairs, to Create an Indian Emancipation Commission, and for Other Purposes, H.J. Res. 506, 74th Cong. (1936); Bill to Abolish the Bureau of Indian Affairs, to Abolish the Office of Commissioner of Indian Affairs, to Create an Indian Emancipation Commission, and for Other Purposes, H.J. Res. 114, 75th Cong. (1937).

5. See, for example, Ellinghaus, *Blood Will Tell*; Stremlau, *Sustaining the Cherokee Family*; Chang, *Color of the Land*; Barker, *Native Acts*. For more on blood quantum and competency and Osage citizenship, see Dennison, *Colonial Entanglements*.
6. See, for example, Philp, *Termination Revisited*, 76; Grillot, *First Americans*, 219–21; Fixico, *Termination and Relocation*, 58.
7. Adams, *Who Belongs?*, 17.
8. Barker, *Native Acts*, 89.
9. The bills included Bill to Emancipate the Indians of the United States, H.R. 5115, 78th Cong. (1944); Bill to Provide for Removal of Restrictions on Property of Indians Who Serve in the Armed Forces, H.R. 3681, 79th Cong. (1945); Bill to Emancipate Certain Indians of the United States Who Served in the Armed Forces During World War I and World War II, H.R. 2165, 80th Cong. (1947); Bill to Emancipate the Indians of the United States and to Establish Certain Rights for Indians and Indian Tribes, H.R. 2958, 80th Cong. (1947); Act to Emancipate United States Indians in Certain Cases, H.R. 1113, 80th Cong. (1947); Bill to Emancipate United States Indians in Certain Cases, S. 186, 81st Cong. (1949); Bill to Provide a Decree of Competency for United States Indians in Certain Cases, H.R. 2724, 81st Cong. (1949); Bill to Provide a Decree of Competency for United States Indians in Certain Cases, H.R. 457, 82nd Cong. (1951); Bill to Provide a Decree of Competency for United States Indians in Certain Cases, S. 485, 82nd Cong. (1951); Bill to Provide a Decree of Competency for United States Indians in Certain Cases, S. 335, 83rd Cong. (1953); and Bill to Provide a Decree of Competency for United States Indians in Certain Cases, H.R. 4985, 83rd Cong. (1954).
10. The only bill to pass the House was H.R. 1113 in 1947. See Philp, *Termination Revisited*, 76.
11. Act to Emancipate United States Indians in Certain Cases, H.R. 1113, 80th Cong. (1947). The subsequent bills included S. 186 (1949), H.R. 2724 (1949), H.R. 457 (1951), S. 485 (1951), and S. 335 (1953).
12. Committee on Interior and Insular Affairs, Report to Accompany H.R. 4985, Providing a Certificate or Decree of Competency for United States Indians in Certain Cases, H.R. Rep. No. 836, at 9 (1953); NCAI, Series 6, Committees and Special Issues Files, Box 256, Federal Indian Policy and Legislation Files, Competency Bill (H.R. 4985); NMAI.
13. Committee on Interior and Insular Affairs, Report to Accompany H.R. 4985.
14. O'Connor, *Poverty Knowledge*, 4, 8, 6.
15. Jennings, *Out of the Horrors*, 8.
16. O'Connor, *Poverty Knowledge*, 15.
17. Fox, *Three Worlds of Relief*, 10.

18. Kerber, *No Constitutional Right*, 80.
19. Jennings, *Out of the Horrors*, 6.
20. Mittelstadt, *From Welfare to Workfare*, 59. See also Jennings, *Out of the Horrors*, 5 for a discussion of rehabilitation for disabled men.
21. See Gordon, *Pitied but Not Entitled*, 45, 61, 304; Ladd-Taylor, *Mother-Work*, 88–89; Koven and Michel, *Mothers of a New World*.
22. Baynton, *Defectives in the Land*, 2.
23. F. Cohen, "Indian Wardship" (1953), in *Legal Conscience*, 331–32.
24. Berger, "Red," 603–17. See also Robert Williams, *Like a Loaded Weapon*.
25. Berger, "Red," 629.
26. See Porter, "Demise of the *Ongwehoweh*," 122; Hoxie, *Final Promise*, 70–72.
27. See Chang, *Color of the Land*; Hoxie, *Final Promise*; Stremlau, *Sustaining the Cherokee Family*; Tonkovich, *Allotment Plot*.
28. Otis, *Dawes Act and the Allotment*, 8.
29. Berger, "Red," 629.
30. The 1928 Brookings Institution report, "The Problem of Indian Administration" (also known as the Meriam Report), documented loss of land, poor living conditions, abuse at federal boarding schools, and health issues as a result of allotment policy. The publication of this report led to the passage of the Indian Reorganization Act in 1934. For more on the Meriam Report, see Ramirez, *Standing Up to Colonial Power*, 121–31; Critchlow, "Lewis Meriam"; Harmon, *Rich Indians*, 210–12.
31. Indian Commissioner Morgan on Indian Policy, Extract from the *Annual Report of the Commissioner of Indian Affairs*, 1889, in Prucha, *Documents of United States Indian Policy*, 177, emphasis added.
32. Prucha, *Documents of United States Indian Policy*, 177.
33. Prucha, *Documents of United States Indian Policy*, 177.
34. Bederman, *Manliness and Civilization*, 183.
35. Bederman, *Manliness and Civilization*, 195.
36. See, for example, Fox, *Three Worlds of Relief*; Katznelson, *When Affirmative Action Was White*; Poole, *Segregated Origins of Social Security*; Canaday, *Straight State*.
37. Fox, *Three Worlds of Relief*, 2.
38. Fox, *Three Worlds of Relief*, 5–6, 285.
39. Act to Emancipate United States Indians in Certain Cases, H.R. 1113, 80th Cong. (1947). This phrase was included in all subsequent competency bills: S. 186, H.R. 2724, H.R. 457, S. 485, S. 335, and H.R. 4985.
40. Wardship was thus equated with the system of old poor laws that associated relief as charity or gratuity, not something to which Native people were entitled due to a legal relationship with the United States. See Tani, *States of Dependency*, 10.
41. See chapter 6 for a discussion of assumptions about Native people and taxes.

42. This clause was included in H.R. 1113, S. 186, H.R. 2724, H.R. 457, S. 485, S. 335, and H.R. 4985.

43. Unpublished Hearing, "Emancipation of Indians," House of Representatives Subcommittee on Indian Affairs of the Committee on Public Lands, June 20, 1947, 80th Cong., at 9, HRG-1947-PLH-0317, ProQuest Congressional.

44. Unpublished Hearing, "Emancipation of Indians," at 29.

45. Testimony of Felix S. Cohen on H.R. 4985, House Committee on Interior and Insular Affairs, July 7, 1953, Folder 8, Correspondence Regarding Various Tribal Legal Matters 1952–1961, Box 3, William Zimmerman Papers, CSR-UNM.

46. All-Pueblo Council Resolution Opposing H.R. 4985, Folder 26, Indian Affairs All-Pueblo Council 1950–1960, Box 134, Dennis Chavez Papers, CSR-UNM.

47. Twobulls to Miller, 1954, NCAI, Series 6, Committees and Special Issues Files, Box 256, Federal Indian Policy and Legislation Files, Competency Bill (H.R. 4985), NMAI.

48. Statement by Senator Hugh Butler in Explanation of Bills Introduced to Remove All Restrictions on the Indian Tribes, 1947, Indian Bureau Liquidation, Box 15, SEN 83A-F9 (1928–1953), Committee on Interior and Insular Affairs Indian Affairs Investigating Subcommittee, RG 46, NAB.

49. McKay to LaFarge, 1955, NC 16/4/1, Correspondence on Various Subjects, Box 2, Series 4, U.S. Bureau of Indian Affairs 1934–1959, Collection No. 16, PLP, UNR.

50. Statement by Senator Hugh Butler in Explanation of Bills Introduced to Remove All Restrictions on the Indian Tribes.

51. Report of Survey Team, Bureau of Indian Affairs, 1954, 5, Folder 15, Bureau of Indian Affairs 1954, Box 136, Dennis Chavez Papers, CSR-UNM.

52. Dillon Myer Memo to Secretary of Interior, 1953, 1950–1953 Commissioner of Indian Affairs Memoranda and Reports (2 of 4), Box 2, DM, HSTL.

53. Myer Memo to Secretary of Interior.

54. Myer Memo to Secretary of Interior.

55. LaFarge to Lesser, 1954, Association on American Indian Affairs File—Competency, Box 75, Philleo Nash White House/Association on American Indian Affairs Files, HSTL.

56. Omaha Tribe Response to NCAI Survey, NCAI, Series 6, Committees and Special Issues Files, Box 257, Emergency Conference 1954–General Material, NMAI. See Ellinghaus, *Blood Will Tell*, 45–69, for more on fee patents and competency certificates of the early twentieth century.

57. Unpublished Hearing, "To Provide a Decree of Competency for U.S. Indians in Certain Cases," House of Representatives Subcommittee on Indian Affairs; Committee on Interior and Insular Affairs, May 7, 1954, 83rd Cong., at 8–9, HRG-1954-IIA-0084, ProQuest Congressional.

58. Bill to Emancipate the Indians of the United States and to Establish Certain Rights for Indians and Indian Tribes, H.R. 2958, 80th Cong. (1947), at 5–6.

59. Act to Emancipate United States Indians in Certain Cases, H.R. 1113, 80th Cong. (1947), at 5–6.

60. Bill to Emancipate United States Indians in Certain Cases, S. 186, 81st Cong. (1949), at 3–4.

61. Council of Laguna Pueblo, Resolution, December 12, 1953, NCAI, Series 4, Tribal Files, Box 111, Tribal Files Laguna (Pueblo—New Mexico), 1948–1961, NMAI.

62. Twobulls to Miller, 1954, NCAI, Series 6, Committees and Special Issues Files, Box 256, Federal Indian Policy and Legislation Files, Competency Bill (H.R. 4985), NMAI.

63. Quoted in W. V. Eckardt, "Terminating the Indians," *New Leader*, April 26, 1954, 17, Folder 14, New Mexico Association on Indian Affairs 1955, Box 83, Dennis Chavez Papers, CSR-UNM.

64. "From Our Mail, Escondido, California," National Congress of American Indians, *Washington Bulletin*, vol. 2, no. 2, March–April 1948, National Congress of American Indians (1 of 4), Box 26, SEN 83A-F9 (1928–1953), Committee on Interior and Insular Affairs Indian Affairs Investigating Subcommittee, RG 46, NAB.

65. James Curry Memo to Bronson, 1951, NCAI, Series 8, Attorneys and Legal Interest Groups, Box 457, Curry, James E.—Attorney, Correspondence 1951, NMAI.

66. Joseph Garry, "What Is the Competency Bill—H.R. 4985?" May 4, 1953, NCAI, Series 6, Committees and Special Issues Files, Box 256, Federal Indian Policy and Legislation Files, Competency Bill (H.R. 4985), NMAI.

67. "Indian Citizenship Occupies Indian Affairs Subcommittee," unknown newspaper, Selective Service Miscellaneous, Box 201, Sells Indian Agency Files of Community Worker, RG 75, NARA–Pacific Region (R).

68. These hearings addressed H.R. 1113, H.R. 2165, and H.R. 2958.

69. The issue of automatic conferral of competency on spouses was not directly inserted into the bills until H.R. 4985 in 1954.

70. Unpublished Hearing, "Emancipation of Indians," House of Representatives Subcommittee on Indian Affairs of the Committee on Public Lands, June 20, 1947, 80th Cong., at 26, HRG-1947-PLH-0317, ProQuest Congressional.

71. Unpublished Hearing, "Emancipation of Indians," at 27.

72. Unpublished Hearing, "Emancipation of Indians," at 37–38.

73. Committee on Interior and Insular Affairs, Report to Accompany H.R. 4985, Providing a Certificate or Decree of Competency for United States Indians in Certain Cases, H.R. Rep. No. 836, at 9 (1953), NCAI, Series 6, Committees and Special Issues Files, Box 256, Federal Indian Policy and Legislation Files, Competency Bill (H.R. 4985), NMAI.

74. Committee on Interior and Insular Affairs, Report to Accompany H.R. 4985.

75. AAIA Draft Competency Bill, 1954, Association on American Indian Affairs File—Correspondence April 1954, Box 76, Philleo Nash White House/Association on American Indian Affairs Files, HSTL.

76. AAIA Draft Competency Bill, 1954.

77. Singh, *Black Is a Country*, 193.

78. Summary of Addresses, Evening Session, Emergency Conference of American Indians on Legislation, February 25, 1954, NCAI, Series 6, Committees and Special Issues Files, Box 257, Emergency Conference 1954–General Material, NMAI.

79. Garry, "What Is the Competency Bill?"

80. AAIA Petition to President and Congress Requesting Disapproval of H.R. 1113, Association on American Indian Affairs Files—Correspondence 1947–1948, Box 75, Philleo Nash White House/Association on American Indian Affairs Files, HSTL.

81. Garry, "What Is the Competency Bill?"

82. Bill to Emancipate the Indians of the United States, H.R. 5115, 78th Cong. (1944). The only bill in which this kind of language did not appear was H.R. 3681, which only targeted Native veterans.

83. Act to Emancipate United States Indians in Certain Cases, H.R. 1113, 80th Cong. (1947). This paragraph also appeared in S. 186, H.R. 2724, H.R. 457, H.R. 485, S. 335, and H.R. 4985.

84. LaFarge to O'Mahoney, 1949, Indian File 1946–1952 Association on American Indian Affairs, Box 24, Harry S. Truman Staff Member Office Files Philleo Nash Files, HSTL.

85. Vigil to President Eisenhower, 1954, Folder 26, Indian Affairs All-Pueblo Council 1950–1960, Box 134, Dennis Chavez Papers, CSR-UNM.

86. Vigil to President Eisenhower.

87. These kinds of arguments were especially like the claims made by local government agents in Newburgh, New York, and Louisiana that poor Black welfare recipients were "immoral," "freeloaders," and "social parasites." See Mittelstadt, *From Welfare to Workfare*, 86–97; Chappell, *War on Welfare*, 70; Tani, *States of Dependency*, 1–7.

88. Mittelstadt, *From Welfare to Workfare*, 42.

3. EVERY DAY WITH THE BIA

1. On race and the welfare state, see Brown, *Race, Money*; Chappell, *War on Welfare*; Fox, *Three Worlds of Relief*; Gordon, *Pitied but Not Entitled*; Katznelson, *When Affirmative Action Was White*; Kornbluh, *Battle for Welfare Rights*; Lieberman, *Shifting the Color Line*; Mettler, *Dividing Citizens*; Mittelstadt, *From Welfare to Workfare*; Quadagno, *Color of Welfare*.

2. Ramirez, *Standing Up to Colonial Power*, 11.

3. Mittelstadt, *From Welfare to Workfare*, 12.

4. Orleck, *Storming Caesar's Palace*, 87, emphasis added.

5. Nadasen, *Welfare Warriors*, 114.

6. Bruyneel, *Third Space of Sovereignty*, 9–10.

7. Letter from Albert Aleck, Chairman of Tribal Council, to Office of Dependency Benefits, NC 16/12/8, Welfare Case Records Ca-Cl late 1930s, Box 9, Series 12, Tribal Society and Daily Life 1930s–1964, Collection No. 16, PLPT, UNR.

8. Letter from Major H. A. Lake, Officer in Charge, Special Inquiries Branch, to Pyramid Lake Tribal Council, Records of the Pyramid Lake Paiute Tribe, NC 16/12/8, Welfare Case Records Ca-Cl late 1930s, Box 9, Series 12, Tribal Society and Daily Life 1930s–1964, PLPT, UNR.

9. Letter from Gelvin, Superintendent of Carson Agency, to Steve Ryan, BIA, NC 16/12/8, Welfare Case Records Ca-Cl late 1930s, Box 9, Series 12, Tribal Society and Daily Life 1930s–1964, PLPT, UNR.

10. Letter from Gelvin, Superintendent of Carson Agency, to Steve Ryan.

11. Monthly Allowances for the Dependents of Soldiers Pamphlet, Veteran's Rehabilitation, Box 165, CRCC Files, Records of the Bureau of Indian Affairs, RG 75, NARA–Pacific Region (R).

12. Howard Moore would have been expected to contribute $22 per month, deducted from his wages. The governmental contribution for a wife with one child was $40, with $10 for each additional child.

13. Letter from Gelvin, Superintendent of Carson Agency, to Steve Ryan.

14. Orleck, *Storming Caesar's Palace*, 89, 95.

15. Gensler to Office of Dependency Benefits, 1944, Military Activities—Registration—Selective Service, Box 165, CRCC Files, RG 75, NARA–Pacific Region (R).

16. Gensler to Office of Dependency Benefits, 1944.

17. Arizona State Department of Social Security and Welfare Policies and Procedures 1948, Welfare—Woodruff, Box 149, Pima Indian Agency Records Relating to Welfare, RG 75, NARA–Pacific Region (R).

18. Arizona State Department of Social Security and Welfare Policies and Procedures 1948.

19. Navajo Assistance Inc. to Littell, 1949, NCAI, Series 4, Tribal Files, Box 114, Navajo Tribe (Arizona), 1949, NMAI.

20. Jackson to Bronson, October 5, 1948, NCAI, Series 4, Tribal Files, Box 120, Gila River (Pima-Maricopa, Arizona), 1948–1955, NMAI.

21. Ahkeah to Bronson, October 28, 1948, NCAI, Series 4, Tribal Files, Box 113, Navajo Tribe (Arizona), 1948, NMAI.

22. Woodruff Memo on Indian Relief 1948, Welfare—Woodruff, Box 149, Pima Indian Agency Records Relating to Welfare, RG 75, NARA–Pacific Region (R).

23. Letter from Robinson to Commissioner Regarding Relief 1948, Welfare—Woodruff, Box 149, Pima Indian Agency Records Relating to Welfare, RG 75, NARA–Pacific Region (R).

24. In this context, the Red Cross acted as a quasi-governmental agency that mediated communication between the military, the BIA, Native servicemen, and their families. The American Red Cross, first founded by Clara Barton in 1881, is, as historian Julia Irwin writes, "officially connected to the state but not fully part of it." The organization first received its congressional charter in 1900. Not only does the Red Cross provide international aid in the event of disasters; officially it also acts as "a medium of communication between members of the American armed forces and their families." See Irwin, *Making the World Safe*, 5; American Red Cross, "Brief History."

25. Ahkeah to Littell, 1948, NCAI, Series 4, Tribal Files, Box 113, Navajo Tribe (Arizona), 1948; NMAI.

26. Ahkeah to Littell, 1948, emphasis in original.

27. Ensor to Daniels, April 13, 1944, Folder 36, War Department Relations, Box 23, Series 6, Subject Numeric Correspondence Files 1926–1952, Cherokee Indian Agency Records, RG 75, NARA–Southeast (A).

28. Jones to Youngbird, May 25, 1944, Folder 36, War Department Relations, Box 23, Series 6, Subject Numeric Correspondence Files 1926–1952, Cherokee Indian Agency Records, RG 75, NARA–Southeast (A).

29. Letter to Social Security Board from E. B. Hudson, January 1944, NC 16/12/9, Welfare Case Records Co-Cu late 1930s, Box 9, Series 12, Tribal Society and Daily Life 1930s–1964, PLPT, UNR.

30. Letter to Nina Winnemucca from the Navy Department, undated, NC 16/12/9, Welfare Case Records Co-Cu late 1930s, Box 9, Series 12, Tribal Society and Daily Life 1930s–1964, PLPT, UNR.

31. Letter to Veteran's Administration from E. B. Hudson, January 1944, NC 16/12/9, Welfare Case Records Co-Cu late 1930s, Box 9, Series 12, Tribal Society and Daily Life 1930s–1964, PLPT, UNR.

32. Letter to Slater from E. B. Hudson, January 1944, NC 16/12/9, Welfare Case Records Co-Cu late 1930s, Box 9, Series 12, Tribal Society and Daily Life 1930s–1964, PLPT, UNR.

33. Letter to E. B. Hudson from Veterans' Service Commission, February 1944, NC 16/12/9, Welfare Case Records Co-Cu late 1930s, Box 9, Series 12, Tribal Society and Daily Life 1930s–1964, PLPT, UNR.

34. Letter to Don Foster from E. B. Hudson, February 1944, NC 16/12/9, Welfare Case Records Co-Cu late 1930s, Box 9, Series 12, Tribal Society and Daily Life 1930s–1964, PLPT, UNR.

35. Letters from Veterans' Service Commission to E. B. Hudson, June 1944 and July 1944, NC 16/12/9, Welfare Case Records Co-Cu late 1930s, Box 9, Series 12, Tribal Society and Daily Life 1930s–1964, PLPT, UNR.

36. Don Foster, Memorandum to All Field Employees and Tribal Councils 1943, NC 16/2/2, Bulletins Memos Etc., Box 2, Series 2, Carson Indian Agency 1941–1963, PLPT, UNR.

37. Gordon, *Heroes of Their Own Lives*, 6.

38. Letter to E. B. Hudson from Tephia Slater, August 1943, NC 16/12/10, Welfare Case Records D late 1930s, Box 9, Series 12, Tribal Society and Daily Life 1930s–1964, PLPT, UNR.

39. Letter to E. B. Hudson from Tephia Slater, August 1943.

40. Letter from E. B. Hudson to Mrs. Coulson of Red Cross, March 1944, NC 16/12/9, Welfare Case Records Co-Cu late 1930s, Box 9, Series 12, Tribal Society and Daily Life 1930s–1964, PLPT, UNR.

41. Letter from Celestia Coulson of Red Cross to E. B. Hudson, May 1944, NC 16/12/9, Welfare Case Records Co-Cu late 1930s, Box 9, Series 12, Tribal Society and Daily Life 1930s–1964, PLPT, UNR.

42. Letter to Joe and Bessie Greene from Veteran's Administration, May 1944, NC 16/12/9, Welfare Case Records Co-Cu late 1930s, Box 9, Series 12, Tribal Society and Daily Life 1930s–1964, PLPT, UNR.

43. Letter to Tephia Slater from E. B. Hudson, September 1944, NC 16/12/9, Welfare Case Records Co-Cu late 1930s, Box 9, Series 12, Tribal Society and Daily Life 1930s–1964, PLPT, UNR.

44. Letter to Tephia Slater from E. B. Hudson, September 1944.

45. See Gouveia, "'We Also Serve,'" 165; Child and White, "'I've Done My Share,'" 199; Rosier, *Serving Their Country*, 47; Carroll, *Medicine Bags and Dog Tags*, 223.

46. Social Security Act Indian Amendments of 1949, S. 691, 81st Cong. (1949).

47. Dennis Chavez Press Release, Social Security Bill, January 27, 1949, Folder 34, Bill to Include Indian Wards of Government in Social Security Program 1949, Box 82, Dennis Chavez Papers, CSR-UNM.

48. Jackson to Bronson, February 5, 1949, NCAI, Series 4, Tribal Files, Box 120, Gila River (Pima-Maricopa, Arizona), 1948–1955, NMAI, emphasis in original.

49. "Crow Indians Ask for Equality," *Great Falls Tribune*, January 8, 1946, Indian Policy (2 of 4), Box 16, SEN 83A-F9 (1928–1953), Committee on Interior and Insular Affairs Indian Affairs Investigating Subcommittee, Records of the U.S. Senate, RG 46, NAB.

50. Bronson to Altmeyer, 1949, NC 16/6/3, National Congress of American Indians 1943–1949, Box 4, Series 6, Inter-Tribal Indian Organizations 1930–1959, PLPT, UNR.

51. Curry to Bronson, 1949, NC 16/6/3, National Congress of American Indians 1943–1949, Box 4, Series 6, Inter-Tribal Indian Organizations 1930–1959, PLPT, UNR.

52. DeWitt, Béland, and Berkowitz, *Social Security*, 14.

53. *Southwest Indian Newsletter*, February 1951, Indians—Southwest Indian Newsletter, February 1951–February 1952, Box 44, PNWH, HSTL.

54. Colorado River Resolution for Needy Indians 1938, Minutes, Tribal Council 1936–1938, Box 19, CRCC Files, RG 75, NARA–Pacific Region (R).

55. Letter from Robinson to Commissioner, 1948, Welfare—Woodruff, Box 149, Pima Indian Agency Records Relating to Welfare, RG 75, NARA–Pacific Region (R).

56. "Indians Seek Changes on Vets' Loans," *Great Falls Tribune*, March 30, 1946, National Congress of American Indians (2 of 4), Box 26, SEN 83A-F9 (1928–1953), Committee on Interior and Insular Affairs Indian Affairs Investigating Subcommittee, RG 46, NAB.

57. Statement of Kizzie Yazzie, Minutes of Navajo Tribal Council, December 18–20, 1945, 31, Navajo Tribal Council—Organization—Minutes of Meetings 12-18-45, 6-23-46, 1-7-47, Box 408, Phoenix Area Office Division of Extension and Industry Files, Minutes of Navajo Tribal Council, RG 75, NARA–Pacific Region (R). For more on GI Bill loans for education, see chapter 5. For more on Native veterans' lack of access to GI Bill loans for housing, see Keeler, "Putting People Where They Belong."

58. Letter from Robinson to Daiker 1948, Welfare—Woodruff, Box 149, Pima Indian Agency Records Relating to Welfare, RG 75, NARA–Pacific Region (R).

59. Mirabal to Bronson, 1948, National Congress of American Indians Records (NCAI), Series 4, Tribal Files, Box 132, Taos Pueblo (New Mexico), 1947–1959, NMAI.

60. Baltazar to Bronson, 1948, NCAI, Series 4, Tribal Files, Box 94, Jicarilla (Apache—New Mexico), 1933–1961; NMAI.

61. Johnson to LaFarge, 1949, NCAI, Series 4, Tribal Files, Box 120, Gila River (Pima-Maricopa, Arizona), 1948–1955, NMAI.

62. Ahkeah to Bronson, August 27, 1948, NCAI, Series 4, Tribal Files, Box 113, Navajo Tribe (Arizona), 1948, NMAI. Navajo poverty was in no small part rooted in the livestock reduction program employed during 1933–46. Sheep herds were dramatically reduced based on studies that linked overgrazing to soil erosion, which officials feared would damage the recently constructed Hoover Dam. This not only caused economic devastation but revealed government officials' disregard of the spiritual and cultural significance of sheep and livestock for Navajo people. For more on livestock reduction see Weisiger, "Gendered Injustice"; Denetdale, *Reclaiming Diné History*, 169, 174; Benally, *Bitter Water*, 69–73.

63. Mapatis v. Ewing Complaint filed in U.S. District Court for District of Columbia, 4, Folder 1, *Mapatis, Frank et al. v. Ewing, Oscar R* (Federal Social Security), 1948–1949, Box 332, AAIA Papers, MML.

64. Mapatis v. Ewing Complaint, 4.

65. Mapatis v. Ewing Complaint, 4.

66. Mapatis v. Ewing Complaint, 4.

67. Letter from AZ and NM Congresspeople to Altmeyer 1948, Social Security Legislation Correspondence, Box 168, CRCC Files, RG 75, NARA–Pacific Region (R).

68. Letter from AZ and NM Congresspeople to Altmeyer 1948.

69. Letter from AZ and NM Congresspeople to Altmeyer 1948.

70. For more see Mink, *Wages of Motherhood*; Katznelson, *When Affirmative Action Was White*; Gordon, *Pitied but Not Entitled*; Chappell, *War on Welfare*.

71. Amicus Brief of All-Pueblo Council, Mescalero Apache Tribe, Jicarilla Apache Tribe and the NCAI, Folder 1, *Mapatis, Frank et al. v. Ewing, Oscar R* (Federal Social Security), 1948–1949, Box 332, AAIA Papers, MML.

72. Bennet Statement, Proceedings of the Meeting of the Navajo Tribal Council, July 23–26, 1946, 47, Navajo Tribal Council—Organization—Minutes of Meetings 12-18-45, 6-23-46, 1-7-47, Box 408, Phoenix Area Office Division of Extension and Industry Files, Minutes of Navajo Tribal Council, RG 75, NARA–Pacific Region (R).

73. Bennet Statement, Proceedings of Meeting of the Navajo Tribal Council, 47.

74. Bennet Statement, Proceedings of Meeting of the Navajo Tribal Council, 50.

75. Franco, *Crossing the Pond*, 197.

76. Bernstein, *American Indians and World War II*, 171.

77. Godfrey Feature Radio Address, WTOP, November 22, 1946, Indian Policy (4 of 4), Box 17, SEN 83A-F9 (1928–1953), Committee on Interior and Insular Affairs Indian Affairs Investigating Subcommittee, RG 46, NAB.

78. Johnson to McCarran, 1947, Appropriations—Interior 1947, Box 47, McCarranalia II, Nevada Historical Society.

79. Johnson to McCarran, 1947.

80. Lone Eagle to Truman, 1951, Indians Navajo-Hopi Rehabilitation Bill S.1407, Box 1079, HST Official, HSTL.

81. Red Cloud to Truman, 1952, , Box 1079, HST Official, HSTL.

82. Statement of Zuni Indian Veterans of World War II and the Korean Conflict, Adopted February 17, 1954, Emergency Conference of American Indians on Legislation Program, Prepared Resolutions 9–10, Indians—National Congress of American Indians Report—Washington Conference February 1954, Box 42, PNWH, HSTL.

1. Henry Cypress to Kenneth Marmon, October 1952, and Marmon to Cypress, October 27, 1952, Folder 790, Welfare 1950–1952, Box 15, Series: Seminole Agency Subject Files Correspondence, Records of the Seminole Indian Agency, RG 75, NARA–Southeast (A).

2. On the history of caseworkers' surveillance and monitoring of welfare recipients' behavior and "morality" in the twentieth century, see Gordon, *Pitied but Not Entitled*; Roberts, *Killing the Black Body*; Orleck, *Storming Caesar's Palace*; Nadasen, *Welfare Warriors*; Mittelstadt, *From Welfare to Workfare*; Chappell, *War on Welfare*; Katz, *Undeserving Poor*; Kornbluh, *Battle for Welfare Rights*; Fox, *Three Worlds of Relief*; Tani, *States of Dependency*. Native people rarely factor into studies of the welfare state (with the exception of Tani's *States of Dependency*, which covers Natives' battle for Social Security benefits in Arizona). However, historians Brianna Theobald and Margaret Jacobs have examined the intersections between Native women's mothering and reproductive rights and state caseworkers. See Theobald, *Reproduction on the Reservation*; Jacobs, *Generation Removed*. In addition, Julie Davis has examined community activism around social services, especially education, in conjunction with the American Indian Movement's founding in Minneapolis. See Davis, *Survival Schools*. And lastly, Julie Reed's study of nineteenth-century Cherokee social welfare establishes the long-intertwined history of social services and sovereignty. See Reed, *Serving the Nation*. On the history of the federal welfare state and American colonialism, see Amador, "Women Ask Relief."

3. Fraser and Gordon, "Genealogy of Dependency," 310–11.

4. Fraser and Gordon, "Genealogy of Dependency," 327.

5. Theobald, *Reproduction on the Reservation*, 6; Margaret Jacobs, *Generation Removed*, 52–53. See also Gurr, *Reproductive Justice*; Lawrence, "Indian Health Service"; Schoen, *Choice and Coercion*; Silliman et al., *Undivided Rights*; Ladd-Taylor, *Fixing the Poor*.

6. Theobald, *Reproduction on the Reservation*, 6.

7. Roberts, *Killing the Black Body*, 17–18. Rhetoric about "innocent taxpayers" took on additional connotations when it was applied to Native people and land. Chapter 6 addresses this rhetoric in more detail.

8. Roberts, *Killing the Black Body*, 17, 209.

9. Theobald, *Reproduction on the Reservation*, 10.

10. Gordon, *Pitied but Not Entitled*, 11.

11. Mettler, *Dividing Citizens*, 5–6.

12. Tani, *States of Dependency*, 19.

13. Circular Letter from Fred A. Daiker, Director of Welfare, March 1943, War Pamphlets, Box 202, Sells Indian Agency Files of Community Worker, Records of the Bureau of Indian Affairs, RG 75, NARA–Pacific Region (R).

14. Hudson was the teacher at the Nevada Day School in Nixon, Nevada. From the records, it seems that he was often employed by the Carson Agency superintendent to follow up with individual Native people.

15. Letter to Doris Shaw from E. B. Hudson, October 1944, NC 16/12/9, Welfare Case Records Co-Cu late 1930s, Box 9, Series 12, Tribal Society and Daily Life 1930s–1964, Collection No. 16, PLPT, UNR.

16. Roberts, *Killing the Black Body*, 209.

17. The assimilationist framing of BIA engagement with Native people over welfare benefits is the subject of chapter 5.

18. See Fraser and Gordon, " Genealogy of Dependency," 317.

19. Letter to E. B. Hudson from Celestia Coulson, Red Cross, July 1942, NC 16/12/10, Welfare Case Records D late 1930s, Box 9, Series 12, Tribal Society and Daily Life 1930s–1964, PLPT, UNR.

20. Letter to E. B. Hudson from Celestia Coulson, Red Cross, July 1942.

21. Letter to E. B. Hudson from Celestia Coulson, Red Cross, July 1942, emphasis added.

22. Sells Community Worker Monthly Reports, October 1944 and December 1945, Monthly Report to Superintendent of Sells 1944–1945, Box 215, Sells Indian Agency Health and Social Welfare Correspondence of Community Worker Files, RG 75, NARA–Pacific Region (R). The Sells Agency (located in Sells, Arizona) is now known as the Papago Agency and serves the Tohono O'odham Nation.

23. Theobald, *Reproduction on the Reservation*, 7.

24. Letters between Jonah Welch, Joe Jennings, Jarrett Blythe, and Office of Dependency Benefits, October 10–16, 1945, Folder 36, War Department Relations, Box 23, Series 6, Subject Numeric Correspondence Files 1926–1952, Records of the Cherokee Indian Agency, RG 75, NARA–Southeast (A).

25. Ute Junior Jumper to Navy, November 2, 1945, Folder 36, War Department Relations, Box 23, Series 6, Subject Numeric Correspondence Files 1926–1952, Records of the Cherokee Indian Agency, RG 75, NARA–Southeast (A).

26. Jennings to Navy, November 13, 1945, Folder 36, War Department Relations, Box 23, Series 6, Subject Numeric Correspondence Files 1926–1952, Records of the Cherokee Indian Agency, RG 75, NARA–Southeast (A).

27. Jarrett Blythe to Harry Snyder, January 31, 1946, and Harry Synder to Red Cross, January 21, 1945, Folder 36, War Department Relations, Box 23, Series 6, Subject Numeric Correspondence Files 1926–1952, Records of the Cherokee Indian Agency, RG 75, NARA–Southeast (A). In the records Betty Ann Johnson is also referred to as Betsy Ross Johnson.

28. Hickel, "War, Region, and Social Welfare."
29. In the case of the Johnson marriage, divorce proceedings were initiated after Betty Ann Johnson pleaded guilty to adultery in Superior Court. In addition to accepting the dependency allotment for Johnson's child, Jarrett Blythe, principal chief, also noted that they would "attempt to secure the child" and place him or her with Lloyd Johnson's sister. Jarrett Blythe to Harry Snyder, January 31, 1946, Folder 36, War Department Relations, Box 23, Series 6, Subject Numeric Correspondence Files 1926–1952, Records of the Cherokee Indian Agency, RG 75, NARA–Southeast (A).
30. This freedom of choice was encapsulated by a more ambiguous and critical stance against mothers of soldiers, which led to a "more decisive repudiation of the iconic middle-aged mother" after the war. Rebecca Plant has shown that although mothers of servicemen killed in action were lauded for their sacrifices, such sentimentality was increasingly linked to the United States' "political and psychological immaturity." Plant, *Mom*, 78–80.
31. Letter to Arthur Dunn from E. B. Hudson, June 1944, NC 16/12/9, Welfare Case Records Co-Cu late 1930s, Box 9, Series 12, Tribal Society and Daily Life 1930s–1964, PLPT, UNR.
32. Letters to Levi and Arthur Dunn from E. B. Hudson, June 1944, NC 16/12/9, Welfare Case Records Co-Cu late 1930s, Box 9, Series 12, Tribal Society and Daily Life 1930s–1964, PLPT, UNR.
33. Letter to Arthur Dunn from E. B. Hudson, June 1944.
34. Ensor to Calhoun, November 9, 1942, Folder 36, War Department Relations, Box 23, Series 6, Subject Numeric Correspondence Files 1926–1952, Records of the Cherokee Indian Agency, RG 75, NARA–Southeast (A).
35. Ensor to Driver, October 31, 1942, Folder 36, War Department Relations, Box 23, Series 6, Subject Numeric Correspondence Files 1926–1952, Records of the Cherokee Indian Agency, RG 75, NARA–Southeast (A).
36. Orleck, *Storming Caesar's Palace*, 81.
37. Orleck, *Storming Caesar's Palace*, 94–95.
38. Snell to Marmon, August 17, 1951, Folder 790, Welfare 1950–1952, Box 15, Series— Seminole Agency Subject Files Correspondence, Records of the Seminole Agency, RG 75, NARA–Southeast (A). It is unclear from the correspondence whether Tiger actually received ADC payments in 1948 when she first applied.
39. Snell to Marmon, August 17, 1951, emphasis added.
40. Marmon to Snell, August 29, 1951, Folder 790, Welfare 1950–1952, Box 15, Series— Seminole Agency Subject Files Correspondence, Records of the Seminole Agency, RG 75, NARA–Southeast (A).
41. Snell to Marmon, October 21, 1952, Folder 790, Welfare 1950–1952, Box 15, Series—Seminole Agency Subject Files Correspondence, Records of the Seminole Agency, RG 75, NARA–Southeast (A), emphasis added.

42. Snell to Marmon, October 21, 1952.
43. Snell to Marmon, August 17, 1951, Folder 790, Welfare 1950–1952, Box 15, Series—Seminole Agency Subject Files Correspondence, Records of the Seminole Agency, RG 75, NARA–Southeast (A).
44. Wilson to Marmon, December 1, 1952, Folder 790, Welfare 1950–1952, Box 15, Series—Seminole Agency Subject Files Correspondence, Records of the Seminole Agency, RG 75, NARA–Southeast (A).
45. Marmon to Osceola, December 15, 1952, Folder 790, Welfare 1950–1952, Box 15, Series—Seminole Agency Subject Files Correspondence, Records of the Seminole Agency, RG 75, NARA–Southeast (A).
46. Marmon to Wilson, December 17, 1952, Folder 790, Welfare 1950–1952, Box 15, Series—Seminole Agency Subject Files Correspondence, Records of the Seminole Agency, RG 75, NARA–Southeast (A).
47. Boehmer to Snell, December 30, 1952, Folder 790, Welfare 1950–1952, Box 15, Series—Seminole Agency Subject Files Correspondence, Records of the Seminole Agency, RG 75, NARA–Southeast (A).
48. Boehmer to Snell, February 13, 1951, Folder 790, Welfare 1950–1952, Box 15, Series—Seminole Agency Subject Files Correspondence, Records of the Seminole Agency, RG 75, NARA–Southeast (A).
49. Mittelstadt, *From Welfare to Workfare*, 46.
50. McClelland and Eby, "Child Support Enforcement," 25–26; Handler and Hollingsworth, "Reforming Welfare," 1167n3.
51. Virtue, "Operative Relationships," 30.
52. Virtue, "Operative Relationships," 34.
53. Handler and Hollingsworth, "Reforming Welfare," 1167n3.
54. Jones to Marmon, June 27, 1951, Folder 790, Welfare 1950–1952, Box 15, Series—Seminole Agency Subject Files Correspondence, Records of the Seminole Agency, RG 75, NARA–Southeast (A).
55. Jones to Marmon, June 27, 1951.
56. Marmon to Jones, July 16, 1951, Folder 790, Welfare 1950–1952, Box 15, Series—Seminole Agency Subject Files Correspondence, Records of the Seminole Agency, RG 75, NARA–Southeast (A).
57. Snell to Boehmer, February 12, 1951, Folder 790, Welfare 1950–1952, Box 15, Series—Seminole Agency Subject Files Correspondence, Records of the Seminole Agency, RG 75, NARA–Southeast (A).
58. Boehmer to Snell, October 23, 1950, Folder 790, Welfare 1950–1952, Box 15, Series—Seminole Agency Subject Files Correspondence, Records of the Seminole Agency, RG 75, NARA–Southeast (A).

59. Marmon to Smith, May 23, 1951, Folder 790, Welfare 1950–1952, Box 15, Series —
Seminole Agency Subject Files Correspondence, Records of the Seminole Agency,
RG 75, NARA–Southeast (A), emphasis added.

60. Smith to Marmon, June 21, 1951, Folder 790, Welfare 1950–1952, Box 15, Series —
Seminole Agency Subject Files Correspondence, Records of the Seminole Agency,
RG 75, NARA–Southeast (A).

61. Smith to Marmon, June 21, 1951.

62. Marmon to Smith, May 23, 1951.

63. Wilkerson, *To Live Here*, 6, emphasis added.

64. Theobald, *Reproduction on the Reservation*, 133, emphasis added.

65. "Help for Indian GIs," National Congress of American Indians, *Washington Bulletin*, vol. 1, no. 4, June–July 1947, Indian Affairs [Trudeau] 1947–1948, Box 16,
Papers of William Brophy and Sophie Aberle Brophy, HSTL.

66. White to Hunsicker, 1947, Relief Welfare Navajo 7-13-48, 11-30-47, Box 1, Phoenix
Area Office District Director's Classified Files, RG 75, NARA–Pacific Region (R).

67. United Pueblos Agency, Meeting of Division Heads on Re-Employment of War
Veterans, War Pamphlets, Box 202, Sells Indian Agency Files of Community
Worker, RG 75, NARA–Pacific Region (R).

68. United Pueblos Agency Memo, Re-Employment of War Veterans, 1944, War
Pamphlets, Box 202, Sells Indian Agency Files of Community Worker, RG 75,
NARA–Pacific Region (R).

69. Veterans' Resolution on GI Bill, Proceedings of the Meeting of the Navajo Tribal
Council, July 23–26, 1946, 48–49, Navajo Tribal Council — Organization —
Minutes of Meetings 12-18-45, 6-23-46, 1-7-47, Box 408, Phoenix Area Office
Division of Extension and Industry Files, Minutes of Navajo Tribal Council, RG
75, NARA–Pacific Region (R).

70. Jennings to Hemingway, October 8, 1946, Folder: Veterans Training — General
1945–1949, Box 7, Series 36, Veterans Training Files 1944–1952 (Education Branch),
Records of the Cherokee Indian Agency, RG 75, NARA–Southeast Region (A).

71. Jennings to VA Vocational Rehabilitation and Education Division, May 12, 1948,
Folder: Veterans Training — General 1948, Box 8, Series 36, Veterans Training
Files 1944–1952 (Education Branch), Records of the Cherokee Indian Agency,
RG 75, NARA–Southeast Region (A).

72. Jennings to VA, January 23, 1947, Folder: Veterans Training — General 1945–1949,
Box 7, Series 36, Veterans Training Files 1944–1952 (Education Branch), Records
of the Cherokee Indian Agency, RG 75, NARA–Southeast Region (A).

73. Jennings to Brown, April 22, 1946, Folder: Veterans Training — General 1945–
1949, Box 7, Series 36, Veterans Training Files 1944–1952 (Education Branch),
Records of the Cherokee Indian Agency, RG 75, NARA–Southeast Region (A).

74. VA Suggested Talk to Be Given at Student Assembly, April 15, 1948, Folder: Veterans Training—General 1948, Box 8, Series 36, Veterans Training Files 1944–1952 (Education Branch), Records of the Cherokee Indian Agency, RG 75, NARA–Southeast Region (A).
75. For more on the bureaucracy and waiting involved in GI reentry, see McEnaney, *Postwar*, 103–5.
76. There is also a historiography of this line of thinking, as mentioned in chapter 3.
77. John Adair, "The Navajo and Pueblo Veteran: A Force for Culture Change," *American Indian* 4, no. 1 (1947): 10–11, Association on American Indian Affairs publication, Reference File—Assoc. On American Indian Affairs, Inc., Box 23, RG 220, Records of the President's Commission on Civil Rights, HSTL.
78. United Pueblos Agency Memo, Readjustment Problems of Returning Pueblo Indian War Veterans, 1945, Corres Re Loans World War II—Indians in United States Army—Monthly Military Service Report, Box 165, Colorado River Agency Central Classified Files, RG 75, NARA–Pacific Region (R).
79. BIA Circular No. 3604, Indian Service Assistance for Returned Veterans, 1945, Welfare—Social Security, Box 216, Sells Indian Agency Health and Social Welfare Correspondence of Community Worker, RG 75, NARA–Pacific Region (R).
80. BIA Circular No. 3604, Indian Service Assistance for Returned Veterans, 1945.
81. Jennings to Hyatt, January 21, 1948, Folder: Veterans Training—General 1948, Box 8, Series 36, Veterans Training Files 1944–1952 (Education Branch), Records of the Cherokee Indian Agency, RG 75, NARA–Southeast Region (A).
82. The Cherokee Indian School is referred to in the records also as Cherokee High School and Cherokee Central High School. It was a boarding school operated by the BIA until 1954. Jennings to VA, March 3, 1949, Folder: Edwin Walkingstick, Box 10, Series 37, Veterans Training Folders (Education Branch), Records of the Cherokee Indian Agency, RG 75, NARA–Southeast Region (A). The period of four days of unexcused absences seemed incredibly short at first read. However, according to other correspondence, it seems as though this was according to VA regulations.
83. Jennings to VA, July 3, 1947, and January 22, 1948, Folder: Edwin Walkingstick, Box 10, Series 37, Veterans Training Folders (Education Branch), Records of the Cherokee Indian Agency, RG 75, NARA–Southeast Region (A).
84. Jennings to VA, March 31, 1949, Folder: Edwin Walkingstick, Box 10, Series 37, Veterans Training Folders (Education Branch), Records of the Cherokee Indian Agency, RG 75, NARA–Southeast Region (A).
85. List of Veterans at Cherokee Central 1946, Folder: Veterans Training—General 1945–1949, Box 7, Series 36, Veterans Training Files 1944–1952 (Education Branch), Records of the Cherokee Indian Agency, RG 75, NARA–Southeast Region (A).

86. Welch to VA, October 22, 1947, Folder: Jonah H Welch, Box 10, Series 37, Veterans Training Folders (Education Branch), Records of the Cherokee Indian Agency, RG 75, NARA–Southeast Region (A).

87. Hyatt to Jennings, November 7, 1947, Folder: Jonah H Welch, Box 10, Series 37, Veterans Training Folders (Education Branch), Records of the Cherokee Indian Agency, RG 75, NARA–Southeast Region (A).

88. Willett to Welch, March 22, 1946, Folder: Jonah H Welch, Box 10, Series 37, Veterans Training Folders (Education Branch), Records of the Cherokee Indian Agency, RG 75, NARA–Southeast Region (A).

89. Jennings to VA, October 22, 1947, Folder: Jonah H Welch, Box 10, Series 37, Veterans Training Folders (Education Branch), Records of the Cherokee Indian Agency, RG 75, NARA–Southeast Region (A).

5. IMPROVING FARMS AND HOMES

1. Bradley to Willett, August 19, 1946, and Willett to Bradley, August 8, 1946, Folder: Bradley, Richard L., Box 1, Series 37, Veterans Training Folders (Education Branch), RG 75, Cherokee Indian Agency, NARA–Southeast (A).

2. Reeves to Bradley, October 15, 1947, Folder: Bradley, Richard L., Box 1, Series 37, Veterans Training Folders (Education Branch), RG 75, Cherokee Indian Agency, NARA–Southeast (A).

3. Firkus, "Agricultural Extension," 474.

4. Margaret D. Jacobs, "Working on the Domestic Frontier," 166; Fixico, *Indian Resilience and Rebuilding*, 51.

5. Olson, "G.I. Bill and Higher Education," 600; Murray, "When War Is Work," 990.

6. McEnaney, *Postwar*, 100.

7. See Murray, "When War Is Work," 994–95.

8. Murray, "When War Is Work," 991.

9. BIA Circular Letter April 7, 1948, Folder 790, Welfare 1950–1952, Box 15, Series— Seminole Agency Subject Files Correspondence, RG 75, Seminole Agency, NARA–Southeast (A), emphasis added. On the connections between the G.I. Bill and Relocation, see Keeler, "Putting People Where They Belong." On the gendered nature of relocation programming, see Theobald, *Reproduction on the Reservation*, 103–4.

10. BIA Circular Letter April 7, 1948, Folder 790, Welfare 1950–1952, Box 15, Series— Seminole Agency Subject Files Correspondence, RG 75, Seminole Agency, NARA–Southeast (A).

11. Hemingway to Jennings, December 15, 1948, Folder: Jonah H Welch, Box 10, Series 37, Veterans Training Folders (Educational Branch), RG 75, Cherokee Indian Agency, NARA–Southeast (A).

12. Throughout the 1940s, Jonah Welch and Olive McCoy Welch experienced turmoil in their marriage. By 1950 they had had three more children together, but the couple's relationship was fragile, as evidenced by Welch's communication to the VA and BIA. What we know is filtered through bland bureaucracy—the VA's need for official documentation in order to determine the appropriate subsistence allowance payments. Especially important is the fact that the VA corresponded with Jonah and Olive indirectly, as their responses were filtered through Joe Jennings of the BIA. Jennings was not a member of the family, although he was familiar with the family's dynamics. The Welch family's story (or rather, the story captured in Joe Jennings's archive) ends with an official reconciliation. In December 1950 Jonah and Olive Welch signed an affidavit testifying that they were "living together as man and wife" and had joint custody over their now eight children. Hyatt to Welch, April 22, 1948; Jennings to Veterans Administration, May 25, 1948; Hyatt to Jennings, June 18, 1948; Jonah and Olive Welch Affidavit, December 5, 1950, Folder: Jonah H Welch, Box 10, Series 37, Veterans Training Folders (Educational Branch), RG 75, Cherokee Indian Agency, NARA–Southeast (A).
13. Clapsaddle, *Even as We Breathe*, 59.
14. Altschuler and Blumin, *GI Bill*, 82.
15. Olson, "G.I. Bill and Higher Education," 600.
16. L. Cohen, *Consumers' Republic*, 140, emphasis added.
17. Altschuler and Blumin, *GI Bill*, 134. See also Katznelson, *When Affirmative Action Was White*.
18. "Help for Indian GIs," National Congress of American Indians, *Washington Bulletin* 1, no. 4 (June–July 1947), Indian Affairs [Trudeau] 1947–1948, Box 16, WBSB, HSTL.
19. Beatty to BIA School Superintendents and Principals, 1944, Education Servicemen's Readjustment Act, Box 201, Sells Indian Agency, Files of Community Worker, RG 75, NARA–Pacific Region (R).
20. 78 Cong. Rec. H4, 345 (1944), emphasis added.
21. 78 Cong. Rec. H4, 345 (1944).
22. Dean Smith, Analysis and Comparison of Provisions of Part VIII of Senate and House Bills (S.1767) Providing for Education of Veterans, S.1767 (2 of 2 folders), 78th Cong., Box 64 (SEN 78A-E1), Records of the U.S. Senate, RG 46, NAB.
23. Beatty to BIA School Superintendents and Principals, 1944, and Stirling to Veterans Administration, March 31, 1947, Veterans Service Committee—War Veterans Education, Box 165, Colorado River Agency Central Classified Files, RG 75, NARA–Pacific Region I.
24. Keith Olson's 1973 article on the success of the G.I. Bill in the *American Quarterly* provides some interesting reflections on the initial reactions of college

administrators to an incoming class of veteran students, many of whom would be married with families of their own. Olson quotes from University of Chicago dean A. J. Brumbaugh: "in all seriousness . . . What will we do with married students on the campus? How will we house them? . . . Will we be embarrassed by the prospects of babies and by their arrival?" Olson, "G.I. Bill and Higher Education," 603.

25. *A Bill Establishing a Joint Congressional Committee to Make a Study of Claims of Indian Tribes Against the United States, and to Investigate the Administration of Indian Affairs: Hearings on S.J. Res. 79, Before the Committee on Indian Affairs United States Senate*, 79th Cong. 17 (1946) (Resolution of Navajo Veterans of Foreign Wars and American Legion), Navajo, Box 93, SEN 83A-F9 (1928–1953), Committee on Interior and Insular Affairs Indian Affairs Investigating Subcommittee, RG 46, NAB.

26. The school system became tribally operated in 1990, renamed as Cherokee Central Schools. "History of Cherokee Central Schools," Cherokee Central School, https://www.ccs-nc.org/apps/pages/index.jsp?uREC_ID=373900&type=d& pREC_ID=851868.

27. Willett Memo to Jennings, June 18, 1947, Folder: Veterans Training—General 1946–1948, Box 7, Series 36, Veterans Training Files 1944–1952 (Education Branch), RG 75, Cherokee Indian Agency, NARA–Southeast (A).

28. Brown to Jennings, November 1, 1946, Walker to Jennings, March 7, 1946, and Jennings to Stone, August 23, 1948, Folder: Veterans Training—General 1945– 1949, Box 7, Series 36, Veterans Training Files 1944–1952 (Education Branch), RG 75, Cherokee Indian Agency, NARA–Southeast (A).

29. Jennings Report on Cherokee Veterans Training Program, Folder: Veterans Training—General 1946–1948, Box 7, Series 36, Veterans Training Files 1944– 1952 (Education Branch), RG 75, Cherokee Indian Agency, NARA–Southeast (A).

30. Jennings to Stone, August 23, 1948, Folder: Veterans Training—General 1945– 1949, Box 7, Series 36, Veterans Training Files 1944–1952 (Education Branch), RG 75, Cherokee Indian Agency, NARA–Southeast (A).

31. Jennings to Danielson, January 17, 1946, Folder: Veterans Training—General 1945–1949, Box 7, Series 36, Veterans Training Files 1944–1952 (Education Branch), RG 75, Cherokee Indian Agency, NARA–Southeast (A).

32. Willett Memo to Jennings, June 18, 1947.

33. Willett Memo to Jennings, June 18, 1947; Jennings to Danielson, January 17, 1946, Folder: Veterans Training—General 1945–1949; Box 7, Series 36, Veterans Training Files 1944–1952 (Education Branch), RG 75, Cherokee Indian Agency, NARA–Southeast (A).

34. Willett Memo to Jennings, June 18, 1947.

35. Jennings Report on Cherokee Veterans Training Program, Folder: Veterans Training—General 1946–1948, Box 7, Series 36, Veterans Training Files 1944–1952 (Education Branch), RG 75, Cherokee Indian Agency, NARA–Southeast (A).

36. See, for example, Lomawaima, "Estelle Reel," 17–18. White women's reform organizations such as the Women's National Indian Association and the General Federation of Women's Clubs advocating for the "preservation" of certain aspects of Native culture, including arts and crafts in the early twentieth century. See Huebner, "Unexpected Alliance," 350. On Native people's contested history with cultural tourism, see R. Phillips, *Trading Identities*; Raibmon, *Authentic Indians*; Cothran, "Working the Indian Field Days;" K. Phillips, *Staging Indigeneity*; Klann, "Babies in Baskets."

37. For more on the relationship between the WRA and BIA at the Poston Internment Camp, see Drinnon, *Keeper of Concentration Camps*; Okimoto, *Sharing a Desert Home*; Byrd, *Transit of Empire*, 185–94; Phu, "Double Capture." For more on the WRA and BIA in other locations, see Horiuchi, "Spatial Jurisdictions;" Leong and Carpio, "Carceral Subjugations."

38. Beatty to Gensler, January 24, 1947, Folder: WRA—Poston (Disposition of Buildings), Box 64, Irrigation District Number 4 Colorado River Irrigation Project, Records of Shepard, RG 75, NARA–Pacific Region (R).

39. Gensler to Beatty, April 9, 1947, Folder: Veterans Service Committee—War Veterans Education, Box 165, Colorado River Agency Central Classified Files, RG 75, NARA–Pacific Region (R).

40. Beatty to Gensler, January 24, 1947; Gensler to Commissioner, March 2, 1948, Folder: WRA—Poston (Disposition of Buildings), Box 64, Irrigation District Number 4 Colorado River Irrigation Project, Records of Shepard, RG 75, NARA–Pacific Region (R). However, Gensler also wanted to ensure that the buildings would be available for housing for Hopi and Navajo families who would move under the colonization plan; he even requested that a provision be written into legislation that specified that the BIA could retain buildings it needed. Without this provision, Gentler predicted "considerable extra work put on us in dealing with the tribe for these buildings."

41. Gensler Report, "Proposed Veterans' Vocational Training School," Folder: Veterans Service Committee—War Veterans Education, Box 165, Colorado River Agency Central Classified Files, RG 75, NARA–Pacific Region (R).

42. Gensler to Veterans Administration, February 10, 1947, Gensler to Veterans Administration, March 6, 1947, and Gensler to Beatty, April 9, 1947, Folder: Veterans Service Committee—War Veterans Education, Box 165, Colorado River Agency Central Classified Files, RG 75, NARA–Pacific Region (R). Moreover, Public Works specified that they couldn't allocate the funds until the BIA owned

the buildings, which entailed an additional bureaucratic process before money could be dispensed.

43. Stirling to Veterans Administration, March 31, 1947, Folder: Veterans Service Committee—War Veterans Education, Box 165, Colorado River Agency Central Classified Files, RG 75, NARA–Pacific Region (R).

44. Beatty to Munsen, January 30, 1948, Folder: Veterans Service Committee—War Veterans Education, Box 165, Colorado River Agency Central Classified Files, RG 75, NARA–Pacific Region (R).

45. Gensler Report, "Proposed Veterans' Vocational Training School."

46. Stirling to Veterans Administration, March 31, 1947, Folder: Veterans Service Committee—War Veterans Education, Box 165, Colorado River Agency Central Classified Files, RG 75, NARA–Pacific Region (R), emphasis added.

47. Stirling to Veterans Administration, March 31, 1947.

48. Max Drefkoff, "An Industrial Program for the Navajo Indian Reservation," Report to the Commissioner of Indian Affairs, 1948, 6, Box 93, SEN 83A-F9 (1928–1953), Committee on Interior and Insular Affairs Indian Affairs Investigating Subcommittee, RG 46, NAB.

49. Thompson Statement, Minutes of Navajo Tribal Council, December 18–20, 1945, 60, Folder: Navajo Tribal Council—Organization—Minutes of Meetings 12-18-45, 6-23-46, 1-7-47, Box 408, Phoenix Area Office Division of Extension and Industry Files, Minutes of Navajo Tribal Council, RG 75, NARA–Pacific Region (R).

50. United Pueblos Agency Memo, Benefits to War Veterans under the "G.I. Bill of Rights," 1944, Folder: War Pamphlets, Box 202, Sells Indian Agency Files of Community Worker, RG 75, NARA–Pacific Region (R).

51. Colorado River Jurisdiction, Indian Veteran Training Questionnaire, Folder: Veterans Service Committee—War Veterans Education, Box 165, Colorado River Agency Central Classified Files, RG 75, NARA–Pacific Region (R).

52. Statistics Pertaining to Papago Servicemen and Servicewomen, 1946, Folder: Indians at Work, Box 201, Sells Indian Agency Files of Community Worker, RG 75, NARA–Pacific Region (R).

53. Monthly Report to Commissioner of Indian Affairs, Navajo Agency, April-May 1946, Folder: Monthly Report to Commissioner of Indian Affairs 1946, Box 14, Colorado River Agency Central Classified Files, RG 75, NARA–Pacific Region (R); Fort Yuma Sub-Agency, Quarterly Report of Indian Men and Women Returning from Military Service and War Employment, 1945, Corres Re Loans World War II—Indians in United States Army—Monthly Military Service Report, Box 165, Colorado River Agency Central Classified Files, RG 75, NARA–Pacific Region (R).

54. Walkingstick to Veterans Administration, January 23, 1950, Folder: Edwin Walk-ingstick, Box 10, Series 37, Veterans Training Folders (Education Branch), RG 75, Cherokee Indian Agency, NARA–Southeast (A).

55. Husbands to Jennings, January 19, 1951, and Jennings to Veterans Administra-tion, January 4, 1951, Folder: Edwin Walkingstick, Box 10, Series 37, Veterans Training Folders (Education Branch), RG 75, Cherokee Indian Agency, NARA–Southeast (A).

56. Edwin Walkingstick, "What the School Could Do," February 28, 1946, Folder: Edwin Walkingstick, Box 10, Series 37, Veterans Training Folders (Education Branch), RG 75, Cherokee Indian Agency, NARA–Southeast (A).

57. Walkingstick to Veterans Administration, January 23, 1950.

58. Roland to Davis, July 15, 1947, Folder: Veterans Training—General 1947–1949, Box 7, Series 36, Veterans Training Files 1944–1952 (Education Branch), RG 75, Cherokee Indian Agency, NARA–Southeast (A).

59. Brown to Davis, July 15, 1947, Folder: Veterans Training—General 1947–1949, Box 7, Series 36, Veterans Training Files 1944–1952 (Education Branch), RG 75, Cherokee Indian Agency, NARA–Southeast (A).

60. Blanton to Veterans Administration, July 11, 1947, and Willett to Jennings, July 11, 1947, Folder: Veterans Training—General 1947–1949, Box 7, Series 36, Veterans Training Files 1944–1952 (Education Branch), RG 75, Cherokee Indian Agency, NARA–Southeast (A).

61. Anthony to Veterans Administration, September 29, 1950, Folder: Anthony, Char-lie 1947–1950, Box 1, Series 37, Veterans Training Folders (Education Branch), RG 75, Cherokee Indian Agency, NARA–Southeast (A).

62. Jennings to Veterans Administration, October 2, 1950, Folder: Anthony, Charlie 1947–1950, Box 1, Series 37, Veterans Training Folders (Education Branch), RG 75, Cherokee Indian Agency, NARA–Southeast (A).

63. Bennett to Gensler, March 3, 1947, Folder: Veterans Service Committee—War Veterans Education, Box 165, Colorado River Agency Central Classified Files, RG 75, NARA–Pacific Region (R).

64. Gensler to Veterans Administration, March 6, 1947, and Gensler to Beatty, April 9, 1947, Folder: Veterans Service Committee—War Veterans Education, Box 165, Colorado River Agency Central Classified Files, RG 75, NARA–Pacific Region (R).

65. Gensler to Davis, June 19, 1947, Davis to Gensler, June 27, 1947, and Mathie-sen to Commissioner of Indian Affairs, July 1, 1948, Folder: Veterans Service Committee—War Veterans Education, Box 165, Colorado River Agency Central Classified Files, RG 75, NARA–Pacific Region (R).

66. In 1947 the Colorado River Tribal Council "urgently requested" information about the status of the Veterans School and expressed interest in lobbying the

state government about the plan. Zeh to Zimmerman, November 7, 1947, Folder: WRA Poston (Disposition of Buildings), Box 64, Irrigation District Number 4 Colorado River Irrigation Project, RG 75, NARA–Pacific Region (R).

67. H. A. Mathiesen, "Progress Report on the School for Indian Veterans at Cherokee, North Carolina," Folder: Veterans Training, Box 7, Series 36, Veterans Training Files 1944–1952 (Education Branch), RG 75, Cherokee Indian Agency, NARA–Southeast (A).

68. Mathiesen, "Progress Report on the School for Indian Veterans."

69. For a larger discussion of vocational rehabilitation after World War II, see Jennings, *Out of the Horrors*; McEnaney, *Postwar*, 97–134.

70. See Enoch, "Resisting the Script," for quotes from Richard Henry Pratt, founder of the Carlisle Indian School, and Zitkala-Ša's strong responses.

71. Mathiesen, "Progress Report on the School for Indian Veterans."

72. Pima Indian Agency Jurisdiction, Combined Narrative Extension Report, October 1947, Monthly Reports 1942–1948 Pima Agency, Box 361, Phoenix Area Office Division of Extension and Industry Files, RG 75, NARA–Pacific Region (R). The Pima Agency serves the Gila River Indian Community and the Ak-Chin Indian Community and is headquartered in Sacaton, Arizona.

73. Robert Hackenberg, *An Analysis of Tribal Economics and Tribal Government on the Gila River Reservation*, John Hay Whitney Foundation, 1955, 119–20, Arizona–Gila River Tribes (Pimas), Box 84, William Brophy General File, HSTL.

74. Hackenberg, *Analysis of Tribal Economics*, 120.

75. Mathiesen, "Progress Report on the School for Indian Veterans."

76. Okimoto, *Sharing a Desert Home*, 7. See Byrd, *Transit of Empire*, 187, for a discussion of the "colonization" terminology.

77. Krakoff, "Settler Colonialism and Reclamation," 264.

78. Minutes of Special Meeting with John Collier and Colorado River Tribal Council, October 30, 1939, Series 4, Addresses and Writings, Part 2, 1933–1945, John Collier Papers (University Microfilms International, Reel 32), Arizona State University Law Library.

79. The 2018 documentary produced by the Colorado River Indian Tribal Council, *In Our Voice*, describes in detail the intersecting processes of Japanese American internment and colonization. At 10 minutes 45 seconds into the documentary, Amelia Flores (Mohave) notes that World War II delayed the colonization program, but that the program was "in the background" of the experience of the Colorado River Indian Tribes and the WRA camp on their reservation. Wright, *In Our Voice*.

80. R. H. Rupkey, "Narrative for Final Report," March 31, 1945, Folder: Colorado River Gravity Project–Japanese Internment General (1 of 2), Box 7, Phoenix Area Office Irrigation Files 1935–1961, RG 75, NARA–Pacific Region (R).

81. Woehlke to Collier, March 18, 1942, War Relocation Authority—Internment of Japanese on Indian Lands 1942 Part 1 (February–August 1942), Native Americans and the New Deal—The Office Files of John Collier 1933-1945 (University Microfilms International, Reel 17), Labriola National Indian Data Center, Arizona State University.

82. Interview of Amelia Flores, at 13 minutes 8 seconds, in Wright, *In Our Voice.* Four tribes (the Chemehuevi, Mohave, Navajo, and Hopi) officially constitute the Colorado River Indian Tribes today.

83. Summary of Indian Irrigation Projects in the Colorado River Basin, 1945, Indian Affairs 1945, Box 16, WBSB, HSTL.

84. Gensler to Commissioner of Indian Affairs, February 11, 1947, Folder: Veterans Service Committee—War Veterans Education, Box 165, Colorado River Agency Central Classified Files, RG 75, NARA–Pacific Region (R).

85. Gensler Report, "Proposed Veterans' Vocational Training School," Folder: Veterans Service Committee—War Veterans Education, Box 165, Colorado River Agency Central Classified Files, RG 75, NARA–Pacific Region (R).

86. Gensler Report.

87. Gensler Report.

88. Gensler Report.

89. Brophy to Gurney, May 3, 1946, Commissioner of Indian Affairs—Correspondence May 1946, Box 15, WBSB, HSTL.

90. Annual Report of the Commissioner, Office of Indian Affairs, to the Secretary of the Interior, Fiscal Year Ended June 30, 1946, 356, Folder: Correspondence with Institutions, Organizations, Etc.—National Congress of American Indians, Box 12, RG 220 Records of the President's Commission on Civil Rights, HSTL.

91. Jennings to Stone, August 23, 1948; Nichols to Jennings, May 22, 1948, Folder: Veterans Training—General 1945-1949, Box 7, Series 36, Veterans Training Files 1944-1952 (Education Branch), RG 75, Cherokee Indian Agency, NARA–Southeast (A).

92. Jennings to Stone, August 23, 1948.

93. McKinney, "From Canning to Contraceptives," 58.

94. Report on Foods and Nutrition, 1940, Extension and Industry Narrative Reports and Program of Work, 1937-1952, Box 2, Agricultural Extension Program, Carson Agency, RG 75, NARA–Pacific Region (SF).

95. Ladies Home Improvement Club Report, 1940, Extension and Industry Narrative Reports and Program of Work, 1937-1952, Box 2, Agricultural Extension Program, Bishop Sub-Agency, RG 75, BIA, NARA–Pacific Region (SF).

96. Farm Surveys of Robert Reed, George Walker, and Noah Ledford, Folder: Completed Visit Sheets by Agricultural Instructors to Trainee Farms, Box 1, Series

36, Veterans Training Files 1944–1952 (Education Branch), RG 75, Cherokee Indian Agency, NARA–Southeast (A).

97. Jennings to Stone, August 23, 1948.

98. Reports of Instructor Hyatt on Freeman Lambert, March 18, 1948; Lou Brady, March 9, 1948, Folder: Completed Visit Sheets by Agricultural Instructors to Trainee Farms, Box 1, Series 36, Veterans Training Files 1944–1952 (Education Branch), RG 75, Cherokee Indian Agency, NARA–Southeast (A).

99. Sawyer to Burge, March 18, 1946, Folder: Veterans Administration, Box 202, Sells Indian Agency Files of Community Worker, RG 75, NARA–Pacific Region (R).

100. Statistics Pertaining to Papago Servicemen and Servicewomen, 1946, Indians at Work, Box 201, Sells Indian Agency Files of Community Worker, RG 75, NARA–Pacific Region (R).

101. Drefkoff, "Industrial Program for the Navajo Indian Reservation."

102. Farm Loans Instruction Plan, Folder: Veterans Training—Class Instruction Plans 1950–1952, Box 10, Series 36, Veterans Training Files 1944–1952 (Education Branch), RG 75, Cherokee Indian Agency, NARA–Southeast (A).

103. Gensler Report, "Proposed Veterans' Vocational Training School."

104. Select Committee to Investigate Indian Affairs and Conditions in the United States, An Investigation to Determine Whether the Changed Status of the Indian Requires a Revision of the Laws and Regulations Affecting the American Indian (H.R. 166), H.R. Rep. No. 2091 at 14 (1944), Folder 19, Congressional Report Addressing Changed Status of American Indian 1944, Box 16, William Zimmerman Papers, Center for Southwest Research, University of New Mexico.

105. Select Committee to Investigate Indian Affairs and Conditions in the United States, An Investigation.

106. All four of the competency bills proposed by Francis Case between 1944 and 1947 focused on the "emancipation" of Native veterans. To Case, military service was such a clear fulfillment of the duties of citizenship that it merited direct conferral of competency onto a Native applicant.

107. Frank C. Waldrop, "Let 'Em Go," *Washington Times-Herald*, July 23, 1947, Indian Bureau Liquidation, Box 15, SEN 83A-F9 (1928–1953), Committee on Interior and Insular Affairs Indian Affairs Investigating Subcommittee, RG 46, NAB.

108. Waldrop, "Let 'Em Go."

6. NEBULOUS SHAME

1. "Shameful," *Arizona Times*, October 31, 1947, Folder 28, Rehabilitation of Navajo and Hopi Tribes 1947, Box 82, Dennis Chavez Papers, CSR-UNM.

2. Hill to Hayden, 1947, Folder 28, Rehabilitation of Navajo and Hopi Tribes 1947, Box 82, Dennis Chavez Papers, CSR-UNM.

3. Simpson to Chavez, September 5, 1951, Folder 23, Bureau of Indian Affairs 1950–1951, Box 134, Dennis Chavez Papers, CSR-UNM.

4. Shreve, *Red Power Rising*, 119–38.

5. Dudas, *Cultivation of Resentment*, 21.

6. Dudas, *Cultivation of Resentment*, 22.

7. Kiel, "Nation vs. Municipality;" Cramer, *Cash, Color, and Colonialism*; Cramer, "Common Sense of Anti-Indian Racism"; Harmon, *Rich Indians*.

8. Kiel, "Nation vs. Municipality," 64.

9. Michelmore, *Tax and Spend*, 11.

10. Michelmore, *Tax and Spend*, 31, 21.

11. Tani, *States of Dependency*, 184.

12. Hill to Hayden, 1947, Folder 28, Rehabilitation of Navajo and Hopi Tribes 1947, Box 82, Dennis Chavez Papers, CSR-UNM.

13. Simpson to Chavez, September 24, 1951, Folder 23, Bureau of Indian Affairs 1950–1951, Box 134, Dennis Chavez Papers, CSR-UNM.

14. Barker, *Native Acts*, 30–31.

15. Felix Cohen, Amicus Brief of Association on American Indian Affairs, Hualapai Tribe of Arizona, and San Carlos Apache Tribe of Arizona, State of Arizona v. Oscar R. Ewing, Civil Action No. 2008-52, 11 (United States District Court for District of Columbia 1952), Folder 20: *Arizona v. Ewing, Oscar R.* (Federal Social Security), 1952, Box 328, AAIA Papers, MML.

16. "Reservations Perfect Example of the Welfare State," *Los Angeles Herald-Express*, May 16, 1950; Myer, Dillon S. Commissioner of Indian Affairs, Box 26, SEN 83A-F9 (1928–1953), Records of the Committee on Interior and Insular Affairs Indian Affairs Investigating Subcommittee, Records of the U.S. Senate, RG 46, NAB.

17. "Reservations Perfect Example of the Welfare State."

18. Margaret D. Jacobs, *Generation Removed*, 40; V. Deloria, *Custer Died for Your Sins*, 9.

19. Jacobs, *Generation Removed*, 41–42.

20. Jacobs, *Generation Removed*, 39.

21. Jacobs, *Generation Removed*, 59.

22. H. Scudder Mekeel, "The American Indian as a Minority Group Problem," *American Indian* 2, no. 1 (Fall 1944), Indians—Pamphlets and Reports (2 of 3), Box 43, PNWH File, HSTL.

23. Extension of Remarks of Hon. Hugh Butler of Nebraska, "Wards of the Government." Address by Dean Russell, S. Rep. No. 81 (1950), Indian Bureau Liquidation, Box 15, SEN 83A-F9 (1928–1953), Committee on Interior and Insular Affairs Indian Affairs Investigating Subcommittee, RG 46, NAB.

24. Russell, "Wards of the Government."

25. United States Commission on Civil Rights, *Justice*, 1961, p.149, Publications—Civil Rights (Folder 2), Box 111, Files of Indian Health, WBSB, HSTL.

26. Russell, "Wards of the Government."

27. Essie Skillern, "A New Day for Indian Americans," in "The Rights and Liberties of the American Indian: Background Information," 161, Background Information—The Rights and Liberties of American Indians (Folder 1), Box 78, Files of the Commission on the Rights, Liberties, and Responsibilities of the American Indian, WBSB, HSTL.

28. Skillern, "New Day for Indian Americans," 167, emphasis added.

29. L. S. Cressman, "The Rights and Liberties of the American Indian: Background Information," p. 63, Background Information—The Rights and Liberties of American Indians (Folder 1), Box 78, Files of the Commission on the Rights, Liberties, and Responsibilities of the American Indian, WBSB, HSTL.

30. Skillern, "New Day for Indian Americans," 170.

31. Skillern, "New Day for Indian Americans," 165.

32. Kiel, "Nation vs. Municipality," 64.

33. Emmons Address to Annual Meeting of AAIA, May 5, 1954, Folder 13, Indian Affairs Speeches 1954, Box 2, Glenn Emmons Papers, CSR-UNM.

34. S. Lyman Tyler, "A Work Paper on Termination: With an Attempt to Show Its Antecedents," iii, Memo #55–Agenda for 7th Meeting San Francisco Work Paper on Termination Its Antecedents 8-28-58, Box 69, William Brophy Commission on the Rights, Liberties, and Responsibilities of the Indian Papers, HSTL.

35. Ruth Bronson, "Outreach," NCAI, Series 3, Correspondence, Box 64, Correspondence Name Files—Bronson, Ruth (Treasurer of NCAI and Consultant to Executive Director), NMAI, emphasis added.

36. V. Deloria, *Custer Died for Your Sins*, 20.

37. V. Deloria, *Custer Died for Your Sins*, 23.

38. V. Deloria, *Custer Died for Your Sins*, 15.

39. Taylor to Hayden, December 27, 1946, WRA—Poston [Disposition of Buildings], Box 64, Irrigation District Number 4 Colorado River Irrigation Project Records, Records of the Bureau of Indian Affairs, RG 75, NARA–Pacific Region (R).

40. Taylor to Hayden, December 27, 1946.

41. Letter from Gensler to Zimmerman 1941, Social Security Legislation Correspondence, Box 168, Colorado River Central Classified Files (CRCC Files), RG 75, NARA–Pacific Region (R).

42. V. Deloria, *Custer Died for Your Sins*, 46.

43. William Brophy, "Story of the Indian Service," 1946, 4, Correspondence with Institutions, Organizations, Etc.-National Congress of American Indians, Box 12, RG 220, Records of the President's Commission on Civil Rights, HSTL.

44. Brophy, "Story of the Indian Service," 2.

45. Welke, *Law and the Borders* 70–71; P. Deloria, *Indians in Unexpected Places*, 26.
46. Welke, *Law and the Borders* 75.
47. Welke, *Law and the Borders*, 86.
48. "A Federal Problem," *Phoenix Gazette*, February 25, 1953, Folder 21, *Arizona v. Hobby, Oveta Culp* (Hualapai and San Carlos), 1952–1954, Box 328, AAIA Papers, MML.
49. "A System Long Outgrown," *Arizona Republic*, March 3, 1953, Folder 21, *Arizona v. Hobby, Oveta Culp* (Hualapai and San Carlos), 1952–1954, Box 328, AAIA Papers, MML.
50. United States Commission on Civil Rights, *Justice*, 1961, 156, Publications — Civil Rights (Folder 2), Box 111, WBSB, HSTL.
51. United States Commission on Civil Rights, *Justice*, 149.
52. United States Commission on Civil Rights, *Justice*, 156.
53. New Mexico: 1961 Report to the Commission on Civil Rights from the State Advisory Committee, p. 418, Publications — Civil Rights (Folder 4), Box 112, WBSB, HSTL.
54. P. Deloria, *Indians in Unexpected Places*, 27.
55. P. Deloria, *Indians in Unexpected Places*, 27–28.
56. Berger, "Red," 635.
57. United States Commission on Civil Rights, *Justice*, 117.
58. Berger, "Red," 635.
59. Thomas S. Shiya, "What Indian Tribes Can Do to Assume Their Responsibilities," Phoenix Area Land Operations Conference, 1955, Publicity Ethnology, Box 6, Phoenix Area Office Central Classified Files, RG 75, NARA–Pacific Region (R).
60. Shiya, "What Indian Tribes Can Do."
61. Shiya, "What Indian Tribes Can Do."
62. Department of the Interior, Office of the Solicitor, "The Applicability of the Social Security Act to the Indians," 1936, 4–5, Social Security Legislation Correspondence, Box 168, CRCC Files, RG 75, NARA–Pacific Region (R).
63. Felix Cohen, Amicus Brief, 11.
64. Statement by Senator Hugh Butler in Explanation of Bills Introduced to Remove All Restrictions on the Indian Tribes, 1947, Indian Bureau Liquidation, Box 15, SEN 83A-F9 (1928–1953), Committee on Interior and Insular Affairs Indian Affairs Investigating Subcommittee, RG 46, NAB, emphasis added.
65. Weaver to Myer, 1950, Personal Correspondence 1950 (1 of 2), Box 4, Personal Correspondence File, DM Papers, HSTL.
66. Commission on the Rights, Liberties, and Responsibilities of the American Indian, chapter 1, 29, 28, Memo #110 — Memorandum to Accompany Chapter 1 of Commission Report 11-11-59, Box 72, Files of the Commission on the Rights, Liberties, and Responsibilities of the American Indian, WBSB, HSTL.

67. V. Deloria, *Custer Died for Your Sins*, 23.
68. Senate Committee on Indian Affairs, Survey of Conditions among the Indians of the United States, S. Rep. No. 78-310, pt. 1 (1948), at 5.
69. *A Bill Establishing a Joint Congressional Committee to Make a Study of Claims of Indian Tribes Against the United States, and to Investigate the Administration of Indian Affairs: Hearings on S.J. Res. 79, Before the Committee on Indian Affairs United States Senate*, 79th Cong. 24–25 (1946) (Statement of AIDA). AIDA was founded in 1923 by future commissioner of Indian Affairs John Collier. It was one of many "Friends of the Indians" organizations made up of primarily non-Native, white, members.
70. Court Proceedings, Arizona v. Hobby, Civil Action No. 2008-52, February 20, 1953, 12, Folder 21, *Arizona v. Hobby, Oveta Culp* (Hualapai and San Carlos), 1952–1954, Box 328, AAIA Papers, MML.
71. Court Proceedings, Arizona v. Hobby, 12, emphasis added.
72. Court Proceedings, Arizona v. Hobby, 12.
73. Koontz to Robinson, 1951, Welfare—1949-1951 Correspondence of James A. Helm, Box 149, Pima Indian Agency Records Relating to Welfare, RG 75, NARA–Pacific Region (R).
74. Robinson to Koontz, 1951, Welfare—1949-1951 Correspondence of James A. Helm, Box 149, Pima Indian Agency Records Relating to Welfare, RG 75, NARA–Pacific Region (R).
75. "The No-Man's-Land of Indian Slums," *Indian Affairs*, Newsletter of the American Indian Fund and the AAIA, April 21, 1950, Association on American Indian Affairs (2 of 2), Box 8, SEN 83A-F9 (1928–1953), Committee on Interior and Insular Affairs Indian Affairs Investigating Subcommittee, RG 46, NAB.
76. "No-Man's-Land of Indian Slums."
77. "No-Man's-Land of Indian Slums."
78. F. Cohen to Officers of All Pueblo Council and Pueblo Governors, 1950, Folder 26, Indian Affairs All-Pueblo Council 1950–1960, Box 134, Dennis Chavez Papers, CSR-UNM. For more on Natives' ineligibility for housing improvement programs, see Kwak, *World of Homeowners*, 180–82.
79. Altschuler and Blumin, *GI Bill*, 187–88.
80. L. Cohen, *Consumers' Republic*, 141.
81. Altschuler and Blumin, *GI Bill*, 201.
82. Altschuler and Blumin, *GI Bill*, 199, 201.
83. Sawyer to Burge, 1946, Veterans Administration, Box 202, Sells Indian Agency Files of Community Worker, RG 75, NARA–Pacific Region (R).
84. Keeler, "Putting People Where They Belong," 87.
85. April 7, 1948, BIA Circular Letter, Folder 790, Welfare 1950–1952, Box 15, Seminole Agency Subject Files Correspondence, RG 75, NARA–Southeast (A).

86. Kimmis Hendrick, "Bureaucracy Hit; Near-Famine Cited," *Christian Science Monitor*, December 3, 1947, NCAI, Series 4, Tribal Files, Box 113, Navajo Tribe (Arizona), 1946–1947, NMAI.

87. The BIA had stated in 1945, "Indian agency superintendents may authorize the use of income from [trust] lands as security for loans partially guaranteed by the Veteran's Administration," as well as "other liberal provisions." However, despite these provisions, lending agencies remained wary of granting loans to Native applicants. In the early 1950s BIA officials changed bureau regulations to "permit mortgaging of such lands under certain conditions." BIA Press Release, "Indian Bureau Moves to Transfer Functions," 1953, Myer Dillon S Commissioner of Indian Affairs, Box 26, SEN 83A-F9 (1928–1953), Committee on Interior and Insular Affairs Indian Affairs Investigating Subcommittee, RG 46, NAB. However, many lenders were still reluctant to extend loans to Native applicants because they "feared that the Secretary [of the Interior], under existing statutes, had no right to permit the execution of mortgages on restricted lands by a regulation." Felix Cohen Memo to Clients, Public Law 450, 1956, Folder 8, Correspondence Regarding Various Tribal Legal Matters 1952–1961, Box 3, William Zimmerman Papers, CSR-UNM. Without "specific legislative authority," banks and lenders "refused to accept Indian lands as security for loans" until President Dwight Eisenhower signed a law authorizing mortgages and deeds of trust on individual Indian trust or restricted lands in 1956. Under this new law, trust status was not removed, but "trust was lifted to the extent of the debt and the lender may levy upon the land as if it were owned in fee simple." Although advocates argued that this law would make it easier for Natives to obtain credit, because "restrictions on alienation are removed in cases of foreclosure," there was a risk that borrowers could lose their land entirely. Indeed, Keeler notes that Native people on reservations *still* have limited access to home loans because "trust land cannot be used as collateral in case of mortgage default." Keeler, "Putting People Where They Belong," 92.

88. "Amendment to GI Bill Asked to Aid Indian Vets," *Great Falls Tribune*, October 23, 1945, National Congress of American Indians (2 of 4), Box 26, SEN 83A-F9 (1928–1953), Committee on Interior and Insular Affairs Indian Affairs Investigating Subcommittee, RG 46, NAB.

89. Commissioner's Meeting, Te-Moak, 1956, Folder 3, Indian Affairs Commissioner's Conferences Phoenix Area, Box 3, Glenn Emmons Papers, CSR-UNM.

90. Kiel, "Nation v. Municipality," 66.

7. CARE TAKEN TO INFORM

1. Peterson to Hastings, February 20, 1957, NCAI, Series 6, Committees and Special Issues Files, Box 307, Folder: Special Issues—Health and Welfare—Montana Department of Public Welfare, NMAI.

2. *Cherokee Indians, North Carolina, Hearings on H. Res. 30, September 17, Before the Subcommittee on Indian Affairs of the Committee on Interior and Insular Affairs House of Representatives*, 84th Cong. 50 (1955) (James Haley to Helen Peterson).

3. Cobb, "Introduction: A Reflexive Historiography," in Cobb, *Say We Are Nations*, 5.

4. Hemmings, *Why Stories Matter*, 20.

5. Cited in Powell, "Political Grammar," 949–50.

6. Mansfield, *Political Grammar*, viii.

7. Bruyneel, *Third Space of Sovereignty*, 128. For more on Native self-determination and economic development in the mid- to late twentieth century, see Goldstein, *Poverty in Common*, 87, 149–50.

8. Theobald, *Reproduction on the Reservation*, 140.

9. Native women have a long history of advocating for their people and voicing their concerns to the U.S. government. Just a few examples of scholarly work on this topic in the late nineteenth through the twentieth centuries include (but are not limited to) Winnemucca, *Newspaper Warrior*; Zitkala-Ša, *Help Indians Help Themselves*; A. Deer, *Making a Difference*; selections from Cobb, *Say We Are Nations*, including speeches and testimonies by Christine Galler (also known as Christal Quintasket), Elizabeth Peratrovich, Tillie Walker, Marie Sanchez, and others; Guise, "Who Is Doctor Bauer?"; Margaret D. Jacobs, *Generation Removed*; Margaret D. Jacobs, *White Mother*; S. Deer, *Beginning and End of Rape*.

10. Fixico, *Call for Change*, 19.

11. King, *Earth Memory Compass*, 5.

12. TallBear, "Caretaking Relations," 32. See also Harris, "Whiteness as Property," 1707–91.

13. V. Deloria, "We Were Here," 135.

14. Reed, *Serving the Nation*, 5–6.

15. Reed, *Serving the Nation*, 3.

16. Reed, *Serving the Nation*, 6.

17. Harjo, *Poet Warrior*, 7.

18. N. Scott Momaday, "The Delight Song of Tsoai-talee," cited in Harjo, *Poet Warrior*, 114, Poetry Foundation, https://www.poetryfoundation.org/poems/46558/the-delight-song-of-tsoai-talee.

19. Statement of D'Arcy McNickle, 1954, 9, Correspondence with Institutions, Organizations, Etc.—National Congress of American Indians, Box 12, Records of the President's Commission on Civil Rights, RG 220, HSTL.

20. Statement of D'Arcy McNickle, 8. John Dickey was the committee member who made this statement.

21. Memo: "Civil Rights of American Indians," Prepared by Milton Steward and Rachel Sady, 1947, 5, Staff Memoranda, Witnesses, Statements to the Committee, and Other Committee Documents, Box 16, RG 220, HSTL.

22. Oliver La Farge, "The Year of Confusion," AAIA Annual Meeting, May 5, 1954, 6, Association on American Indians File—Correspondence May 1954, Box 76, Philleo Nash White House / Association on American Indians Files, HSTL.

23. Letter from James Curry to Ruth Bronson, 1949, Indian Legislation 1947–49 Proposed Legislation—Senatorial, Box 28, Senatorial Records, J. Howard McGrath Papers, HSTL.

24. Curry to Bronson, 1949.

25. Ruth Bronson, "Outreach," NCAI, Series 3, Correspondence, Box 64, Correspondence Name Files—Bronson, Ruth (Treasurer of NCAI and Consultant to Executive Director), NMAI.

26. In Nevada, Native land adjacent to towns and cities was referred to as "colonies." For more demographic information on Native people in Nevada, see Elliott, *History of Nevada*, 396–99; Forbes, *Nevada Indians Speak*.

27. *Termination of Federal Supervision over Certain Tribes of Indians: Joint Hearing on H.R. 7552, Part 10, before the Subcommittees of the Committees on Interior and Insular Affairs*, 83rd Cong., 1235 (1954) (Testimony of Eleanor Myers, Representative of Lovelock Indian Colony), Nevada Indians, Box 90, General File—Indians, WBSB, HSTL.

28. Testimony of Eleanor Myers, 1235.

29. Testimony of Eleanor Myers, 1237–38.

30. Testimony of Eleanor Myers, 1238, emphasis added.

31. Cragun to Montana Delegation, January 15, 1957, NCAI, Series 6, Committees and Special Issues Files, Box 307, Folder: Special Issues—Health and Welfare—Montana Department of Public Welfare, NMAI.

32. Wilkerson, *To Live Here*, 6.

33. Helen Peterson, Statement before Constitutional Rights Subcommittee, September 1, 1961, NCAI, Series 3, Correspondence, Box 67, Folder: Correspondence Name Files—Peterson, Helen (Executive Director, NCAI), NMAI. For the history of the NCAI's founding, see Cowger, *National Congress of American Indians*, 3.

34. Cowger, *National Congress of American Indians*, 3.

35. Ramirez, *Standing Up to Colonial Power*, 219.

36. The Constitutional Rights Subcommittee was established in 1955 to survey "the extent to which the Constitutional rights of the people of the United States were being respected and enforced." When Peterson testified, the committee was chaired by Sam Ervin (D-NC). Ervin was an advocate for civil liberties, but he opposed civil rights legislation (a Southern Democrat, Ervin contributed to the "Southern Manifesto" of 1956, which opposed school desegregation). Thus, the subcommittee played no role in the passage of the 1964 Civil Rights Act. The committee investigated constitutional rights such as fair trials, rights to bail and speedy trials, and the rights of mentally ill Americans, civil servants, and

Native people. In 1977 the subcommittee was folded into the Subcommittee on Constitutional Amendments. United States Senate, "Sam Ervin: A Featured Biography," https://www.senate.gov/senators/FeaturedBios/Featured_Bio_ErvinSam .htm; Donald A. Ritchie, "Senate Subcommittee on Constitutional Rights," Encyclopedia.com, 1992, https://www.encyclopedia.com/politics/encyclopedias -almanacs-transcripts-and-maps/senate-subcommittee-constitutional-rights.

37. Moreton-Robinson, *White Possessive*, 50.
38. Peterson, Statement before Constitutional Rights Subcommittee.
39. Peterson, Statement before Constitutional Rights Subcommittee.
40. Peterson, Statement before Constitutional Rights Subcommittee.
41. Peterson, Statement before Constitutional Rights Subcommittee, emphasis added. In this statement Peterson foreshadows future efforts by Native people to establish a system of restorative justice. See S. Deer, "Decolonizing Rape Law."
42. Peterson, Statement before Constitutional Rights Subcommittee.
43. Moreton-Robinson, *White Possessive*, 57.
44. Peterson, Statement before Constitutional Rights Subcommittee.
45. Peterson and Jemison, "This Resolution," 103.
46. Peterson and Jemison, "This Resolution," 104.
47. Bronson, "Outreach."
48. *Constitutional Rights of the American Indian, Hearings on S. Res. 53, Part 1, Before the Subcommittee on Constitutional Rights of the Committee on the Judiciary United States Senate*, 87th Cong. 188 (1961) (statement of Mrs. Helen Peterson, Executive Director, National Congress of American Indians; Accompanied by John W. Cragun, General Counsel, National Congress of American Indians).
49. National Congress of American Indians, "Emergency Conference of American Indians on Legislation," 1954, Association on American Indians File—Correspondence 1953–1954, Box 75, Philleo Nash White House/Association on American Indians Files, HSTL.
50. "Emergency Conference of American Indians on Legislation."
51. Commissioner's Conference, Nambe Pueblo and Tesuque Pueblo, 1956, Folder 5, Indian Affairs Commissioner's Conferences Gallup Area First Session, Box 3, Glenn Emmons Papers, CSR-UNM.
52. "Emergency Conference of American Indians on Legislation."
53. Quoted in Speech of George Malone, "Tear Up the Indian Bureau by the Roots— Set the Indian Free," S. Rep. No. 81 (1949), Indian Bureau Liquidation, Box 15, SEN 83A-F9 (1928–1953), Committee on Interior and Insular Affairs Indian Affairs Investigating Subcommittee, Records of the U.S. Senate, RG 46, NAB, emphasis added.
54. Commissioner's Meeting, Reno-Sparks, 1956, Folder 3, Indian Affairs Commissioner's Conferences Phoenix Area, Box 3, Glenn Emmons Papers, CSR-UNM.

55. See Altschuler and Blumin, *GI Bill*, 61; Mettler, *Soldiers to Citizens*, 10.

56. Felix Cohen, Amicus Brief of Association on American Indian Affairs, Hualapai Tribe of Arizona, and San Carlos Apache Tribe of Arizona, State of Arizona v. Oscar R. Ewing, Civil Action No. 2008-52, 7 (United States District Court for District of Columbia 1952), Folder 20, *Arizona v. Ewing, Oscar R.* (Federal Social Security), 1952, Box 328, Association on American Indian Affairs Papers, MML.

57. Commission on the Rights, Liberties, and Responsibilities of the American Indian, *A Program for Indian Citizens: A Summary Report*, 1961, 3, A Program for Indian Citizens—A Summary Report January 1961, Box 78, William Brophy Commission on the Rights, Liberties, and Responsibilities of the Indian Papers, HSTL, emphasis added.

58. Bronson, "Outreach."

59. Michelmore, *Tax and Spend*, 39.

60. *Constitutional Rights of the American Indian, Hearings on S. Res. 53* (statement of Helen Peterson), emphasis added.

61. "Current Policy of the Montana Department of Public Welfare Relating to State Child Welfare Services on Indian Reservations," January 27, 1957, NCAI, Series 6, Committees and Special Issues Files, Box 307, Folder: Special Issues—Health and Welfare—Montana Department of Public Welfare, NMAI.

62. Newton to Cragun, July 3, 1956, NCAI, Series 6, Committees and Special Issues Files, Box 307, Folder: Special Issues—Health and Welfare—Montana Department of Public Welfare, NMAI.

63. *Unpublished Hearing in Connection with House Concurrent Resolution 108 at Flathead Agency, Dixon, Montana, October 16, Before Congressional Subcommittee on Interior and Insular Affairs*, 83rd Cong. 1 (1953) (statement of William Henry Harrison of Wyoming, Chairman of Hearing), HRG-1953-IIA-0306, ProQuest Congressional.

64. *Unpublished Hearing in Connection with House Concurrent Resolution 108 at Flathead Agency* (statement of Chief Paul Charlo, interpreted by Stevens Matt), HRG-1953-IIA-0306, ProQuest Congressional.

65. Statement of Chief Paul Charlo, 23.

66. Cooper, Greenfield, and O'Connell to Metcalf, January 28, 1957, NCAI, Series 6, Committees and Special Issues Files, Box 307, Folder: Special Issues—Health and Welfare—Montana Department of Public Welfare, NMAI.

67. Cooper, Greenfield, and O'Connell to Metcalf, January 28, 1957.

68. *Constitutional Rights of the American Indian, Hearings on S. Res. 53* (statement of Helen Peterson).

69. Unpublished Hearing, "Emancipation of Indians," House of Representatives Subcommittee on Indian Affairs of the Committee on Public Lands, June 20,

1947, 80th Cong., 26, HRG-1947-PLH-0317, ProQuest Congressional. See chapter 2 for full discussion of these hearings.

70. Johnnie Tillmon, "Welfare Is a Women's Issue," *Ms. Magazine*, Spring 1972, https://msmagazine.com/2021/03/25/welfare-is-a-womens-issue-ms-magazine-spring-1972/.

71. Nadasen, *Welfare Warriors*, 32, 167.

72. Wilkerson, *To Live Here*, 6.

73. Kornbluh, *Battle for Welfare Rights*, 17, emphasis added.

74. Bronson, *Indians Are People, Too*, 2.

75. Harjo, *Poet Warrior*, 74.

76. Stryker, "Transgender Feminism," 87. Many thanks to Leslie Dunlap for pointing me toward this article.

CONCLUSION

1. F. Cohen, "Indian Wardship" (1953), in *Legal Conscience*, 331–32.

EPILOGUE

1. Belcourt, *History of My Brief Body*, 77.

2. Hartman, *Scenes of Subjection*, 3.

3. Margaret D. Jacobs, *Generation Removed*, 4.

4. Will Rogers Jr., "Starvation without Representation," *Look Magazine*, February 17, 1948, 36, NCAI, Series 4, Tribal Files, Box 113, Folder: Tribal Files Navajo Tribe (Arizona), 1948, NMAI.

5. Rogers, "Starvation without Representation," 38.

6. Margaret D. Jacobs, *Generation Removed*, 40.

7. James Estrin, "Behind the Scenes: Still Wounded," *New York Times*, Lens (blog), October 20, 2009, https://archive.nytimes.com/lens.blogs.nytimes.com/2009/10/20/behind-22/index.html.

8. Estrin, "Behind the Scenes."

9. For more on Native child removal see Margaret D. Jacobs, *Generation Removed*; Margaret D. Jacobs, *White Mother*; Harness, *Bitterroot*; King, *Earth Memory Compass*; Child, *Boarding School Seasons*; Child, "Boarding School as Metaphor."

10. James Estrin, "Photographing, and Listening to, the Lakota," *New York Times* Lens (blog), August 17, 2012, https://archive.nytimes.com/lens.blogs.nytimes.com/2012/08/17/photographing-and-listening-to-the-lakota/.

11. Estrin, "Photographing, and Listening."

12. Estrin, "Photographing, and Listening."

13. As of 2022, John S. Knight fellows received a stipend of $85,000 and a $5,000 housing supplement. Fellows also receive free Stanford tuition for the year

of their fellowship. "JSK Journalism Fellowships," accessed August 30, 2022, https://jsk.stanford.edu/become-a-fellow/.

14. Pine Ridge Community Storytelling Project.

15. See Neeta Lind, "First Nations News & Views: Huey's Nat Geo Cover, Lakota People's Law Project, Jim Thorpe's Body," *Daily Kos* August 12, 2012, https://www.dailykos.com/stories/2012/8/12/1119352/-First-Nations-News-Views-Huey-s-Nat-Geo-Cover-Lakota-People-s-Law-Project-Jim-Thorpe-s-Body.

16. Aaron Huey, "America's Native Prisoners of War," TEDxDU 2010, video, accessed August 30, 2022, https://www.ted.com/talks/aaron_huey_america_s_native_prisoners_of_war.

17. Huey, "America's Native Prisoners of War," TEDxDU 2010, 14:35.

18. Huey published photographs of the Lakota Sun Dance, which drew criticism of a different sort from those who opposed publication of this sacred ceremony in a national magazine, to be consumed by a primarily non-Lakota readership.

19. Fuller and Huey, "In the Shadow," 42. See Huey's complete collection of photographs from Pine Ridge at his website, https://www.helloprototype.com/projects-pineridge.

20. Fuller and Huey, "In the Shadow," 46–47.

21. *Tiospaye* is a Lakota social and political concept. A *tiospaye* is a group linked by kinship; in Ella Deloria's words, "a larger family, constituted of related households." Deloria notes that in the closeness of the *tiospaye* lay "such strength and social importance as no single family, however able, could or wished to achieve entirely by its own efforts." E. Deloria, *Waterlily*, 20.

22. Thank you to the University of California, San Diego students in my fall 2020 class, "Native Americans and American Politics," for their thoughtful observations and critiques.

23. Enrique Limón, "The Faces of My People: Photographer Matika Wilbur Redefines Contemporary Native Life," *Santa Fe Reporter*, August 19, 2014, https://www.sfreporter.com/news/coverstories/2014/08/20/the-faces-of-my-people/. Wilbur's photographic project, "Project 562," is based on her desire to photograph faces from all 562 federally recognized tribes. (She started the project in 2012; in 2022 there are 574 federally recognized tribes.)

24. V. Deloria, *Custer Died for Your Sins*, 148.

25. Deloria, *Custer Died for Your Sins*, 149.

26. Fuller and Huey, "In the Shadow," 50.

27. Fuller and Huey, "In the Shadow," 50.

28. Long Soldier, *Whereas*, 44.

29. Long Soldier, *Whereas*, 44.

BIBLIOGRAPHY

ARCHIVES/MANUSCRIPT MATERIAL

Arizona State University Law Library, Tempe

    John Collier Papers, University Microfilms International

Center for Southwest Research, University of New Mexico, Albuquerque (CSR-UNM)

    Dennis Chavez Papers
    Glenn Emmons Papers
    William Zimmerman Papers

Harry S. Truman Library, Independence, Missouri (HSTL)

    Dillon S. Myer Papers (DM)
    Harry S. Truman Official File 296 (HST Official)
    Harry S. Truman Staff Member Office Files, Philleo Nash Files
    J. Howard McGrath Papers
    Joel D. Wolfsohn Papers
    Philleo Nash White House / Association on American Indians Files
    Philleo Nash White House Files (PNWH)
    Record Group 220, Records of the President's Commission on Civil Rights
    William Brophy and Sophie Aberle Brophy Papers (WBSB)
    William Brophy Chronological File
    William Brophy Commission on the Rights, Liberties, and
        Responsibilities of the Indian Papers
    William Brophy General Files

Labriola National Indian Data Center, Arizona State University, Tempe

Native Americans and the New Deal—The Office Files of John Collier, University Microfilms International

National Archives and Records Administration (NARA), Legislative Archives, National Archives Building (NAB), Washington DC

Papers Relating to Specific Bills and Resolutions (SEN 78A-E1)

Records of the Committee on Interior and Insular Affairs Indian Affairs Investigating Subcommittee (SEN 83A-F9 1928–1953)

Records of the U.S. Senate, Record Group 46

National Archives and Records Administration, Pacific Region, Riverside, California (NARA–Pacific Region [R])

Records of the Bureau of Indian Affairs, Record Group 75

Colorado River Agency Central Classified Files (CRCC)

Files of Papago Agency, Sells, Arizona

Phoenix Area Office Central Classified Files

Phoenix Area Office District Director's Classified Files

Phoenix Area Office Division of Extension and Industry, Minutes of Navajo Tribal Council Files

Pima Indian Agency Records Relating to Welfare

Sells Indian Agency Files of Community Worker

Sells Indian Agency Health and Social Welfare Correspondence of Community Worker Files

National Archives and Records Administration, Pacific Region, San Francisco, California (NARA–Pacific Region [SF])

Records of the Bureau of Indian Affairs, Record Group 75

Bishop Sub-Agency Files

Carson Agency Files

National Archives and Records Administration, Southeast Region, Atlanta, Georgia (NARA–Southeast [A])

Records of the Bureau of Indian Affairs, Record Group 75

Cherokee Indian Agency Files

Seminole Agency Files

National Museum of the American Indian Archive Center, Smithsonian Institution, Suitland, Maryland (NMAI)

Records of the National Congress of American Indians (NCAI)

Nevada Historical Society, Reno

McCarranalia II (Papers of Pat McCarran)

Seeley G. Mudd Manuscript Library, Princeton University, Princeton, New Jersey
(MML)

Association on American Indian Affairs Papers

Special Collections, University of Nevada, Reno (UNR)

Collection No. 16, Records of the Pyramid Lake Paiute Tribe (PLPT)

PUBLISHED WORKS

Adams, Mikaëla. *Who Belongs? Race, Resources, and Tribal Citizenship in the Native South.* Oxford: Oxford University Press, 2016.

Altschuler, Glenn C., and Stuart M. Blumin. *The GI Bill: A New Deal for Veterans.* Oxford: Oxford University Press, 2009.

Amador, Emma. "'Women Ask Relief for Puerto Ricans': Territorial Citizenship, the Social Security Act, and Puerto Rican Communities, 1933–1939." *Labor: Studies in Working-Class History of the Americas* 13, no. 3–4 (December 2016): 105–29.

American Red Cross. "A Brief History of the American Red Cross." Accessed August 30, 2022. https://www.redcross.org/content/dam/redcross/National/history-full-history.pdf.

Arnold, Laurie. *Bartering with the Bones of Their Dead: The Colville Confederated Tribes and Termination.* Seattle: University of Washington Press, 2012.

Barker, Joanne. *Native Acts: Law, Recognition, and Cultural Authenticity.* Durham NC: Duke University Press, 2011.

Barkley Brown, Elsa. "Negotiating and Transforming the Public Sphere: African American Political Life in the Transition from Slavery to Freedom." *Public Culture* 7 (1994): 107–46.

Baynton, Douglas. *Defectives in the Land: Disability and Immigration in the Age of Eugenics.* Chicago: University of Chicago Press, 2016.

Beck, David. *The Struggle for Self-Determination: History of the Menominee Indians since 1854.* Lincoln: University of Nebraska Press, 2005.

Bederman, Gail. *Manliness and Civilization: A Cultural History of Gender and Race in the United States, 1880–1917.* Chicago: University of Chicago Press, 1995.

Belcourt, Billy-Ray. *A History of My Brief Body.* Columbus OH: Two Dollar Radio, 2020.

Benally, Malcolm. *Bitter Water: Diné Oral Histories of the Navajo-Hopi Land Dispute.* Tucson: University of Arizona Press, 2011.

Berger, Bethany R. "Red: Racism and the American Indian." *UCLA Law Review* 56 (2009): 591–656.

Bernstein, Alison R. *American Indians and World War II: Toward a New Era in Indian Affairs.* Norman: University of Oklahoma Press, 1991.

Blansett, Kent, Cathleen Cahill, and Andrew Needham, eds. *Indian Cities: Histories of Indigenous Urbanization*. Oxford: Oxford University Press, 2022.

Brings Plenty, Trevino L. "Red-ish Brown-ish." In *New Poets of Native Nations*, edited by Heid E. Erdrich, 115. Minneapolis: Graywolf Press, 2018.

Bronson, Ruth Muskrat. *Indians Are People, Too*. New York: Friendship Press, 1944. HathiTrust, https://babel.hathitrust.org/cgi/pt?id=wu.89058379140&seq=9.

Brown, Michael K. *Race, Money, and the American Welfare State*. Ithaca NY: Cornell University Press, 1999.

Bruyneel, Kevin. "Challenging American Boundaries: Indigenous People and the 'Gift' of US Citizenship." *Studies in American Political Development* 18 (Spring 2004): 30–43.

——. *The Third Space of Sovereignty: The Postcolonial Politics of US-Indigenous Relations*. Minneapolis: University of Minnesota Press, 2007.

Bureau of Indian Affairs. "Answers to Your Questions on American Indians." Pamphlet 2: "Questions on Education, Health, Land, Citizenship, Economic Status, Etc." Washington DC: Interior Department, c.1948–50. Google Books.

Burt, Larry W. *Tribalism in Crisis: Federal Indian Policy, 1953–1961*. Albuquerque: University of New Mexico Press, 1982.

Byrd, Jodi A. *The Transit of Empire: Indigenous Critiques of Colonialism*. Minneapolis: University of Minnesota Press, 2011.

Cahill, Cathleen D. *Federal Fathers and Mothers: A Social History of the United States Indian Service, 1869–1933*. Chapel Hill: University of North Carolina Press, 2011.

Canaday, Margot. *The Straight State: Sexuality and Citizenship in Twentieth-Century America*. Princeton NJ: Princeton University Press, 2009.

Capozzola, Christopher. "Legacies for Citizenship: Pinpointing Americans during and after World War I." *Diplomatic History* 38, no. 4 (2014): 713–26.

Carroll, Al. *Medicine Bags and Dog Tags: American Indian Veterans from Colonial Times to the Second Iraq War*. Lincoln: University of Nebraska Press, 2008.

Chang, David A. *The Color of the Land: Race, Nation, and the Politics of Landownership in Oklahoma, 1832–1929*. Chapel Hill: University of North Carolina Press, 2010.

Chappell, Marisa. *The War on Welfare: Family, Poverty, and Politics in Modern America*. Philadelphia: University of Pennsylvania Press, 2010.

Cherokee Central School. "History of Cherokee Central Schools." https://www.ccs -nc.org/apps/pages/index.jsp?uREC_ID=373900&type=d&pREC_ID=851868.

Child, Brenda. "The Boarding School as Metaphor." *Journal of American Indian Education* 57, no. 1 (2018): 37–57.

——. *Boarding School Seasons: American Indian Families, 1900–1940*. Lincoln: University of Nebraska Press, 1998.

Child, Brenda J., and Karissa E. White. "'I've Done My Share': Ojibwe People and World War II." *Minnesota History* 61, no. 5 (Spring 2009): 196–207.

Clapsaddle, Annette Saunooke. *Even as We Breathe*. Lexington KY: Fireside Industries Books, 2020.

Cobb, Daniel. *Native Activism in Cold War America: The Struggle for Sovereignty*. Lawrence: University Press of Kansas, 2008.

———, ed. *Say We Are Nations: Documents of Politics and Protest in Indigenous America since 1887*. Chapel Hill: University of North Carolina Press, 2015.

Cohen, Felix. *Handbook of Federal Indian Law*. 1982 ed. Charlottesville VA: Michie Bobbs-Merrill, 1982.

———. *The Legal Conscience: Selected Letters of Felix S. Cohen*. Edited by Lucy Kramer Cohen. New Haven CT: Yale University Press, 1960.

Cohen, Lizabeth. *A Consumers' Republic: The Politics of Mass Consumption in Postwar America*. New York: Vintage Books, 2003.

———. *Making a New Deal: Industrial Workers in Chicago, 1919–1939*. 2nd ed. Cambridge: Cambridge University Press, 2009.

Commission on the Rights, Liberties, and Responsibilities of the American Indian. *A Program for Indian Citizens: A Summary Report*. Albuquerque NM: The Commission, 1961.

Cothran, Boyd. "Working the Indian Field Days: The Economy of Authenticity and the Question of Agency in Yosemite Valley." *American Indian Quarterly* 34, no. 2 (March 2010): 194–223.

Cowger, Thomas. *The National Congress of American Indians: The Founding Years*. Lincoln: University of Nebraska Press, 1999.

Cramer, Renée Ann. *Cash, Color, and Colonialism: The Politics of Tribal Acknowledgment*. Norman: University of Oklahoma Press, 2008.

———. "The Common Sense of Anti-Indian Racism: Reactions to Mashantucket Pequot Success in Gaming and Acknowledgment." *Law and Social Inquiry* 31, no. 2 (Spring 2006): 313–41.

Critchlow, Donald T. "Lewis Meriam, Expertise, and Indian Reform." *The Historian* 43, no. 3 (May 1981): 325–44.

Davis, Julie L. *Survival Schools: The American Indian Movement and Community Education in the Twin Cities*. Minneapolis: University of Minnesota Press, 2013.

Deer, Ada. *Making a Difference: My Fight for Native Rights and Social Justice*. With Theda Perdue. Norman: University of Oklahoma Press, 2019.

Deer, Sarah. *The Beginning and End of Rape: Confronting Sexual Violence in Native America*. Minneapolis: University of Minnesota Press, 2015.

———. "Decolonizing Rape Law: A Native Feminist Synthesis of Safety and Sovereignty." *Wicazo Sa Review* 24, no. 2 (Fall 2009): 149–67.

Deloria, Ella Cara. *Waterlily*. Lincoln: University of Nebraska Press, 1988.

Deloria, Philip J. *Indians in Unexpected Places*. Lawrence: University Press of Kansas, 2004.

Deloria, Vine, Jr. *Custer Died for Your Sins: An Indian Manifesto*. New York: Avon Books, 1969.

———. "We Are Here as Independent Nations" (1965). In Cobb, *Say We Are Nations*, 133–38.

Deloria, Vine, Jr., and Clifford Lytle. *The Nations Within: The Past and Future of American Indian Sovereignty*. New York: Pantheon Books, 1984.

Denetdale, Jennifer Nez. *Reclaiming Diné History: The Legacies of Navajo Chief Manuelito and Juanita*. Tucson: University of Arizona Press, 2007.

Dennison, Jean. *Colonial Entanglement: Constituting a Twenty-First Century Osage Nation*. Chapel Hill: University of North Carolina Press, 2012.

DeWitt, Larry W., Daniel Béland, and Edward D. Berkowitz. *Social Security: A Documentary History*. Washington DC: CQ Press, 2008.

Drinnon, Richard. *Keeper of Concentration Camps: Dillon S. Myer and American Racism*. Berkeley: University of California Press, 1987.

Dudas, Jeffrey R. *The Cultivation of Resentment: Treaty Rights and the New Right*. Stanford CA: Stanford University Press, 2008.

Ellinghaus, Katherine. *Blood Will Tell: Native Americans and Assimilation Policy*. Lincoln: University of Nebraska Press, 2017.

Elliott, Russell R. *History of Nevada*. 2nd ed. Lincoln: University of Nebraska Press, 1987.

Enoch, Jessica. "Resisting the Script of Indian Education: Zitkala Ša and the Carlisle Indian School." *College English* 65, no. 2 (November 2002): 117–41.

Erdrich, Heid E. "Introduction: Twenty-One Poets for the Twenty-First Century." In *New Poets of Native Nations*, edited by Heid E. Erdrich, xi–xvi. Minneapolis: Graywolf Press, 2018.

Erdrich, Louise. *The Night Watchman*. New York: Harper Collins, 2020.

Field, Corinne. "Frances E. W. Harper and the Politics of Intellectual Maturity." In *Toward an Intellectual History of Black Women*, edited by Mia E. Bay, Farah J. Griffin, Martha S. Jones, and Barbara D. Savage, 110–26. Chapel Hill: University of North Carolina Press, 2015.

———. *The Struggle for Equal Adulthood: Gender, Race, Age, and the Fight for Citizenship in Antebellum America*. Chapel Hill: University of North Carolina Press, 2014.

Firkus, Angela. "Agricultural Extension and the Campaign to Assimilate the Native Americans of Wisconsin, 1914–1932." *Journal of the Gilded Age and Progressive Era* 9, no. 4 (October 2010): 473–502.

Fixico, Donald L. *Call for Change: The Medicine Way of American Indian History, Ethos, and Reality*. Lincoln: University of Nebraska Press, 2013.

———. *Indian Resilience and Rebuilding: Indigenous Nations in the Modern American West*. Tucson: University of Arizona Press, 2013.

———. *Termination and Relocation: Federal Indian Policy, 1945–1960*. Albuquerque: University of New Mexico Press, 1986.

Forbes, Jack D., ed. *Nevada Indians Speak*. Reno: University of Nevada Press, 1967.

Fox, Cybelle. *Three Worlds of Relief: Race, Immigration, and the American Welfare State from the Progressive Era to the New Deal*. Princeton NJ: Princeton University Press, 2012.

Franco, Jere' Bishop. *Crossing the Pond: The Native American Effort in World War II*. Denton: University of North Texas Press, 1999.

Fraser, Nancy, and Linda Gordon. "A Genealogy of Dependency: Tracing a Keyword of the US Welfare State." *Signs* 19, no. 2 (Winter 1994): 309–36.

Frickey, Philip P. "Marshalling the Past and Present: Colonialism, Constitutionalism, and Interpretation in Federal Indian Law." *Harvard Law Review* 107, no. 2 (December 1993): 381–440.

Fuller, Alexandra, and Aaron Huey. "In the Shadow of Wounded Knee." *National Geographic* 222, no. 2 (August 2012): 30–53.

Goeman, Mishuana. *Mark My Words: Native Women Mapping Our Nations*. Minneapolis: University of Minnesota Press, 2013.

Goldstein, Alyosha. *Poverty in Common: The Politics of Community Action during the American Century*. Durham NC: Duke University Press, 2012.

Gordon, Linda. *Heroes of Their Own Lives: The Politics and History of Family Violence: Boston, 1880–1960*. New York: Viking, 1988.

——. *Pitied but Not Entitled: Single Mothers and the History of Welfare, 1890–1935*. New York: Free Press, 1994.

Gouveia, Grace Mary. "'We Also Serve': American Indian Women's Role in World War II." *Michigan Historical Review* 20, no. 2 (Fall 1994): 153–82.

Grillot, Thomas. *First Americans: U.S. Patriotism in Indian Country after World War I*. New Haven CT: Yale University Press, 2014.

Guise, Holly Miowak. "Who Is Doctor Bauer? Rematriating a Censored Story on Internment, Wardship, and Sexual Violence in Wartime Alaska, 1941–1944." *Western Historical Quarterly* 53, no. 2 (Summer 2022): 145–65.

Gurr, Barbara. *Reproductive Justice: The Politics of Health Care for Native American Women*. New Brunswick NJ: Rutgers University Press, 2015.

Handler, Joel F., and Ellen Jane Hollingsworth. "Reforming Welfare: The Constraints of the Bureaucracy and the Clients." *University of Pennsylvania Law Review* 118, no. 8 (July 1970): 1167–87.

Haney-López, Ian. *White by Law: The Legal Construction of Race*. New York: New York University Press, 2006.

Harjo, Joy, *Poet Warrior: A Memoir*. New York: W.W. Norton, 2021.

Harmon, Alexandra. *Rich Indians: Native People and the Problem of Wealth in American History*. Chapel Hill: University of North Carolina Press, 2010.

Harness, Susan Devan. *Bitterroot: A Salish Memoir of Transracial Adoption*. Lincoln: University of Nebraska Press, 2018.

Harris, Cheryl I. "Whiteness as Property." *Harvard Law Review* 106, no. 8 (June 1993): 1707–91.

Hartman, Saidiya. *Scenes of Subjection: Terror, Slavery, and Self-Making in Nineteenth-Century America*. New York: Oxford University Press, 1997.

Hemmings, Clare. *Why Stories Matter: The Political Grammar of Feminist Theory.* Durham NC: Duke University Press, 2011.

Hickel, K. Walter. "War, Region, and Social Welfare: Federal Aid to Servicemen's Dependents in the South, 1917–1921." *Journal of American History* 87, no. 4 (March 2001): 1362–91.

Horiuchi, Lynne. "Spatial Jurisdictions, Historical Topographies, and Sovereignty at the Leupp Isolation Center." *Amerasia Journal* 42, no. 1 (2016): 82–101.

Hoxie, Frederick E. *A Final Promise: The Campaign to Assimilate the Indians, 1880–1920*. Lincoln: University of Nebraska Press, 1984.

Huebner, Karin L. "An Unexpected Alliance: Stella Atwood, the California Clubwomen, John Collier, and the Indians of the Southwest, 1917–1934." *Pacific Historical Review* 78, no. 3 (August 2009): 337–66.

Huey, Aaron. "America's Native Prisoners of War." TED Talks. TEDxDU 2010. https://www.ted.com/talks/aaron_huey_america_s_native_prisoners_of_war.

Irwin, Julia. *Making the World Safe: The American Red Cross and a Nation's Humanitarian Awakening*. Oxford: Oxford University Press, 2017.

Jacobs, Margaret D. *A Generation Removed: The Fostering and Adoption of Indigenous Children in the Postwar World*. Lincoln: University of Nebraska Press, 2014.

——. *White Mother to a Dark Race: Settler Colonialism, Maternalism, and the Removal of Indigenous Children in the American West and Australia, 1880–1940*. Lincoln: University of Nebraska Press, 2009.

——. "Working on the Domestic Frontier: American Indian Domestic Servants in White Women's Households in the San Francisco Bay Area, 1920–1940." *Frontiers: A Journal of Women Studies* 28, no. 1/2 (2007): 165–99.

Jacobs, Meg. *Pocketbook Politics: Economic Citizenship in Twentieth-Century America*. Princeton NJ: Oxford: Princeton University Press, 2005.

Jennings, Audra. *Out of the Horrors of War: Disability Politics in World War II America*. Philadelphia: University of Pennsylvania Press, 2016.

Katz, Michael. *The Undeserving Poor: America's Enduring Confrontation with Poverty* 2nd ed. Oxford: Oxford University Press, 2013.

Katznelson, Ira. *When Affirmative Action Was White: An Untold History of Racial Inequality in Twentieth-Century America*. New York: W.W. Norton, 2005.

Keeler, Kasey. "Putting People Where They Belong: American Indian Housing Policy in the Mid-Twentieth Century." *Native American and Indigenous Studies* 3, no. 2 (2016): 70–104.

Kerber, Linda K. *No Constitutional Right to Be Ladies: Women and the Obligations of Citizenship.* New York: Hill and Wang, 1998.

Kessler-Harris, Alice. *In Pursuit of Equity: Women, Men, and the Quest for Economic Citizenship in 20th-Century America.* Oxford: Oxford University Press, 2001.

Kiel, Doug. "Nation vs. Municipality: Indigenous Land Recovery, Settler Resentment, and Taxation on the Oneida Reservation." *Native American and Indigenous Studies* 6, no. 2 (Fall 2019): 51–73.

King, Farina. *The Earth Memory Compass: Diné Landscapes and Education in the Twentieth Century.* Lawrence: University Press of Kansas, 2018.

Klann, Mary. "Babies in Baskets: Motherhood, Tourism, and American Identity in Indian Baby Shows, 1916–1949." *Journal of Women's History* 29, no. 2 (Summer 2017): 38–61.

Kornbluh, Felicia. *The Battle for Welfare Rights: Politics and Poverty in Modern America.* Philadelphia: University of Pennsylvania Press, 2007.

Koven, Seth, and Sonya Michel, eds. *Mothers of a New World: Maternalist Politics and the Origins of Welfare States.* New York: Routledge, 1993.

Krakoff, Sarah. "Settler Colonialism and Reclamation: Where American Indian Law and Natural Resources Law Meet." *Colorado Natural Resources, Energy, and Environmental Law Review* 24, no. 2 (2013): 261–86.

Kwak, Nancy. *A World of Homeowners: American Power and the Politics of Housing Aid.* Chicago: University of Chicago Press, 2015.

Ladd-Taylor, Molly. *Fixing the Poor: Eugenic Sterilization and Child Welfare in the Twentieth Century.* Baltimore: Johns Hopkins University Press, 2017.

———. *Mother-Work: Women, Child Welfare, and the State, 1890–1930.* Urbana: University of Illinois Press, 1994.

Lambert, Valerie. "The Big Black Box of Indian Country: The Bureau of Indian Affairs and the Federal-Indian Relationship." *American Indian Quarterly* 40, no. 4 (Fall 2016): 333–63.

———. *Native Agency: Indians in the Bureau of Indian Affairs.* Minneapolis: University of Minnesota Press, 2022.

Lawrence, Jane. "The Indian Health Service and the Sterilization of Native American Women." *American Indian Quarterly* 24, no. 3 (2000): 400–419.

Lee, Erika. *At America's Gates: Chinese Immigration in the Exclusion Era, 1882–1943.* Chapel Hill: University of North Carolina Press, 2003.

Leong, Karen J., and Myla Vicente Carpio. "Carceral Subjugations: Gila River Indian Community and Incarceration of Japanese Americans on Its Lands." *Amerasia Journal* 42, no. 1 (2016): 103–20.

Lieberman, Robert C. *Shifting the Color Line: Race and the American Welfare State.* Cambridge MA: Harvard University Press, 1998.

Lomawaima, K. Tsianina. "Estelle Reel, Superintendent of Indian Schools, 1898–1910: Politics, Curriculum, and Land." *Journal of American Indian Education*, 35, no. 3 (Spring 1996): 5–31.

Long Soldier, Layli. *Whereas*. Minneapolis: Graywolf Press, 2017.

Mansfield, Edward Deering. *The Political Grammar of the United States; or, A Complete View of the Theory and Practice of the General and State Governments, with the Relations between Them*. Cincinnati: Truman & Smith, 1840. Google Books.

McClelland, Muriel, and Lynn Cianci Eby. "Child Support Enforcement: The New Mexico Experience." *New Mexico Law Review* 9, no. 1 (Winter 1978–79): 25–43.

McCool, Daniel, Susan M. Olson, and Jennifer L. Robinson. *Native Vote: American Indians, the Voting Rights Act, and the Right to Vote*. Cambridge: Cambridge University Press, 2007.

McDonald, Laughlin. *American Indians and the Fight for Equal Voting Rights*. Norman: University of Oklahoma Press, 2011.

McEnaney, Laura. *Postwar: Waging Peace in Chicago*. Philadelphia: University of Pennsylvania Press, 2018.

McKinney, Amy. "From Canning to Contraceptives: Cooperative Extension Service Home Demonstration Clubs and Rural Montana Women in the Post–World War II Era." *Montana: The Magazine of Western History* 61, no. 3 (Autumn 2011): 57–70.

Mettler, Suzanne. *Dividing Citizens: Gender and Federalism in New Deal Public Policy*. Ithaca NY: Cornell University Press, 1998.

———. *Soldiers to Citizens: The GI Bill and the Making of the Greatest Generation*. Oxford: Oxford University Press, 2005.

Michelmore, Molly C. *Tax and Spend: The Welfare State, Tax Politics, and Taxing State*. Philadelphia: University of Pennsylvania Press, 2011.

Mihesuah, Devon Abbott. *So You Want to Write about American Indians? A Guide for Writers, Students, and Scholars*. Lincoln: University of Nebraska Press, 2005.

Miller, Douglas K. *Indians on the Move: Native American Mobility and Urbanization in the Twentieth Century*. Chapel Hill: University of North Carolina Press, 2020.

Mink, Gwendolyn. *The Wages of Motherhood: Inequality in the Welfare State, 1917–1942*. Ithaca NY: Cornell University Press, 1995.

Mitchell, Pablo. *Coyote Nation: Sexuality, Race, and Conquest in Modernizing New Mexico, 1880–1920*. Chicago: University of Chicago Press, 2005.

Mittelstadt, Jennifer. *From Welfare to Workfare: The Unintended Consequences of Liberal Reform, 1945–1965*. Chapel Hill: University of North Carolina Press, 2005.

———. *The Rise of the Military Welfare State*. Cambridge MA: Harvard University Press, 2015.

Molina, Natalia. *Fit to Be Citizens? Public Health and Race in Los Angeles, 1879–1939*. Berkeley: University of California Press, 2006.

———. "'In a Race All Their Own': The Quest to Make Mexicans Ineligible for US Citizenship." *Pacific Historical Review* 79, no. 2 (May 2010): 167–201.

Momaday, N. Scott. "The Delight Song of Tsoai-talee." In *In the Presence of the Sun: Stories and Poems, 1961–1991*. New York: St. Martin's Press, 1992. Poetry Foundation, https://www.poetryfoundation.org/poems/46558/the-delight-song-of -tsoai-talee.

Moreton-Robinson, Aileen. *The White Possessive: Property, Power, and Indigenous Sovereignty*. Minneapolis: University of Minnesota Press, 2015.

Murray, Melissa. "When War Is Work: The G.I. Bill, Citizenship, and the Civic Generation." *California Law Review* 96, no. 4 (August 2008): 967–98.

Myles, Eileen. "An American Poem." In *Not Me*. New York: Semiotexte, 1991. Poetry Foundation, https://www.poetryfoundation.org/poems/53965/an-american -poem.

Nadasen, Premilla. *Welfare Warriors: The Welfare Rights Movement in the United States*. New York: Routledge, 2005.

Nash, Philleo, Sol Tax, R. David Edmunds, Gary Orfield, and Ada Deer. "Federal Indian Policy, 1945–1960." In *Indian Self-Rule: First-Hand Accounts of Indian-White Relations from Roosevelt to Reagan*, edited by Kenneth R. Philp, 129–41. Logan: Utah State University Press, 1995.

Nelson, Robert A., and Joseph F. Shelley. "Bureau of Indian Affairs Influence on Indian Self-Determination." In *American Indian Policy in the Twentieth Century*, edited by Vine Deloria Jr., 177–96. Norman: University of Oklahoma Press, 1985.

Ngai, Mae. *Impossible Subjects: Illegal Aliens and the Making of Modern America*. Princeton NJ: Princeton University Press, 2004.

O'Connor, Alice. *Poverty Knowledge: Social Sciences, Social Policy, and the Poor in Twentieth-Century U.S. History*. Princeton NJ: Princeton University Press, 2002.

Odem, Mary E. *Delinquent Daughters: Protecting and Policing Female Sexuality in the United States, 1885–1920*. Chapel Hill: University of North Carolina Press, 1995.

Okimoto, Ruth. *Sharing a Desert Home: Life on the Colorado River Indian Reservation, Poston, Arizona, 1942–1945*. Berkeley: News from Native California, 2001.

Olson, Keith W. "The G.I. Bill and Higher Education: Success and Surprise." *American Quarterly* 25, no. 5 (December 1973): 596–610.

Orleck, Annelise. *Storming Caesar's Palace: How Black Mothers Fought Their Own War on Poverty*. Boston: Beacon Press, 2005.

Otis, D. S. *The Dawes Act and the Allotment of Indian Lands*. Edited by Francis Paul Prucha. Norman: University of Oklahoma Press, 1973.

Parman, Donald. "Indians and the Civilian Conservation Corps." *Pacific Historical Review* 40, no. 1 (February 1971): 39–56.

Peterson, Helen, and Alice Jemison. "This Resolution 'Gives' Indians Nothing" (1954). In Cobb, *Say We Are Nations*, 103–6.

Phillips, Katrina M. *Staging Indigeneity: Salvage Tourism and the Performance of Native American History.* Chapel Hill: University of North Carolina Press, 2021.

Phillips, Ruth. *Trading Identities: The Souvenir in Native North American Art from the Northeast, 1700–1900.* Seattle: University of Washington Press, 1998.

Philp, Kenneth R., ed. *Indian Self-Rule: First-Hand Accounts of Indian-White Relations from Roosevelt to Reagan.* Logan: Utah State University Press, 1995.

———. *John Collier's Crusade for Indian Reform, 1920–1954.* Tucson: University of Arizona Press, 1977.

———. *Termination Revisited: American Indians on the Trail to Self-Determination, 1933–1953.* Lincoln: University of Nebraska Press, 1999.

Phu, Thy. "Double Capture: Native Americans in WRA Internment Photography." *Amerasia Journal* 42, no. 1 (2016): 16–40.

Pine Ridge Community Storytelling Project. Accessed August 30, 2022. http://cowbird .com/huey/collection/171/stories/. (The Cowbird site is no longer available; see https://cowbird.com/.)

Plant, Rebecca. *Mom: The Transformation of Motherhood in Modern America.* Chicago: University of Chicago Press, 2010.

Pommersheim, Frank. *Broken Landscape: Indians, Indian Tribes, and the Constitution.* Oxford: Oxford University Press, 2009.

Poole, Mary. *The Segregated Origins of Social Security: African Americans and the Welfare State.* Chapel Hill: University of North Carolina Press, 2006.

Porter, Robert. "The Demise of the *Ongwehoweh* and the Rise of the Native Americans: Redressing the Genocidal Act of Forcing American Citizenship upon Indigenous Peoples." *Harvard BlackLetter Law Journal* 15 (1999): 107–83.

Powell, H. Jefferson. "The Political Grammar of Early Constitutional Law." *North Carolina Law Review* 71, no. 4 (April 1993): 949–1010.

President's Committee on Civil Rights. *To Secure These Rights.* Washington DC: Government Printing Office, 1947.

Prucha, Francis Paul, ed. *Documents of United States Indian Policy.* Lincoln: University of Nebraska Press, 1975.

Puisto, Jaakko. *"This Is My Reservation; I Belong Here": The Salish and Kootenai Indian Struggle against Termination.* Pablo MT: Salish Kootenai College Press, 2016.

Quadagno, Jill. *The Color of Welfare: How Racism Undermined the War on Poverty.* New York: Oxford University Press, 1994.

Raibmon, Paige. *Authentic Indians: Episodes of Encounter from the Late Nineteenth-Century Northwest Coast.* Durham NC: Duke University Press, 2005.

Ramirez, Renya. *Native Hubs: Culture, Community, and Belonging in Silicon Valley and Beyond.* Durham NC: Duke University Press, 2007.

———. *Standing Up to Colonial Power: The Lives of Henry Roe and Elizabeth Bender Cloud.* Lincoln: University of Nebraska Press, 2018.

Reed, Julie. *Serving the Nation: Cherokee Sovereignty and Social Welfare, 1800–1907*. Norman: University of Oklahoma Press, 2016.

Riseman, Noah. *Defending Whose Country? Indigenous Soldiers in the Pacific War*. Lincoln: University of Nebraska Press, 2012.

Risling Baldy, Cutcha. *We Are Dancing for You: Native Feminisms and the Revitalization of Women's Coming-of-Age Ceremonies*. Seattle: University of Washington Press, 2018.

Ritter, Gretchen. "Jury Service and Women's Citizenship before and after the Nineteenth Amendment." *Law and History Review* 20, no. 3 (Autumn 2002): 479–515.

Roberts, Dorothy. *Killing the Black Body: Race, Reproduction, and the Meaning of Liberty*. 2nd ed. New York: Vintage Books, 2017.

Roediger, David R. *Working toward Whiteness: How America's Immigrants Became White; The Strange Journey from Ellis Island to the Suburbs*. New York: Basic Books, 2005.

Rollings, Willard Hughes. "Citizenship and Suffrage: The Native American Struggle for Civil Rights in the American West, 1830–1965." *Nevada Law Journal* 5 (Fall 2004): 126–40.

Rosenthal, Nicolas. "Painting Native America in Public: American Indian Artists and the New Deal." *American Indian Culture and Research Journal* 42, no. 3 (July 2018): 47–70.

———. *Reimagining Indian Country: Native American Migration and Identity in Twentieth-Century Los Angeles*. Chapel Hill: University of North Carolina Press, 2012.

Rosier, Paul. *Serving Their Country: American Indian Politics and Patriotism in the Twentieth Century*. Cambridge MA: Harvard University Press, 2009.

Rusco, Elmer. *A Fateful Time: The Background and Legislative History of the Indian Reorganization Act*. Reno: University of Nevada Press, 2000.

Schoen, Johanna. *Choice and Coercion: Birth Control, Sterilization, and Abortion in Public Health and Welfare*. Chapel Hill: University of North Carolina Press, 2005.

Shah, Nayan. *Contagious Divides: Epidemics and Race in San Francisco's Chinatown*. Berkeley: University of California Press, 2001.

Shreve, Bradley. *Red Power Rising: The National Indian Youth Council and the Origins of Native Activism*. Norman: University of Oklahoma Press, 2011.

Silliman, Jael, Marlene Gerber-Fried, Elena Gutiérrez, and Loretta Ross. *Undivided Rights: Women of Color Organize for Reproductive Justice*. Cambridge MA: South End Press, 2004.

Simonsen, Jane. *Making Home Work: Domesticity and Native American Assimilation in the American West, 1860–1919*. Chapel Hill: University of North Carolina Press, 2011.

———. "'Object Lessons:' Domesticity and Display in Native American Assimilation." *American Studies* 43, no. 1 (Spring 2002): 75–99.

Singh, Nikhil Pal. *Black Is a Country: Race and the Unfinished Struggle for Democracy*. Cambridge MA: Harvard University Press, 2004.

Skocpol, Theda. *Protecting Soldiers and Mothers: The Political Origins of Social Policy in the United States*. Cambridge MA: Harvard University Press, 1992.

Sparrow, James T. *Warfare State: World War II Americans and the Age of Big Government*. Oxford: Oxford University Press, 2011.

Stein, Gary C. "The Indian Citizenship Act of 1924." *New Mexico Historical Review* 47, no. 3 (1972): 257–72.

Stremlau, Rose. *Sustaining the Cherokee Family: Kinship and the Allotment of an Indigenous Nation*. Chapel Hill: University of North Carolina Press, 2011.

Stryker, Susan. "Transgender Feminism: Queering the Woman Question." In *Feminist Frontiers*, edited by Verta Taylor, Nancy Whittier, and Leila J. Rupp, 83–89. Lanham MD: Rowman & Littlefield, 2019.

TallBear, Kim. "Caretaking Relations, Not American Dreaming." *Kalfou* 6, no. 1 (Spring 2019): 24–41.

Tani, Karen M. *States of Dependency: Welfare, Rights, and American Governance, 1935–1972*. Cambridge: Cambridge University Press, 2016.

———. "States' Rights, Welfare Rights, and the 'Indian Problem': Negotiating Citizenship and Sovereignty, 1935–1954." *Law and History Review* 33, no. 1 (February 2015): 1–40.

Taylor, Graham. *The New Deal and American Indian Tribalism: The Administration of the Indian Reorganization Act, 1934–45*. Lincoln: University of Nebraska Press, 1980.

Theobald, Brianna. *Reproduction on the Reservation: Pregnancy, Childbirth, and Colonialism in the Long Twentieth Century*. Chapel Hill: University of North Carolina Press, 2019.

Tillmon, Johnnie. "Welfare Is a Women's Issue." *Ms. Magazine*, Spring 1972, https://msmagazine.com/2021/03/25/welfare-is-a-womens-issue-ms-magazine-spring-1972/.

Tonkovich, Nicole. *The Allotment Plot: Alice C. Fletcher, E. Jane Gay, and Nez Perce Survivance*. Lincoln: University of Nebraska Press, 2012.

Townsend, Kenneth William. *World War II and the American Indian*. Albuquerque: University of New Mexico Press, 2000.

United States Commission on Civil Rights. *Justice*. Washington DC: Government Printing Office, 1961.

United States Department of the Interior, Indian Affairs. "Our Nation's American Indians and Alaska Native Citizens." Frequently Asked Questions, modified August 19, 2017. https://www.bia.gov/frequently-asked-questions.

Virtue, Maxine Boord. "Operative Relationships among Various Courts, Law Enforcement, and Welfare Agencies in the City of Detroit." *Michigan Law Review* 49, no. 1 (November 1950): 1–38.

Weisiger, Marsha. "Gendered Injustice: Navajo Livestock Reduction in the New Deal Era." *Western Historical Quarterly* 38, no. 4 (Winter 2007): 437–55.

Welke, Barbara Young. *Law and the Borders of Belonging in the Long Nineteenth Century United States*. Cambridge: Cambridge University Press, 2010.

Wilkerson, Jessica. *To Live Here, You Have to Fight: How Women Led Appalachian Movements for Social Justice*. Urbana: University of Illinois Press, 2019.

Williams, Rhonda Y. *The Politics of Public Housing: Black Women's Struggles against Urban Inequality*. Oxford: Oxford University Press, 2004.

Williams, Robert A. *Like a Loaded Weapon: The Rehnquist Court, Indian Rights, and the Legal History of Racism in America*. Minneapolis: University of Minnesota Press, 2005.

Wilson, Diane. *The Seed Keeper*. Minneapolis: Milkweed Editions, 2021.

Winnemucca, Sarah. *The Newspaper Warrior: Sarah Winnemucca Hopkins's Campaign for American Indian Rights, 1864–1891*. Edited by Cari M. Carpenter and Carolyn Sorisio. Lincoln: University of Nebraska Press, 2015.

Wright, John, dir. *In Our Voice: The Chemehuevi, Mohave, and Navajo Perspectives*. Colorado River Indian Tribes Film Series, Jux Films, 2018. https://critfilms.org/film3/. (Video is no longer available at this site.)

Zitkala-Ša. *Help Indians Help Themselves: The Later Writings of Gertrude Simmons Bonnin (Zitkala-Ša)*. Edited by P. Jane Hafen. Lubbock: Texas Tech University Press, 2020.

INDEX

and practices of Native women, 116, 183–84, 195, 265n9
Carson Indian Agency, 71, 78–79
Case, Francis, 42, 44, 56, 58–59, 205–6
Charlo, Paul, 204
Chavez, Dennis, 82, 117, 131, 158
Chemehuevi, 135, 146. *See also* Colorado River Indian Tribes; Colorado River Reservation
Cherokee Indian Agency, 76, 105, 118, 120
Cherokee Indian High School. *See* Cherokee Indian School
Cherokee Indian School: use of agricultural extension agent, 133–34, 145, 149–50; as boarding school, 128–29, 133; as veterans training center, 120, 121, 125, 128–29, 130, 133–35, 139–42, 143, 144–45, 149–50, 153, 214
Cherokee Nation, 186
Cherokee Nation v. Georgia, 12, 20
Cherokee, NC, 125, 130, 140
Cheyenne River Sioux, 55
child removal, 161, 221
children: as depicted in poverty photographs, 219–24
child welfare, 203
Christianson, Theodore, 27
citizenship: and assimilation, 5–6, 9, 24, 47; dual, 20, 24, 171, 190; duties of, 31; and employment, 9, 56, 123, 127–28; equal, 5, 45, 53, 83, 192, 196, 198–200; and gender, 9–10, 43, 49, 58–61, 107, 139; language of, 142, 181, 182, 184, 192; and marriage, 59–61, 78; and military service, 16, 23, 37, 58, 90, 93, 118, 152; and productivity, 48, 56; and taxpaying, 58, 157–58, 161, 167, 192–94, 196; tribal, 86, 171; as uplift, 29, 61, 134; wardship as an impediment to, 20, 22, 24, 31, 62, 157

civilization: and assimilation, 48, 170; and the Dawes Act, 48; and individualism, 16; in opposition to "savagery," 8, 21, 47, 168, 170, 172
civil rights, 3–4, 38, 87, 182, 183, 189, 199
Clapsaddle, Annette Saunooke, 125, 130, 153
Cloud, Elizabeth Bender, 195
Cohen, Felix, 47, 52, 87, 175, 201, 211
Collier, John, 25–28, 34, 146–47
colonialism, 37–38. *See also* settler colonialism
Colorado River Indian Agency, 73
Colorado River Indian Tribes, 84, 135–36, 257n79
Colorado River Reservation, 73, 130, 135, 143, 146–48, 214; "colonization of," 147, 254n40
Commission on the Rights, Liberties, and Responsibilities of the American Indian, 171–72, 202
Committee on Civil Rights (Truman's), 189–90
competency: adjudication of, 40, 42; and allotment, 41–42; exploitation of, 50, 54; history of within Indian policy, 41, 212; and improbability of using welfare benefits, 41, 42, 43, 52, 60, 93; as legal status, 40, 234n4; and marriage, 42, 58–61, 205–6; "moral and intellectual" qualifications of, 43, 44–50, 64; and property, 28, 40, 45, 55, 56, 123, 146, 150; and termination, 41, 46, 54, 64
competency bills, 12, 40, 42, 55–62, 171, 211
Confederated Salish and Kootenai Tribes (Flathead Reservation), 31, 194, 204

conscience, 161–62, 165, 178. *See also* guilt

Constitution, 21, 27, 181; commerce clause, 199; "Indians not taxed," 159

Constitutional Rights Subcommittee of the Senate Judiciary Committee, 182, 185, 195–98, 266–67n36

Coulson, Celestia, 102, 106

Council of Laguna Pueblo, 1, 3, 57

Council of the Pueblo of Laguna. *See* Council of Laguna Pueblo

Cragun, John, 179, 194

credit, 100, 139, 151

Crow, 83

Curry, James, 57, 83, 87, 190–91

Custer Died for Your Sins (Deloria), 224, 226

Cypress, Henry, 95–96

Cypress, Mrs. Futch, 95–96

Dawes Allotment Act. *See* allotment

Dawes, Henry, 48

debt, 101, 102; and definitions of wardship, 183; owed to Native people, 44, 191

Declaration of Independence, 63

Deloria, Vine, 161, 166–67, 172, 186, 224–26

democracy, 38, 46, 92, 127

Department of the Interior, 24, 26–27, 87, 136

dependency: *doxa* of, 13, 96–97, 123, 181, 199, 213; and gender, 13, 58–61, 68, 96, 213; good and bad, 101; and Native identity, 64; and the plight narrative, 161–62; on welfare benefits, 40, 46; and work, 8

dependency allotments. *See* dependency allowances

dependency allowances, 35; amount, 72; and Native men's control over, 80, 103–5; and oversight of BIA agents, 70–73, 99–107, 213; as welfare, 67

De Mers, Stephen, 90, 177

D'Ewart, Wesley, 42, 52

Dock, Henry, 73

Dock, Ione, 73, 97

"domestic dependent nations," 21

Driver, Nick, 106

Ducheneaux, Frank, 55

Dunn family, 105–6

Eastern Band of Cherokee, 76, 103, 125–26, 133, 139–40, 146, 149–52, 181

Eid, Troy, 32

Eisenhower, Dwight, 63–64

Elk, John. See *Elk v. Wilkins*

Elk v. Wilkins, 22

emancipation: of competent Native people, 40, 62, 64, 212; and the Indian Reorganization Act, 27; and payment of taxes, 174; and termination, 18, 31, 168, 212

Emmons, Glenn, 164, 165, 177, 200, 201

employment, 8, 123, 127, 176, 191–92

Ensor, William, 76, 106

entitlement, 34, 98

equality, 83, 89

Ervin, Sam, 179, 199, 202, 266–67n36

Evans, John, 117, 119, 137–38

Ewing, Oscar, 79

Extension Service. *See* Agricultural Extension Service

"fair play," 185, 198–201, 208, 215

Farm Home Administration, 150, 175

farming, 127, 138, 141, 145–46, 147, 151. *See also* agricultural training fathers: gendered responsibility of, 58–61, 115–16; "legal harassment" of, 112; and Native women's receipt of ADC, 108–16

federal government, 35, 89; dependence upon, 43–44, 50; growth of, 15, 65; relationship with tribes, 21–23, 29–30, 32, 39, 41, 48, 89. *See also* state, the

Federal Housing Administration, 118, 119

Federal Security Agency, 83

federal welfare state: expansion of, 4, 15, 33, 34, 38, 50, 67, 158–59, 160–61, 165; feminization of, 158; and relationship to state governments, 52, 87–89, 155–57; as slavery, 162; and social control, 6, 46, 68, 79, 101; and taxpayers, 158, 178; two-track system, 34, 98–99, 117; wardship as, 5, 51, 177–78, 201–2

first-class citizenship: and civil rights, 3; and competency, 39, 41, 42–44, 62, 152, 211–12; definitions of, 2, 4, 6, 9, 11, 12, 40, 44, 55, 103, 200, 215, 227n5; and gender, 58–61, 103, 110, 120, 140, 207; and the GI Bill, 120, 126, 129–30, 144, 152; and guilt, 164; and government assistance, 4, 201–3, 206; and Indian policy, 4, 47; and individualism, 5, 6, 12, 16, 40, 41–42, 45, 46, 64, 144, 198; and land ownership, 6, 58, 169, 173, 178, 192–93; and termination, 5, 46, 54, 192–93, 215; and voting rights, 3, 227n5

Florida Department of Public Welfare, 95, 108, 111; and surveillance of Seminole welfare recipients, 108–16

Foster, Don, 78

French, Josie, 79–80, 97

full citizenship, 1, 9, 31, 42, 46, 58, 158, 227n5. *See also* full-fledged citizenship

full-fledged citizenship, 39, 171. *See also* first-class citizenship

Garry, Joseph, 57, 62

Gelvin, Ralph, 71–73, 79

Gensler, C.H., 72–73, 135–37, 143, 167

GI Bill, 12, 19, 70; access to, 14, 36, 67, 89–90, 213; educational benefits of, 14, 35, 130–31, 213, 252–53n24; and employability of veterans, 14, 127; and first-class citizenship, 127–28; and gendered self-sufficiency, 14, 126–27, 146, 148–50; home loans, 35, 150–51, 175–77; and housing, 118; Native veterans' eligibility for, 93, 118; promotion of by BIA, 117, 120, 137–39; and race, 36, 131; redlining, 36, 176; restrictions on federal agencies, 132; as "rights-based" welfare, 98–99, 127; and vocational training, 131, 137–38, 143, 148, 214

Gila River Pima-Maricopa Community. *See* Pima-Maricopa Indian Community

Goldwater, Barry, 54

Gosar, Paul, 31–32

government by consent, 63, 83, 200

grandmothers, 114–16

greed, 155–56, 160, 163, 206

Greene family, 80–82, 105

guardianship: and citizenship, 27; over estate, 28; over wives and children, 58–61, 104, 205–6. *See also under* wardship

Moore, Howard, 71–72
Moore, Sarah, 71–72, 78–79, 97
Morgan, Thomas J., 49
mothers: of soldiers, 105–6, 247n30; on welfare, 8, 10, 65, 68, 73, 86, 95–97, 99, 107, 111–12, 206–7
Murdock, John, 132
Myer, Dillon, 53–54, 171
Myers, Eleanor, 191–94, 200, 205

National Congress of American Indians, 15, 82–83, 89, 91, 194–95; Congressional testimony of, 189; meetings, 117, 177; 1954 Emergency Conference of (1954), 57, 62, 92, 200; surveys, 55
National Geographic, 218–19, 221, 223–25
National Welfare Rights Organization, 206
Navajo Assistance, Inc., 74
Navajo Nation, 76, 137, 151, 169, 186; livestock reduction program, 243n62; as part of the Colorado River Indian Tribes, 135, 147; poverty of, 74, 91, 161, 219–20
Navajo Treaty of 1868, 133
Navajo Tribal Council, 75, 85
Navajo Veterans of Foreign Wars, 133
Navy, 79
NCAI. *See* National Congress of American Indians
need-based welfare, 8, 33, 73, 82, 88, 98, 228n9. *See also* welfare dependency
New Deal: and expansion of the welfare state, 33, 160, 202; and Native people, 34; and rights, 33
New Mexico, 169; and resistance to granting Social Security benefits to Native people, 73, 82–84, 87–89,

93, 156, 159, 178; welfare officials of, 74, 156–57
NOLEO. *See* Notice to Law Enforcement Officials
Northwestern Band of Shoshones, 190
Notice to Law Enforcement Officials, 111–12, 114
nuclear family, 59, 127, 205, 207; morality of, 8, 113; in opposition to Native kinship, 68, 111, 115; and relationality, 188

OAA. *See* Old Age Assistance
ODB. *See* Office of Dependency Benefits
Office of Dependency Benefits, 71, 73, 78–79, 99, 213; and "squandering" of benefits, 99–104, 213
Office of Indian Affairs. *See* Bureau of Indian Affairs
Oglala Lakota Nation, 91–92, 221–23, 225
Oglala Lakota Tribal Council, 52, 57
Oglala Sioux Tribal Council. *See* Oglala Lakota Tribal Council
oil, 57, 166
Old Age Assistance, 13, 24, 33, 67, 74, 76, 82, 84, 86, 87, 95
Old Age Insurance, 33
Omaha Tribe of Nebraska, 55, 196
O'Mahoney, Joseph, 63
Osceola, Bill, 108

Papago. *See* Tohono O'odham
patent fees, 55–57, 59, 64
pauperism, 48–50, 88
Pete, Mrs. George, 101–2
Peterson, Helen: as Executive Director of NCAI, 179–80, 194, 199; use of political grammar, 15, 180–81,

196–98, 202–3, 215; presence at Congressional hearings, 179, 180–81, 185, 194–99, 216; relational framework, 180, 194, 197–98, 199, 205, 209, 215

photography, 219–24

Pierce, Lucy, 114–16

Pima. *See* Akimel O'odham

Pima Indian Agency, 75

Pima-Maricopa Indian Community, 75, 82, 85, 86, 87, 174

Pinal County, 75

Pine Ridge Reservation, 91, 218, 220, 221

PL 280. *See* Public Law 280

plenary power, 22, 26, 32, 211

plight narrative, 159, 160–66, 172, 173, 177, 214, 219–20, 222–23

plural wives, 113

police brutality, 198

political grammar, 181–82, 184, 189–94, 200, 206–7, 215

Poston Veterans' Vocational School, 130, 135–37, 138, 142–43, 144, 148, 153, 214

Poston War Relocation Center, 130, 135, 147

poverty: and the American Dream, 218; federal government's fault for, 88–89, 156–57, 162–63, 165; as a moral problem, 46, 65, 88, 218, 239n87; as perpetual, 5, 40, 43, 158, 178, 214, 217; as racialized, 52; relationship to wealth, 166–67, 172, 173; research of, 45; as shameful, 160; signifying Native identity, 64, 156–57, 159, 162, 166, 215, 218, 223; tropes of, 29, 30, 161, 185, 193, 198, 219–24

poverty knowledge, 12, 45, 117, 186–87, 195

prejudice, 52, 133, 189,

privilege: and protection of wardship, 51, 156–57, 160, 173, 175, 214

property: and allotment, 168; as income for Native families, 47; individual rights of, 49, 59, 64, 173; loss of, 57; taxes on, 57, 192; tribal, 56–57; trust restrictions on, 55

Public Law 280, 28–29, 185, 195–98

public services, 52, 172, 192, 194

Pyramid Lake Paiutes, 71, 80

Pyramid Lake Tribal Council, 71

Qualla Boundary, 133

racism, 52–53, 88, 155, 160, 170, 175–76, 178, 194, 205, 214

Rankin, John, 132

Red Cloud, Joseph, 91–92

Red Cross, 75, 78, 80, 241n24; communications with the military, 106; and interactions with BIA, 102, 106; investigations of dependency allowances, 80, 100, 101–2

red tape, 19, 20, 35, 70

rehabilitation: and poor people, 8, 46, 65, 201; and veterans, 144

relationality: being "in good relation," 16, 186, 216; and care, 116, 181, 182, 187–88, 194, 203, 215; definitions of, 185–89; as Native history, 186–88; and sovereignty, 4, 17, 195, 197, 208; and the state, 186, 188–89, 195–97, 204–5, 208, 215; and wardship, 180, 185, 188, 195, 197, 199, 200, 205, 207, 215; and welfare, 15, 180, 185, 188, 195, 207, 215; and the welfare rights movement, 185, 206–7

relocation: and employment, 128, 153; and housing, 176; as policy, 29, 128, 176; "voluntary," 128, 143, 153

wardship (*cont.*)

51, 65, 162–63, 165, 211, 214, 224; as disability, 19, 40, 42, 47, 64, 189; as example of welfare state, 4, 67, 160–63, 201–2, 212, 234n3; and gender, 123; as gratuitous, 6, 18, 42, 43, 51, 61, 69, 200; and incompetency, 19, 41, 53; and Indian poverty knowledge, 50, 64, 101, 214; and the Fourteenth Amendment, 22; as a legal relationship, 61, 68–70, 75, 89, 190–91, 200–201, 211; as lived experience, 13, 14, 99, 100, 103–16, 126, 129, 130, 152–53, 177, 211; as a "magic work," 47, 211; and manhood, 49–50; of Native children, 19; Native definitions of, 5, 68, 86, 193, 225; as protection for Native property, 62, 91, 168, 174; and pupilage, 20–21; and reservation residence, 160, 170; termination of, 5, 25, 29, 31, 61, 160, 164, 166, 196; and veterans, 119, 132–33; Zitkala-Ša on, 38

War Relocation Authority, 135–36

water, 203–4

Welch, Jonah, 103–5, 121–22, 128–29, 252n12

Welch, Olive McCoy, 103–5, 110, 121–22, 128–29, 252n12

welfare benefits: Cherokee definitions of, 186; Mexican Americans' access to, 50; and Native peoples' persistence, 73–79; as paternalism, 79; as transactional, 185, 187, 194, 203, 206–7, 215

welfare caseworkers: and competency legislation, 42, 52; and contentious attitudes towards Native people, 69, 74–76, 109, 180; disagreements with BIA, 109, 112–16; gendered

perceptions of, 68, 101, 111; and stalling tactics, 74–75; and use of BIA to investigate claims, 69, 73–74, 107–16; and use of "suspense files," 75

welfare dependency, 224; fears of, 43, 61, 161, 165, 215; gendered, 13, 123; and moral failings, 8, 44, 96, 123; state's definitions of, 11, 40, 175, 213; wardship as, 64, 67, 69, 93, 99, 212, 214

welfare policy: historiography of, 6, 34; and Native people, 67; and race, 34, 67, 101. *See also* federal welfare state

welfare recipients, 97; claims on the state of, 10, 68, 206; government officials' moral suasion over, 96; surveillance of, 68, 97, 100, 107–8, 206, 213; taking more than deserved, 52–54, 72–73, 88, 239n87; as wards, 68

welfare rights, 98, 206–7

welfare rights activists, 10, 206–7

welfare state. *See* federal welfare state

Wesley, Clarence, 84

westward migration, 30, 155–56, 164

Werner, Theodore, 27

"white man," the, 172, 196–97, 200, 216

white men, 20, 38, 89, 113, 130, 155–56, 160, 163, 193, 196

Wilbur, Matika, 224

Willett, Prentice, 122–23, 125–26, 141–42,

Wilson, Eva, 108–10

Winnebago, 196. *See also* Ho-Chunk

Winnemucca, Nina, 76–77

Winnemucca, Pete, 76

Winnemucca, Stanley, 76–77

wives, 58–61

In the New Visions in Native American
and Indigenous Studies series

Standing Up to Colonial Power:
The Lives of Henry Roe and
Elizabeth Bender Cloud
Renya K. Ramirez

Walking to Magdalena: Personhood
and Place in Tohono O'odham
Songs, Sticks, and Stories
Seth Schermerhorn

To order or obtain more information on these or other University
of Nebraska Press titles, visit nebraskapress.unl.edu.

www.ingramcontent.com/pod-product-compliance
Lightning Source LLC
Chambersburg PA
CBHW020909290125
21027CB00030B/141/J